Proletarian Order

To tell the truth, to arrive together at the truth, is
a communist and revolutionary act. – *Antonio Gramsci, 21 June 1919*

Illusion is the most tenacious weed in the collective consciousness.
History teaches, but it has no pupils. – *Antonio Gramsci, 11 March 1921*

Gwyn A. Williams

Proletarian Order

**Antonio Gramsci, Factory Councils
and the Origins of Italian Communism
1911-1921**

Pluto  Press

First published 1975 by
Pluto Press Limited
Unit 10, Spencer Court
7 Chalcot Road
London NW1 8LH

ISBN 0 902818 65 1 paperback
ISBN 0 902818 66 X hardback

Printed in Great Britain by
Bristol Typesetting Co Ltd
Barton Manor,
St Philips Bristol

Designed by Richard Hollis, GrR

Cover photographs: Collection Moro, Rome

Contents

Preface

I have written this book in the hope that it will prove of service to the British working-class and marxist movements. The experiences of communists in the Italy of 1911-21 seem to me central to the historical patrimony of workers and revolutionary socialists – in Europe generally and in the British Isles in particular. One major purpose of the book is to make as much as possible of that experience directly available to comrades who use the English language.

The book is in no sense an attempt at a full marxist 'reading' (whether innocent or guilty, to quote comrade Althusser) of the crisis. To borrow an expression from that old curmudgeon Georges Sorel, the book is a 'diremption': a selection of essentials, which I hope is vital and living even if a trifle contradictory, in accordance with the spirit of its subject.

The focus is, of course, Antonio Gramsci and the Turin council movement. With Gramsci, the book begins, in effect with the publication of *L'Ordine Nuovo* in May 1919, when his thinking became an historically operative force. It makes no effort to examine his earlier thought, which requires a volume or volumes to itself. My friend Stephen Overy, who is writing such a volume, has helped me here, as in many other ways. I have, however, given almost as much weight to Amadeo Bordiga and his movement; they seem to me equally important and require further examination. Around this communist core, the essay tries to sketch in enough of the general background, but, obviously, whole areas – bourgeois politics generally, fascism, even other sectors of the left, from reformists to syndicalists – are treated much less fully. The subject of the book, however, does, I think stand in its own right. While there are references ahead, I have done my best not to read back later writings into those of 1919-20. I think it very important to remain imprisoned within a strict chronology, at least at this stage, particularly with Gramsci's writings, but also with Bordiga's.

I have tried to indicate my debts in the footnotes and bibliography. In English, I owe most to the thesis of Martin N. Clark on the Italian labour movement which opens up the dimensions of the real and the practical and without which I could not have written as I have. In Italy, of course, Paolo Spriano towers over the history of communism almost as tall as Benedetto Croce did once in another world. It has been a pleasure to read so much of him. It is probably Luigi Cortesi, above all, who has most moved my mind, often against the grain, together with the work of Andreina de Clementi, Rosa Alcara and others associated with the *Rivista storica del socialismo*. It seems to me that their work is a major marxist and communist enterprise whose significance is European – and, braving the wrath of sundry cohorts of comrades – European includes British.

The book began as a short introduction to a translation of one of Paolo Spriano's and I am deeply grateful to Richard Kuper and Pluto Press for stoicism, heroism and generosity well beyond the call, to Neil Middleton and Allen Lane the Penguin Press for tolerating a deviation in the hope that it might prove ultimately productive, and to Lawrence and Wishart for allowing me to quote extensively from Gramsci's political writings. Chic Maisels, a comrade of the Communist Organization in the British Isles, was responsible for the remarkable Gramsci numbers of the *New Edinburgh Review* and accepted translations and drafts apparently without end, as well as introducing me to Hamish Henderson, a Sorelian diremption in his own right. My wife suffered in getting this book out almost as much as Pia Carena must have done in getting out *L'Ordine Nuovo*. I hope they all get their reward in a better world.

I have taken the liberty of dedicating the book to an anarchist comrade of Gramsci's in the Turin council movement. The dedication comes from someone who is neither anarchist nor Italian but who thinks (as I hope we all think) that he knows a good comrade when he sees one.

Gwyn A. Williams
York 1974

To the memory of Pietro Ferrero of Turin, metal-worker and anarchist, who was a student at the study circle of the Barriera di Milano, who served as secretary to the Turin section of FIOM, who led in the April struggle and the Occupation of the Factories, who led the resistance to the referendum in September 1920, who led the last struggle of the councils in April 1921 and who was killed by the fascists on 18 December 1922.

1. Structure: Italy in the Age of Imperialism and Democracy

> It is necessary, with bold spirit and in good conscience, to save civilization. We must halt the dissolution which corrodes and corrupts the roots of human society. The bare and barren tree can be made green again.
>
> Are we not ready?[1]

Antonio Gramsci, a Sardinian of 28 who had made his home in the socialist movement of Turin, nervous, caustic, with a hunched back and a brain like a burning-glass, directed his summons to his socialist comrades on 15 May 1919, a few weeks after groups of ex-officers and *Arditi* shock troops, inspired by Benito Mussolini, burned the offices of the socialist newspaper *Avanti* in Milan.

Gramsci's was the most distinctive voice to make itself heard above the tumult of Italy in the crisis which broke the liberal state and the socialist movement. It is a voice historically associated with the revolutionary council movement of the Turin workers, itself perhaps the most distinctive of all the council communisms of Europe after 1917. Both the movement and the marxism of Gramsci, whose progressive elaboration it accelerated and deeply influenced, form part of the historical patrimony of the revolutionary working-class movement. They are essential to that 'usable past' which the movement must mobilize if it is ever to throw off the 'corpses of the dead generations', to break the bourgeois hegemony, as omnipresent as pollution.

A sense of catastrophe informs Gramsci's writing as it does that of so many others in these years. But the Italian crisis of 1919-20, however cataclysmic, is recognizably one of a series which stretch back at least to the shocks of 1911-12, which unhinged the system of Giovanni Giolitti. Giolitti, the Old Fox of Dronero, had contrived to construct an effective liberal and parliamentary 'consensus' out of the congeries of interest-groups in politically invertebrate and nationally unintegrated Italy. He had presided over the decade which registered the decisive advance of modern industry in the North. In 1911-12, the tight-rope snapped. In June 1911, under pressure, Giolitti introduced a bill for near-universal manhood suffrage. The 'amorphous masses', whose threatening presence loomed behind so much of the political discourse of Italians, were to be incorporated into the political system. In September, Italy went to war with Turkey for the possession of Libya, as imperialism and chauvinism, in a variety of voluntarist and anti-rationalist ideologies, established a hegemony over the imagination and the intellect. During 1911-12, the small but disproportionately influential Socialist Party, which had settled into the Giolittian system, was itself unhinged by a massive revolt of the left, which purged the party, dislocated its unity and swept to leadership its charismatic militant Benito Mussolini. In 1912, the anarcho-syndicalists founded their union federation, the Italian syndicalist union, USI, while in Naples, a young engineering student, Amadeo Bordiga, himself a charismatic figure among socialist youth, began to use language and concepts which socialists later called Leninist.

The shocks of 1911-12 announced the impact on marginal Italy of European capitalism as it passed into its imperialist phase. It was the impact of growth, quantitative and qualitative, which transformed social life ; of imperialist expansion, finance and monopoly capitalism ; of new forms of technology and organization and of a multiplicity of new ideologies which tried to assimilate the human meaning of the change. Functionally inherent in this mutation of capitalism was the process of mass 'socialization' : the incorporation of much of the working population into civil society, into 'the nation' and nationalism ; its technical education and fragmentation, its ordering into democratic and parliamentary forms based on universal or near-universal manhood suffrage even in the authoritarian monarchies. In its intensifying crises, this 'mass society' encountered mass rebellion, which increasingly by-passed a social democracy disappearing into the absorbent new liberal democracy, and expressed itself in direct action and anti-parliamentary responses, in variants of syndicalism. This was the crisis, with World War as its climax, which in the socialist world signalled the passage from the Second to the Third International.

The Trajectory of Italian Capitalism

It was in 1899 that Fiat (*Fabbrica Italiana Automobili Torino*) was founded in Turin, by the ingenious and enterprising Giovanni

Agnelli. Lancia opened up there, Romeo and Bugatti in Milan ; they were followed by scores of others. By 1907, there were 40 motor-car firms, with a capital of 90 million lire, 38 million of it in Turin. The automobile industry was a luxury craft, the sports-car its prototype, dramatic in its audacious technology and ambitious road-races. Working out from the established engineering schools and industries of Turin and Milan, Italians swiftly colonized this most advanced sector of European production. A severe slump eliminated the insecure and by 1914 the industry was stabilizing at 44 firms, 12,000 employees and assets of 67 million lire. There were 21,000 cars on Italian roads, three times the 1910 total, and over 3,000 a year were being exported. The War forced a colossal expansion. Production rose from some 9,000 vehicles in 1914 to 20,000 in 1918. There was mass production of utility vehicles and trucks, a move into aircraft, submarine engines, railway material, machine-guns ; lesser firms were absorbed, as steel and engineering experienced a parallel and monstrous growth. Turin was transformed into a classic industrial monolith of a city. Fiat's capital rose from 17 million lire to 200 million. After the war, it ran into headlong collision with a militant and original working-class movement which made Fiat-Centro the pilot-plant of the Occupation of the Factories in September 1920, when a despairing Agnelli offered to turn the firm into a co-operative. But it weathered the depression of 1920-21, rode the fascist destruction of the working-class movement and settled into the Mussolini regime, swallowing its rivals and, with its holding company IFI-Fiat, establishing a virtual monopoly by 1927.[2]

Modern enterprises, with their highly-skilled cadres, mushroomed out of the established but restricted industrial complex of the Milan-Turin-Genoa triangle, in response to the demands of the new capitalism. Typewriters became an Italian specialism when Olivetti opened at Ivrea in 1908 and from 1906 the production of printing presses and type-setting machines focused on Turin. Similarly cement and concrete grew into a major sector of the building industry, itself growing in response to urbanization and expansion. The chemical industry, established and growing during the 1900s, developed into the monster Montecatini enterprise and stimulated the development of dynamite production, photography and above all, rubber, as Pirelli and its kin moved into vehicle tyres and, increasingly, into the supply of the fast-growing electrical industry.

Electricity was perhaps the most striking pioneering enterprise. The first electric power station in Europe was opened in Milan in 1884; hydro-electric plants were rapidly developed. Production increased from some 100 million kilowatt hours around 1900 to over three thousand million by 1914, easing the dependence on British coal. During the War, production of this 'white coal' rose to 4.3 thousand million kilowatt hours, spawning a cluster of subsidiary industries and speeding the adoption of the electronic furnace. For around these novel industries and interpenetrating with them, rose the whole complex of steel – which having increased its production twelve-fold between 1896 and 1913, rose by 50 per cent during the War – and large-scale engineering, with its machine tools and enterprises of high technicity. From 1896 all the graphs begin to rise; they turn sharply upwards during the first decade of the twentieth century, to climax in the stupendous growth of the War years. In the ten years before the War, Italian industrial production, in large measure based on the most recent technology, increased by 87 per cent against a European average of 56 per cent. The vulnerable body of a relatively retarded society suddenly sprouted a monstrous head.[3]

In brief, the capitalist mode of production established its dominance in Italy during its most advanced phase, the phase Lenin, Hilferding, Luxemburg, Bukharin got to grips with in socialist theory. Industries grounded in a frontier technology, instinct with the dynamic of trust and cartel, mushroomed in the north and north-west around a firm but limited base and were from birth enmeshed in banks and insurance consortia, finance capital, the state. In vertical and horizontal expansion, trusts and finance-industrial complexes interlocked with the state apparatus. Northern Italy rapidly developed into a sector of European bourgeois civilization driving into revolutionary technical change, monopoly capitalism, imperial expansion and state integration.

It was driving also into crises of ideology and the intellect, of popular mobilization and mass socialization. Its rise dislocated an Italian polity grounded in a plurality of modes of production, lacking a national-popular integration and a bourgeois 'civic spirit'. This was a polity held together by the exclusion of the peasant and much of the working-class population from 'civil society' and the 'juridical' life of the state, by the more or less effective exercise of oligarchical skills in the politics of bland and irresponsible corruption, by the more or less frequent resort to bloody police and military repression. The rise of the new capitalism dislocated no less the other-world of this society, a working population in which passionate, communal, often elemental revolt was endemic, the kind of revolt commentators called *anarchoid* : a quasi-Bakuninist, populist tradition, stiffening into revolutionary syndicalism, out of which a marxist socialist movement was struggling to grow.

When Giolitti tried to outflank the socialists and his opponents with a sudden rush into manhood suffrage in 1911, a good three million of the new electorate of 8.6 million (an increase of over 5 million) were expected to be illiterate. Illiteracy might be only 11 per cent in Piedmont, but it was 90 per cent in some areas of the South and the Islands and 54-70 per cent in the South as a whole. The national average was 37.6 per cent.[4] The 'amorphous masses' were to enter political life.

For the South remained essentially a region bearing all the stigmata of backwardness, poverty, illiteracy, its people suffering from a sense of almost colonial, indeed near-racist subordination to the North. There was a zone of industrial development, shipbuilding and some engineering around Naples, with pockets at Rome and elsewhere ; strips south of Naples and in Sicily had developed a commercial agriculture in citrus fruits and vegetables comparable in intensity to that of the Po valley in the North ; there were ripples of 'improvement', intensive but localized cultivation of vines and olives. But much of the region and over 30 per cent of its cultivatable land was locked into the traditional and immobile society of the vast estates, the latifundia, with their big villages full of wretched tenants and clusters of landless labourers trapped in under-employment and insecurity. It was a society of poverty, illiteracy, mass emigration, repellently 'priest-ridden' to anti-clericals. It supported, however, a swollen urban bourgeoisie and petty-bourgeoisie which was instructed, white-collar, 'intellectualist' and aspiring ; broad, often parasitic ranges of agents, lawyers, fixers in the crevices, merchants, journalists. Here the clientelism and endlessly-shifting alliances which characterized Italian political life acquired a peculiar permanence and intensity, often inter-penetrating with the shadow-world of criminality and occult influence, the world of *camorra* and *mafia*, the Freemasonry of the anti-clericals. Its educated and frustrated classes colonized the bureaucracy and all the agencies of development, improvement and education ; its writers and thinkers enjoyed a disproportionate influence, generating much of the nation's 'intellectual energy'. Naples was the metropolis, with its minority industry and industrial classes, its vast, huddled, often pre-industrial sub-proletariat, its complex, Byzantine politics and polished society, buttressing aristocratic clans who were often the nursery of notable intellect. Most notable of all was the Idealist philo-sopher Benedetto Croce who, as he modestly put it, 'burned through' marxism in five years, wrote a history of Italy punctuated by his own biography and, in his books, his journal *Critica*, his sheer intellectual presence, exercised a kind of tyranny, at once stimulating and stifling, over Italian thought: 'a species of lay Pope', as Gramsci once called him.[5]

Central Italy, dominated by the swelling administrative, political, clerical and intellectual capital of Rome and pockmarked by patchy industrial development, was largely spaced out between lati-fundia and share-croppers ; rural society, moving up an Appenine spine of wretched and small-scale peasant proprietorship, achieved some stability in the relatively more affluent *mezzadria* share-croppers of Tuscany. In Lombardy and along the Po valley, farming was com-mercial and intensive ; on the Lower Po, it became industrial, with its teeming hired labourers, *braccianti,* organizing in tough unions against tenant farmers and the big agrarian owners in sugar-beet, hemp and an agriculture heavily penetrated by entrepreneurial capital. Emilia-Romagna had been one of the earliest working-class conquests of the socialist movement.

In terms of absolute numbers of the active population, agri-culture remained dominant to the War and beyond. The population of Italy grew from 31.7 million in 1891, to 33.7 million in 1901, 36.7 million in 1911 and 37.5 million in 1921. In 1881, agriculture account-ed for over 35 per cent of the active population. The proportion fell steadily, from 30 per cent in 1901, to 27.7 per cent in 1911 and 25.7 per cent in 1921. Over the same period, the proportion of the active popu-lation attributed to 'industry' inched up from 11 to 11.4 per cent ; that in the 'tertiary' sector of commerce, transport, services, registered a sharper increase from 7.9 per cent to 9 per cent. These figures are deceptive. An estimate for 1911 allots 57 per cent of the population to the land, 28 per cent to industry. Not only were important sectors of the labouring population included in the 'tertiary' category ; the agri-cultural population itself was complex in its sub-division. In 1871, owner-operated farms accounted for 18 per cent of Italy's productive land, tenant farms for nearly 8 per cent and share-cropping for some 17 per cent. By the eve of the War, peasant proprietors were 21.2 per cent of all farmers, a proportion which increased sharply during and after the War, to over 35 per cent in 1921, as many labourers acquired some land.[6] But agriculture entered a quasi-permanent crisis from the 1880s, when the great depression in European rural economy hit, despite considerable efforts by the state. Emigration, which mounted to a peak in 1913 and which severely affected the social and family structure of many areas in the South and Venetia, was acute in rural society ; there was much migration from country to town, from south to north. Whole sectors of the agrarian population were strictly proletarian ; many non-proletarian groups were not far removed from them in predicament and response. During the trade-union upsurge of 1920, nearly 900,000 rural workers joined the socialist federation. Gramsci could group three and a half million 'workers, peasants and white-collars' as members of the socialist movement in 1919.[7] But he had to pay careful attention to the variety of groups within it. The striking feature of the plebeian classes in Italy was their *fragmentation,* often stiffened by contradictory ideologies. There was a wide range of occupational experiences, artisan, seasonal migrant, rural proletarian, 'proprietor', tenant, white-collar worker – all 'proletarian' in predicament if not always in status and outlook, workers of mixed status. What is true is that the industrial working class and the factory proletariat in particular, while strategically placed, were a minority within the plebeian and labouring population.

The industrial focus, of course, was the Milan-Turin-Genoa triangle and its hinterland. Established in embryo even before the unification of Italy, it was the base for a first abortive thrust into imperialism and mass industrialization in the 1880s, accompanied, characteristically and prophetically, by an extension of the franchise, an agrarian crisis and by popular revolt scudding from south to north. Textiles had been the original basis for industrialization in Piedmont, Lombardy, and to a lesser degree, Venetia, but the European crisis of the 1870s confronted the new state with the threat of permanent imprisonment within an under-developed economy and a subordinate political status. From the beginning, the state, often working through the precociously developed banking system, deliberately forced the pace of industrial growth in the service of great-power ambitions.

Italy was desperately short of coal and iron ore, but steel was obviously essential to an imperial power and the state, which owned sub-soil mineral rights (and extended the principle to water with the growth of the hydro-electric system), exploited the ore deposits of Elba and the twin sites of Piombino and Portoferraio, to encourage the growth of massive trusts and consortia, closely linked to the armed forces and national policy – the pilot plant at Terni, the Falck and Dalmine firms, above all the massive Ilva trust and its associated cartels. Ship-building was similarly sponsored and seen through the transition to steel and coal; railways were controlled and ultimately nationalized.

In response to the crisis of the 1870s, the *Sinistra* (Left) came to power, supported by new industrialists, middle bourgeoisie, anticlericals, committed to imperial expansion and mass mobilization. Under the intransigent Crispi, 1887-1896, high tariff walls were erected around industry and in imperialist conflict with France over Tunis, a fierce tariff war waged against French trade from 1888. There was a thrust forward in Africa, and at home the franchise was extended to give two million the vote. The multiplication of parliamentary groups which resulted transformed political government into an exercise in the manipulation and harmonization of interests, *trasformismo*, extending deeply into political society and giving it its characteristic form.

The imperialist thrust ran into disaster. Without doubt, many sectors of heavy industry got a boost, but exporters generally and southerners in particular suffered. The structure of the economy could not stand the pace. Italy plunged into deep depression until 1893 and there were massive bank failures in 1893-94. Popular unrest broke into virtual insurrection and the invasion of Ethiopia failed miserably. In 1895 the socialists won 12 seats in the Chamber. The Left was displaced, the restored Right attempted reconstruction, with some degree of success, but was confronted with continuing popular resistance which climaxed in the massive insurrections of 1898. Repression proved self-defeating and after the elections of 1900 the Left returned to government. Power in fact passed to the Piedmontese Giovanni Giolitti, the first major statesman not to be associated with the original unification of Italy, the *risorgimento*, a genius in the practice of *trasformismo*. Premier five times and Minister of the Interior twice, it was Giolitti who caught the tide of recovery, turned the political system into an effective instrument and presided over the advance of modern industry in the North.

Around this northern core, Giolitti built his system of patronage and manipulation. Within the protectionist system, he tried to embrace and harmonize as many conflicting interests as possible. He met resistance. Nationalists denounced his prosaic pacifism ; southerners fumed at the continuing 'conquest' of the South by the North, the continuing 'bribery' of southern landlords and bourgeoisie with 'compensation' within the system. The celebrated southern radical Gaetano Salvemini, who challenged and deeply influenced many young socialists, was particularly fierce in his attacks on Giolitti's electoral and parliamentary manipulation, which he pilloried as a corruption of Italian life. But the 'statesman of Dronero' was effective enough to acquire a reputation for political magic. A particular success was his handling of the socialist movement. Giolitti curbed repression and attempted a measured and reformist recuperation of the popular forces. A whole socialist world of parliamentary deputies, craft federations, co-operatives, local communes, was gradually being absorbed into a skilfully balanced and finely tuned system which tended to operate at the expense of consumers, tax-payers and southerners. It was this Chinese vase (as Benjamin Franklin called an 18th century British empire which operated on similar principles) which was broken by the relatively sudden rise of modern capitalism.

At every stage, that capitalism was powered by the state and the unusually fecund banking and financial system, which tended to absorb the agrarians and provide a focus of class solidarity, transcending sectional conflicts of interest. Around the state-owned coal of Elba the great steel consortia formed ; the nationalization of the railways in 1905 was an armature for the engineering industry ; shipping was dominated by the *Banca Commerciale Italiana*, with German capital, Giolittian policies, and intimate connections with government. The first agrarian and industrial confederations organized themselves. A network of tariffs, subsidies, bounties, contracts and deals, bound banks, industries and state into a system laced with the corruption and scandal typical of liberal parliamentary democracy in its golden age.

Italy's entry into the War, which displaced Giolitti, enormously accelerated the process. During the War and particularly in the frenetic revival after the military disaster of Caporetto, October-

November 1917, expansion was breakneck and almost blind, in a context of voracious demand for armaments and supply, loose contracting with the state, huge profits, scandal, and a working class subjected to near-military discipline and falling real wages. Steel production climbed from 5 per cent to 10 per cent of total national output ; engineering from 21 per cent to 31 per cent. New methods of mass production were introduced as profits averaged out at 16 per cent, sometimes rising much higher. The capital of companies increased by an average of 56 per cent, in engineering by 152 per cent. The capital of Ilva soared from 30 million to 300 million lire, Breda from 14 to 114 million, Terni from 27 to 137 million. The colossus was Ansaldo, 'the monster with a thousand gullets'. A shipbuilding firm in Liguria, it drove forward in dramatic speed after Caporetto, taking over iron and steel works, erecting plants, hydro-electric stations, producing enormous quantities without too much regard for cost or efficiency. Its capital mushroomed from 30 million to 500 million lire and in its myriad plants it employed 110,000 workers. Before the war ended, in full robber-baron style, it took over its support, the *Banca di Sconto*, in a classic coup.[8]

Ansaldo's key men, the Perrone brothers, Pio and Mario, could have served communists as a veritable caricature of scaly and venomous mastodons in the capitalist jungle. Bold, arrogant, passionately, even hysterically nationalist (most heavy industry, after all, was directed to the home market), they denounced the *Banca Commerciale Italiana* as Giolittian, pro-German and unpatriotic (their own foreign capital was French). They bought up newspapers wholesale, deputies too ; they directly financed the nationalist journal *L'Idea Nazionale* as they did Mussolini.

They were typical of a new breed of finance-industrial capitalists who met the post-war crisis of reconversion with grandiose and breathtaking speculations on the stock exchange. The Perrone brothers' onslaught on the *Banca Commerciale* was a struggle of titans ; Fiat, Ilva were drawn after them. Funds which might have solved many of their serious production problems were thrown into empire-building. It was their aggression which provoked the most serious conflicts in industry, while more 'traditional' sectors looked for a return of Giolittian stability. Among the agrarians, similarly, it was the pushing, new entrepreneurs heavily involved in financial transactions, who made the pace against the traditionals, men like Lino

Carrara who broke the syndicalist strike in Parma in 1908 with squads which were fascist in everything but name and who was impatient with his association's president Cavazza with his talk of 'balance'.[9]

In the industrialists' confederation *Confindustria*, reorganized effectively in March 1920, the militant workers' movement faced a formidable enemy which could override the tentative democratic-reformist policies of a Giolitti, who returned to office in June 1920. Heavy industry and armaments first seriously financed the fascists, the agrarians first turned them loose – though as fascism grew through the provinces, it drew support from a wide range of sources.[10] The workers' movement had already been stopped by 1921 and crippled by unemployment, and fascism did not save the industrialists from the quasi-permanent inflation. The years 1921-23 were loud with spectacular crashes. Heavy industry and armaments lost half their strength as the lead passed to chemicals, electrical engineering, the newer industries. Before the War, there had been a host of small firms: 244,000 of which 160,000 employed no more than five people. The rise of the trusts before and during the War had cut into their number; numbers, and bankruptcies, increased again during the first years of fascist rule, with its financial orthodoxy. But in the 'battle of the lira' and the 'battle for wheat', the capitalist logic of industrial re-organization coincided with the logic of fascist thinking on nationalist self-sufficiency. *Confindustria*, recognized as a fascist 'corporation', thrust its organization down into the lower reaches of industry; there was a slaughter among the lesser breeds; mergers which had averaged some 16 a year, reached 266 in 1928; state enterprises intervened as directive elements. Settling to a lower level of production and sharing it out in quotas, Italian industry hardened into a form of state monopoly capitalism, which toughened in the siege conditions of the 1930s.[11]

There is a logic, the logic of imperialism – state monopoly capitalism *and* popular mobilization – in the arc of development which curves from 1900 into the fascist regime. A critical moment was the immediate post-war crisis when an aggressive sector of this new capitalism, in town and country, clashed head-on with socialist and populist movements emerging from the War in wholly unprecedented strength, while Giolitti tried to 'manage' both in the style which had worked well enough before 1912. The socialist movement, and the Turin council movement within it, struggled to achieve success in this confrontation, and in the intellectual ferment which accompanied it.

Italian Socialism

During the insurrectionary crisis of *Red Week* in the summer of 1914, the reformist Giovanni Zibordi protested in the socialist journal *Critica Sociale* against Benito Mussolini's 'dictatorship' over the Socialist Party and denounced it as a radical betrayal of the whole tradition of Italian socialism, which he derived from the marxism of Frederick Engels and the evolutionary practice of the Second International.[12]

Zibordi's evocation of 'tradition' was partisan polemic. The socialist party was in many ways a characteristic party of the Second International, in some senses, indeed, a direct product of the International itself. But several other essential features of the movement need to be grasped. Socialism in Italy first conquered a sector of the middle class; it emerged from a left wing of the republican and democratic movement and assimilated its own official marxism with difficulty. Its first serious and sustained popular support, from the beginning, came from the *rural* workers of the Lower Po in their embattled unions. It never fully succeeded in unifying its component elements. Both the party and its trade-union federation were, of necessity, drawn into parliamentary and collaborationist activity, despite their intransigent programmes, and they found it extraordinarily difficult to integrate popular masses, frequently rebellious and frequently suppressed in blood, into their political action. Above all, the party had to struggle desperately hard to establish an identity and emerge from an *anarchoid* context and a 'Bakuninist' tradition of radical dissent.[13]

Filippo Turati towered over the political spokesmen of the movement. The virtual creator of parliamentary socialism and author of the Workers' Hymn, he was the epitome of reformism. In 1920-21 the Comintern was repeatedly to call on the party to expel him, in vain. The son of a very Catholic prefect, he developed an interest in criminology in Bologna university (a common route into socialism at the time) converted to the cause in the company of the Russian exile Anna Kuliscioff, broke with the democrats of Milan and formed a socialist league there in the year of the Second International, in 1889.

In 1891, he launched *Critica Sociale*, one of the great journals of social democracy.

He was fulfilling a Milan tradition. With the fading of the Bakuninist International, a number of leading intellectuals converted to political action and, enmeshed with republicans, democrats and radicals, clustered around the journal *La Plebe* in the Lombard capital. Foremost among them was Andrea Costa, who, in the service of a radical programme for a working-class party published by *La Plebe* in 1880, threw himself into action among the hard-pressed rural workers of the Po valley. He was joined by journalists and lawyers of the region, men like Camillo Prampolini and Leonida Bissolati. The rural workers, the *braccianti,* had early been active, along with printers, railwaymen, building and textile workers, in mutual aid societies and from 1882 to 1886, there was a massive drive into unions, producer and consumer co-operatives and peasant leagues, in fierce struggles and sporadic repression.

Most active in the campaign were militants of the *Partito Operaio* (Workers' Party) which emerged in Milan in 1882. This had grown out of a cluster of local unions in revolt against 'half-deranged' Bakuninists and patronizing middle-class democrats. In what became a recurrent and characteristic style of the Italian movement, these workers were instinctually proletarian, anti-intellectual, anti-middle class, suspicious of parliament. Their leading spokesman, who detested Turati, was a tough, deeply ouvrierist, self-educated printer Costantino Lazzari. Government exploited his movement of 'the blistered hands' against the Milan socialists and democrats but in 1886, when the army was sent against the rural workers, the party was suppressed. Its struggle for life during the next few years propelled it towards the legalitarian socialists.

The terrible slump of the tariff war against France after 1888 was the forcing house and the formation of the Second International the catalyst. The great international May Day of 1890 generated a thrust for working-class unity. More, it was in response to the International that the characteristic organization of Italian labour emerged: the *camera del lavoro*. Osvaldo Gnocchi-Viani, one of Italy's earliest marxists, returned from the International's founding congress full of enthusiasm for the French union organization (initially syndicalist in inspiration) of the *bourses du travail* (literally, labour exchanges). In direct imitation, the first *camera del lavoro* (literally, chamber of labour) was formed in Milan. By 1893, there were 14, linked in a national organization ; by 1904, there were ninety.

The *camera* pre-dated union federations by craft on the German or British model, and for long commanded greater loyalty. It provided a centre for all the local unions and workers' institutions of a particular commune or district, and as time passed, these came to embrace unions, local leagues, co-operatives, savings banks. The focus was the *casa del popolo* (literally, people's house or home). This functioned as a hiring hall and workers' labour exchange, club, educational centre and headquarters, and was to be a prime target for the fascists in 1921-22. Union members were always a minority among workers, union dues irregular, organization often sketchy. Unions had to 'lead' a non-union 'mass'. Local conflicts were often handled by an ad hoc committee of agitation and the best weapon was generally a mobilization of the whole working class of an area, and its institutions, against employers. The local 'general strike' became a distinctive weapon of Italian labour and the real focus of action was the *camera* rather than the union.

The *camera* connected the traditional, localized revolt in *anarchoid* style to the newer labour movement. It tended to breed a populist and communal, sometimes a class, rather than a trade or craft, mentality. It embraced a much wider range of workers. Unions tended to appeal to the more skilled, prosperous and sophisticated. National craft federations grew more slowly. They were at first very much a labour aristocracy: printers, railway workers, black-coats, state employees. They long retained an elitist outlook. They became more representative as mass industry struck roots. When the socialist national federation of land workers (*Federterra*) was formed in 1901, it claimed 240,000 members. By 1902, there were 24 national federations of trade unions with a membership of some 480,000. By this time, they were beginning to colonize the *camere* themselves. But the latter were generally more responsive to impulses of popular revolt and the creation of a central 'resistance' secretariat at Milan in 1902 imperfectly integrated the two sectors of the labour movement.[14]

The socialist *party* emerged from the conjuncture of slump, repression and International. At a workers' congress in Milan in 1891 the decision was taken. At once there was a struggle with numerous and influential anarchist militants. At the Genoa congress of 1892, the anarchists withdrew and the Party of Italian Workers adopted a programme of class war, the socialization of the means of production and exchange, organized resistance to capital and totally independent action at elections and in parliament. In 1893 the rural unions of the Po came over en masse under their bourgeois leaders and the congress of Reggio Emilia ended with a march past by 10,000 peasants, carrying their socialist banners like religious images.

In that year the party took the title 'socialist' and during the decade which followed there was an influx of marxists and of people who thought themselves marxist. This was the intellectual decade of Antonio Labriola, a Neapolitan philosopher who became a professor at Rome in 1874, and discovered Marx in 1890, promptly publishing the first Italian translation of the Communist Manifesto. Labriola was a brilliant, caustic man, one of Engels's regular correspondents. He was the first Italian to present marxism as scientific socialism, not as an outgrowth from the *risorgimento*.[15] Yet though his influence was to prove profound, he was soon angrily alarmed at the shuffle of the party into collaboration with democratic forces. It was Turati above all who focused the party's action on the achievement of democratic rights and who presided over the influx of middle-class 'marxist' youth who entered the party in the spirit of a crusade.

The socialists had to fight hard for ten years. In the collapse of the first Italian imperialism, there were waves of repression, bitter and bloody struggles in the streets, outbreaks of anarchist terrorism. The king was assassinated in 1900. In 1894 the party was suppressed and its leaders arrested. It re-emerged in 1895, took the title Italian Socialist Party (PSI) opened its ranks to individual membership and won 13 seats in the Chamber. It played a leading part in the struggle against repression, was suppressed again in the mass insurrections of 1898, fought back as a central force in the democratic resistance and emerged in the elections of 1900, which virtually initiated the Giolittian era, with 33 seats in the Chamber, reformist leadership and the makings of the first mass political party in Italian history.

By this time, the contradiction between its marxist theory and its democratic practice was becoming intolerable and the party tried to resolve it with the familiar Second International device of 'minimum' and 'maximum' programmes.[16] At the Rome congress of 1900, the maximum Genoa programme of 1892 was reaffirmed as 'the compass by which the party should keep its direction', but a minimum democratic programme was adopted: universal suffrage for both sexes, proportional representation, abolition of indirect taxation, decentralization, freedom for the workers' movement, free, secular education, an end to repression and the nationalization of transport and mines. The nationalization of land was dropped in the hope of winning small-peasant support. Turati was now convinced that the first task of the party was to win democracy and, throughout the Giolitti decade, there was a steady drift of the parliamentary group into a form of collaboration.

The reformist leadership of the middle-class intellectuals had to struggle against the instincts of the rank and file and against periodical outbreaks of revolt. For Giolitti's blandness was episodically contradicted by brutal police and military action. During the early 1900s, reformist leadership was threatened by Enrico Ferri, a flamboyant criminologist and the very type of adventurist demagogue who so beset the movement. Far more serious was the impact of revolutionary syndicalism, for Georges Sorel struck many resonant frequencies in Italy.[17] A powerful group of syndicalists at one stage threatened to capture the party. Their rigorously intransigent doctrine, scorning 'politics', preaching direct action and total class war, captured many sectors, appealed to Lazzari and other veterans and disrupted the *camere* in particular. The leader was Arturo Labriola, a Neapolitan professor of acute and powerful intellect, with a command of oratory and political psychology. Many of his comrades were southerners; they were nearly all petty-bourgeois; Enrico Leone, Agostino Lanzillo, Alceste de Ambris.[18] They even unhinged the reformists' grip on Milan and it was they above all who precipitated the first national general strike of 1904, which paralyzed Italy for four or five days. Giolitti, however, simply sat out the storm, in a style which anticipated his equally effective 'positive inaction' during the Occupation of the Factories of 1920. The strike ended in collapse and recrimination, a severe weakening of the union movement. The syndicalist intellectuals themselves entered an ideological crisis. They tended to disperse: Labriola ended up as Minister of Labour in a Giolittian cabinet, while some of the others joined the fascists. During the last years of Giolitti's decade, as the PSI itself began to acquire a more strictly proletarian character, so syndicalism began to rebuild itself on a more coherent working-class base. But by 1908, the power of syndicalism within the Socialist Party was broken and the reformists were imprinting a democratic character upon it. In the 1909 elections, the party won 44 seats.

They were enormously reinforced by the formation of the General Confederation of Labour, the CGL. This emerged in 1906 in reaction against the syndicalist experience. It integrated the union federations (its real strength) with the *camere* in a complicated federal structure which had to take account of Italy's intense localism. The structure rose from the base to a representative national council and a small directive council, nominally controlled by congresses, which did not however, directly create the leadership: this evolved out of the union network. The CGL proclaimed itself politically 'neutral'. In terms of parliamentary democracy – or 'democracy' *tout court* in current socialist parlance – this meant a theoretical commitment to socialism and the class war. The first secretary was the skilful and committed Rinaldo Rigola, whose ideal was the British Labour Party. The CGL's relations with the PSI strictly followed the practice recommended by the 1907 Stuttgart congress of the Second International. 'Economic' struggles were to be led by the CGL, 'political' struggles by the PSI. The PSI reserved to itself the right to call a general strike whenever workers were killed by the police or the military, as they frequently were, and to 'associate itself' with popular rebellions even if these had no organic socialist meaning. In practice, the two organizations worked by joint consultation and differences became acute only at times of crisis and mass revolt.

The CGL under Rigola expanded smoothly. By 1911 it had enrolled nearly 384,000 workers. The syndicalists set up a headquarters in Parma and in 1912 founded their own federation, USI (*Unione Sindacale Italiana*), with about 100,000 members, concentrated among lower-paid workers in Emilia, though it was very active in Liguria and entered a career of vigorous growth. USI was hostile to bureaucracy; its dues and strike pay were low; it relied on a quasi-anarchist spontaneity. Its organization was horizontal, in contrast to that of the CGL, in that it focused action on the *camera*; its objective was the 'expropriating general strike'. Syndicalist and quasi-anarchist influence was also strong in the autonomous railway and maritime unions. Catholic unions, 103,000 strong in 1914, and independent (generally republican) unions at 176,000 offered no serious challenge to the 680,000 enrolled that year in the CGL, USI and the autonomous organizations. But while some 7 million workers remained un-

unionized, it was the CGL, with its disciplined, financially sound, strong central organization and effective co-ordination, which was the core power of the organized working class.[19] It lent immeasurable support to the reformists of the party. Both CGL and PSI moved swiftly into a position which was deeply, almost functionally reformist.

The Predicament of the Socialist Party

It is important to realize, then, that opposition to a quasi-traditional 'anarchism' was central to socialist identity. It was this fundamental *denial* of the *anarchoid* which *defined* socialism in Italy.

Anarchists, syndicalists, populist rebels, were identified with a 'mindless', futile revolt of 'amorphous' and unconscious masses, inimical to socialist purpose and ultimately counter-revolutionary. This, of course, was often a crude caricature of their rivals, particularly the syndicalists. The anarcho-syndicalist movement, permanently 'revolutionary', produced union militants and shop-stewards second to none, as Gramsci was wryly to discover in his factory councils. On the other hand, the movement was susceptible to 'Sorelian' deviations. It was a hard core of syndicalists, rallying to Mussolini in his war interventionism, who put bone into the first fascist organizations. And the negative reaction of the socialist unions was so deep-rooted as to be virtually 'structural'. The metalworkers' union, FIOM (*Federazione Italiana Operai Metallurgici*) in particular, built itself up in hostile reaction to disastrous syndicalist or quasi-syndicalist strikes in the Turin complex in the years before the War.[20] After the War, to Turati, whose career was founded on the crucial break with anarchism, and to many even of the 'maximalist' union leaders, 'Bolshevism' in its Italian translation and the factory council movement, simply seemed the perennial enemy in fashionable new guise.

By 1914, the socialist movement had 52 deputies in the Chamber and commanded a million votes in elections. It had won control of 300 communes and four provinces. It had built up a whole apparatus of institutions – co-operatives, credit institutions, defence organizations. In Emilia, these were shaping into a state within a state. The parliamentary deputies – the GPS – inevitably became the leadership focus, and the whole movement was in fact steeped in reformist practice, thinking – and perhaps more important, reformist *instincts*. The party structure, however, a complex one, rising from urban sections, with their ward 'circles', provincial federations and a youth movement to a national council and a Directorate, gave congress the right to elect that Directorate. The official Directorate, then, tended to reflect opinion in the local sections, which often fluctuated wildly in response to the grinding reformism of the socialist deputies, communes and unions. The Directorate was theoretically the guardian of the marxism and *ultimate* programme, the *maximum* programme of the party, the socialization of the means of production and exchange, holding it to its destiny through all the vicissitudes of bourgeois politics. In practice, the recruitment of leading cadres was haphazard and undisciplined, weak in marxist education and exposed to the opportunism, careerism and demagogy of middle-class individualists and déclassés. In the 'marxist' decade of the 1890s and the 'syndicalist' troubles before the War, leadership of the socialist movement quite often served as a phase in the personal biographies of agile men en route to quite different destinations.

For the party's leadership and even much of its active membership, was intensely middle-class and intellectual. *Critica Sociale* was a landmark in the intellectual geography of Italian bourgeois civilization. The leadership was quick to respond to movements of fashion in the university and intellectual world. It had precious little *direct* contact with working people (in sharp contrast to the CGL leadership). Its sphere tended to be propagandist – from the crudest street level to sophisticated debate in the journals – and increasingly *electoral*. In the middle of the Giolittian decade, whereas socialist party membership was about 70 per cent working class, socialist parliamentary representation and even local leadership was 80 per cent middle class. Periodically there were waves of working-class, *ouvrierist* protest against this condition ; endless complaints about the superfluity of *lawyers* (occupational disease of parliamentary democracy) demands for a purge of *Freemasons* (who played the occult role proper to them in Catholic countries).[21] But the *parliamentary* perspective of the PSI in the Giolittian era rooted leadership in the middle class, the intellectuals, the educated orators. Significantly, as the PSI grew more working-class, just before the outbreak of war, its Directorate grew more anti-parliamentary.

A particular casualty of this incorporation into Giolitti's protectionist democratic reformism was socialist penetration of the South. The South remained largely impervious to socialism (as it was to fascism). The PSI and the CGL did very little to bridge the gap between North and South which at times acquired a quasi-racial character. It was this which drove Gaetano Salvemini out of the party in 1910, to denounce the whole labour movement as a species of subsidized aristocracy in Giolitti's protectionist bloc, scorning the desperate working people of the South and the Islands. Gramsci the Sardinian was peculiarly responsive to this charge. He was one of the movers in a scheme to find Salvemini a socialist seat in Turin. His later communist paper took the title of Salvemini's famous 'meridionalist' journal – *l'Unità*. But the PSI-CGL signally failed to penetrate the South or to move from the rural proletariat into the potentially serviceable ranks of small tenants and petty proprietors – a failure which was to be decisive in 1919-20 and, as neo-fascist success currently proves, remains a major obstacle to communist advance.

This middle-class and intellectual dominance of the party, however, was not merely a reformist block to revolutionary progress; it was a factor of instability. 'They are trying to import Mexican stuff into our country,' complained one militant in 1920.[22] In fact socialist intellectuals' susceptibility to academic and literary *fashion* was painfully unsettling – a peculiarly strong local reflection of the intellectual-ideological instance of the global crisis of European capitalism which first registered (as it does today) precisely in such circles, with precisely this essentially 'petty-bourgeois' effect. The extraordinarily 'plastic' quality of Italian response to new ideas and new ideologies was almost Latin American in style, probably for similar structural reasons.

The story is probably apocryphal which has *both* the fascist Italian and the Soviet Russian ambassadors to Paris turning up with offers of help on hearing that the grave of Georges Sorel had fallen into neglect, but it carries a punch in Italy, where Sorel *registered*.[23] Sorelian notions on the general strike, the directive myth, marxism as social poetry, action, the morality of the producers, were as influential on Gramsci as on Mussolini, to name only two of the younger militants. Corradini the nationalist coolly raided marxism to erect an image of Italy as a 'proletarian nation'. The absorption of 'marxism' into the mainstream of European thought (after a surgical operation on its revolutionary and unifying core-concepts) reduced it to a current of useful ideas. Pareto, Mosca, Croce, many others juggled 'marxist' concepts wholesale. Indeed the 'revisionist' movements in

Italian marxism, both social-democratic and radical, are infinitely more interesting than the dreary Bernstein slog which fills the text-books. With the Croce-Sorel correspondence, perhaps, as their core, they cut back ('fashionable' ahead of their time, like the contemporary drama of Pirandello) to the quasi-idealist roots of the doctrine and resurrected its stress on creative *action*, its unity of theory and practice (translated in terms of the voluntarist doctrines of the *will* then current), its character as a political *art*. This was how the relatively ignorant Gramsci responded in 1917 – he called October 1917 the revolution *against* Das Kapital, meaning the *Capital* of an arid, mech-anistic and positivist Second International 'marxist' determinism. More seriously the evolution of Gramsci's marxism paralleled, in its dialectic with Croce, Marx's own life-long wrestling match with Hegel.

The socialist leadership had itself been formed initially by the celebrated 'marxist' decade of the 1890s in the universities, with the philosopher Antonio Labriola as presiding genius. But with the crises of imperialism and popular mobilization and the coincident decline of positivism, liberalism, parliamentarianism, it was varieties of anti-positivist, neo-Hegelian, idealist and anti-democratic thought which captured the literary and university world, Croce as weighty and respectable guru, D'Annunzio the poet as energumen. Parallel to it were more vulgar and activist varieties of the philosophy of 'action', 'Bergsonianism', voluntarism, 'creative élites', from D'Annunzio's posturing to the frenetic dynamism of Marinetti and the Futurists and all the pseudo-Sorelian cults of the war-lovers.[24]

Benito Mussolini, a product of the Romagna which was alleged to make an export industry out of flamboyant and *anarchoid* agitators, all bombs and *braggadocio* – those loud-mouthed Stentor-ellos and Masaniellos of the Land of Pulcinella in Gramsci's pained prose – struck a resonant frequency on the left between 1912 and 1914 and was probably a sight more representative than official socialist historiography can bring itself to admit. The youth of Italian socialism were Mussolini's before they were Bordiga's. Not only Gramsci but Palmiro Togliatti himself, were distinctly 'Mussolinian' in the fine rapture of their first socialism. The *Duce* – as *socialists* were begin-ning to call him before 1914 – was editor of *Avanti* after all, and all the efforts of reformists and worried centrists could not get him out of the editor's chair. His defection to the interventionist cause in 1914, even more with Italy's actual entry into the War in 1915, carried sectors of the syndicalist movement and several socialists with him. They gave the first fascism its 'professional' core. Mussolini himself dropped the word 'socialist' from his newspaper *Il Popolo d'Italia* when he got a handout from the Perrone godfathers.[25]

Mussolini's career is well-known. But there were many other examples of the flexibility, the 'availability', the plasticity of the intellectual leadership of the socialist party. The case of Nicola Bombacci is in some ways more striking. Like Mussolini a schoolmaster from the Romagna, he was, with his golden voice, hair and beard, a rattled-brained 'red' on the left of the party, creating 'soviets' with a wave of his histrionic hand. A leading 'revolutionary' and imprisoned during the war, he joined the communist party, served as deputy and worked for the Soviet embassy. He was expelled at the end of the 1920s for sympathy with fascism. He hung around the fringe of fascism, producing a 'left-fascist' journal with government subsidy. He went into eclipse, like most of the fascist 'left' after Mussolini's détente with the establishment, but again like his kin, re-emerged in the desperate days of the Salò Republic 1943-45, in the happy absence of the monarchy and the unhappy presence of the partisans. He became one of Mussolini's closest confidants in his last days, trying to 'revive' the 'revolutionary' spirit of fascism. He seems to have been influential in the elaboration of the Eighteen Points of Mussolini's political 'testament' which are today the ideological foundation for the fascist revival. He died a traitor's death with Mussolini in 1945. As he came out of the Milan prefecture while they were burning the papers, in pinstripe trousers and carrying a small suitcase, he is reported to have said to his doomed companions: 'What else would I need? ... I am expert in such matters. I was in Lenin's office in Petersburg when the White troops of Yudenich were advancing on the city and we were preparing to leave as we are doing today ...'![26]

Victor Grayson figures were an occupational disease of Italian socialism. Confronted with Bombacci and Mussolini, with Ferri and so many others before them, the party leaders' obsession with unity, discipline, order, becomes more understandable. In Bordiga's case, the reaction was a demand for the total eradication of any and every petty-bourgeois trait in a rigidly purist and disciplined communism which almost shunned contact with the filthy and polluted society outside.

Alfred Rosmer in his *Lenin's Moscow* makes an interesting

comment. He mentions someone in the Soviet 'hierarchy' and adds, 'of course at that time no one would have dreamt of using such a term ; it took Mussolini's fascism to establish it and Stalinism to pick it up.'[27] In fact, the very word was as popular with Gramsci as with Mussolini and it bid fair to become a commonplace of socialist discourse. Certainly the *thing* if not the word, was *central* to the response of most committed socialist leaders. Fear of both the meteor-like creatures who used the socialist movement as some kind of rite of passage and of the 'amorphous masses 'outside, so prone to *anarchoid* impulse and yet so necessary to socialist mobilization, was ingrained, from Turati to Bordiga. Serrati was to denounce Gramsci's council theory in virtually the same terms as he had Mussolini's 'Sorelian' kinship with anarchistic action.

It was not only the 'anarchic' left which had to be tied down ; the permanent threat came from reformism and its molecular incorporation into bourgeois democratic radicalism, with Giolitti as necromancer-in-chief. Consequently a *functional centrism* became a permanent feature of the socialist Directorate. Periodically, waves of popular discontent 'outside', provoking a 'democratic' response from reformists, stirred the left into 'marxist' protest. The Directorate's repeated reaction was a re-affirmation of the *maximum* and revolutionary programme of the party to curb the reformists, a shuffle leftwards to embrace the mutinous in a 'revolutionary' recuperation which did not in fact seriously affect the parliamentary, trade-union and reformist *reality* of party practice. This reaction was so regular as to become a 'tradition' – an indication of its *structural* character. The classic socialist crisis of 1919-20, personified in the agony of Serrati (whose position in practice, as Bordiga acutely pointed out in a lost letter to Lenin, was close to that of the German Independents, the USPD) while critically intense, was in a very real sense 'traditional'. The fact that Serrati did ultimately and too late expel the reformists and die a militant in the new communist party is itself testimony to the death of a 'tradition'.

In these circumstances, *symbolism* came to carry excessive weight in the socialist party, as a defence against the 'betrayal' inherent in social democracy. An audience with the king was the kiss of death. Bissolati was expelled even though he wore a soft hat and lounge suit to restore his socialist virginity. The *maximalism* of the party Directorate tended to acquire a distinctly symbolic, mythic character. Even Bordiga's abstentionism from parliamentary elections had something of this quality. His response to a pluralist, intellectually polyglot Italian society, with a socialist party harassed by loose-limbed Stentorellos and moving inexorably into a 'fireman' reformist role, was a total break with *every* bourgeois institution, a rigid communist party with a revolutionary programme and action which *nobody* and *nothing* could *blur*. Total abstention from elections, like total abstention from alcohol, was both a practical proposal with purgative consequences and a Sorelian myth of communist purity.

The Italian Socialist Party was therefore trapped in a permanent tension between the overpowering reformism which was propelling the movement steadily into bourgeois democracy, and the pulses of popular discontent which it failed to channel and whose explosions outside the party provoked an anti-reformist reaction within. With the breaking of the imperialist crisis, the endless pas-de-deux of the socialist Directorate suddenly became a ritual fire-dance.

2. Conjuncture: Italy in the Crisis of Imperialism and Democracy

The Seminal Crisis of 1911-12

In the Italian sector, the imperialist crisis broke in 1911. In its reformist assimilation into the Giolittian system, the PSI had won valuable gains in labour and social legislation, the establishment of labour as a recognized interest, the civilizing of conflict and the gradual extension of 'citizenship' to the working class. The main target of this first phase of democratization remained universal male suffrage. In the process, however, the party had run into stagnation. From 1910 its membership started to decline; it fell by 2,000 to around the 30,000 mark in 1911 and registered another fall to around 27,000 by 1912. The CGL which had achieved spectacular increases under its reformist leader Rigola, reached its peak in 1911 with a membership of nearly 384,000. In the next year, it fell dramatically by nearly 75,000, staged only a limited recovery in 1912-13 and fell again, by 87,000, during the run-up to war in 1914-15. The syndicalist USI, however, founded in 1912, enrolled 150,000 very rapidly, half the CGL's strength, and presented a continuous challenge to the outbreak of war. Most ominous, perhaps, was the decline in the circulation of the socialist organ *Avanti* which had built up a national reputation since its inception in 1896. By 1911, it had plummeted to little over 10,000, under the editorship of the ultra-reformist Bissolati and the first phase of that of the more left-wing reformist Claudio Treves.[1]

A severe slump in 1907-8 provoked unrest, while the perennial tension in rural society worsened. The outbreak of the Libyan war in 1911 stirred all the latent but deep anti-militarism of the peasant and working classes, imperfectly if at all integrated into the patriotism and nationalism which were universal among the middle and lower-middle classes. The consequent explosions of popular protest were exploited by USI and the anarchists rather than the CGL and the Socialist Party. And the protests were vividly symptomatic of a relatively under-developed country in the throes of mass industrialization. Almost simultaneously, for example, the workers of the steel plants at Elba-Piombino went into action, not primarily over wages, although inflation was a strain, but in 'modern' protest against the formation of a steel trust with state support, while the rural population of Cosentino in the South, ravaged by cholera and totally bereft of the most elementary health services, staged a communal revolt almost 'medieval' in its elemental character – and both were hammered by police repression. To Turati, this simply re-inforced the urgency with which he pressed for a planned economy in which a mobilized and properly educated working class, in manhood suffrage, would work for the democratic remaking of Italy. Syndicalists could call out a more immediate response.[2]

A series of scandals had unseated Giolitti ; a successor ministry failed and in a style which was typical of him, Giolitti installed one of his own men, Luzzatti, as caretaker premier, while the 'statesman of Dronero' prepared a suitably spectacular come-back. Luzzatti proposed a suffrage bill which was so restricted that it drove the socialist deputies into opposition. At that point, in June 1911, Giolitti stepped forward as saviour with a new deal, including virtually universal suffrage embracing illiterates, and the nationalization of life insurance. He made a determined effort to incorporate the socialists into his government. Bissolati actually had an audience with the king, though he ultimately refused office. The parliamentary group, the GPS, however, saw no offence and rallied behind the Giolitti government.

Within months, Giolitti took the country into imperialist war with the annexation of Libya. Intended as a limited operation, it in fact unleashed an explosion of nationalist and chauvinist frenzy which anticipated the 'radiant days of May' in 1915, mobilized the middle and lower-middle classes and split republican, radical and syndicalist groups. It was widely suspected that universal suffrage had been a bribe to lure socialists into a democratic-imperialist consolidation. In fact, Bissolati proclaimed himself 'not anti-colonial' ; the majority of socialist deputies voted for annexation and there were plenty of voices on the left to talk of a civilizing and hence essentially 'socialist' mission in Africa, just as in 1915, many leftists saw the world war as a 'revolutionary' occasion. In 1911, it looked as if the PSI were finally about to disappear into bourgeois democracy. Croce in an essay in February talked of the 'death of socialism'; Giolitti himself in April, had said that Karl Marx had been 'banished to the attic'.

In response, there was a powerful revolt of the rank and file. A fraction calling itself *intransigent revolutionary* had formed in October 1910; on 1 May 1911 it launched a new periodical *La Soffitta (The Attic)* to re-affirm marxism. Little concerned with marxism in fact, it was a spokesman for 'marxist' activism. The movement spread; it won two deputies, 200 party sections, eight weeklies. It cultivated a style new in socialist circles, simple, direct, mobilizing opinion around the cost of living, in competition with the syndicalists – a reflection of the emergence of a new generation of working-class militants, *simplist*, direct and effective, especially in Turin, Milan and Naples.[3] The outbreak of the Libyan War precipitated a general strike, in which syndicalists joined. It was only partly effective – the power of the 'political nation' was overwhelming, but there was an explosion of verbal protest from every working-class and many peasant centres and a ripple of direct action. Mussolini, the rising young socialist star of the Romagna, joined Pietro Nenni, then a republican, in tearing up railway tracks. They turned prison into a sacramental experience by reading Georges Sorel to each other in their cell.[4]

At the Modena congress of the party in October 1911 there was a head-on collision.[5] When Cabrini publicly hoped for a victory 'for the flag of our people' in Libya, Seratti broke into the Workers' Hymn. The intransigents were not powerful enough to break the opposition – they scored about 40 per cent in the voting – but the reformists split, Turati and Treves holding out for the independence of the party, while Bissolati and his followers accepted the logic of democratic and patriotic affiliation. In consequence the Directorate was largely divided between the two reformist groups, the intransigents pinned down to the base and the PSI paralyzed. During 1912, as syndicalists made the pace in mass actions among the people and socialist membership continued to fall, followed now by that of the CGL, Mussolini began to register on the youth movement and the party as a mass-orator of genius, and intransigent militants set to work at grass-roots level. At the congress of Reggio Emilia in July 1912, they were strong enough to carry the day. In a tightly-fought congress, with a powerful intervention from Mussolini, the party finally expelled the Bissolati reformists, who promptly formed a

Reformist Socialist Party. A further drive to expel Freemasons, however, split the intransigents and failed.[6]

The intransigents were in fact a heterogeneous and incoherent group ; their only unity lay in opposition to reformism and absorption in democracy. The coup at Reggio Emilia, however, transformed the character of the party.

For a while, paralysis continued. The intransigents of the Directorate were hamstrung by the persistent strength of the reformists. Bacci, the new editor of *Avanti*, now moved to Milan, was a stalking-horse for Treves. Bissolati's new Reformist Socialist Party was a challenge. It was to win a score of seats in the 1913 elections and Rigola intended to swing the CGL to its support. The great wave of popular unrest which broke over Italy as it did most of western Europe in these years, was still by-passing the socialist movement. A terrible strike of the un-unionized racked Turin for a couple of months early in 1912 and was taken over by the syndicalists ; its failure was blamed on FIOM. The syndicalists created USI in November. It enrolled 150,000 very rapidly. In 1913, its secretary, de Ambris, was elected to the Chamber with a half-dozen syndicalists and independent revolutionaries.

As a new generation of proletarian and some student militants entered left-wing politics, a potential source of strength was identified. How to tap it? Giacinto Menotti Serrati who, with his companion the Russian-Italian Angelica Balabanoff, was developing a coherently marxist radicalism, argued for a total ideological re-equipment of the party. Salvemini in his *Unità* was already dismissing the movement, its youth in particular, as intellectually primitive. An alternative was a demagogic drive to displace the syndicalists as the voice of the masses. In a sense the party's choice was made for it. Bacci gave up the editorship of *Avanti*. Lazzari tried to get Salvemini to take over, offered the journal to Serrati, in vain. Desperate to revivify the party, he proposed Mussolini, who took over in December.

The man from the Romagna immediately struck the right frequency, with a confused but passionate 'subversive' propaganda which deployed, in his customary vivid but jackdaw style, all the fashionable activist themes then current. He had connections with the high-toned and 'energetic' nationalists of *La Voce* of Florence ; he used Salvemini – both anxious to rid Italian culture of its 'provincialism'. Mussolini's own writing was steeped in pseudo-Sorelian notions; it reflected Pareto's new theory of 'elites'. He threw open the journal to non-party activists, the syndicalists in particular: Labriola, Leone, Lanzillo. The democratization of Italy, argued Mussolini, had been achieved; reformists no longer had any reason to exist. The Libyan War and the massive struggles in industry presaged a new phase of violent struggle against imperialist capitalism. Italian socialism had behind it no Commune like the French, no years of illegality like the German. The Italian proletariat needed to 'live a heroic and historic day'. He scorned 'concretism' and directed his fire against democracy, liberalism, Rigola and the 'labourism' of the CGL. He projected 'a rebellious Utopia' as an energizing myth.[7]

The immediate results were spectacular. A police massacre in January 1913 brought Mussolini roaring out of *Avanti*. A second struggle in Turin, led this time by FIOM, was victorious and a remarkable display of class solidarity transcending craft interests. Savage strikes broke out in Milan, with the syndicalist Corridoni prominent. Mussolini swung *Avanti* to support for USI. Its attacks on the CGL were so merciless that they forced the temporary resignation of its leadership. In the elections of 1913, Mussolini supported the candidature of an old Communard in Milan at the head of a coalition of socialists, anarchists and syndicalists. By this time, the rapidly growing socialist youth movement was his to a man and the left made him a hero. The circulation of *Avanti* rocketed, as it became a semi-insurrectionary journal.

His weakness was the essentially transient character of any identification of socialism with most of the popular actions he supported. The reformists were soon in full cry against him and many other militants became alarmed. In July 1913, he offered his resignation to the Directorate. They called for greater discipline, but confirmed him in office. The syndicalists in Milan were defeated and Mussolini patched up a truce with the CGL. *Avanti* toned down its editorials. To find his own voice again, Mussolini launched a personal fortnightly, characteristically called *Utopia*, in which he preached a revolutionary revision of marxism, with a stress on revolution as an 'act of faith' by minority elites.

And by the Ancona congress of the PSI in July 1914, the circulation of *Avanti* was passing the 60,000 mark, having doubled in a year and a half since its take-over by Mussolini and quintupled since its move from Rome to Milan. Membership of the party was passing the 50,000 mark. The youth federation, FGS, topped 10,000 for the first time and was recruiting able militants. At the elections of 1913, the socialist vote rose over the million (an increase from 8 to 11 per cent) and 52 deputies were elected. In the local elections of 1914, an important sector of the national territory passed under the administration of socialists, as the party won four provinces and 300 communes, including Bologna, Cremona, Novara, Piombino and Milan itself, where Mussolini got a seat.

It was with immense satisfaction that Mussolini wrote of the Ancona congress: 'Italian socialism becomes more and more proletarian and less and less populist, more and more class-ist, less and less democratic.'

A New Generation: Turin and Naples

In the process which Mussolini exalted, the party had lost, through the defection of ultra-reformists and syndicalists, whole sectors of its middle-class and lower-middle-class leadership. There had been a largely instinctive re-assertion of ideological rigour which, after nearly twenty years of immersion in democratic action, in the electoral experience of alliances and 'blocs', particularly at the local level, in anti-clerical and anti-militarist propaganda common to radical groups, the party was unprepared for. To oppose the relatively coherent democratic ideology of the reformists and the froth of transient demagogues, there was little but the 'nineteenth-century ouvrierism' of such as Lazzari. The influx of tough, new proletarian militants, many of them women in the north, did little for the party's ideological and cultural autonomy. 'Culture' tended to be identified with reformist leadership and absorption into bourgeois society.

In Turin, for example, to complaints that the socialist paper *Il Grido del Popolo* (The Cry of the People) was becoming too simple, its editor Maria Giudice, a primary schoolteacher and an intransigent, replied: '*Il Grido* is not yet simple enough, easy enough, clear enough . . . Theories or no theories, when the masses *feel* like socialists, they will act like socialists.' The intransigent militants coming to the fore in Turin as it rapidly grew into a centre of the newer mass industry, were similar in temper: Francesco Barberis, a 'tribune of the people', Pietro Rabezzana, who moved over from the republicans and often talked like a syndicalist, Giovanni Boero, with his deep-rooted distrust

of intellectuals, Elvira Zocca the women's leader who 'came to socialism mainly through feeling . . . through that instinct for rebellion
common to all members of the working class'. It was the perennial,
and perennially false, distinction between 'theory' and 'action' which
Mussolini was able to exploit.[8]

In fact, the Turin militants and their kin elsewhere were
voicing, albeit in a negative manner, the equally perennial and crucial
problem of any revolutionary socialist movement in bourgeois society,
the need to achieve a socialist identity and autonomy within the overpowering intellectual hegemony of capitalist society. An elementary
form of marxism was by now widespread, but its quality was pathetic
even by the standards of the Second International. In many localities,
'marxism' was simply an economic gloss on democratic rhetoric, on
that petty-bourgeois, street-corner anti-clericalism which was the
stock-in-trade of radicals, particularly after Giolitti's Gentilone Pact
with the catholics for the first elections based on near manhood
suffrage in 1913.

Furthermore, in sharp contrast to the 'marxist' decade of
the 1890s, the student population was moving en masse into the newer
activist, anti-positivist, elitist styles ; students, as in so many countries,
were usually the belligerent vanguard of nationalist demonstrations
which generally took on an anti-working-class character. Among the
student minority which rallied to the working class, 'marxism' was the
mechanistic determinism of the Second International's creed, lost in
the positivism prevalent outside intellectual circles. As Tasca said
about the first generation of self-taught working-class intellectuals in
Turin : 'In our great trinity of Darwin, Spencer and Marx, the latter
tended to lose out.'[9]

On the other hand, many of the newer movements of the
intellect, which could be refreshment and liberation in terms of personal psychology and formation, were being channelled into the popular movement in 'Sorelian' forms by the syndicalists who offered the
challenge of permanent rebelliousness. Any working-class intellectual
or student committing himself to the proletariat was inevitably exposed to them. The Turin youngsters were soon avid readers of
Prezzolini's *La Voce,* Salvemini's *L'Unità,* enthusiastic supporters of
Mussolini, a process which significantly distanced them from their
elders.[10]

The socialist youth federation, the FGS, was most seriously

affected, as it formed the cadres who were to rejuvenate the party. Its action was manly and often heroic, particularly against militarism, where it responded promptly to the tough anti-war resolutions of the Basle congress of the International in 1912 and to the vehement propaganda of such as Gustave Hervé in France. But its own propaganda in its journal *Avanguardia* tended to be *simplist* and moralist, competing in radicalism with the syndicalists but essentially a *protest* against the sheer sordid exploitation and corruption of the Giolittian regime. The South and its wretched condition was a touch-stone and Salvemini, with his passionate crusade, became a hero second only to Mussolini. In a striking gesture in Turin, Tasca and Ottavio Pastore with the support of the young Gramsci, then entering politics very much a Sardinian, offered Salvemini a northern seat after he'd been defeated by Giolitti's unscrupulous manipulation of catholics and southern clienteles. When he refused, it was natural to offer the seat to Mussolini.[11]

In brief, the socialist movement, in the democratic culture of its leading figures, *and* in the 'anti-culture' of its proletarian militants, in the contradictory ideologies of its youth movement, even in its rebellion, remained a prisoner of the bourgeois intellect.

The issue was brought to the forefront in 1912 when Salvemini denounced the quality of *Avanguardia*, the poverty of its theoretical elaboration. Angelo Tasca in Turin, already launched on his enterprise to 'revivify' marxism through 'modernization', broadly agreed and, shedding Salvemini's 'intellectualism', nevertheless proposed a radical change in the nature of the youth paper. But in a classic debate at the youth congress in Bologna in September 1912, he was defeated by Amadeo Bordiga of Naples.[12]

Bordiga, said Giuseppe Berti who knew him well, 'hadn't read a page of Croce or Gentile, and boasted of it. And it was true. He found positivism inadequate and clumsy. It seemed to him that, for a philosophy, marxism largely sufficed.'[13] This kind of comment on Bordiga was made frequently. In view of later distortions of his thinking, it is important to stress that his was in no sense the 'anti-culture' of a Maria Giudice. What he was seeking, at first in an inevitably crude and clumsy manner, was the creation, in combat, of a proletarian, marxist 'culture' in total rupture with the bourgeois world. In his total commitment to a totally *class*, proletarian action in every field of human experience, he was led, largely through experience rather than through study, to adopt rigorous positions, virtually unique in Italy (though there were other examples elsewhere in Europe, including Britain) which later commentators would recognize as 'communist', indeed, in some senses 'Leninist'.

Bordiga's central theme was the inescapable necessity of *political* action in *proletarian* autonomy, no matter what the immediate context. His hammering on marxism was perhaps narrow and could become *simplist,* near-sectarian. But in the circumstances of Italy, and of Naples in particular, this was probably a functional necessity. It was certainly powerful, consistent and historically effective. Through the turmoil of Italy in crisis, from 1912 onwards, it carried him remorselessly to the leadership of a new communist party.

In 1912, he argued against Tasca that no effort at reform could change the class basis of culture and education. Against the 'cultural crisis' of Tasca and Salvemini, he posited the existence of a much deeper crisis of ideas and principles inherent in the crisis of a capitalist society, a crisis which could be resolved only by the regeneration of the marxist consciousness of class and in struggle. The causes of socialist malaise were localism, particularism, craft and trade egoism, the absence of unity of class purpose. In this context 'working-class culture' could figure in a *democratic* programme but was of little use in the necessarily 'subversive' action of socialism. He did not deny 'socialist culture', but believed the only way to develop it was to leave it to individual initiative, while avoiding at all costs the prison of the academic and the scholastic. And such initiatives could bear fruit only if they were directly related to the basic social conflict and the proletarian struggle.[14]

Bordiga, who had been an anonymous voice shouting in support of Mussolini's call to expel Bissolati at the congress of Reggio Emilia, was 23 in 1912, the son of an agronomist of Piedmontese origin who taught at the agricultural college at Portici, near Naples.[15] Naples was tough territory for a socialist. There had been industrial development, particularly after the special laws of 1904 in the city's favour. A belt of ship-building, engineering shops, Ilva, Armstrong, the Miani-Silvestri plants, together with *pasta* manufactories, stretched from Castellammare to Torre del Greco, with Torre Annunziata earning the nickname of 'little Manchester'. But while the hinterland escaped somewhat from the overpowering presence of clientele politics, the Freemasons and respectable criminality and corruption, the socialist movements in the city were trapped in the electoral bloc system which was prevalent in much of the South and which installed reformist socialists in local power at Rome as members of a coalition presided over by the celebrated Mason Ernesto Nathan. The national PSI turned a blind eye to the deviations of the local section even when it came out in support of the Libyan War. The threat had come from the syndicalists. Arturo Labriola's journal *Propaganda* had at one time displaced *Avanti* among militants of the hinterland ; his removal and the secession of syndicalists from the party had reduced both socialists and syndicalists to a rump, increasingly absorbed in a popular bloc and penetrated by Freemasonry in an unnervingly non-proletarian environment.

It was in revolt against this condition that the *Karl Marx* circle was formed in April 1912, around Bordiga and a group of friends, in part drawn from the Portici college – Ruggero Grieco who was long to be Amadeo's left hand, Ortensia de Meo, who was to become his wife, Mario Bianchi. They began their long, minority struggle for marxist principle. In 1913 class conflict erupted in popular action against an increase in tariffs ; the manhood-suffrage elections were a labyrinth of manipulation, corruption and violence. The *Karl Marx* circle came out against the local socialist union, against mere rebellion without marxist awareness, against the abstention from parliamentary elections preached by disgusted purists. The elections, argued Bordiga, must be fought by a totally independent socialist party precisely in order to expose the class character of democracy. Difficult though it was to distinguish socialists from the parliamentary practice of the bourgeoisie, the effort had to be made – 'The social revolution is a political fact and is prepared on the political terrain.' Abstentionism was a renunciation of the only method which could equip the proletariat with a consciousness which would protect it from the politicking of bourgeois opportunists . . . 'Electoral neutralism means neutralism of consciousness and opinion.' Social problems, while economic in essence, invariably assumed political form.[16]

Bordiga had not yet reached the position of seeing electoral practices themselves as a source of bourgeois hegemony, but in two journals which the group produced locally, argued for a strictly *proletarian* participation.

At the Ancona congress of the party in July 1914, his thinking acquired a new dimension. The left, better organized than ever before, directed its efforts towards an expulsion of the Freemasons and the ending of all electoral alliances. Bordiga threw himself into the struggle. He ran up against the rooted Socialist policy towards the South, of which Ettore Ciccotti was the major exponent. In orthodox Second International terms, this argued, from the backwardness of the region, for socialist effort in support of its bourgeois modernization, its capitalist 'maturation', its bourgeois 'revolution', in almost Menshevik terms. Bordiga came out for a totally *proletarian* policy. His perspective was national, indeed international. He rejected any perspective which based policy on the 'peculiarity' of the South. The crisis of the South was an integral element of a general capitalist crisis which was registering in Italy. Even if the development of the proletariat were retarded in the South, the party must in no way renounce its 'necessary continuity' in revolutionary ideology. The bourgeois revolution had begun first in a determinate country and then spread, but as this historical process developed, its phases became 'simultaneous' in all countries. The socialist party of the international proletariat was universalizing its propaganda throughout the inhabited world despite disparities in local conditions . . . 'If we renounced this historical simultaneity of the revolutionary process, we would have renounced our very *raison d'être* as a party.' The duty of socialists was to create a global opposition to a global capitalism, and the opposition was to be total: the Socialist Party was not 'a patient process of reconstruction of the disintegrating organizations of present society ; it is a process of demolition of the present organization of society in its entirety'.

The South still lacked a proletariat in the strict marxist sense of the term, but if the southern bourgeoisie was economically retarded, it had achieved its *political* victory simultaneously with the victory of the bourgeoisie in Italy as a whole . . . 'it has achieved the democratic regime, which is the political regime of the bourgeois class.' Any adaptation of socialist policy in the South to the relatively under-developed character of its own local proletariat would be a denial of the *political* revolution of the proletariat. 'The Socialist Party cannot halt before the corpse of an impotent bourgeoisie lying inert across its path.' The Socialist Party had to be the party of the *proletariat*, the *Italian* proletariat, indeed the European, the world proletariat, or it was nothing.[17]

This argument, schematic though it was, certainly introduced into the Italian party something of the tone of the great debates in the Russian movement. At the time, Bordiga's was an isolated voice, but in the turmoil of the insurrections of Red Week and the radicalization of socialist policy at Ancona, the leadership of the Naples socialist union at Naples was displaced. Bordiga assumed the editorship of its journal *Il Socialista* and was making it the organ of his rigid and principled marxism when war broke out.[18]

The response of his opponent in the 'culture' debate, Angelo Tasca, was very different. Turin, of course, in the years before the War was rapidly growing into the most characteristically industrial city in Italy.[19] It had been relatively backward, compared to the Lombard centres and even the smaller industrial centres in Piedmont. Textiles and the dress industry were the foundation, with many women workers ; the professional middle classes and artisan groups were relatively weak. Its university, while prestigious, was not renowned for marxism or even for Crocean idealism, until Umberto Cosmo took the chair of Italian literature in 1913. The working class, rather passive, *was* renowned for its mutual aid societies and co-operation. Turin's general association of workers, the AGO, was the first labour organization in Italy to create a retail co-operative and in 1899 it joined with the railway workers' co-operative to form the extremely powerful Turin Co-operative Alliance, ACT. Reformists were strong in the PSI section, but this was itself numerically weak ; in 1910 it had only 600 members.

While militancy was on the increase from 1900, it was the impact of the automobile industry, with associated engineering and chemical plants, which transformed the city. Modern mass industry quite suddenly mushroomed ; by 1911, there were some 93,000 industrial workers in the city, over 30,000 of them metalworkers. FIOM, created in 1901, soon made Turin its base, as did the CGL at first. Most of the skilled workers were creamed off into automobiles and there was an increasing migration into unskilled work from the countryside, though the rapid multiplication of enterprises of high technicity generated a good deal of mobility.

Moreover, the swift rise of new firms, the crashes of 1907-8, the revival of prosperity from 1911 in a context of general political militancy plunged Turin into struggles of the fiercest intensity which made its working class a by-word for solidarity and combativity.

FIOM won its first celebrated contract with Fiat in 1906, which recognized the 10-hour day as normal and authorized the election of ad hoc grievance committees called 'internal commissions', a small number of workers, elected by union men within the factory to handle everyday problems of discipline and arbitration. In the same year the whole working class of the city struck in support of the textile workers and, in response, the employers formed a Turin Industrial League. FIOM won a contract with the Itala car firm at this time which, in return for a no-strike pledge for three years, authorized a permanent internal commission and a union shop. In the following year, however, the organized employers struck back, extended their cartel to the province, tried to co-ordinate action with Genoa, Milan and Terni, and ran into headlong collision with syndicalist-inspired resistance. A series of shattering defeats for the workers coincided with the onset of the depression which 'rationalized' the car industry. On the ruins of working-class militancy, the first *Confindustria*, general confederation of industrialists, formed at Turin on the model of the League. From 1911, however, orderly and rapid growth was resumed, a process which the outbreak of War transformed into breakneck industrialization. On this rising curve, working-class militancy swept into a series of titanic struggles as, after the Reggio congress, *intransigent revolutionary* militants captured the local Socialist Party section. A struggle of the un-unionized in 1912 precipitated a 65-day strike, one led by FIOM the following year brought the men out for 75 days and secured a settlement in which skilled men accepted some sacrifice to help the unskilled. Turin began to outstrip Milan and Emilia-Romagna as a stronghold of socialist militancy, working-class solidarity and ambitious proletarian spirit.

It was at the beginning of this process, in 1909, that Angelo Tasca, the son of a worker, and only 17 years old, joined with Giuseppe Romita, later a reformist and Gino Castagno, a centre socialist, to found a section of the FGS.[20] There had earlier been study circles and even a Francisco Ferrer modern school (named after the Spanish anarchist martyr) in Turin, but the new central section, intensely serious and puritanical (it broke with the local party stalwarts over the drink question) captured the loyalties of several dozen zealous young workers, most of them of recent rural origin. One of their first activities was the establishment of circles in the periphery and the organization of 'red cyclist' expeditions, Clarion style, into the countryside. It was the bleak response of the country people which drove them to 'escape from positivism' and eradicate their own inadequacies.

According to Piero Gobetti, the 'revolutionary' liberal who knew him well, Tasca was something of an apostle with a messianic conception of popular redemption. He committed himself to an exploration of socialist history, in an effort to 'modernize' marxism in an activist sense and free it from positivism. In later years he was meticulously to edit the Labriola-Engels correspondence and to write a perceptive history of fascism.[21] He and his group plunged into *La Voce*, Salvemini, the most advanced bourgeois culture, in an effort to eliminate their 'provincialism'. The Turin section developed into a highly distinctive sector of FGS. It was overwhelmingly working class; Tasca and Romita were the only students. Tasca indeed was totally involved in the great battles of 1912-13, alongside FIOM men and against the syndicalists.

It was from 1913 or so that some students from Turin university were drawn into the section, Umberto Terracini, precocious in 'political' skills, Palmiro Togliatti, distinctly dilettante and detached at this stage, and Antonio Gramsci. Gramsci[22] had come to the university in 1911 from Sardinia and had been struggling with a range of courses, concentrating on linguistics, literature and philosophy, despite extreme poverty and ill-health, 'a headache every day for three years'. Socialist in a style which was at once 'intellectualist' *and* deeply committed to the 'popular', more sharply Sardinian and 'southern' in his pre-occupations, he was then essentially 'Crocean', open to the whole world of the mind, profoundly 'ethico-political' in motive. He had read 'some things by Marx' but was repelled by positivism and it is difficult to see him at this stage as in any meaningful sense a serious marxist. In 1914-15, his linguistics teacher introduced him to a philosopher with the words . . . 'he wants to find out more about Marx'; this *after* his first major political article, which damned him, virtually for life, as a 'Mussolinian', voluntarist, 'Bergsonian' exponent of intervention in the War. According to that philosopher, what drove Gramsci in 1914-15 was an urge 'to understand how culture developed, for revolutionary reasons . . . He wanted to find out how thinking can lead to action . . . how thought can make hands move.'[23]

It was after his experience of the manhood suffrage elections of 1913 in Sardinia that Gramsci joined the socialist movement.

He was an instant success at small-group teaching at the FGS centre. The night streets were loud with argument as he and his class talked their way home, a perennially familiar scene in working-class history. The arguments Gramsci developed, however, were scarcely familiar. In essence, he, like Tasca, was trying to mobilize the whole of 'culture' in the service of revolution – and of a slowly strengthening marxism. Almost inevitably, it was a problematic fixed by Croce, Gentile, Salvemini, the literary critic de Sanctis, a breath-taking range of bourgeois thinkers, which registered on his readers. Gramsci's theatre criticism and running commentary in *Il Grido del Popolo* and the Turin edition of *Avanti*, in the late War years, brilliant, caustic, oblique, probably represent a unique moment in the history of the socialist movement. But he presented his work as a building of 'the new socialism, full of moral and revolutionary energy, in which there is not a party and a proletariat but a single mass moving rapidly towards a goal . . .'[24] Like all the youth, he was Mussolinian in 1913-14 ; Sorel's style flits elusively through much of his work. As late as 1917, he could bring out his first pamphlet *La Città Futura*, still 'instrumentally' Crocean, and greet the Bolshevik revolution as the revolution 'against' *Das Kapital*. In a sense, despite his personal distinction, he represented, in extreme form, certain characteristics of the Turin group as a whole, activist, enterprising, revivifying, but rather uneasy and marginal among the Rabezzanas and Giudices even of Turin. The contrast with Bordiga is stark. No historical phenomenon, however, is simple, as Gramsci so frequently pointed out. It was after the cataclysm of the Turin rising of 1917 which precipitated him into local leadership that Gramsci's writing acquired new, and marxist, dimensions. And at that point, it is necessary to note, he found his natural place alongside Bordiga's men.

The difference between the two most serious centres of 'regeneration' in the youth movement becomes almost painfully evident at the dramatic moment of Mussolini's defection. Both Bordiga and Tasca had contributed to Mussolini's *Utopia* ;[25] the Turin group had wanted him as their deputy. In October 1914, the editor of *Avanti* published his notorious article *From an Absolute to an Active and Operative Neutrality*, in which he, in effect, advocated entry into the War on the side of the Entente, so that socialism, committing itself to the 'nation' and its problems, might achieve their 'revolutionary' solution. With the International in collapse and the PSI almost alone in its official opposition to war, Mussolini's article was a shock. In November, he was expelled, after he had launched his paper *Il Popolo d'Italia* which developed the fascist ideology.

For the left and the youth movement, this was a catastrophe. The Turin group, in fact, disintegrated. Togliatti supported intervention, left the Socialist Party and when Italy entered the war in 1915, having been rejected on health grounds, volunteered for service with the medical corps. He believed the establishment of a *pax Britannica* through war would advance socialism. Terracini on the other hand opposed war and was imprisoned for distributing anti-war leaflets. Tasca developed an argument in the Turin paper, favouring opposition to the war as a 'negative myth', to prise the working class free from authority.[26] Gramsci wrote his first political article for *Il Grido* on 31 October. It was almost his last. Under the title *Active and Operative Neutrality*, he denounced the reformists for their passivity in face of the war. The Italian proletariat, whose party was a 'state in embryo', must seek the conditions most favourable for a decisive social 'dislocation' or 'wrench' (*strappo*) and exert pressure on its adversary. If the Italian bourgeoisie felt summoned to war by its own destiny, this might present the opportunity for a series of 'wrenches'. And while the article did not in fact advocate intervention, it was, with reservations, obviously sympathetic to Mussolini's argument. Notable in it is the rooted influence of a 'voluntarism' which was not simply Mussolinian, the notion of a 'dislocation', of 'new values a reborn socialist party has put into circulation' and a certain concentration on the nation and on nation-making which was common in intellectual discourse: the question 'we, Italian socialists' must ask themselves was: 'What must be the function of the *Italian* socialist party (note, not the *proletariat* or *socialism* in general) in the present moment of *Italian* life?'.[27]

Gramsci never really recovered from the effect of the article. He was labelled an interventionist. His brother Mario volunteered for war service and ended up a fascist and this, too, was used against Antonio. Gramsci withdrew from the active life of the party, tried to immerse himself in his studies, seriously considered a teaching career, and collapsed into a nervous breakdown. It was a year before he resumed socialist activity as a committed anti-war militant.[28]

From Naples, the response was clear-cut. On 22 October, *Il Socialista* carried an article whose title was its message, *For an*

Active and Operative Anti-militarism. And Bordiga never wavered an inch from a total proletarian and anti-nationalist opposition to capitalist war. By 1917 he was arguing for armed insurrection. As the Socialist Party floundered and the interventionists whipped up their campaign, Bordiga and his group were isolated in Naples. The journal ceased publication; it struggled briefly to life again in May 1915, as the street campaigns for intervention reached fever pitch and as the call for working-class resistance met no response in the southern city. The last number of *Il Socialista* on 22 May 1915 carried the head-line: 'It is War. Down with the War!'[29]

The Outbreak of War

At the Ancona congress of the party in 1914, the radicaliza-tion and internationalization of the PSI were carried a stage further. Freemasons were finally expelled, amid harrowing scenes; electoral alliances were renounced; parliamentary deputies were to be sub-jected to party control. Preparatory measures for the August meeting of the Second International were made the occasion for linking the struggles in Italy directly to those in Europe as a whole. Serrati joined the Directorate, Mussolini was confirmed in his editorship of *Avanti* and Lazzari was made secretary in an attempt to achieve some kind of unity. For the reformists remained powerful at all levels. They had been reinforced by the election results and at the CGL congress in May, they had won all along the line.

The implicit paralysis of the party leadership became ex-plicit with the explosion of Red Week. On 7 June, an anti-militarist, anti-nationalist, anti-capitalist demonstration in Ancona organized by Nenni and the anarchist hero Malatesta was fired on by the police and three were killed. The PSI, in accordance with its policy, called a general strike. This was the signal for insurrectionary outbreaks. Ancona was held by rebels for ten days. Barricades went up in all the big cities. In Emilia and the Marches, authority collapsed. Local leaders established the dictatorship of the proletariat; red flags were raised, churches attacked, railways torn up, villas sacked, taxes abol-ished and prices reduced. The socialist state within a state in Emilia became reality and it took ten thousand troops to reduce Ancona. The extent and the intensity of the strike were without precedent. There was no effective central leadership; socialists, anarchists, syndicalists, republicans, joined in a melée. The PSI Directorate was paralyzed after its first call. Mussolini revelled in the movement with 'that legitimate joy with which the craftsman contemplates his creation . . . Workers, I would like to be the poet of the general strike.' In fact, the loyalty of the army and the police had generally held, white guards had appeared at Bologna and elsewhere, and, in the local elections, reactionary candidates triumphed in Turin, Genoa and Rome. The CGL had been appalled by the virulence of the rising and on 11 June intervened to call off the strike, an action which Mussolini denounced as a 'felony'.[30]

The reformists in *Critica Sociale* and the whole parliamentary group moved to an all-out attack on Mussolini and his 'dictatorship'. 'The emancipation of the proletariat is not to be achieved by outbursts by disorganized mobs' declared the deputies. Claudio Treves accused Mussolini of treachery and hooliganism. The Directorate was trapped. Mussolini had in fact followed the official *policy* of the party leadership; his 'error' lay in the intangible quality of style. The leadership once again confirmed him in his editorship and took a strong anti-government line; even the GPS obstructed legislation. But with its instinct for unity and deep suspicion of the syndicalists, the leadership shuffled to the right and subjected Mussolini to discipline.[31]

It was, then, on a movement whose local militants were being hounded by the police and whose leadership had patched up an internal truce that the War crisis broke.[32] The first to react was Mussolini. 'Down with war!' he wrote in *Avanti* on 26 July, 'Not a man! Not a penny!' The next day Turati and Treves gathered the parliamentary deputies in Milan, re-affirmed support for absolute neutrality and called on the International. Balabanoff and Morgari went to the last desperate meetings of the International at Brussels. The Directorate launched an anti-war manifesto on 28 July and held an extraordinary convention on 3-4 August, attended by the CGL, the autonomous maritime and railway unions and even USI. This re-affirmed absolute neutrality but, ominous symptom, added a condemnation of the central powers.

Lenin hailed the PSI as the 'happy exception' to the dismal collapse of the Second International. This is true, in the sense that the PSI rejected the war, refused to support it and worked hard to rebuild an International. But it is true only up to a point. The Salandra government (Giolitti had prudently withdrawn earlier in the year) decided on neutrality, fearing German-Austrian hegemony. This decision killed the Triple Alliance, made possible an Austrian attack on Italy and propelled the government, behind the back of a parliament, many of whose members supported the neutralist stand of Giolitti, into negotiations with the Entente to sell Italian intervention. A great surge of interventionist emotion built up, fuelled by the old irredentism against Austria, pro-Belgian and pro-French feeling, all the old great-power lusts and romantic-revolutionary passion of the democratic nationalists. It was the democratic left above all, radicals, republicans, Mazzinians, varieties of socialists and syndicalists who moved the crowds in the streets, with D'Annunzian rhetoric ; heavy industry partly mobilized behind the more nationalist of the new capitalists, though Turin as a whole stayed Giolittian and neutralist.

The gale of patriotic passion blew across the socialist movement. Could socialists stand by if Austria attacked? How could a socialist be neutral in a war between imperial Germany and France, 'cradle of a hundred revolutions', home of the revolutionary proletariat, of syndicalism, of that Hervé, the super pacifist who had just volunteered as a private? The syndicalist split, de Ambris and Corridoni urging intervention ; a UIL union federation was to break from USI and attract 'revolutionary' patriots. Salvemini went over. Turati and the reformists, anxious to incorporate the working class into a democratic rebuilding of Italy, were equally anxious not to have it alienated from 'the nation'. All the old arguments over defensive against offensive war were rehearsed ; as German socialists pointed to the threat from the Russian Tsar, Italians talked of Germanic repression. What was revealed in the crisis was the essential unity of the Italian intelligentsia, of the middle and lower-middle classes. The line of class division over adherence to 'the nation' ran through the socialist movement.

Already in early August, there was talk of a truce in the class war ; the CGL declared itself ready to resist an Austrian invasion. German social democrats on mission were coldly received and the Italian-Swiss conference in Lugano in September took up a defensist-pacifist position. As the interventionist forces built up, Mussolini shifted further and further towards them, finally to explode in his October article. The Directorate censured him and he resigned. On 15 November, having secured financial backing from a range of sources, including France, he launched *Il Popolo d'Italia*, with slogans from Blanqui and Napoleon: 'He who has steel, has bread! Revolution is an idea which has found bayonets!' A group of syndicalists rallied round him, mobilized 5,000 in 50 *fasci*, and his paper became the mouthpiece of an increasingly frenetic interventionist left.

The PSI expelled him as a traitor and never forgave him (they refused to accept his surrender even in 1945, the surrender of an 'old comrade' as he whimsically called himself!).[38] The shock was profound, since he had been virtually the leader of the mass party. There was a ripple of defections, but militants and the youth on the whole stood firm, grounded in the rooted anti-militarism of the working class and the peasantry. Serrati took over *Avanti*, to begin his heroic and often lonely struggle to maintain the unity of the party, the epic which made him the most loved of all its leaders.

But he had to struggle to maintain that unity as defensism eroded the party's neutrality. Through the winter, as intervention came closer, the reformists shuffled closer to the nation and talked of 'relative neutrality' and a truce in the class war. Intransigents organized mass demonstrations in the new year against the cost of living, unemployment, the threat of war, but the only truly intransigent voice was Bordiga's. By December, he was preaching the need to break free of any and every association with capitalism's war, the need to intensify 'social discord'; the proposal to turn national into civil war, while never made explicit, became implicit in his writing.

But from February, government took action against socialist demonstrations and Serrati himself was arrested, as the interventionists took to the streets. The approaching climax of negotiations with the Entente, the revolt in parliament and the re-appearance of Giolitti as a possible focus for neutralism, galvanized the interventionists. With D'Annunzio in the van, a passionate, near-hysterical chauvinist frenzy mobilized masses against parliament, against Giolitti, against the 'traitor' socialists, in the 'radiant days of May'.

The PSI was reduced to a state of siege. As the Directorate, oscillating desperately, tried to organize resistance to the interventionist street campaign, the parliamentary group warned equally desperately against the threat of civil war and total isolation from the nation. The Directorate lost its nerve. It dropped the general strike against the war proposed for 19 May and told sections to hold protest meetings instead. But at Turin, with middle-class opinion largely formed by the Giolittian *La Stampa* and the section controlled by proletarian militants in close contact with working-class life, they went ahead, into a general strike on 17-18 May, which led to prolonged and bloody clashes with the police. There were other sporadic outbreaks across Italy, but they could be swept aside. Peasantry and working class were dragooned into war by an exultant middle class and petty bourgeoisie.

As the state of siege clamped down, the PSI, to preserve its unity, adopted the rather negative slogan: 'Neither support nor sabotage'. The PSI voted solidly against war credits in the Chamber and then Turati went to see his friend, Camillo Corradini, Giolittian *chef de cabinet* to the minister Orlando, to offer 'dignified collaboration' in holding the masses steady to the national cause.

The War and the Working Class

In a sense, the war created both peasant militancy and a conscious working class.[34] Some 5,750,000 men were drafted ; 600,000 were killed, 700,000 permanently disabled. Of the conscripted, 46 per cent were peasants or rural workers. It proved easy to whip up their hatred against exempted industrial workers. Sardinian peasants in uniform had no hesitation in shooting down Turin workers in August 1917. The rural labour force of males over 18 fell from 4.8 million to 2.2 million. Women and children went more extensively to work, but food production fell sharply, agricultural prices doubled while industrial prices trebled ; there were requisitions and controls. On the other hand, the black market flourished and it is clear, as Gramsci pointed out, that many peasant households fought free of debt and mortgage.[35] In northern Italy the number of peasant proprietors rose from 26 to 36 per cent of the total number of farmers.[36] The net effect, particularly during the national mobilization after the Caporetto disaster, with its sweeping promises of land reform, was to generate an intense and quasi-political land-hunger and militancy among the rural population. Their rebellion was registering during 1918 and when the war ended, the peasants exploded into history.

On the working class, the most obvious impact was that of sheer expansion. Italian production, particularly after Caporetto, achieved near-miraculous levels. At the end of the war, Italy had more artillery than Britain ; it was exporting trucks and aircraft to its allies. Steel and engineering production increased by 50 per cent; the output of electric power doubled. Large firms became monsters; Ilva, Fiat, Ansaldo straddled northern Italy like a colossus. In the last year of the war, there were dramatic financial take-overs. The labour force expanded abruptly. Engineering embraced 500,000; Fiat's workers alone rose from 7,000 to 30,000; the worker population of Turin doubled. In the immediate aftermath of the war, well over three million workers flooded into the liberated trade unions.

Their living conditions during the war generated contradictory effects which were as explosive as those in agriculture. All firms deemed essential to the war effort were designated 'auxiliary' and subjected to quasi-military discipline. Some of their workers were considered to be on military duty, others were exempted from military service. Over 300,000 of some 900,000 workers in auxiliary factories were considered military or exempted and over 760 of the 1,976 auxiliary firms were in the metal industry. It has been estimated that over a third of the labour force was excused service at the front. Their wages rose to nominally high levels. There were more opportunities for women. There was a widespread popular prejudice against the 'well-paid shirkers'.

In fact, their lives were frequently wretched. Prices rocketed; there was massive inflation. Note circulation rose from 3,454 million lire in 1913 to 14,465 million in 1918. One estimate records a rise in the cost-of-living index from 132.7 in 1915 (1913=100) to 409.1 in 1918, while the index for daily earnings rose from 3.54 lire to 6.04 lire in the same period. Another estimates the fall in real wages at over a quarter. It is clear from social-service institution figures that in Milan, where wages were higher than average, a family of two adults and three children would need two wage-earners in the family simply to keep going. In Turin, consumption of meat per inhabitant fell by a third, that of sugar by a half.[37] Food shortages were chronic, general living and working conditions grim, the breakneck growth of industry and the general dislocation caused intense suffering. And while the government made belated efforts to impose equality of sacrifice in the national revival after Caporetto, 1917 and 1918 were a black period. Shortly before the Turin workers rose in revolt in August 1917, Giolitti himself made a speech denouncing the blatant inequality.

For industrial profits were monstrous and the black market

nauseating. Serrati regularly published the balance sheets of companies despite censorship and police harassment. In 1917, 313 leading firms made a net profit of almost 1,331 million lire, two and a half times as much as in 1916. Pirelli made 7 millions in 1917 alone – and Pirelli tyres were said to have been found on captured Austrian trucks. One scholar estimates that between 1914 and 1917, the profit rate in steel rose from 6.3 to 16.5 per cent, in wool, from 5.1 to 18.7 per cent, chemicals and rubber from around 8 to near 16 per cent. Motor-cars were said to have risen from 8.2 to 30.5 per cent.[38] The average is placed at around 16 per cent and profits of 20 per cent and 40 per cent were common. And there was a miasma of scandal, corruption and even treason, around these war profits of the 'sharks'. In 1918, industrialists who had exported silk to Germany via Switzerland were arrested ; Pirelli was subjected to enquiry ; *La Stampa* waged a campaign against the corruption of the shop-keepers' co-operative. After the war, Giolitti could win massive support for his campaign to gouge these profits out of the 'sharks'.[39]

The net result was a monstrous increase in class hatred. It was intensified and turned into militancy by the mobilization of industry for the war.[40] The instrument was committees of industrial mobilization created in August 1915. These imposed a form of military feudalism on the factories. Workers were tied to the job under threat of imprisonment, demotion to lower-paid jobs, posting to the front. But this forced labour was accompanied by a near-compulsory arbitration system. The committees undertook the settlement of disputes. They settled 948 conflicts directly and decreed settlement in 458 other cases. Members of the committee were active in pacifying yet others. Union leaders were enmeshed in this process. Indeed, Bruno Buozzi, secretary of FIOM, found the system reasonably effective. Unions could no longer protect their members from disciplinary action, but they had a myriad jobs to perform over wages, health, safety. Their participation in the system brought them recruits. Membership of FIOM rose from some 11,000 to 47,000 at a time when union propaganda was impossible.

On the other hand, the service of union leaders generated suspicion and opened a breach between workers and labour organizations. The stresses and strains of wartime growth in any event vastly multiplied the frictions of daily work. Some kind of safety valve was needed and, in these circumstances, the 'internal commissions' which had enjoyed a sporadic existence pre-war became ubiquitous. At times, the mobilization committees encouraged them and they were often successful in disciplinary matters. They enjoyed some independence of the formal union structure and the mobilization committees often entrusted the local enforcement of agreements to them. But, while they were becoming essential to workers on the shop-floor and their members were beginning to act like shop-stewards, there was little system or uniformity in their selection. In the Turin area, they were usually five in number, often 'obvious' candidates from the 'leading workers' in the shops. Only union members had the right to vote in their election, but such procedures were often merely formal, union officials and dues-collectors doing the choosing. The influence of FIOM was paramount, but inevitably it was on the commissions that discontent came to a focus.[41]

It was during 1917 that the atmosphere became brittle. To check the rising tide of discontent, government urged a conciliatory policy on wages and grievances but at the same time, opened the committees to representatives of catholic and interventionist unions. There was a sharp increase in tension and the internal commissions began to acquire a certain independence in hostility to the trade unions. Much the same process was happening in all the institutions of the working class. While official socialist policy remained 'Neither support nor sabotage', the socialist-controlled communes had plenty of jobs they could do, in defence of the standard of living, in assistance, in securing exemption, in what the party called 'human solidarity'. Their actions were supported by deputies in the Chamber, the co-operatives, the land workers' union. All the institutions of the working class drifted into collaboration with the state and the reformist movement emerged immensely strengthened by the war. On the other hand, popular discontent was, by 1917, reaching insurrection point.

1917 and the Polarization of the PSI

'The colossal historical error of the men who, from the outbreak of the world war to the present have controlled the governing organs of our association,' wrote Gramsci in October 1920, 'has been the belief that they could preserve the old structure of the party from its inner dissolution.'[42]

The most striking feature of the PSI during the War and

immediately after it is the fact that it preserved a unity, despite an internal polarization which would logically appear to have been intolerable. Serrati, in fact, saw this task as his historical duty. The roots of the 'failed revolution' of 1919-20 in Europe clearly lie in the war period itself, particularly in those decisive months between the mass revolts against the War in 1917 and the 'rally to the nation' which followed the last German offensive, itself made possible by the Soviet tactical surrender at the peace of Brest-Litovsk, which precipitated the first serious conflict between Lenin and the revolutionary 'left'. In Italy, the Caporetto disaster had this effect in late 1917. Despite intense popular disaffection and the attempt to create a revolutionary political movement, the reformists, and with them much of the structure of official socialism, rallied to the nation and to an international perspective which was essentially democratic, with the February revolution in Russia and the internationalism of Woodrow Wilson as its parameters. The precise temper of the insurrectionary masses remains elusive. After the War, during the critical debate over revolution in the CGL at the climax of the Occupation of the Factories in 1920, Buozzi of FIOM proposed a compromise resolution which in effect ratified the use of 'revolutionary' means to achieve ends which, however dramatic, remained essentially 'democratic'. It may well be that this, in fact, accurately reflected popular temper not only in 1920 but in 1917. Certainly the social-democratic spirit remained very strong, even in parties which had formally ceased to be social-democratic. If it were conceded that the issue of 'communist' revolution was in fact settled in Europe in the critical months between the first Russian revolution and the peace of Brest-Litovsk, then the post-war crisis, Comintern policy, particularly in the 1920-21 switch to a 'united front', and the thinking of that 'ultra-left' which Lenin dismissed as 'infantile' would require radical re-assessment.[43]

This is speculation. What is certain is that popular discontent reached the point of insurrection in some areas of Italy in 1917, but failed to create a revolutionary instrument ; the revolutionary wing of the PSI failed to be effective and moreover, remained within a party in which reformism and a commitment to democracy had strengthened. However devoted and heroic the unitary labours of Serrati, the results surely suggest more permanent and structural causes. Despite its international role, the PSI did not achieve qualitative change after the crack of the Second International.

The PSI, despite its ambiguity over the Libyan War, had been strong in the International and after 1914, through its roving ambassadors, Balabanoff and Morgari, it strove hard to rebuild it.[44] It resolutely refused to countenance any reshaping of the International as an instrument of the Entente and the first Zimmerwald conference of the anti-war left in September 1915 owed a great deal to its efforts. There, the Italian delegation which included Serrati, made contact with Lenin and Trotsky. They did not join the proto-communist minority in its 'revolutionary defeatism', but rallied to the majority call for peace without annexations or indemnities. At the second conference in Kienthal in April 1916, where the Italians were more numerous, Serrati moved more decisively to the left (Bala-banoff was moving even further) but Morgari took the chance to talk to the Henry Ford peace mission and elaborated a Wilsonian argu-ment. There is no cause to doubt the 'internationalism' of *any* sector of the PSI, but most of them would qualify for Lenin's dismissive appellation of 'centrist'. Interestingly enough – and symptomatically – Lenin saw Turati and Treves as the Kautskys and Adlers of Italy. It was Bordiga who was to identify Serrati himself, in whom Lenin had some faith, as the real centrist.[45]

The PSI was far less active inside Italy. Fifteen northern provinces were declared a war zone, censorship was severe (though Serrati often managed to circumvent it), militants were harassed and called up. Serrati got the message of Zimmerwald through – there was an epidemic of Zimmerwald pins at one stage – but in practice the Directorate found it very difficult to maintain the party as a unit. Action shrank to the localities. Gramsci was now active in socialist journalism in Turin and Bordiga was holding to his lonely stand in the South, but it was very difficult for the party as a national force, with war service, prison, defection and exile eroding its cadres, to establish effective contact with the mounting popular exasperation. Only the deputies and the union leaders enjoyed any real freedom of manoeuvre. In June 1916 the Salandra government fell and Turati's personal contact Orlando became Minister of the Interior. The de facto collaboration of socialist institutions openly increased.

It was in 1917 that contradictions became acute.[46] President Wilson's peace message of 23 January was welcomed warmly by the reformists and circumspectly by Serrati, but at an ad hoc convention which managed to meet in Rome in February, a split threatened.

There were enough section delegates there to make it something close to a congress. After much agonizing debate, the conduct of the Directorate was approved by nearly 24,000 votes to over 6,000, but there was much discontent over the behaviour of the deputies. Bordiga was present and moved a tough motion which was only narrowly defeated, by 17,000 to 14,000. But the fiercest opposition came from the delegates of Turin, where popular exasperation was intense. Rabezzana, Barberis and Maria Giudice called for action. None was forthcoming, though the party re-affirmed its Zimmerwald allegiance. The Turin delegates were thrown back on their own resources.

The situation was transformed by news of the February revolution in Russia, followed by America's entry into the War. To reformists and democrats this revolutionized the character of the war, made it now unmistakably a war for democracy. The parliamentary wing and their supporters began to rally en masse to a Wilsonian doctrine and support for Russian moderates. On the other hand, the *fact* of revolution encouraged the intransigents. A vague but powerful desire to 'do like they did in Russia' gripped many. *Avanti* at this time was misinformed on the actual situation in Russia ; not until May did Balabanoff get to Petrograd. In these circumstances, the reformists took the lead in two critical meetings of the Directorate in April and May attended by representatives of the GPS and CGL. The April meeting issued a statement written by Turati which talked of a Russo-American democratic bloc confronting imperial autocracies which were bound to disintegrate. Only Bordiga protested, in a letter to *Avanti* and Serrati minimized the statement as an expression of the personal views of 'one or two of us'.

But, in May, Milan and nearby centres exploded into protest and riot against shortages and the general misery. The Directorate-CGL meeting which took place in the shadow of this, the most serious rebellion since the outbreak of war, virtually ignored it. It published instead a fully democratic programme of post-war reconstruction which called for universal suffrage in proportional representation, abolition of the senate, tax reforms, the 8-hour day, a state insurance scheme, civil service reform, socialization of the land and parliamentary control over foreign policy. The programme was presented in terms of a Wilsonian Europeanism. It was supported by speeches and articles by Turati and Treves which went further than the bulk of the deputies were prepared to go, hinting at socialist support for 'a better government', talking of a democratic peace and 'no-one in the trenches next winter'.[47]

These developments seem to have spurred the intransigents into action. Serrati himself, strengthened by a flow of accurate intelligence from Balabanoff in Petrograd, moved left. Lenin's name figured more and more prominently in *Avanti*. Serrati's perception of Lenin at this point, like Gramsci's, was more visionary and mythical than correct, but it registered a strengthening commitment to revolution. On 20 August, *Avanti* carried the headline *Viva Lenin*! which threw the reformists into consternation.

More serious work was in hand. In the spring the Naples section, led by Bordiga, issued an important statement of principle: socialists in every country must direct their efforts to one end, an immediate stop to the war, by an intransigent class action to resolve the crisis by achieving the revolutionary ends of socialism. This call to revolution, Leninist in tone, summoned the party to shed all ambiguity, to discipline and direct mass agitation, to make itself the vanguard of the proletariat in mass struggle against capitalism and bourgeois militarism.[48]

From Bordiga's Naples the summons to form a revolutionary movement circulated in semi-clandestine manner. About a hundred sections seem to have rallied. Groups of dedicated revolutionaries were now emerging in the most embattled centres. Florence was a stronghold, under the editor of the local journal *Difesa*, Egidio Gennari. In Milan, there were Luigi Repossi, Bruno Fortichiari and Abigaille Zanetta. In this nascent 'communist' movement, Turin was to the fore: its 'rigids' included Rabezzana, Barberis, Giudice, Giovanni Boero, Elvira Zocca.

In April, the youth movement began to move. The April number of *Avanguardia* projected a revolution in Germany and added, 'From the trenches to the streets! . . . Truth is on the march. It marches inexorably and victoriously from Russia to Germany. The socialist youth of Italy await it.'[49] In May, the FGS secretary sent a memorandum to the Directorate and the GPS demanding that they impose a 'clear class policy' on the CGL, for the preparation of a general strike on the slogan 'immediate peace and not victory'.

In May, Rabezzana was urging the collection of arms and both he and Barberis resigned from the national leadership of the party. In July the revolutionaries held a semi-secret meeting in Florence ('fifty extremists' according to the police) which constituted a fraction under the old 1910 name of *intransigent revolutionary* and took a clearly anti-patriotic line, summoning the party to abandon the 'bourgeois fatherland', adopt a strictly revolutionary line and re-affirm that violence was the mid-wife of social transformation. On 12 August, Lazzari the party secretary himself circulated socialist mayors on the proposal that they resign en masse if the War were not stopped.

The visit of a Russian delegation of Mensheviks and Social Revolutionaries seems to have struck the spark. They toured Italy, to a rapturous welcome from the crowds. Serrati may have interpreted their speeches rather freely, for everywhere they went they were greeted, to their visible dismay, with cries of *Viva Lenin!* The sudden emergence of mass, popular 'subversion' was a shock. The most tense moment was in Turin. In response to the news from Russia, the city's middle class had become more assertive in their neutralism. Giolitti spoke against inequality of sacrifice in August. The mayor of Turin made speeches in his support and was forced to resign. In Turin the Russians got their most enthusiastic reception. A little over a week later, the city rose in revolt.[50]

On the morning of 21 August, eighty bakeries failed to open in yet another breakdown in bread supplies. The streets filled with protesting women and children. Large supplies of wheat were rapidly imported but it was too late. The factories exploded into an anti-war demonstration. Clashes between police and workers were followed by pitched battles between workers and soldiers. The working-class quarters were barricaded, barracks attacked for arms, two churches sacked. The immediate uprising seems to have been entirely spontaneous. But the militants of the section, anarchists and syndicalists, quickly moved in to organize defence. In an effort to break out of encirclement, the workers advanced on the centre of the city ; on 24 August they nearly broke through. But they were finally beaten back by machine-guns and tanks.

On the 23rd some thirty socialist and union leaders, both in-transigent and reformist, had hurriedly met to give some order to the movement. No-one knew what to do. They issued a statement praising the workers' courage and asking them to give up any further 'useless violence'. On the 26th, socialist deputies asked the workers to return to their jobs and by the 28th it was all over. At least 50 workers had been killed and several hundred wounded. Over 800 socialists and anarchists were arrested, including the whole of the section leadership, and nearly 200 were shipped off to the front. The trial of alleged ringleaders was scheduled for the summer of 1918. In truth the movement had risen spontaneously from below. Moreover, not only was it one of the fiercest and bloodiest conflicts in Italian working-class history ; it was *consciously internationalist* and revolutionary. Lenin himself described the Turin rising as part of 'the development of the world revolution'. The fact that Serrati rushed to Turin so that the PSI should be 'associated with the movement' speaks volumes. A mass movement of workers well to the left of the PSI had suddenly emerged on the streets.

The Turin rising dislocated whatever plans the intransigents may have had. In the decimated Turin movement Gramsci was propelled into leadership. He became editor and 'only reporter' of *Il Grido del Popolo*. In a tough fight, he saved the funds of the Turin co-operative alliance from dispersal and began to rebuild the movement again.[51] Apart from Serrati's action, the PSI had shown 'no sign of life' during the rising. It evoked no response elsewhere. The deputies and the reformists immediately exploited it to reinforce their case and began to attack Serrati for his 'Leninism'. The secretary Lazzari oscillated. At the end of August Italian delegates went to the London conference of Entente socialists in breach of their Zimmerwald commitment. The leadership exerted itself to calm the movement. In September, Lazzari went to the FGS congress at Florence to urge prudence and respect for national sentiment. The congress rejected him, voted a revolutionary motion and made Bordiga editor of *Avanguardia*. But the next month, the Boselli government fell, Orlando took office and Turati's relations with authority tightened. And at that point disaster struck. Between 24 October and 4 November, the Italian army suffered a crushing defeat, Caporetto. Losing 300,000 men and an equal number in desertions, as well as masses of equipment, the army reeled back before the invaders. The enemy were finally fought to a stop at the Piave and Monte Grappa. Almost at once, the first confused news came through of the Bolshevik revolution in Russia.

The immediate response, 'in a gale of fear and patriotism', was a national, almost tribal rally against the invader. A massive and organized campaign for national revival was launched ; the country was swept by patriotic fervour. The socialist deputies and much of the movement were caught up in the rally. While they theoretically maintained their position, they in fact rallied to the nation as well. Turati, outrunning most of his colleagues, virtually committed them to support of the war effort.

The revolutionaries drove resolutely in the opposite direction. On 18 November, a date often taken to signal the birth of 'communism' in Italy, the fraction met in clandestine conference in Florence. Gramsci attended his first national convention. Bordiga dominated the meeting. 'The time for action has come. The workers in the fields and factories are armed. They are tired of it all. We must act.' Gramsci supported him, but was attacked for his 'Bergsonianism' and 'interventionist' past. Lazzari and Serrati intervened. They, too, were anxious to curb the right wing, but they counselled against immediate action. The country was going through a patriotic spasm ; the peasant army had not hesitated to open fire in Turin. They carried the day and Bordiga was defeated. The outcome was a reaffirmation of the official slogan 'Neither support nor sabotage' in stronger antiwar terms.[52]

In effect, in a situation of total ambiguity, the reformists were given a free run. Under the spur of the interventionists, government subjected the Giolittians to police surveillance and the 'subversives' to repression. Lazzari was arrested for his letter to the mayors ; Bombacci followed. Serrati was arrested for 'moral responsibility' for the Turin rising. Bordiga was called up. *Avanti* was obstructed, militants harassed.

At the same time, the parliamentary group, working to the official slogan but in practice lending passive support to the war effort, enjoyed a measure of governmental benevolence. Together with the communes and the unions, it was busy saving the remnants of the movement from destruction. Membership had fallen from the 58,000 of 1914 to some 25,000.

New recruits began to come in during 1918, however, after the national rally had spent itself. The last months of the war were in many ways the worst, as industrialization and popular misery reached a climax. In industry there was growing opposition to the collaboration of the unions. During 1918, all the pent-up frustrations of the war years threatened to break over their heads. FIOM began to denounce 'enemies' who were using the internal commissions. In Turin, in *Il Grido del Popolo*, Gramsci began to popularize the British shop-steward movement. In the last months of the war USI began to grow. In the summer of 1918 the unions themselves moved to take over the internal commissions and render them harmless. Demands for recognition of the commissions figured regularly in every wage claim and they began to serve as a focus for a militant reaction against union policy.[53]

In the meantime, Turati, in his zeal to commit the party to full participation in the post-war democratic reconstruction of Italy, was going to extreme lengths. 'Monte Grappa is our fatherland', he declared in one of a series of patriotic speeches, which gave great offence even to moderates. The problem came to a head when Orlando created a commission to draft proposals for the democratic reconstruction of Italy after the War. The interventionist left had been pressing for a Constituent Assembly to reconstruct the country and evoked some response in the CGL which interpreted the proposal in terms of a labour parliament and union control over industry. Much of the CGL, the parliamentary group and the right wing generally favoured participation in the commission, popularly known as *Commissionissima*. Rigola got a favourable vote through the CGL's national council.

The Directorate, appalled at the drift into democracy, determined to stop the process. It was regaining strength. The commission proposals were published just as the trials of the Turin leaders opened. The Bolshevik revolution was beginning to register, despite censorship. A rising tide of militancy was battering FIOM and the unions and the movement was beginning to catch the first tide of popular anger and hope which was bubbling up as the war ended. The government was compelled to lift its ban on the holding of a socialist congress and the Directorate forbade all participation of socialists in the commission.

In a tightly-fought struggle at the CGL's national council, the rural workers, probably feeling the wind of the impending peasant revolt, swung to the Directorate and the delegates voted to withdraw from *Commissionissima*. Rigola, warning against servitude to the party, resigned. He was succeeded by Ludovico D'Aragona, scarcely less reformist. Foreseeing trouble ahead, the CGL tried to protect itself against a 'maximalist' party. At the end of September 1918, it signed its celebrated Pact of Alliance with the PSI, which was to prove of constitutional significance during the Occupation of the

Factories two years later. This was a reversion to Second International practice, in its drawing of a line of demarcation between 'political' and 'economic' strikes. All economic strikes were to be called and led by the CGL, after it had heard the views of the party Directorate ; the PSI pledged itself not to interfere once the decision had been taken. A similar agreement was to apply, in reverse, to political strikes.[54]

Scarcely less Second International in tone was the congress of the party which finally assembled in Rome in September. Despite the lacerations of the war years, a new vista of post-war opportunity was opening up. There was a surge of emotional support for unity, a rally around Serrati's long and arduous labour. Lazzari organized a group to achieve unification. The GPS was recalled to its duties under the 1913 regulations which tried to impose party control over deputies. Only Turati's conduct was condemned outright and the congress went no further. The more radical motions from the left were curbed. The party committed itself once more to its maximum programme: the socialization of the means of production and distribution.[55]

Gramsci in Turin hailed the congress as a clear-cut victory for socialism and a commitment to build a party which could make the revolution. He was over-sanguine. In November, as the war ended, the CGL came out in support of a Constituent Assembly. The party Directorate immediately repudiated it. It declared a commitment to the socialist republic and the dictatorship of the proletariat. In Naples, Bordiga brought out a new journal, *Il Soviet*. In its first numbers, he called for the expulsion of reformists from the party.[56]

The ritual fire-dance was about to re-commence.

3. Biennio Rosso

'This is not revolution' wrote Benito Mussolini in *Il Popolo d'Italia* on 4 December 1919, 'it is the unconscious St Vitus's dance of maximalist epilepsy.'[1]

The celebrated *biennio rosso* (Red Two Years) of 1919-20 appeared to many at the time as chaos and to many in retrospect as the great lost opportunity for socialist revolution. What emerges, at an historical distance, is the essentially ideological, moral, spiritual quality of the crisis. In a more precise sense than the word usually carries, it was a crisis of social identity, as in the momentary breakdown of the capitalist mode of production and bourgeois civil order, hitherto dumb and instrumental classes struggled, in often clumsy, unseeing, sometimes hysterical action, to establish an historical autonomy. No 'economic' analysis will suffice. During 1920, there were 1,881 strikes in Italy. Strikers totalled 1,267,953, according to the official figures (whose precision must surely be counted heroic: in 1920 perhaps even bureaucracy needed its Sorelian myths?); 16,398,227 working days were lost.[2] These were the highest figures ever recorded. Any treatment of them under the rubric 'capital-labour relations' would rank as the highest academic lunacy.

During 1919 wave after wave of strikes, land occupations, demonstrations, street actions, conflict, broke over the country. Nationalists defied the law, launched commando raids, seized Fiume. In the Lower Po valley, marches with songs and banners, direct and extra-legal action, convinced agrarians that the dictatorship of the proletariat had come. Socialist municipalities hauled down the national flag, hoisted the scarlet banner, insulted soldiers as well as officers. Public services struck. The army groaned and grumbled. Mass movements of catholics, socialists, syndicalists, peasants, rural workers, mushroomed. In June and July authority collapsed before a nation-wide popular action over food prices. A momentary lull in the autumn preceded a general election which swept socialists and catholic *popolari* to mass power and threatened to paralyze the state. The early months of 1920 were the most disturbed Italy had known since 1898. What the bourgeoisie, already organizing 'white guards', experienced as a strike frenzy reached a climax in a general strike in April in the Turin region which brought out half a million workers and affected four million people. In the summer of 1920 the syndicalists were claiming 800,000 members for their union organization and in September, conflict in the metal industry led to an occupation of factories throughout Italy which brought the country to a halt and created a situation in which the Socialist Party formally proposed a revolution to the union movement, to have it rejected by 591,245 votes to 409,569. This democratic exercise (which must surely be unique in history) was nullified by an economic crisis which crippled the working-class movements. As the dissident mass forces largely maintained their numerical strength in the local elections of November, unemployment cut a swathe into militancy and in that same month, the fascist squads moved into action. Within a couple of years they had destroyed both the popular movements and the liberal, democratic state.[3]

The great strike in Turin in April 1920 was not over wages or hours. It was a battle in defence of the workers' new factory councils which were threatening managerial autocracy. These workers, no less than the peasant ex-servicemen seizing lands in the South, the small owners organizing in passion in the North, were trying to assert an historical *presence,* to establish a 'new order'. The 'economic' struggles have little meaning unless they are set in the context of a widely diffused, exasperated, sometimes ferocious, hopefully expectant mood: what Italians called *diciannovismo* – '1919-ism'.

Revolt

There was certainly an economic crisis. Exports had collapsed, imports had swollen, emigration had ceased, the transport system was run down. There had been a serious fall in food production. Grain fell from 52 million quintals in 1911-13 to 45 million in 1919, 38 million in 1920; maize from 25 to 22 million in the same period. There were acute shortages through much of 1919. The coal shortage was no less desperate. The price index for coal reached 1666 in 1920 against 100 for 1913. The abandonment of controls by the

Entente's economic council broke the lira; the rate against the dollar leaped from 6.34 at the end of 1918 to 13.7 in 1919, and 28.27 in 1920. Production fell by 15 per cent in mining, 40 per cent in engineering, 20 per cent in chemicals.[4]

Masses of capital were locked up in installations now unprofitable and reconversion to peacetime rhythms proved very difficult. The budget deficit was appalling and inflation intensified. Demobilization was slow, employers anxious to get into peacetime production. The wave of strikes which broke over northern Italy early in 1919 struck at the right moment, often using novel techniques like the sit-in. The employers generally offered little resistance. The 8-hour day was won and everywhere, in town and country, employers and agrarians were forced to retreat. In many sectors of the industrialist class, indeed, there was a widespread loss of confidence, typified by Agnelli's despairing offer to surrender Fiat to a workers' co-operative in 1920. During 1919-20, the belief that a transition to some form of socialist ownership was 'inevitable' took a grip on whole sectors of opinion outside the socialist movement.

On the other hand, it was precisely in this period that some of the large trusts launched their more dramatic financial enterprises in bank take-overs and stock exchange speculation. Funds were massively mis-applied in a battle between giants. These aggressive groups, Ansaldo in the van, refused to accept the fall in profits, which dropped to an average 7 per cent in 1920; after the first shocks of 1919 had passed, they moved to the offensive in labour conflicts during 1920 and their persistence precipitated a wave of bankruptcies and failures during 1921-22: the *Banca di Sconto* fell, the *Credito Italiano* met disaster as Fiat tried to take it over, and even Ansaldo broke in 1923. For Italian industry had suffered far less material damage than the French and in purely 'economic' terms the crisis was one of adjustment.

What gave it its peculiarly intense and 'global' character was the spirit in which conflicts were fought. The crisis, in brute terms, registered first among the popular classes as food shortage, later and quasi-permanently, as a crisis of inflation. In Milan for example, the retail food price index rose from 287.5 to 344.9 between April and June 1919 (1912=100). In 1920, the weekly expenditure of an 'average' working-class family on 'commodities of prime necessity' alone, rose from 124.7 lire to 167.9 between January and September.[5] The burden of the transition was falling on the backs of the labouring classes. An explosion of discontent was inevitable.

The form it took, however, was quasi-revolutionary. Workers climbing out of the militarized labour of the war years ; peasants, coming out of the army, were seized with a hatred of the war and of all who had profited from it. There was an instinctive, and often a quite conscious, rejection of the capitalist system as such. Strikes were fought to the limit to dislocate it ; the newly-awoken peasantry and the mutinous rural labourers ran into brutal collision with it. There was a general thirst for 'revolution – through Constituent Assembly, a new catholic justice, the dictatorship of the proletariat.

The worst moment, for the bourgeoisie, was probably the earliest. Protests against food prices exploded into riots in the syndicalist stronghold of La Spezia ; they spread, through June and July, at first along the syndicalist and anarchist network into Liguria and the Romagna and then into the North and Emilia. They developed into an insurrectionary, quasi-revolutionary movement. After shops had been sacked and hoarders attacked, citizens' committees sprang up to regulate prices. In some areas 'soviets' were formed. Authority caved in. Power passed to the local committees and, in effect, to the CGL which was the only organization which could cope. Shopkeepers brought their keys to the *camere del lavoro* and entrusted their stocks to the union organizations. In July, in one vital sector of supply, a virtual anti-state grew out of the ground.[6]

This was certainly the most insurrectionary moment of the post-war crisis. It probably was a 'revolutionary opportunity'. Had a party on the Leninist model – or even a Bordighist model – existed at that moment, it is conceivable that it could have 'taken power'. Whether it could have held it, is another matter. This is speculation, because the Socialist Party was not in a position to take over. The PSI in fact warned the CGL off 'collaboration' with the state in the food committees ; it was suspicious of the syndicalist tone of the movement. Its organization could not cope. Nor could any other party's. And during the international strike of 20-21 July, called to support the embattled soviet republics of Russia and Hungary, the railwaymen defected and the CGL clamped down on any 'excess' of revolutionary feeling. It was this experience that convinced Serrati that a revolution was possible only after the organization of a disciplined striking force. After July, the energies of both the socialists and the *popolari* focused on the general elections in the autumn.[7]

The forces of dissidence and rebellion were in fact totally fragmented and disparate. Most striking was the entry of the rural population into historical action.[8] In the national mobilization which followed Caporetto, government had made sweeping promises of land reform and it was the ex-servicemen's associations in particular which began to translate these into reality, especially in the South. Their organizations led processions of landless labourers, often in a ritual exercise, to take possession of uncultivated lands on the great estates. In September, the government permitted the requisition of uncultivated land and its transfer to peasant co-operatives for four years. In fact only some 27,000 hectares were transferred by April 1920, but the agitation intensified, involving catholic unions and local priests.

In the North and Centre, peasant parties and catholic unions multiplied. The share-croppers of rich Tuscany moved into an organized offensive, and the union movement marched through peasant districts. In northern Italy the number of proprietors had increased by 50 per cent by 1921, largely as a result of the investment of wartime savings ; illegal seizures of land were rare. Neither the southern land-occupations (often arising out of ancient quarrels) nor the small proprietor-tenant movements in the north and centre were inherently revolutionary. In Emilia, where the socialists were well-entrenched among labourers and where the government's recognition and subsidizing of labour exchanges in effect gave local power to the socialist union in the desperate struggle for work, the catholic unions embraced the richer farmers, the Popular Party the middle class. A highly complex and bitter triangular struggle developed. In Lower Lombardy however, Guido Miglioli had his stronghold in Cremona and fought for collectivization and the formation of estate councils to give the labourer a voice. And through the early months of 1919 the activities of catholic unions and co-operatives amounted to a vast organizational drive which mobilized masses of the rural population against landowners and in rejection of the structure of rural society. By May 1919 prefects' reports spoke of landowners being denounced even from pulpits and talked of 'a real class war'.[9]

With the relaxation of the papal bans on political participation and the high temper of 1919, the catholic movement mushroomed with incredible speed. The catholic union federation, CIL, had been approved by the Pope in March 1918. With 162,000 members at the end of the War, it shot over the million mark by 1920 and 80 per cent of its membership was rural. The Popular Party, the PPI, published its programme in January 1919, launched a journal and held its congress in June. It swallowed up the lesser catholic parties and tried to marshal its forces in the cause of Christian Democracy. It was riddled with contradiction, embracing reactionary landlords and rebellious small-holders alike. Gemelli, a Milan priest, wanted a confessional movement, the leader Luigi Sturzo, supported by De Gasperi, stood for a non-confessional movement committed to reform in a context of Wilsonian democracy. The party's core-support were the 'small men' – small owners, tenants, share-croppers, artisans, small business-men and industrialists (it scored some surprising successes in the towns). Miglioli, the 'white bolshevik', for some time held aloof, but his tendency developed into a left wing of the movement, eager to mobilize a Christian proletariat against capitalism.[10]

In the general elections of November 1919 the *popolari* won 100 seats, second only to the socialists. But like the socialists, they lacked inner cohesion. In April 1920 the government's failure to ex-tend the land grants in the south and provide the necessary financial and technical aid to the co-operatives, the party's stand in favour of individual proprietorship as against collectivization, and its refusal to work with the socialists, provoked a Miglioli revolt at the party congress. His motion for expropriation in the South and for co-opera-tion with the PSI was rejected by 106,000 votes to 27,000. Indeed the PPI joined Giolitti's government in June 1920 and one of its men, Micheli, became Minister of Agriculture.

The party in fact lived in contradictions which, in a sense, paralleled those of the socialists. Its alliance with Giolitti and rejection of the socialists directed a potentially explosive movement into demo-cratic action and away from revolution, but it could not escape its own contradictions. Micheli in October 1920 gave permanent tenure to the occupiers in the South, while the catholic unions denounced share-cropping agreements in the North and Miglioli's estate councils threatened to take over in Upper Cremona. An alarmed and angry agrarian class swung into action. The fascist reaction in fact began at the time of the November local elections (when land occupations had to be countenanced in speeches) and in the rural areas of the North.[11]

The catholic rural movement was thus both divorced from

the socialist movement and contradictory in itself. This was to be one of the key issues between Serrati and Lenin.[12] Serrati's dismissal of Lenin's proposals for uniting urban and rural workers carried weight as a reflection of Italian reality. The division between socialist *braccianti* and catholic *mezzadri* and small proprietors was structural. But Serrati's attitude seemed to pre-suppose a *permanence* in this division, which the Miglioli movement's success in fact challenged. It also involved a certain surrender to the fixed position of the social-ist rural-workers' federation *Federterra*. What Serrati's argument lacked was any sense of a *developing* crisis in which the 'democratic dictatorship of the proletariat and the poor peasants' was *immanent* and *realizable*. This Gramsci the 'southerner' had in full measure and this demand for a clear-cut *class* line, which could yet embrace flexible policies directed at the disintegration of the PPI and the in-corporation of sizeable sectors of the rural population, was the essential meaning of the Comintern's apparently contradictory direc-tives. The responsibility for effecting an alliance was the Socialist Party's and no other's. Its failure is a measure of its failure to develop into a 'communist' party despite its adherence to the Third Inter-national.

In practical terms, however, such communist policies would have had to be *long-term*. In the circumstances of 1919-20, the mush-room growth of the CIL and the PPI in fact removed a vital sector of society from the revolutionary equation.

A similar failure to communicate cut the socialists off from ex-servicemen's associations and even some of the militant *fasci*. Like the Freikorps in Germany, not all such movements were necessarily reactionary. *Arditi* were to serve in the red guards and the *Arditi del popolo* of 1921 ; the ex-servicemen's groups were vaguely 'revolu-tionary'. The rooted anti-militarism and anti-patriotism of the social-ist movement were so strong that they amounted virtually to 'struc-tural' factors. But again, a genuine sense of the historical potentiality of the developing crisis was missing. Gramsci in 1921 undertook a careful and stimulating analysis of the differences between D'Annun-zio's legionaries and Mussolini's fascists, to bring out the revolu-tionary potentiality of the former. Nothing came of this in the Com-munist Party under Bordiga – the party was ordered to withdraw from the *Arditi del popolo*. There had been even less chance in the Socialist Party.[13] A similar range of arguments can be brought to bear on relations between the PSI and the syndicalists, whose growth during 1919-20 is the most historically neglected factor in the entire crisis.

A revolutionary crisis is not a crisis in which whole classes are necessarily consciously revolutionary: experience of both 1789 and 1917 has made this a cliché. The movements of dissidence in the Italy of 1919-20 were disparate and distinct, separate and often hostile to each other. (So they were in the France of 1789, of course). This evidence, irrefutable in itself, is generally deployed against any argument based on 'lost revolutionary opportunities'. The customary reply is an evocation of 'the absence of a revolutionary party'. This is a truth but only a partial truth. What it omits is the corollary that the creation of such a party would have to be a long-term undertaking. No doubt some kind of tightly-organized communist party might well have seized political power during the food troubles of June-July 1919. Would it have lasted longer than the Soviet republics of Bavaria and Hungary? Without coherent communist construction of the 'revolutionary dictatorship of proletariat and poor peasantry' would it have been anything other than a Blanquist coup?

The real accusation against the Socialist Party is more serious. Granted its inability to 'exploit' the crisis of June-July 1919, it had still adhered to the Third International. This implied the creation of a cohesive communist party and commitment to the dictatorship of the proletariat. This kind of commitment Amadeo Bordiga understood from the first. But in a polycentric society like Italy's, with popular classes in real but fragmented revolt, the Socialist Party could not simply *accept* any divisions which existed, however deeply rooted structurally or ideologically. Necessary were flexible policies grounded in an acute historical awareness of the *developing potential* inherent in a determinant crisis in the mode of production. That developing potential needed to be *realized* by a disciplined communist will. The discipline which was essential was not simply the discipline of the *party*, though this of course was necessary. What was needed was the discipline of the materialist conception of history. Serrati had an acute sense of the historical realities of Italy; he seems to have been lacking in the marxist sensibility to historical *process*. And it was precisely this which lay behind the tortured admonitions of Comintern during 1919-20, particularly the exhortations of Lenin, which were 'wrong' only in terms of empirical reportage.

The translation of Leninist precept into practice would have been arduous and relatively long-term. The PSI never started.

The Crisis of Italian Socialism

'There was once a German high school teacher who was eccentric enough to fall in love. His was the tenderness of the pedagogue.
Do you love me, my little treasure?
Yes.
No, No, No! In the answer, one must repeat the question.
In this manner: Yes, I love you, baby.
Rodolfo Mondolfo is such a professor. His love for the revolution is a grammarian's love. He asks questions and is put out by the answers.
Question: Marx?
Answer: Lenin!
But this is not scientific, *poveri noi*! How can it satisfy the philological sensibilities of scholar and archaeologist? And with professorial and compassionate gravity, Mondolfo marks it:
Fail, fail, fail . . .'

So Antonio Gramsci on a reformist in May 1919.[14] In fact, it was the reformists who were the first to develop a clear and consistent policy to meet the post-war crisis. Turati and his friends had greeted the news of the Bolshevik revolution with dismay. With crowds in Italian streets shouting 'Viva Lenin!' they perceived a real and immediate threat to the structure of Italian socialism which they had built. The summons to a Third International posed a choice in the spring of 1919. They had already made it. It was a rejection of the dictatorship of the proletariat, a rally to democracy.

As soon as the War ended, the mass popular mobilization began.[15] Within a matter of months, the CGL was climbing over the million mark: in 1920, it neared two million; FIOM rose to 120,000, to 160,000. Membership of the PSI rose over 80,000; in 1920, it rose to 200,000 while *Avanti* circulation reached 300,000. The CGL was not prepared for the transformation. Congresses were full of complaints about 'newcomers . . . War socialists' whose turbulent indiscipline dragged the federation into dispute after dispute. The union leaders rode the tide and tried to discipline it. The flurry of strikes in early 1919 they channelled into an organized campaign for the 8-hour day. They looked for a political solution. Both they and the party reformists found it in the Constituent Assembly.

The reformists were agreed not only on the undesirability of revolution but on its impossibility. As the brief Bavarian and Hungarian Soviets flickered out, they pointed to Italy's dependence on imported coal, on the threat of blockade, on American control over finance and foodstuffs. On the other hand, a renewed democracy in a climate of *diciannovismo* was full of the promise of structural reforms. At its meetings to work out a programme for immediate post-war reform in November 1918, the CGL put the Constituent Assembly at the head of the list.

This was a clearcut decision which aligned the union federation with Italian democracy and took the Italian labour movement out of the new socialism which was struggling into existence around the Bolshevik revolution and was to take institutional form in the Third International in the spring of 1919. In the developing European confrontation between imperialist capitalism and the new soviet republics, only the façade of Wilsonian democracy stood between the CGL and a complete surrender of socialist purpose. The Directorate met within a week and issued a statement committing the PSI to the dictatorship of the proletariat and a socialist republic.

In practice, however, this brutal contradiction could not be maintained. There had to be some connection between ultimate purpose and immediate action, in a situation which was still totally unclear. The connection was to hand in the minimum programme of the movement agreed in May 1917, which was wholly democratic. In the very statement which asserted the dictatorship of the proletariat, the Directorate focused attention on the minimum programme as an instrument of mobilization. Around it, some operative unity could be maintained.

In the same period, FIOM at its congress encountered resistance from the Turin delegates in full revolt against collaborationism and demanding greater freedom for internal commissions, more shopfloor control. The unions responded with schemes to use the commissions for restoring contact between officials and members. They developed the argument for a Constituent Assembly as a parliament of labour, establishing workers' control over industry in general. But in January 1919, USI in its congress rejected the Constituent with scorn as a surrender to bourgeois society. It called for strong action in workers' unity. In the early months of 1919 the first great strike wave broke and there were clashes with the police. The popular temper was combative.

It was in this tense atmosphere that the reformists counter-attacked the Directorate. As the Spartacists' rising was crushed in Germany, Turati argued that any immediate insurrection was bound to fail. The answer lay in forcing a series of structural reforms which would strengthen the working class and its institutions. Turati himself saw no point in a Constituent Assembly ; parliament, under manhood suffrage, would serve. The reformists kept up the pressure through a whole series of meetings in January. Serrati, centrally placed as editor of *Avanti*, moved somewhat to the right of the Directorate. He argued that Italy, as a victor nation, could not follow the path of Germany or Russia. Despite the general turmoil, the current mood was basically democratic-reformist not revolutionary. He proposed the use of the Constituent or parliament as a weapon. Through parliamentary pressure, the working class, in a series of escalating demands, would build up its own strength and force the bourgeoisie to the point where it could retreat no further : Turati's programme was thus given a revolutionary twist. In practice, the Directorate could do nothing but accede, though an attempt was made to link this minimum with the maximum programme in a dynamic spirit.[16]

The Constituent was in fact an explosive issue, since it was being pushed by the interventionist left. With the syndicalists ready to scoop up mass support, no socialist political leader could have much to do with it. But no political leader was able to *do* much at all. It was the CGL and the unions who took the lead in an attempt to canalize the seething popular discontent into constructive action. The CGL launched the campaign for an eight-hour day and FIOM won through to success in March.

It was at that point that the appeal of the Third International entered. The first, distinctly ad hoc congress had been held early in March. Hemmed in by the blockade, menaced by the Allied intervention, locked in civil war, the International's summons at that point was little more than a call to arms, but it obviously implied a radical break with traditional socialism. By radio and by courier, its theses penetrated ; a new *communist* order was rising around the embattled soviet republic ; the choice was between it and imperialist capitalism.[17] Every socialist movement in Europe was convulsed. The older socialist parties were trying to rebuild their strength, trying to absorb and direct the new proletarian energy. In whole sectors of society, the natural impulse to rebellion was finding expression in syndicalist and semi-syndicalist modes, in new 'council communisms', in movements calling for a radical and total break with all bourgeois institutions, a rejection of parliaments and trade unions, the formation of communist parties which were strictly proletarian, which given the strength and maturity of the proletariat in western Europe, could take on and defeat the whole of bourgeois society. The western bureau of the Third International itself, at Amsterdam, semi-official and autonomous, was to be full of such talk, and the rise of what was soon to be called 'ultra' leftism disconcerted both socialists and the new communist movements. The immediate crisis, however, was located in the traditional working-class movements, as the European struggle tore them apart into social-democratic and communist organizations.

The reception of the Third International in Italy was singularly haphazard. The Directorate seized on it as an opportunity to recover the initiative lost to the reformists. In a meeting in Milan on 18-22 March, Gennari proposed a final break with the bureau of the Second International and adherence to the Third. There was a confused debate. The secretary Lazzari hailed the 'luminous example of Russia' (a commonplace sentiment at the time) but jibbed at an abrupt rally to Comintern. Serrati supported Gennari. The motion was carried by 10 votes to 3, with the representative of the parliamentary group voting against. There was an immediate clamour against the decision by the parliamentary group (whose 'indiscipline' had been censured) and by reformists in every socialist institution. There is no doubt that the Directorate caught the popular mood. The prestige of the Soviet was immense and there was a widespread and vague determination to 'do what the Russians did'. The vote, however, can hardly be taken as a serious decision to create a communist party.[18]

In Naples, however, the decision had been taken. Bordiga's new journal *Il Soviet* came out in December 1918; it called for an expulsion of reformists from the decision-making centres of the Party. This was long before any such call from Comintern. This and other quasi-Leninist ideas that Bordiga had been developing through the War stemmed from his experience of Italian reality and his sense of the ineluctable and international nature of the conflict. Through the winter, the thinking of *Il Soviet* moved towards intransigence. In

February 1919 it began to develop the theme of abstention from parliamentary elections. In view of later developments, it is important to stress that this was proposed, at this stage, not as a 'principle' but as a tactic. The essential need was to break clearly and decisively with all forms of bourgeois society. Abstention was the logical corollary of the expulsion of reformists from the party. The aim was a rigidly communist party and Bordiga enriched the idea in articles running through May and June 1919. He recognized that the party could not, at that moment, 'create historical situations', but it had to reshape itself in readiness. It had to be the party of the proletariat – and the proletariat was strictly defined: 'The proletarian is not the producer who exercises his craft, but the individual distinguished from anyone who possesses the instruments of production and from anyone free from the need to live by selling his own labour.' This definition ruled out much of the trade-union membership. Unions themselves were instruments of bourgeois society. Consequently the party had to base itself squarely and *solely* on the proletariat and elaborate a clear and precise programme of proletarian dictatorship. There were to be no alliances or blocs. The party's aim must be to mobilize the whole *proletariat* around a 'perhaps schematic and dogmatic definition of communism'.

The major immediate obstacles were the cult of party unity and bourgeois contamination. The party must cut out the cancer of the reformists, a channel for bourgeois democratic deviation, and must transcend organization by category (craft). The decisive weapon was abstention from elections which would break the bourgeois-reformist hypnosis.[19]

At this stage, however, while Bordiga was proposing a purge, he did not advocate the creation of an entirely new party. He wanted the party to 'raise its tone' and 'give clear directives'. Gradually, the makings of a national movement, small in numbers but influentially placed, began to cohere around *Il Soviet*. In Turin, for example, Giovanni Boero became section secretary and during March tried to convert the section to abstentionism. He called for an end to the 'electoral idyll', the use of elections merely to 'expose' capitalism and the creation of soviets. He claimed that a split in the party was inevitable.

He was immediately called to heel by *Avanti* and abstentionism in fact tended to divide the left. The party came out firmly against it and the proposal failed even in the youth congress of FGS in July. Nevertheless, there was a certain radicalization during the early summer. The patent failure of Woodrow Wilson brought the reformists face to face with a grisly choice. Turati and Modigliani called for the resumption of a *united* party struggle ; the former even talked of barricades. On 15 April nationalists and fascists burned the offices of Avanti. The PSI's response was supine ; it relied on the forces of public order. But the membership was infuriated. And on 17 April, Armando Borghi, anarchist secretary of the syndicalist USI, proposed a 'united revolutionary front' formed through revolutionary committees of the PSI, the CGL, USI, the anarchist Union and the railway men. Bombacci and some others in the socialist leadership seemed ready to respond. May Day meetings in Turin and Milan greeted the proposal with enthusiasm and called for the return of Malatesta to Italy.

It is clear that this was a critical moment. It remains obscure. But during May and into June, the PSI turned away from any alliance with the syndicalists. The CGL, of course, was rooted in its opposition. Serrati played a key role and the report of a police spy, transmitted from Paris, gives a valuable account of his thinking at this time.

Serrati, said the agent, 'believes that society is now ripe for a transformation, but that this can only come about through a revolt, an organized revolt which is based on, and has roots among, the middle strata of the bourgeoisie, and especially in the barracks. According to him, revolutionary tendencies are fairly widespread in Italy, but they are not well organized, and hence the main task is to embark on this work of organization so as to have a disciplined force at hand at the decisive moment. The recent workers' agitations can be regarded as a kind of training for the workers towards the goal of revolution, but Serrati has, however, had to admit that at the moment there is no cause for over-optimism, because with the exception of a few big centres in North Italy, some areas near Bologna, and to some extent the Marches, all the rest is incapable even of making any kind of collective gesture.'[20]

The first point to note about this is that the revolution, or rather the revolutionary occasion, is seen as something outside socialist control. When the crash comes, it will throw sectors of the bourgeoisie and the military to the revolutionary camp – evidently then a social 'cataclysm' which has to be 'awaited'; the natural corollary is a 'fleet-in-being' strategy for the socialist movement. Moreover, several of the centres of revolutionary potential that Serrati singled out were in fact *syndicalist* strongholds. Almost every sector of socialist opinion at this time, however 'revolutionary', was developing arguments whose revolutionary logic was inescapably *long-term*.

Serrati had moved to this position even before the June-July outbreak over food prices. This crisis simply confirmed him in his dismissal of the revolutionary potential of street and direct action. The new Nitti government responded to the movement with military and police repression; there were several massacres. But it placed its faith essentially in the CGL and its faith was not misplaced. The CGL duly carried out its 'fireman' role and blamed the disturbances on 'secessionists'. The PSI was virtually motionless throughout. On 5 July, it expressed sympathy with 'the populations' anxious for immediate solutions but warned them against 'facile illusions' and it made no connection between immediate and final solutions. The limited success of the general strike of 20-21 July in support of the Russian and Hungarian Soviets strengthened the trend. Although Bombacci asserted that the reformists 'would have to accept' Lenin or leave the party, in fact during the summer the Directorate and the parliamentary group, together with the CGL, achieved an effective unity, with their sights focused on the general elections.[21]

In these circumstances, the slow-forming Bordiga group was isolated. The abstentionists met in Rome on 6 July, developed a coherent analysis of the crisis but brought it to a focus in abstentionism. They decided to form a fraction at the party congress, scheduled for 5-8 October at Bologna. A week later, the PSI created a commission to draft a new party programme; it was to include Bordiga as well as Serrati, Gennari and Bombacci. For a month Bordiga hesitated, but in August quit the committee. On 17 August *Il Soviet* said the party had to choose: either it was the party of the dictatorship of the proletariat or else simply one more of the parties of democracy. Later in the month the two rival programmes were published. Verbally they differed in little except abstentionism. The official programme looked forward to the violent overthrow of the bourgeois regime and the establishment of proletarian dictatorship and called for the withdrawal of all who did not accept this objective. Parliamentary action was to be co-ordinated with extra-parliamentary in an achievement of the minimum programme and an advance beyond. All candidates were to accept this programme. Bordiga's programme called for the exploitation of elections only for propaganda purposes, the expulsion of social democrats, the dropping of the 1892 programme (still enshrined in party documents) and the changing of the party's name to 'communist'.[22]

The only other 'communist' movement at the time was the developing factory council movement in Turin around the journal *L'Ordine Nuovo*. At that time, however, this movement was only just getting off the ground and it lacked any *party* perspective. The issue of abstention split the left there, as the council movement united it, and *L'Ordine Nuovo's* founder, Angelo Tasca, was easily able to rout Bordiga's men in the section in September.[23] At the Bologna congress, where Turati defended the reformist position ably and prophetically, arguing for structural reforms 'in a revolutionary spirit' and dismissing Bolshevism as a reversion to the 'pre-history of socialism', Serrati swept everything before him. The official motion won over 48,000 votes against 14,000 for a centrist motion and a mere 3,300 for Bordiga, concentrated essentially in Piedmont and Campania.[24] The *abstentionist communist* fraction was formally organized at this congress. At the congress, too, the first steps were taken to establish some more permanent relationship with Comintern. A message from Bukharin was read, basically an appeal for help. Serrati founded a journal *Comunismo* as a theoretical organ of the Third International and received a Comintern representative. Later, the first 'programmatic' letter from Lenin, written at the end of October, reached *Avanti*. It hailed the adherence of the PSI to Comintern (which had been confirmed by acclamation at the congress), supported the decision to take part in the elections and developed the argument against the 'ultra-left' which was taking possession of the Comintern. The letter was taken as a justification for the party's rejection of both Bordiga's policy and the factory council movement in Turin which was now rapidly growing into a threat to trade-union control and which suffered the first attacks from Serrati in November.[25]

The elections were a resounding success. The socialists won over 30 per cent of the popular vote and with 156 seats, emerged as easily the strongest single party in the Chamber. The elections had been fought in a full flood of maximalist rhetoric. At the opening of the session, the socialist deputies walked out on the king; they were promptly attacked by nationalists and there was a general strike. But these high expectations soon evaporated. The increased representation enormously increased the weight of reformist practice and instinct in the party. The Comintern agent strongly supported Serrati's concentration on unity in action and directed communist efforts towards a transformation from within. A new upsurge of popular militancy which plunged northern Italy into near-chaos early in 1920, passed the party by. The syndicalists entered another spiral of growth, USI climbing rapidly towards the 800,000 mark.

The Directorate in fact, in the early months of 1920, was almost totally obsessed with containing a revolt from the ranks. Two developments were decisive. Over the winter of 1919-20, Bordiga addressed two letters to Lenin and Comintern.[26] The first, on 10 November 1919, was in fact the first serious Italian effort to establish contact. It stressed that in Italy, a total labour of 'clarification' had become necessary if adherence to Comintern was not to be meaningless. If the Socialist Party did not 'occupy itself solely and systematically with communist propaganda and preparation in the proletariat', the revolution could be defeated. The Turin council movement he dismissed as 'a reformist modification of trade-union structure' and a deviation from the essential job of creating a homogeneous party. He asked for advice on participation in elections, a split in the party and the tactical problem of creating soviets.

The letter never reached its destination; it was seized by the police. He wrote again on 11 January 1920. This was also confiscated. It was a reply to Lenin's letter to Serrati which had since been published; in a sense it counters, in anticipation, the argument of *Left-wing Communism, an Infantile Disorder*, which became the text of the Second Congress of Comintern six months later. Bordiga asserted that the adherence of the PSI to the Comintern concealed the fact that Adlers and Kautskys still flourished within the party. There was a profound difference from the German situation in that the central maximalists under Serrati in fact corresponded to the German independents, the USPD. The difference between Bordiga and Serrati was therefore not the same as that which separated the German Communist Party from German abstentionists like the KAPD.[27] The Italian maximalists were following a policy which was not communist or even revolutionary, but subservient to parliamentary reformism.

Abstentionism was not therefore sectarian, but a necessary instrument to break the hold of social democracy and create a truly communist party. Bordiga went on to say however that his fraction had decided to split off from the party and form a communist party, even if they took only a minority with them. The split would probably come before the local elections scheduled for July.

The argument was powerful and at this stage, clearly, abstentionism could still be regarded as a tactic rather than a doctrine. Moreover Bordiga in the spring threw out feelers to other left groups. His decision to secede from the PSI, critical enough in itself, meant little unless he could rally support. In February 1920, he was already writing about 'the revolution that failed' and in that same month, he went to Turin, home of the suspect council movement, where nevertheless a local alliance of abstentionists and council communists had captured the party section and drafted a radical national programme. Only at this stage had the *L'Ordine Nuovo* movement begun to develop a perspective on the party, and the programme of the Turin section looked to a capture and 'renewal' of the PSI rather than a breakaway from it.[28]

And during the spring of 1920 it was on Turin rather than Naples that the eyes of the PSI Directorate and the CGL were fixed. For, in a great swoop during November and December 1919, the revolutionary council movement, loudly proclaiming itself 'communist', had won control over much of the Turin complex and unhinged the CGL's control. Both the PSI and the CGL were immersed during the early months of 1920 in devising scheme after scheme for 'soviets' and 'councils' designed expressly to contain the Turin movement and keep it pinned down to Piedmont. The final touches were to be put to their labours at the national council in Turin itself in April. At that point, however, the industrialists of Turin, backed by a reorganized *Confindustria*, launched the first counter-offensive. The PSI was confronted in April 1920 with a lockout and a general strike in Piedmont which brought out half a million workers in a desperate struggle in defence of 'the first affirmation of the communist revolution in Italy'. The workers of Turin had created one of Bordiga's 'historical situations'.

Italy's Petrograd

Italy has three capitals: Rome the administrative centre of the bourgeois state, Milan the commercial and financial centre of the country . . . finally, Turin, the industrial centre where industrial production has reached the maximum level of development. With the transfer of the capital to Rome, all the petty and intellectual middle bourgeoisie migrated from Turin to furnish the new state with the administrative personnel necessary to its functioning: the development of mass industry, on the other hand, attracted to Turin the flower of the Italian working class . . .

The Turin proletariat became thus the spiritual leader of the working masses of Italy, who are tied to this city by multiple bonds: kinship, history, spiritual ties, for the ideal of every worker is to work in Turin . . . they see in this city, the centre, the capital of the communist revolution, the Petrograd of the Italian proletarian revolution.

With the civic and proletarian pride proper to a Sardinian immigrant of impoverished petty bourgeois origins, Antonio Gramsci presented Turin to Comintern in July 1920.[29]

Turin was certainly distinctive and its distinctiveness had begun to register within the socialist movement before the War.[30] It was the War, however, that created its particular character and raised it above Milan as the leading working-class centre. It was of course 'automobile city'. During the war, Fiat's labour force grew from 7,000 to 30,000. By 1919, Fiat was producing 90 per cent of all the vehicles in Italy and was the leading vehicle manufacturer in Europe. Its normal production was 75 vehicles a day ; on one day in 1917, it produced 176. This one firm, in multiple branches, dominated the city. Many other sectors, timber, rubber, were subjected to it. There had been expansion into aircraft and artillery and the growth of subsidiary plants, often of a high technicity. Industry was not only heavy and large-scale ; it was highly modern and efficient and it was essentially unified.

In consequence the city was heavily working-class in character. The number of workers in the city doubled between 1913 and 1918. Of a population of 525,305 at the end of the war, 150,000 or so were factory workers, out of a total of 185,587 wage-earners of all kinds. Given the nature of the industry, there was a high proportion of skilled men. In Turin, then, there was a massive working population, with a great number of skilled men concentrated in a single industry and many of them employed by a single firm. Something of the spirit of a mining village informed a class heavily involved in that engineering industry which, in all European countries, produced the shop-steward movements, the self-management, revolutionary organizations, which characterized the War and post-War period.

Gramsci in his report to Comintern in July 1920 spoke of the metallurgical workers as the vanguard, with 50,000 operatives and 10,000 technicians 'who do not have, however, the petty-bourgeois mentality of the skilled workers of other countries, for example England'. It had one central *camera* (unlike Genoa with its three rivals) with 90,000 members. In July 1920, Gramsci listed communist strength – the PSI section with 1,500 members, 28 ward circles with 10,000 members, 23 youth organizations with 2,000 members. In every firm there was a communist group, federating up through regional groups into a directive committee 'in the bosom of the party section'. The Turin Co-operative Alliance was enormously strong ; the value of its individual shares had risen from 50 to 700 lire. Most of them were owned by the railwaymen who had originally organized it. The party section persuaded them, in the name of socialism, to accept an interest of $3\frac{1}{2}$ per cent on the nominal 50 lire value rather than the real 700. After the defeat of the insurrection of August 1917, a railwaymen's committee was formed with police, bourgeois and reformist support to wrest control from the socialist section by promising members the profits on the 650 lire difference and privileges in food supply. Despite censorship and harassment of the section and the press campaigns of 'traitor reformists', the railwaymen, by 700 votes to 100, supported the socialists and ensured that the co-operative remained 'a weapon of class struggle'.

In that struggle Gramsci himself had played a leading part after having been propelled into local leadership and the editorship of *Il Grido del Popolo* by the mass arrests of August 1917. He had worked for some years among the factory operatives, primarily as teacher and journalist, and served for a while on the provisional executive. In May 1919 he was to be the only intellectual on a section executive composed entirely of proletarian militants. Turin's reputation for militancy had been established just before the war and had been enhanced by the strike against the war in May 1915 and the insurrection of 1917. Its party section was almost permanently in the hands of intransigents of one shade or other. The deputies for the city, however, and many of the local union leaders, particularly of FIOM, were generally moderates or reformists and it was the strain of the war years which generated mass militancy. Almost inevitably this militancy found a focus in the internal commissions.

'We wish to state openly that the leaders should follow the tactics and the paths laid down by, and wanted by, the masses. Otherwise they should quit their posts in favour of men better able to interpret the needs and wishes of the masses.'[31] This was the motif of a manifesto-programme drawn up by Turin delegates to the Rome congress of FIOM, the metalworkers' federation, early in November 1918. The immediate cause of conflict was the decision of Bruno Buozzi, the union secretary, to take part in the work of *Commission-issima*. A meeting of Turin metalworkers in August had condemned him for acting without consulting them. Buozzi replied that 'unions and their secretaries, even if they do not seem to be very militant or class-conscious, are always far more so than the anonymous masses'.

The anonymous masses replied in November with a programme which called for greater participation by workers in deciding union policy, greater combativity and a 'revision' of the role of internal commissions. Demands for a greater say through reformed commissions ran parallel with a rejection of union collaboration with bourgeois society.

In the summer of 1918, union leaders, aware of the growing cleavage between their members and themselves, had begun to move towards re-integrating the commissions into union structure and, at Rome, the FIOM spokesman Colombino supported proposals to turn the commissions into permanent organs of 'workers' control', in the sense of surveillance over wages and discipline, under the supervision of the unions. He presented the project in reformist terms: an improvement in capital-labour relations, the elevation of workers from automata to citizens. He praised the British Whitley councils. This was a classic statement of the CGL case, which informed its support for a Constituent Assembly which would be a 'labour parliament', and which would inform its response to the Occupation of the Factories in 1920. Many reformists supported this line of argument. Modigliani saw the internal commissions as nuclei of the technical organization which would run the factories after socialization. In May 1919, during the brief radicalization of the parliamentary group in the summer, Treves even spoke of them as the nuclei of those fashionable institutions, 'soviets'.[32]

The shop-floor militants had very different views and were

calling for proletarian unity in a fairly clear reference to USI. The issue came to a head with the national agreement which FIOM achieved in March 1919. This won the 8-hour day and substantial wage-increases, but, as a price, it abandoned the Saturday half-day (known as 'the English Saturday') which had applied under the old scheme, carefully restricted the possibilities of rapid strike action and diminished the powers of internal commissions, which were to operate (a crucial provision) only outside working hours. There was violent protest from Liguria, where the USI metal union was strong ; the other focus of resistance was Turin, where militants protested against the limitations on strike action and insisted that internal commissions should have power of decision in all disciplinary issues.[33]

The conjuncture of two other factors charged the argument over internal commissions with a wider meaning. In April there was a technicians' strike in the steel industry, which centred on Turin. Internal commissions were central to the dispute, which resulted in the lock-out of non-technicians. The issues of shop-floor autonomy and a solidarity transcending the division of workers into categories were raised in the sharpest terms and both reformists and radicals pointed the appropriate moral. Hard on the heels of this educative process came the brief radicalization of the early summer. USI's call for a united front evoked a transient response among some members of the socialist Directorate and a stronger, emotional one among the rank and file. A mass meeting in Turin on May Day cheered the name of Malatesta. The local union journal began to warn against syndicalist manipulation of the internal commissions.

There was little echo outside Turin. Distinctiveness bred isolation. As early as December 1918, the Turin socialist movement, weary of a page in the Milan *Avanti*, had secured an *Avanti* edition of their own, under the editorship of Ottavio Pastore, with the assistance of Alfonso Leonetti, Leo Galetto and Antonio Gramsci. And it was Leonetti who, in March, directed an appeal to a wider audience. He wrote an article for the youth paper *Avanguardia* and the subject he chose was the internal commission. He denied any intention of attacking the CGL or any other trade-union body, but he claimed that they lacked the real character of institutions of a new, workers' state. They ought to be given a more revolutionary character through the institution of workers' councils. And he called for the immediate transformation of internal commissions and similar organizations into local 'soviets'. He called his article: *At the Dawn of the New Order*.[34]

On 1 May 1919, as the crowds were cheering Malatesta, a new journal came out in Turin. It bore the title: The New Order – *L'Ordine Nuovo*. It proclaimed itself a journal of the Third International dedicated to the construction of the communist state and the incorporation of Italy into the new communist civilization. In the seventh number on 21 June, in an article called *Workers' Democracy*, written by Antonio Gramsci with some help from Palmiro Togliatti, it called for the radical transformation of internal commissions, through united working-class action, into councils which would be the first cells of the communist revolution and the communist state in Italy.

L'Ordine Nuovo

The journal was launched by the four young men who had become allies in Tasca's youth section in 1912-14. Angelo Tasca, now 28, was once again the leading public figure among them, well-known in union circles after the pre-war struggles. Umberto Terracini, now 24 and a law graduate, was active in political life and, the 'Machiavelli' of the group, was destined to become the most celebrated lawyer in Italy, even after 18 years in a fascist prison. Palmiro Togliatti, now 26, was still, at this stage, somewhat marginal. The most finished academic among them, he made his mark in journalism. Antonio Gramsci, now 28, had stayed in Turin throughout the War, unlike the others. Hopeless in large meetings, he was brilliant and effective in small gatherings. His journalism in *Il Grido* and *Avanti* had been strikingly original and his service during the desperate days of 1917 had won him the respect of militants. In this May, he was to join the executive of the Turin socialist section as its only intellectual.

Gramsci was a complex thinker and a full exploration of the evolution of his early marxism would require a separate volume. In essence, he was trying to free marxism from what he saw as the positivist straight-jacket of Second International determinism, to cut back to the Marx of the political writings and *The Holy Family* – 'It is not History that does these things, it is *men* who do all this', to use his own paraphrase. He spent much of his life wrestling with Croce as Marx had done with Hegel, groping after the materialist core he sensed behind the idealist mystification. Alert to the cultural achievements in train (he was among the first to appreciate Pirandello and was acute on the Futurists) he was particularly well-versed in French writing. At first deeply and directly, later more subtly, influenced by that Georges Sorel who called himself 'a disinterested friend of the proletariat', he was certainly 'Crocean' in his early writings and first responses to the Russian revolution. He had, however, a grasp of some marxist essentials, a southerner's commitment to a multi-class popular integration, a muscular sensitivity to the working class. He was able to relate his projected cultural revolution of socialism to a strengthening marxist appreciation of its relationship to the determinance of the mode of production. At first this was elemental, but it grew into a quite remarkable grasp of a whole complex of inter-related instances.

His experience on *L'Ordine Nuovo* was in fact a point of breakthrough into a new order of marxist elaboration. It was initially achieved through his experience of the factory council movement, which was in no sense a parenthesis in his intellectual biography. On the contrary, in its close and dialectical fusion of theory and practice, it was central to the achievement of that problematic which was to govern his leadership of the Communist Party and, in some senses, his lonely and desperate work in prison. In this process he was to develop into one of the most original and creative, if unfinished, tangential and sometimes ambiguous, thinkers in the marxist tradition.

His Leninism was slower to develop. From the beginning, he had a clear perception of the unity of theory and practice, a global but concrete sense of an emergent communist order, which he was able to relate to the objective and subjective realities of working-class life and to his own pre-occupation with a necessary cultural revolution. His initial vision, however, was distinctly mythic, grandiose, semi-Utopian. His acquisition of Leninism was piece-meal, from his first quasi-idealist perception of Lenin as activist, through his assimilation of Leninism as state-building, to a first approximation of an understanding of the revolutionary strategist. In particular, the idea of the *party*, which was later to fill his whole life, lacked substance at first and the fault was probably structural, inherent in his mode of thinking. The 'absence' of the party (in part) accounts for the externality of his writing in terms of the practice of the council movement in working-class reality; the historically 'accidental' quality of its relationship to the movement on the ground.

Lenin's writings reached him indirectly and in phases. The impact of Lenin's *State and Revolution* is *visible* in his writings and led to a kind of re-possessing of marxism. It is possible to *see* his Marxism and Leninism strengthening. Like Bordiga, he seems to have arrived at some quasi-Leninist positions independently. Like Bordiga, too, in this first, critical period, his assimilation was partial, incomplete.

What is quite striking about his work at least from 1917 onwards is *its very close dependence on daily practice*. From 1917, he was totally immersed in the working-class movement of Turin and the experience registers decisively in his writing. He seems to have closed in on the minutiae of factory organization relatively early. In April 1918, in *Il Grido del Popolo* which he edited, appeared a very detailed anonymous article on English trade unions, which anticipates many of his own criticisms, and a full account of the shop-steward organization. Other articles supplied information on the German movement and developed a European perspective on union role and function.[35] The British and to a degree the American experience seems to have been crucial. Sylvia Pankhurst was to be *L'Ordine Nuovo*'s only regular foreign correspondent. *The Liberator*, edited by Max Eastman, was a prime source on Russia and Lenin himself in the early days. And the influence of Daniel de Leon was quite clearly central. *L'Ordine Nuovo* frequently echoes not only de Leon's arguments but his style. One major interest in its articles is precisely this attempt to 'translate' Leninist experience into the molecular construction of communism in an advanced working class.

The drive, the whole thrust of *L'Ordine Nuovo* was Gramsci's. He it was who had stayed in Turin, had worked ceaselessly in the movement, had proved acceptable to the hard-line proletarians who ran its socialist section, had built up a close-knit circle around his brilliant small-group teaching. It was Tasca, however, who was the public figure. There were practical reasons. It was Tasca who was able to raise the 6,000 lire needed to launch it, Tasca who was the friend and companion of union leaders and local celebrities. Gramsci, caustic, indrawn, with a thin and reedy voice, a diffidence in public assembly, was a marginal man most of his life. Romain Rolland's motto he made his own: pessimism of the intelligence, optimism of the will. Nevertheless, there was something incoherent and haphazard about the formation of the group: Tasca and Gramsci at base radically different in their attitudes, Togliatti until 1920 something of a dilettante, Terracini a politico; all that really united them was a passion for *action*, for work among the factory men and the militants, for cultural revolution: previous student friendship. It reflected an initial incoherence in the thinking of *L'Ordine Nuovo*, which became progressively more obvious after number 7, which launched the factory council movement.

4. L'Ordine Nuovo and its Idea

On 6 September 1919, Antonio Gramsci complained in the editorial 'chronicles' of *L'Ordine Nuovo* that comrades were personalizing the journal; it was forever 'Gramsci, Gramsci . . . etc'. 'The truth is, *L'Ordine Nuovo* is written communistically because the articles are born of the spiritual comradeship and intimate collaboration of three, four, five comrades, of whom Gramsci is one, Angelo Tasca another, Palmiro Togliatti a third.' He begged comrades to shed the 'ugly habits of ideological monotheism' and to make the extra little effort of spiritual liberation required to live ideas as a common patrimony, in themselves, distinct from individuals.[1]

In August 1920, in full polemic with Tasca and abandoned by Togliatti and Terracini, he wrote in very different style . . . 'What was *L'Ordine Nuovo* in its first numbers? It was an anthology, nothing but an anthology; it was a review which could have come out in Naples, Caltanissetta, Brindisi; a journal of abstract culture, abstract information, with a strong leaning towards nasty short stories and well-intentioned woodcuts . . . a mess . . . mediocre intellectualism.' Angelo Tasca had rejected the 'new word' of Italian soviets, the factory councils, as a breach with 'the respectable and peaceable traditions of the happy little family of Italian socialism'; he had filled the first numbers of the journal with learned disquisitions on Louis Blanc and Eugene Fournière, on the Commune 'in the style of Michelet', without reference to Marx and the Soviets. And so, 'Togliatti and I, we staged an editorial coup-d'état.' Gramsci wrote an article on the problem of the internal commissions, got Togliatti to help him and cleared it with Terracini. Under the title, *Workers' Democracy*, it appeared in the seventh number on 21 June and revolutionized the journal.

> Togliatti, Terracini and I were asked to study circles and factory meetings, we were invited by the internal commissions to select gatherings of shop-stewards and dues-collectors. We went ahead. The problem of the development of the internal commission be-

came the central problem, the *idea* of *L'Ordine Nuovo*. It was focused as the fundamental problem of the workers' revolution, of proletarian 'liberty'. *L'Ordine Nuovo* became for us and our followers 'the journal of the factory councils'. The workers loved *L'Ordine Nuovo* . . . because in it, they found something of themselves, the best part of themselves; because in it, they sensed their own inner striving: how can we be free? how can we become ourselves?[2]

This is polemical simplification. Angelo Tasca never remembered any 'coup d'état'.[3] His presence may have diminished after 21 June but he was in no sense excluded. Indeed, on the eve of the critical Bologna congress of the Socialist Party, 5-8 October 1919, he virtually took over the 4 October number of the journal and filled it. Characteristically, this number was essentially 'political' in the precise, practical sense. In so far as the young editors – nicknamed *ordinovisti* – had a 'political' face at this stage, it was Tasca's ; if they had any presence at all at the Bologna congress, it was Tasca's.[4] When Amadeo Bordiga concentrated the fire of *Il Soviet* on the '*Ordine Nuovo* group', Tasca was his real target. Indeed, to set Bordiga's criticisms of this period against articles specifically written by Gramsci is to take a trip through the looking-glass : they simply do not connect. They make more sense in terms of Tasca and, perhaps, of the actual development of the council movement on the ground.[5]

Gramsci was certainly correct to identify a disjuncture between himself and Tasca, which was fundamental (as well as a less radical divergence from Togliatti). The differences were becoming clear by December 1919, led to conflict in January-February 1920 ; after the catastrophe of the great struggle over the councils in Turin and Piedmont in April 1920, the *Ordine Nuovo* group in practice disintegrated (as it had done over Mussolini's interventionist article in October 1914).

The fact that the Tasca-Gramsci tension exploded after April 1920 however, is less significant than the fact that for most of 1919 they could work together in sufficiently effective harmony. This in itself is an indication of the *unformed*, 'plastic', 'available' character of *ordinovista* political thinking at that stage. Moreover, the celebrated 'coup' itself has a largely negative significance. The theory of the councils, as it emerged in the autumn-winter of 1919-20, particularly in its Gramscian formulation, departed quite radically from the argument of the 21 June article *Workers' Democracy*. In fact, the whole point of council theory, particularly its Gramscian form, is that it was the product of *dialectical practice*. Given certain themes of general import whose essential traits were fixed by Gramsci, the theory took shape in an interaction between the handful of young *ordinovisti,* the Turin working class and 'events', themselves largely the consequence of Italian working-class practice. Indeed the intellectual process can often be chronologically punctuated by practice. Much the same can be said of the movement's 'politics' in so far as it tackled the problem of the revolutionary party. In fact, the summer of 1919 witnessed a dual process: a development in contradiction, which exploded during the 'trade-union' crisis of October-December 1919 and the subsequent 'party' crisis in the dialogue with the Bordiga fraction during January-February 1920. A particular Gramscian theory 'emerged' during the process in complex relationship with wider and looser *ordinovista* thinking, and with a highly successful and remarkable, if localized working-class movement. That this theory lent itself to reformist exploitation and failed to integrate itself into original communism, but yet survived, not only 'in suspension' within a political tradition, but as 'folklore' within the workers' movement – as recoverable potential in a new phase (the phase we are living through) of capitalist re-formation and communist response – are all factors essential to the creation of a usable past for the revolutionary working-class movement. But, to be usable, the past has first to be reconstructed in technical autonomy.

The Elaboration of an Argument[6]

Read in the context of the first twenty numbers of *L'Ordine Nuovo*, the celebrated 'coup' article of 21 June falls into place as one item in a series, and an expendable one. In the programme of work printed in the first number, on 1 May, there already figured 'A representative and administrative regime for direct management by producers and consumers'. This was one of nine major themes which the journal intended to explore in an effort to realize the programme of the Third International: the economic and psychological condition of Italians, the socialist organization of production, with particular reference to the problems of raw materials and provisions, finance, small property, education and the formation of an armed nation in defence of the socialist republic. The revolt of the 'amorphous masses' was to be channelled into socialist consciousness and communist organization. And, taking the seizure of power virtually 'as read,' the young editors committed themselves to 'passionate and co-ordinated research' into the elaboration of a maximum programme for the socialist *state*.[7]

Write as if your readers' minds were a blank sheet, its contributors were told – an instruction they promptly and persistently ignored. The style is 'difficult', said an otherwise admiring *Humanité*; and Gramsci cordially agreed. Did they think this was just another rubbishy sheet in 'the glorious tradition of Italian socialism', another Stentorello in the Land of Pulcinella? he asked as he cheerfully printed Aldo Oberdorfer's study of Leonardo da Vinci, in weekly chunks. While the Turin edition of *Avanti* rolled off its 50,000 copies *L'Ordine Nuovo*, by No. 7, reached 3,000, with 300 subscribers, and stuck there.[8]

The first number set the tone. There were the permanent features: the 'chronicles' of self-criticism, the Battle of Ideas book column, where reviews were missiles, the review of the political week and the often brilliant survey of the international scene, usually by Gramsci. Tasca on Louis Blanc was there, but so were Gramsci's keynote editorial on the new proletarian order emerging out of chaos; Max Eastman's study of Lenin as the *statesman* of this new order; an essay on Spain and a piece by Romain Rolland. In the first seven numbers, Fournière's scheme for a socialist state of 1887 vintage was presented in good Tasca style, but it was overshadowed by Lenin on the renegade Kautsky, the Soviet constitution, a massive survey of the problems of creating a Socialist Army by Cesare Seassaro, a fecund if somewhat utopian contributor from Milan, a rather literary 'evocation' by the revolutionary academic Zino Zini and a close analysis of the papal encyclical *Rerum Novarum*. The journal bubbled with Romain Rolland, Henri Barbusse and the *Clarté* group in France, translations from Walt Whitman, and jubilant wrestling matches with Croce and the revolutionary young liberal Piero Gobetti. In one sense, the Gramsci of 1920 was correct; it *was* an anthology with little direct local bite. But it was drenched in the spirit of state-building and squarely directed towards making the working class *think* like a ruling class; it was knit together by leading articles, mostly by Gramsci, charged with a sense of proletarian power, and it struck its characteristic note from the beginning with articles by the anarchist engineer Carlo Petri (Pietro Mosso) and one of its first worker contributors, Enea Matta, with his piece on worker psychology.

With No. 7 on 21 June, *Workers' Democracy* appeared, together with John Reed's *How do Soviets work?* The next number however had an oriental comrade explaining about Asia and a strong critique of Salvemini. Commitment to the Third International; a global coverage of revolutionary movements in Russia and Europe; cultural explorations; all remained permanencies. Themes which were to become central entered gradually. The long debate with anarchists and syndicalists was launched in a triangular argument between Gramsci, Petri and 'For Ever' (Corrado Quaglino) at the end of June; a full description of the English shop-steward movement on 11 July established something of an Anglo-Saxon obsession, with translations of H. N. Brailsford, Bertrand Russell and Arthur Ransome – climaxed by a full series of letters from London by Sylvia Pankhurst. Contributions by workers on factory life, the internal commissions, the problems of white-collar workers, began to thicken during August as the journal's ideas began to register in the factories through the medium of personal discussions in the socialist circles. As FIOM leaders had to concentrate on Lombardy and Liguria for the strike, the pace of penetration accelerated.

The real 'coup' was probably the number for 16 August, when Ottavio Pastore undertook a detailed examination of the revolutionary potential of the internal commissions, with critical comments by Giovanni Giardina and Gramsci. This opened a whole correspondence by factory workers climaxed by another crucial analysis by Andrea Viglongo on 30 August, as the first elections of workshop commissars went through in Brevetti-Fiat and Fiat-Centro. During September, the council movement in the factories began to take possession of the journal; its number of 13 September embodied what was in fact the first really 'programmatic' exposition of council theory. So rapid and powerful was the upsurge of this genuinely working-class movement that the sudden commitment of the journal on 4 October to 'politics' in the sense of a direct, practical concern with the *party*, seems almost an intrusion. A concept of the party was, of course, *implicit*, but only vaguely implicit in comparison with Bordiga's, in the earlier writings, but the first direct argument on party structure and tactics in a more immediate context had been Alfonso

Leonetti's critique of abstentionism on 9 August. The 4 October number, directed to the Bologna congress of the PSI and dominated by Tasca, for the first time established a certain *ordinovista* 'position' in this sense – a position, or to be exact a *non-position*, which was to collapse within a month. For as the council movement inexorably conquered Turin and all its working-class institutions, it ran into head-long collision with the unions. October was really the take-off point for *L'Ordine Nuovo*; it virtually exploded into a new character, a remarkably powerful, rich, vivid journal rooted in the reality of the Turin working class and responding to its every pulse. The climax came with the famous No. 25 on 8 November which printed the *Pro-gramme of the Workshop Commissars* drawn up in full assembly, and launched Gramsci into a directly political, 'party' crisis. By this time, the circulation had reached 5,000. They ran out of the 8 November number on the morning of issue and had to roll off another 5,000 and promise to reprint it as a pamphlet. The slender administrative re-sources of the journal broke down and Gramsci had to plead for 'communist discipline'.[9]

The elaboration of the 'conciliar theory' of the *ordinovisti* then, was directly, and dialectically, integrated into the movement of the factory workers. It was inserted, however, into a global perspective whose master-themes had already been established, largely by Gramsci, even in the earliest numbers of the journal.

The Gramscian Perspective: Master-themes

The Russian revolution has paid its ransom to history, a ransom of death, misery, hunger, sacrifice, indomitable will. Today the struggle reaches its climax. The Russian people has risen to its feet, a giant terrible in its skeletal asceticism, towering over the crowds of pigmies who furiously attack it. It is armed for its Valmy. It cannot be defeated. It has paid its ransom. It must be defended. Its natural allies, its comrades of the whole world, must let it hear that battle-cry which will make its advance irresistible, which will open for it the road to re-enter the life of the world.[10]

Gramsci called the proletariat to battle on 7 June 1919. The battle was a battle for a new civilization. The Russian Revolution, the proletarian revolution, was the maximum revolution, forcing a total transformation, from the 'unicellular to the pluricellular', demanding 'that all men must acquire spiritual and historical consciousness'. Its difficulties were therefore unheard-of.

But the revolution had revealed an 'aristocracy of statesmen' unparalleled in history: 'A couple of thousand men who have devoted their lives to the practical study of revolution . . . tempered like steel' ; living in contact with all forms of capitalism all over the world, 'they have acquired an exact and precise consciousness of responsibility, as cold and sharp as the sword of the conquistadors of empire . . . Lenin is the greatest statesman of contemporary Europe.'

The outstanding achievement of the revolution had been to impose form on chaos, 'to weld communist doctrine to the collective consciousness of the Russian people'. In making the marxist formula of the dictatorship of the proletariat a reality, 'the Bolsheviks have given state form to the historical and social experiences of the international worker and peasant class . . . They have broken with the past but have continued the past, have broken a tradition, but have developed and enriched a tradition . . .'

In the huge disaster which had befallen the human race, capitalism's war which had brought the human race to the lip of destruction, only the state of the soviets offered salvation, in its 'formidable battle against the necessities of history'.

Out of chaos the state of the soviets was creating an army which was becoming 'the dorsal spine of the proletarian state'. This state, the state of the councils, was proving itself immortal because it was 'the form of organized society which adheres plastically to the multiform, permanent and vital necessities of the great mass of the Russian people – and which incarnates the hopes and the aspirations of all the oppressed of the world'.

'The schism in the human race cannot last long. Humanity tends towards interior and exterior unification.' It was historically necessary that other states disappear or transform themselves homogeneously with Russia. 'History is therefore in Russia, life is therefore in Russia . . .' The soviet state, the state of the councils, was a fatal and irrevocable moment in the process of human civilization, the first nucleus of a new human society.

Central to this perspective was an overpowering sense of *calamity*. Capitalism in the age of imperialism had plunged the whole world into unspeakable misery. Millions had died, millions had gone through agonies unheard-of. Production had collapsed. Capitalism could no longer meet even the most elementary needs of the people. It had exhausted its mission in history. 'All the good and all the evil which the bourgeoisie could do has been done.' An impartial historical mind would recognize that its social energy had been the most dynamic and efficient in human history but this eulogy would have to be 'posthumous'. At the present moment, the sum of its evil was immeasurable.[11]

Capitalism and the bourgeoisie had lost the historical initiative. This was central to Gramsci's whole argument. He drove it to dramatic, even ridiculous lengths. If Fiat lost a car race, he seized on the fact as evidence of decay. The rise of finance and monopoly capitalism, the stock exchange exploits of the Perrone brothers, meant that the 'captains of industry' had been displaced by the 'cavaliers of industry' (a pun on the honours' list in Italian) and was itself a symptom of the loss of *creative* power. It was an ordinary worker who invented the typewriter which capitalists cavorting on the stock exchange swooped on.[12] *Historical initiative had passed to the working class.* The human race could no longer be driven through the 'Pillars of Hercules of the historical potential of the capitalist class'. The sheer necessities of production, that *production* which was absolutely essential to human civilization, could be met only if the power and historical initiative of the working class organized themselves. 'In the international class of workers and peasants lies the renaissant youth of human civilization . . . evil will not prevail, disorder and barbarism will not prevail . . . a society, capitalist society, crumbles, a revolution, the communist revolution, arises . . . the triumph of life.'[13]

This apocalyptic vision of human disaster and human renewal came to a focus on the new civilization which was struggling to birth around the nucleus of the 'State of the Councils' in Russia. Everywhere the psychology of the working masses had been transformed. Instinctively, only half-consciously, they were struggling to realize themselves in this new civilization, this new order. All the class energies of the world were focusing on the soviet. Their realization would be a *state*, the proletarian state, the state of the councils.

Everywhere the old political order was breaking down; naked force replaced it. 'The juridical fiction of a statutory contract of pacific co-existence between classes in lawful competition for the conquest of the state has broken down.' Its classic form was parliamentary democracy, which was now the major obstacle to the realization of the new civilization. This was particularly so in Italy, where the democratic form had been imposed by the bourgeoisie on an unformed reality, a state which lacked any national-popular will and commitment. 'It has enabled the possessing classes to digest aristocratic castes and feudal institutions. It has enabled the new proletarian class to find itself again, to lay down the broad lines of its unification. It has become dangerous in as much as the power of the proletariat is already sufficient "legally" to abolish classes and capitalist institutions.' So the contract had been torn up, the state relied on force and the manipulation of the democratic system.[14]

But, 'there exists an organization in becoming, that of the workers and peasants . . . It is not as organized and disciplined as a good philistine would wish . . . But it contains within itself the power to organize and discipline itself.' It was prevented from so doing by 'exterior mechanical violence'. The duty of socialists was to mobilize this capacity for organization and discipline.

'It is supremely ridiculous to give out heart-rending groans because reality is not what we want . . . We must discipline ourselves, organize ourselves, mobilize the proletarian army with its officers, its services, its offensive and defensive apparatus.' But this had to be done in 'an original manner, according to the vital laws of development of communist society'. The history of the class struggle entered a decisive phase, the international revolution acquired form and substance 'from the moment when the Russian proletariat "invented" (in the Bergsonian sense) the State of the Councils, digging out of its experience as an exploited class and extending to the whole collectivity, a system of order, which synthesises the form of proletarian economic life, organized in the factory around the internal committee, and the form of its political life, organized in ward circles, urban and village sections, provincial and regional federations in which the Socialist Party articulates itself. The regime of congresses which elaborates the law is the traditional regime of proletarian social life.'[15]

In this argument, which he was elaborating through May, Gramsci directly translated the Russian soviet experience into Italian terms – internal committees, ward circles, sections, provincial federations. These arose directly out of the process of production itself. In Russia it was these organizations, direct and immediate mediations of the mode of production, which were transformed by revolution into the structure of the new proletarian state. It was over this developing structure that the creative statesmen of the Bolshevik Party presided, releasing it and giving it life.

Was there in Italy nothing which could serve as a focus for a similar development of the proletarian state? a Polish comrade had asked Gramsci. Clearly, there was. The organization which arose directly out of the mode of production was the internal commission of the factory. This, then, was the point of entry for the new civilization. In the microcosm of the factory council were reproduced the lineaments of the macrocosm: the state of the councils, the soviet state, the new proletarian order.

The Gramscian Council: into a Factory Freedom

The article *Workers' Democracy* of 21 June 1919 ran thus:
An urgent problem today faces every socialist with a lively sense of the historical responsibility that rests on the working class and on the party which represents the critical and active consciousness of the mission of this class.

How to harness the immense social forces unleashed by the war? How to discipline them, give them a political form potentially capable of growing and developing normally and continuously into the skeleton of that socialist state which will incarnate the dictatorship of the proletariat? How to weld the present to the future, satisfying the urgent necessities of the one and working effectively to create and 'anticipate' the other?

The aim of this article is to stimulate thought and action. It invites the best and most conscious workers to reflect and, each in the sphere of his own competence and activity, to collaborate in the solution of the problem, to focus the attention of comrades and organizations on it. Only common solidarity in an enterprise of clarification, persuasion and mutual education will produce concrete, constructive action.

The socialist state already exists potentially in the institutions of social life characteristic of the exploited labouring class. To link these institutions, co-ordinating and ordering them in a hierarchy of competences and powers which is strongly centralized, while respecting the indispensable autonomy and articulation of each, means to create a genuine workers' democracy here and now, in effective and active opposition to the bourgeois state; already prepared, here and now, to displace the bourgeois state in all its essential functions in the management and dominion of the national patrimony.

Today, the workers' movement is led by the Socialist Party and the Confederation of Labour, but for the great labouring mass, the exercise of the social power of the party and the Confederation is achieved indirectly, through prestige and enthusiasm, authoritarian pressure and even inertia. The scope of the party's prestige widens daily, spreading to previously unexplored popular strata; it wins consent and a desire to work profitably for the advent of communism among groups and individuals hitherto absent from the political struggle. It is necessary to give permanent form and discipline to these disorderly and chaotic energies. It is necessary to absorb them, organize them, strengthen them, to make the proletarian and semi-proletarian class into an organized society which educates itself, acquires experience, and a responsible consciousness of the duties which fall to classes which achieve State power.

The Socialist Party and the trade unions will absorb the whole labouring class only after years, decades of work. They will not be immediately identified with the proletarian state. In the communist republics, in fact, they have continued to exist independently of the state, as institutions of propulsion (the party) or of control and partial implementation (the unions). The party must continue to be the organ of communist education, the dynamo of faith, the depository of doctrine, the supreme power which harmonizes and leads towards their goal the organized and disciplined forces of the worker and peasant class. Precisely in order rigorously to fulfil this duty, the party cannot throw open its doors to an invasion of new members unused to the exercise of responsibility and discipline.

But the social life of the labouring class is rich in institutions, articulates itself in a multiplicity of activities. These institutions and activities need precisely to be developed, fully organized, co-ordinated in a broad and flexible system which absorbs and disciplines the entire labouring class.

The factory with its internal commissions, the socialist circles, the peasant communities are the centres of proletarian life in which we must work directly.

The internal commissions are organs of workers' democracy which must be freed from the limitations imposed on them by employers, and into which new life and energy must be infused. Today, the internal commissions restrict the power of the capitalist in the factory and perform functions of arbitration and discipline. Tomorrow, developed and enriched, they must be the organs of the proletarian power which replaces the capitalist in all his useful functions of management and administration.

From this moment, the workers must move to elections of large assemblies of delegates, chosen from their best and most conscious comrades, under the slogan: 'All Power in the Factory to the Factory Committees', co-ordinated with another: 'All State Power to the Workers' and Peasants' Councils.'

A vast field of concrete revolutionary propaganda would open up to communists organized in the party and the ward circles. The circles, in agreement with the urban sections, should make a survey of the workers' forces in the zone and become the seat of the ward council of factory delegates, the ganglion which knits together and centralizes all the proletarian energies of the ward. The system of election could be adjusted according to the size of the factories: the aim, however, should be to elect one delegate for every 15 workers, divided by category (as in English factories), rising, through graded elections, to a committee of factory delegates which includes representatives of the whole complex of labour (workers, clerical staff and technicians). The ward committee should also try to incorporate delegates from other categories of workers living in the ward: servants, cab-drivers, tramwaymen, railwaymen, road-sweepers, private employees, clerks, etc. etc.

The ward committee should be an expression of the *whole labouring class* living in the ward, a legitimate and authoritative expression, capable of commanding respect for a spontaneously delegated discipline, charged with power, capable of ordering the immediate and total cessation of all labour throughout the ward.

The ward committees should grow into urban commissariats, controlled and disciplined by the Socialist Party and the craft federations.

Such a system of workers' democracy (integrated with corresponding peasant organizations) would give a permanent form and discipline to the masses. It would be a magnificent school of political and administrative experience. It would mobilize the masses down to the last man, drill them into tenacity and perseverance, into thinking of themselves as an army in the field, which needs strict cohesion if it is not to be destroyed and reduced to slavery.

Every factory would form one or more regiments of this army, with its NCOs, liaison services, officer corps, general staff, powers delegated by free election, not imposed in authoritarian manner. Meetings held inside the factory, ceaseless propaganda and persuasion by the most conscious elements, would effect a radical transformation of workers' psychology. It would make the mass better prepared for, and capable of, the exercise of power. It would diffuse a consciousness of the rights and duties of comrade and worker which is concrete and effective, because spontaneously generated from living and historic experience.

As we have said, these brief proposals are put forward only

to stimulate thought and action. Every aspect of the problem calls for a broad and deep examination, elucidation, subsidiary and co-ordinated study. But the concrete and total solution of the problems of socialist living can be achieved only by communist practice: collective discussion, which sympathetically alters the consciousness of men, unifying them and inspiring them to industrious enthusiasm. To tell the truth, to arrive together at the truth, is a communist and revolutionary act. The formula 'dictatorship of the proletariat' must cease to be a formula, an occasion to parade revolutionary rhetoric. He who wills the end, must will the means. The dictatorship of the proletariat is the installation of a new state, typically proletarian, into which flow the institutional experiences of the oppressed class, in which the social life of the worker and peasant class becomes a system, universal and strongly organized. This state cannot be improvised: the Russian Bolshevik communists laboured for eight months to broadcast and make concrete the slogan 'All Power to the Soviets', and Russian workers had known soviets since 1905. Italian communists must treasure Russian experience and economize in time and labour: the work of reconstruction itself will demand so much time and so much labour that every day and every act must be dedicated to it.[16]

The first point to make about this resonant document is that it presupposes *a strong and communist party*. The leading role of the party is specifically stressed; its 'elite' character is not merely specified, it is made central to the argument. The first purpose of the organization of the masses is to provide this party with its trained, organized and conscious 'army'.

This is wholly in accord with Gramsci's contextual writings with their acute sense of disaster and potential fulfilment. The collapse of bourgeois civilization stemmed from the breakdown of the capitalist mode of production; the communist mode was emerging in embryo; both symptom and cause was the 'tendentially communist' revolt of the 'amorphous masses'. It was the classic marxist crisis. But its fulfilment demanded the exercise of the communist will, as exemplified by Lenin and the Bolsheviks. The first need was to incorporate these masses into an army at the service of the party.

Throughout this period, Gramsci employed the term 'communist' about the Socialist Party. This was his central ambiguity. Formally, there was a case for it. The PSI Directorate had proclaimed its adhesion to the Third International in March; the triumphant maximalists of the majority (the word was often used as a synonym for Bolshevik) were verbally committed to the dictatorship of the proletariat. Gramsci must surely have known that reality was not so clearcut, but throughout his earlier writings, his party is a party with communist commitment; the assumption seems to have been that the PSI was becoming communist. At this stage, he never seriously examined the 'Bolshevization' of the party itself, in actuality.

In his writings, however, the party is the communist directive force. And the style which Bolsheviks often employed in talking about the party, Gramsci extends to the entire working class. His vocabulary is military and authoritarian; the prose marches into the mind by battalions. His mobilization of the masses presupposed a unity of the working class (workers and peasants frequently embraced in a *single* class). Whatever workers' ideologies, the developing crisis in the mode of production was organically incorporating them into the dictatorship of the proletariat. The process was dialectical, linking present and future. Institutions would create the army, *and* they would form the bone-structure of the proletarian state. The party would remain distinct in this state, obviously. So would the unions, but their role ('control and partial implementation') is much more obscure.

For contradictions loom in the process of institution making. Note that the central focus is not in fact the *factory* council, but the *ward* council. This was in accord with the conception of soviets then current in Italy. Bordiga made it central. Dismissing the trade unions as counter-revolutionary, he rejected any organization by category or craft. Soviets, strictly dependent on the party, were to be *territorial* units, representing the 'working class' and transcending all trade and category differentiation.[17] Similar thinking clearly informed Gramsci's first proposal, but the bone structure of his soviets was equally clearly the factory council based on his conception of the English shop-steward system.[18] Moreover, the proletarian state power implicit in these institutions was to become explicit within the factory, *here and now*.

This formulation set loose a horde of doctrinal devils. Most obvious was Bordiga's charge that there could be no proletarian power in the factory *before* the achievement of proletarian power in the state; any attempt to achieve it would lead the workers up a reformist blind alley. The increasing concentration of the *ordinovisti* on factory councils and their long neglect of the practical problem of *making the PSI communist* certainly exposed them to this charge in practice, however inaccurate it may have been in theory.

There was a more immediate, practical contradiction. The factory council was to be formed by craft, but the key unit was the factory labour force as a whole. The scheme was based on the *entire* labouring force, whether unionized or not. The 'un-organized', who were often very numerous, were a nightmare to good union men and *ordinovista* plans were denounced as 'a blacklegs' charter'. Not theoretically central to the scheme, but clearly implicit in it was a version of industrial unionism (in the very same issue Gramsci spoke with approval of the IWW and its 'one big union' – he used the English expression, as he did 'leaders' for the 'labourist' traitors of the reformist unions).

The ward council was presumably designed to counteract 'factory egoism' but the crucial block was the postulate of 'control and discipline' to be exerted by party and craft federations 'at the urban level'. This could only mean the *camera del lavoro* with its entrenched union leaders, often deeply reformist. This confrontation in practice threw up a multitude of projects, with unions trying to control councils, council militants using councils to re-organize unions, and a myriad variations, all inescapably reformist in implication. Gramsci kept the council system (at least in his own mind) clearly separate from both union and party. The party remained central. The role of unions remained unclear. But the communist future was clearly in the councils.

Inevitably, it was the one immediately practical proposal in the article – to work on internal commissions and through 'the English system' turn them into revolutionary organizations for proletarian self-government – which precipitated conflict. Three days after the article appeared, Gramsci spoke in the assembly of the Turin section of the PSI. 'For the revolution to develop from a simple physiological and material fact into a political action which initiates a new era,' he said, 'it must incorporate itself in an already existing power whose development is fettered and constricted by the institutions of the old order' (trade unions were not here explicitly identified as institutions of the old order). This proletarian power had to be a direct, disciplined and systematic expression of the worker and peasant labouring masses. It was necessary, then, to systematize a form of organization which would permanently absorb and discipline the working masses. The elements of this organization had to be sought in the factory internal commissions, 'according to the experience of the Russian and Hungarian revolutions and the pre-revolutionary experience of the English and American working masses, which through the practice of factory committees have begun that revolutionary education and psychological transformation which according to Karl Marx must be considered the most promising symptom of communist realization'. The Socialist Party should deploy its prestige to this end, to make the organization a 'concrete expression of revolutionary dynamism on the march towards maximum achievement'.

He was at once challenged by Bruno Buozzi, leader of the metalworkers' federation FIOM. Factory councils would disorganize the unions and seemed to be simply a disguised version of revolutionary syndicalism. Gramsci in reply was ambiguous. He asserted that trade unions had been born as defensive organizations in a capitalist era. But now the relations of force had been radically transformed in favour of the working class. It was basically a question of *recognizing* an existing fact and giving it 'juridical form'. Implicit here was the displacement of 'old' by 'new', but Gramsci in fact claimed that the new organizations would not weaken the unions but strengthen their base – certainly a reflection of one of the actual processes which constituted the council movement in practice, but clearly an ambiguity in theory and perhaps a tactical concession. For, when the assembly voted to look favourably on the experiment and the *ordinovista* campaign got under way, the contradiction blew up in their faces.[19]

The campaign, which ran an almost subterranean course through July and the first half of August, was conducted through the local circles and the youth sections (*fasci*). Face-to-face discussions built up into a regular exchange through the columns of *L'Ordine Nuovo*, where Gramsci called for a soviet of proletarian culture and arduous, practical, detailed work ; the 'evangelical' phase of socialist propaganda was over ; what was needed now was communist construction : 'more than generous heroism, the revolution needs tenacious, minute, persevering work'.[20] Alfonso Leonetti recalled endless small-group discussions in which the original 'English' scheme was modified in the light of Turin reality. The circulation of the journal was channelled almost entirely through working-class institutions. Of the 1,100 copies being sold in the city in early August, 950 were taken by circles, youth groups, workers' education centres. Gramsci was at one time talking to four meetings in an afternoon.[21]

In circle discussions, union officials proved to be obdurate against the new plans. And in articles of 12 and 26 July, Gramsci noticeably hardened in his public attitude towards the unions. In *The Conquest of the State* on 12 July, he attacked the weaknesses of the revolutionary syndicalists, and stressed the centrality of the state. In developing the attack, he emphasized in particular the transient character of trade unions themselves. Under capitalism, 'the proletarian movement was merely a function of capitalist free competition'; the error of syndicalism and by implication unionism itself, was that it assumed the permanence of the union form. But history was a continuous process; institutions came into existence only if they had a purpose. In the crisis of capitalism, new institutions were necessary. No socialist state could be built on capitalist institutions. The embryonic proletarian state existed in the councils.[22] Two weeks later, in an article *For the Communist International*, in which he called for mass support for beleaguered Russia and Hungary, he singled out the betrayal of the international strike by the French union movement and the Italian railwaymen and dismissing all 'democratic residues', asserted, 'It is necessary to organize an anti-state', a vast network of proletarian institutions in a complex and articulated hierarchy which could effectively wage the class struggle and ultimately fuse with the emergent soviet society of Europe. This task of building mass participation in full consciousness was the job of 'the communist fraction of the socialist party', working out from 'the capillary sources of profit itself'. To build such institutions was to build a communist power which would escape from the good or bad will of 'leaders' and achieve the International.[23]

Within a few days FIOM was locked in struggle in Lombardy and Liguria which engaged its leaders' attention to the end of September. Matta later told the syndicalists that this was a point of breakthrough for the *ordinovista* campaign.[24] The problem of the internal commissions acquired a certain urgency and Gramsci was drawn into controversy in the journal.[25] Ottavio Pastore, on 16 August, stressed the danger of creating institutions which would clash with the trade unions. His solution was to transform the unions, in which a handful ran the organization in mass apathy, by making the factory council their base. Every workshop should elect commissars (he suggested one per 300 or 400 workers). Within the shop they would act as shop-stewards, but as a general assembly, they would name the new internal commission from amongst themselves. Their scope was restricted; an electoral committee (of union stalwarts) would list double the number of commissars required; non-union men would have the vote, but a non-union commissar would play no role within the union. The commissars were to concentrate on discipline, the development of production, the cultivation of a producer consciousness and the acquisition of skills hitherto the preserve of employers, in order to displace them. A particular duty was the creation of commissions for technicians and clerical staff, which were to be embraced in a united commission, to achieve the unity of labour.

This provoked a strong attack from Giovanni Giardina, an abstentionist, which was published in the next number. Pastore's scheme, said Giardina, would merely reform the unions which were trapped in bourgeois society; plans for technicians and specialists would come to nothing, even new cadres from the workers themselves would shift in allegiance for basic class reasons, given bourgeois hegemony. The councils were confusing ends and means. *They* could not achieve the revolution; only the revolution could achieve *them*.

'The communist method is the method of the revolution in permanence', retorted Gramsci, ignoring Pastore's proposal. Institutions were not permanent but the product of history which was 'indefinite dialectical process'. Communist duty, following Lenin, was to identify the essential character of a particular moment and its objective necessities. Giardina's talk of 'ends' and 'means' was empirical. What he called a 'means' was a necessary historical moment of the institution which had to be developed; necessary because dependent on objective, real conditions which could not be changed by an act of will, and immature, to be treated as the first stage of a creative process. What he called an 'end' was a moment of the most intense historical life, 'of maximum identification with the complex reality of the proletarian world as it realizes its idea; communism'.

So, the internal commission was the first link in the chain leading to the dictatorship of the proletariat and communism. The class struggle, at this historical moment, had thrown up a new institution 'based on the factory not the craft, on the unit of production and not a professional union born of the division of labour'. Born of labour, inherent in the very process of production itself, its functions were work functions, 'in which economics and politics blend, in which the exercise of sovereignty is one with the act of production; in it, therefore, all the principles which inform the constitution of the State of the Councils [Soviet Russia – GAW] are realized in embryo'.

At present the internal commission had a determinate form. How to build it up into the complex hierarchy of the council state? 'We have outlined the phases over and over again'. The organic unit of production is the work-team and the workshop. Therefore the commissars must be workshop commissars. The commissars must form a united, single committee, to embrace all workers split into categories by the capitalist division of labour, and eradicate corrupt psychology. Around this nucleus of factory operatives, workers in all other activities of modern life must organize in ward and urban institutions. Such an apparatus can be built 'only if it is firmly based on labour, on production, on the objective realities of production'.

After this lesson, Gramsci was evasive on practical tactics. The workers would have to go through many experiments and learn many lessons. But if you want to arrive, you have to start and you start with what is. So work hard, think hard. Workers still had to fight capitalism through the national craft federations, so it was important not to create confusion. It was necessary to reconcile immediate and long-term demands, bread-and-butter problems and the revolution. His conclusion, however, though tactically blurred, was firm. The new institutions in this historical moment, would indeed strengthen the traditional ones, but the new institutions were the mainspring of the only class struggle which could achieve the revolution, and the increasing resistance they would encounter within the workers' camp itself, as they grew, would have to be overcome.

However firm his general stance, Gramsci had said nothing on the practical issue: the granting of the vote to non-union men. The *workers themselves* had to decide. During August the problem became central. At the main Fiat works, Fiat-Centro, the internal commission resigned and 'commissars' were elected in every work-unit. The action, however, was simply an abortive rank-and-file revolt against union leadership and only union members had been allowed to vote.

This drew an article in *L'Ordine Nuovo* out of Andrea Viglongo, who was to become Gramsci's staunchest supporter.[26] He asserted that the Fiat-Centro workers had followed Pastore's plan in that they had simply turned the new internal commission into a strengthened base for FIOM. This diminished the council and was unacceptable. 'Proletarian government does not mean the dictatorship of a part of the proletariat. In the government of the soviet republic, all workers must share, not just the union men.' It was essential that the vote be universal. On the other hand, as Pastore had claimed, the very constitution of elective internal commissions would probably diminish the number of the un-organized.

To give the vote to non-union men, however, would raise many problems and called for a radical reform of the unions, which at present operated 'outside' the factory. Soviet Russia provided the solution. The soviets, rooted in production, combined political and economic action ; the unions survived, for defence and management liaison, and participated in planning at the top. 'Remembering that we are not yet in a proletarian regime', this was the pattern Viglongo recommended.

The councils, as embryo soviets, had three choices in their policy towards trade unions – to abolish them, to take over their merely 'secondary' functions, or to operate in complete independence of them. Abolition of unions was too dangerous, asserted Viglongo. The majority of the workers were not yet organized in *any* form, economic or political. In bourgeois society, the operation of the internal commissions was still restricted. The council could not take over union functions, since the two institutions were radically distinct – the soviet's work was discipline and preparation for power ; the union's defence and perhaps co-ordination. Furthermore, those who wished to transform the functions of unions were still a minority.

The answer was for the councils to develop in complete autonomy from the unions and to assume a position vis-à-vis unions parallel to that of soviets and unions in Russia. Unions, thus in practice diminished to subsidiary agents, should be integrated into the general movement led by the councils. In the process Viglongo denounced the abstentionist fraction of Bordiga for its assertion that soviets had to be elected by territorial constituencies and not the workplace and cited Bukharin in refutation.[27]

There is no doubt that this was *basically* Gramsci's position. He had several times claimed, however, that the new organizations, whatever their ultimate destiny, would in the short run strengthen the unions and in his comment on Viglongo's piece, after pointing out that in Russia all workers were unionized and so no conflict arose in this particular, Gramsci affirmed his belief that the very process of electing commissars and discussing their role and functions would itself absorb the non-unionized. And he hailed the new elections at Brevetti-Fiat as proof, 'a prime example of the argument of Rosa Luxemburg that so-called political agitations and movements are the most powerful determinants of union strength and solidarity'.

He was right to cite Luxemburg for the Brevetti-Fiat elections on 31 August were a triumph for the 'Luxemburgist' leadership style of the *ordinovisti*. Elections for commissars were held in every work-unit ; the elections took a week and out of 2,000 workers, only three or four abstained.[28] And from this point on, the council movement began to burn through the industrial complex of Turin like a fire-storm.

It is at this moment that *L'Ordine Nuovo* begins to speak with power and assurance. On 13 September, Gramsci greeted the new workshop commissars and, in *The Development of the Revolution,* presented them with eight theses on the concrete revolutionary experiences of the international working class.

> The revolution is not a thaumaturgical act. It is a dialectical process of historical development. Every council of industrial or agricultural workers born in the unity of labour is a point of departure for this development, is a communist achievement. The present duty of communists is to promote and multiply workers' and peasants' councils, to co-ordinate them, systematically to build them into the national unity of a general congress, to conduct an intense propaganda to conquer a majority within them.

The programme of the Socialist Party, fixed at Genoa in 1892, had to be fundamentally revised to base itself on the organization of workers and peasants by unit of production and on incessant and systematic action by communist elements to conquer these organizations and to centralize them in a new type of state (the council state) which would embody the dictatorship of the proletariat after the dissolution of the bourgeois regime.

The new hierarchy of working-class institutions implicit in this as in his earlier statements, he now made explicit. The current system of proletarian organization, craft unions, industrial unions, *camere* and CGL 'emerged to organize competition in the sale of the labour-commodity and is not capable of incarnating the dictatorship of the proletariat'.

Organization by craft had been useful as an instrument of defence and would continue under the dictatorship, as a technical organization to harmonize the different categories of labour and unify the media of communist distribution. Workers' unity achieved some sketchy reality in the *camere* and the federations, but had no effective mass cohesion. But at the workplace, unity is inherent in the very process of production, the creative activity which creates a common and fraternal will. In production the workers' will to power is expressed in terms strictly organic to the relations of production and exchange. So, in the process of elaborating the dictatorship through the intrinsic rhythms of production, all mythical, utopian, religious, petty bourgeois psychology will be stripped away, in revolutionary enthusiasm, 'in tenacious perseverance in the iron discipline of labour and in resistance to every assault, open or insidious, of the past'. In this world of labour, 'the communist party must have no competitors'. It must work to ensure that workers 'no longer express their social will through the tumult and confusion of the parliamentary carnival but in the community of labour face-to-face with the machine which enslaves them today and which tomorrow they will enslave'.

The corollary was obvious. The master-piece of the communist producer was the council.

> The workers' organization which will exercise communist social power and in which the proletarian dictatorship will be incarnated, can be nothing but a system of councils elected at the workplace, flexibly articulated in a manner inherent in the process of industrial and agricultural production, co-ordinated in a local and national hierarchy to realize the unity of the labouring class above and beyond the determined categories of the division of labour.[29]

This extraordinary manifesto, percussant and powerful, confident, riveting, hammers at the mind with such insistence that it becomes difficult to grasp that what it celebrated was the election of workshop commissars in a single factory and that by a compromise. At Brevetti-Fiat, where Gramsci spoke, everyone had the vote but only union men could serve as commissars. This proved to be the key to unlock the factory doors. It resolved the immediate problem the councils had to face.

It clearly represents a compromise between council and union. It is not, however, a compromise which seriously weakens the Gramscian schema. While the two institutions were distinct entities, and while union was to be a technical dependency on council, Gramsci had not ruled out a strengthening of the former by the latter during the transition. Moreover, the *ordinovista* movement was committed to a realization of the workers' will. In his comment on Viglongo, Gramsci had admitted that the problem of non-union men was extremely delicate. He expressly insisted that it could be solved only by the workers themselves.

This spontaneist device clearly opened the way to actions and considerations which were ultimately 'reformist'. The new councils were used by militants to prise FIOM from the moderates. In several factories, on the other hand, workers simply re-elected the old internal commissions. Bordiga's argument that the new system simply strengthened and reformed trade unions within bourgeois society and gave rein to syndicalist and reformist deviations, certainly had some point, especially in the early stages and without the leadership of a communist party.

It was during October, however, and thanks to the device adopted at Brevetti-Fiat, that the council movement began to sweep remorselessly through the metal and engineering plants of Turin. The spirit which informed it, consciously and resolutely 'communist' and charged with Gramsci's style, seemed to rob Bordiga's argument of substance. It was precisely this situation which now lodged in Gramsci's *theoretical* writings, in some of the conciliar statements which have become 'classics'.

In *Unions and Councils* on 11 October, for example, Gramsci detected a 'constitutional crisis' within the unions as the 'leaders' (in English) lost touch with the masses who had acquired a consciousness of their 'historical mission as a revolutionary class'. The union bureaucracy had sterilized the creative spirit of the workers who had now to regain control over 'their own house'. The crisis in the unions strictly paralleled the crisis in the democratic-parliamentary state. The solution to the one was the solution to the other, in that, 'in solving the problem of the will to power within their own class organization, the workers will at the same time create the organic structure of their own state, in victorious confrontation with the parliamentary state'.

The trade union could never be the foundation of this workers' state. It was 'the type of proletarian organization specific to the historical period dominated by capital. In a sense, it can be argued that it is an integral element of capitalist society, exercises a function natural to the regime of private property. During this period, when individuals count only insofar as they own commodities and market their property, the workers too have been subjected to the iron laws of general necessity and have become traders in the only property they have, labour-power and vocational skill.' They have therefore built up their own 'firms', hired or evolved administrative personnel expert in market operations. 'The essential character of the trade union is competitive not communist.'

The proletarian dictatorship, on the other hand, 'realizes itself in the type of organization which is specific to the activity proper to producers, not to wage-earners, the slaves of capital'. The factory council is the first cell of this organization. Unifying all categories of labour, it is a class, a social institution whose *raison-d'être* 'is in labour, industrial production, that is, in a reality which is permanent; no longer in wages, in class division, that is, in a reality which is transient and precisely the reality we intend to transcend'.

There followed one of his memorable evocations of the council:

> The factory council is the model of the proletarian state. All the problems central to the organization of the proletarian state are central to the organization of the council. In the one as in the other, the concept of the citizen declines, that of the comrade takes its place . . . Everyone is indispensable, everyone is at his post, and everyone has a function and a post. Even the most ignorant and backward of workers, even the most vain and 'civil' of engineers eventually convinces himself of this truth in the experience of factory organization: all finally acquire a communist consciousness in grasping the great step forward which the communist economy represents over the capitalist.

It is the council which 'gives the workers direct responsibility for production, persuades them to improve their work, instils a conscious and voluntary discipline, creates the psychology of the producer, the psychology of the maker of history'. The duty of the councils is then clear. They are to 'imprint on the trade unions this positive class and communist purpose . . . The workers will bring this new consciousness to the trade union and, above and beyond the simple activity of class struggle, the trade union will dedicate itself to the fundamental task of imprinting a new pattern on economic life and labour technique, will dedicate itself to the elaboration of the form of economic life and professional technique proper to communist civilization.'

And pointing to the example of the Russian unions, Gramsci summons the workers to their historic duty:

> But to make it possible to imprint on the trade unions this positive class and communist purpose, it is necessary that workers direct all their will and faith to the establishment and advancement of councils, to the organic unification of the working class. On this solid and uniform foundation will rise and grow all the higher structures of the dictatorship and the communist economy.[30]

This article of 11 October is an early example of a practice to which Gramsci was to be prone. A statement of position which in fact represents a certain withdrawal from an original position, is 'recuperated' in the course of an argument which shifts the locus of debate subtly but significantly and presents the new position as a 'stage' *towards* the achievement of the original objective. While strictly separating union and council, he had earlier admitted that the new proletarian organizations might well strengthen the older ones in the short run. Here, one of the main *purposes* of the councils has become a drive to imprint a class and communist purpose on the unions, to bring a new consciousness into those unions. None of the components of the article are new: they had all figured in earlier writing. The emphasis, however, is radically different.

The primacy of the councils as cells of the new proletarian state and authentic agencies of the revolution is made clear in some memorable writing. Particularly notable is the identification of the *producer*, not the wage-slave, with communism and with *the making of history*. This identification of the producer with the producer of history (in a marxism shot through with Hegelian and, more significantly, Sorelian insights) seems to be the first point of entry, in this phase of his work, for the concept of 'historical autonomy' which was to be crucial to the development of Gramsci's marxism.

Central to the argument, of course, is the dismissal of the unions, their bureaucracies and 'worn-out ideologies', and their identification (not yet absolute) with bourgeois society. At this point, however, the argument is not rammed home. The logic of the argument is that of industrial unionism. Gramsci asserts that the making of history was precisely the function of the Russian trade unions, which he interprets as industrial unions elaborating 'the form of economic life and professional technique proper to communist civilization'. The application of industrial-union principles in Russia had reduced the bureaucracy of the textile industry from 100,000 to 3,500 (an instinct, of course, common to the more serious exponents of anarcho-syndicalism: witness the performance of the Spanish CNT in Barcelona during the revolution of 1936).[81]

But at this point, the logic is not pressed home. Unions were, 'it can be argued', an integral element of capitalist society, but only 'in a certain sense'. The Russian unions are left standing as an example. For craft and industrial unions will remain 'the rigid backbone of the great proletarian body'; it is their consciousness which needs to be revolutionized and the growth of the councils will in fact transform them.

This position, stopping short of total industrial unionism but pointing towards it, stopping short of a total identification of trade unions with bourgeois society while pointing towards it, can of course claim a theoretical existence in its own right. But it is an exact reflection of the current position of the council movement in Turin. And through the autumn, as that movement swept to the conquest of the Turin complex, this remained Gramsci's position.

On 25 October, in *Unions and the Dictatorship*, he blamed trade unions for the collapse of the Hungarian Soviet and developed the 'historical' distinction between unions and councils. The communist party organizes the proletarian class to break the whole order of capitalism and every relationship dependent on property (which includes *wages* of course). But it will be hopeless unless it is accompanied by a labour of creation and production. Communist society particularly needs 'intense production'. 'And this is the great and magnificent duty which must be undertaken by the industrial unions. They precisely must achieve socialization.' Once again, however, the reference is specifically to *Russian* experience. The emphasis is stronger, but for Italy, it is still indirect, longer-term.[82]

And in the wildly successful 8 November number of *L'Ordine Nuovo*, in an article *Syndicalism and Councils*, Gramsci carries the argument no further. 'Are we syndicalists?' he asks, to rebut what had become a commonplace charge against the *ordinovisti*. He dismissed syndicalism as false, simply the 'other face' of reformist trade unionism. The latter cultivates in the working class the ideology of the petty bourgeois ; the former restricts itself to a closed circle of 'revolutionaries' ; they both deny the elementary principle of union and of revolution – 'the organization of the whole mass'. 'The Italian practice of pseudo-revolutionary syndicalism, no less than the practice of reformist trade unionism, has been negated by the Turin movement of workshop commissars.'[83]

He could afford to take this line. That very number of *L'Ordine Nuovo* sold out on the morning of issue. The harassed editors, pleading for communist discipline, managed to churn out another 5,000 and had to promise a pamphlet. For this was the number which published *The Programme of the Workshop Commissars*, drawn up on 31 October 1919 by the first general assembly of the workshop commissars of Turin.

5.   Councils and Unions

'We know that our journal has contributed not a little to this movement . . .', Gramsci told the Brevetti-Fiat commissars on 13 September 1919, 'We also know, however, that our work has had value only in so far as it satisfied a need, helped to make concrete an aspiration which was latent in the consciousness of the labouring masses.'[1]

The explosive growth of factory councils in the Turin area during the next few weeks proved him right. However 'reformist' in appearance, the device adopted at Brevetti-Fiat: the vote open to all, the commissariat only to union men, had an effect in practice not unlike that which Bordiga expected from the organization of 'communist groups' within the unions. After the heavy defeat of Bordiga's own motion at the Bologna congress of the PSI in October, the abstentionist fraction officially stopped its propaganda against participation in elections, and *Il Soviet* suspended publication, in accordance with congress decisions.[2] And while supporters of electoral action easily won control of the Turin section of the party, the abstentionist militants threw themselves into the council movement in a working alliance with the *ordinovisti*. The 'communist' left in Turin united around the council movement. They unleashed and rode a mighty surge of working-class revolt and aspiration which drew in anarchists, syndicalists, libertarians and the hitherto apathetic. This revolt, directed in the first instance against union leadership, was to create a situation in which workers, *ordinovisti*, union and party leaders alike lived in a bewildering mesh of contradictions. But it was *L'Ordine Nuovo* and Antonio Gramsci in particular who gave it form and *public style*. Piero Gobetti said that at the climax of their great and exemplary movement, the workers of Turin were 'talking the language of unconscious Hegelians'!

The Programme of the Workshop Commissars

Already in August, the Piedmont youth movement had been

won ; its spokesman Mario Montagnana, a mechanic, committed himself to the campaign and called upon *L'Ordine Nuovo* to become for the working class what *La Voce* was for the bourgeoisie.[8] With support from the PSI section, young socialists went on missions into the working-class suburbs as the *ordinovisti* spoke to meeting after meeting. According to Terracini, the entire proletariat of the city was enthused and there was an outbreak of heated discussion in every working-class gathering.[4] The Brevetti-Fiat workers' election of commissars by workshop, who then elected the new executive of the factory (generally still called 'internal commission' in common parlance) proved the breakthrough point. Through September into October, factory after factory elected its commissars: Fiat-Barriera di Nizza, Fiat-Datto, Fiat-Lingotto, Acciaierie Fiat. Enea Matta, himself a coach-maker at Lancia, helped win Lancia and to interest the coach and body makers. The Itala plant, Savigliano, Ansaldo San Giorgio and Ansaldo Pomilio were won ; there were the first penetrations into chemicals, shoe-making, the timber industry.[5] Turin men took the council spirit to the first national congress of the chemical and rubber workers meeting in Milan on 26-28 October and provoked a heated debate in terms of 'soviets'. Violante, the federation's secretary, pressed the claims of the 'centurion' system practised at the Pirelli works, in which shop-stewards each representing 100 workers were to exercise powers similar to those of the Turin commissars but in which only union members had the vote. The radical motion was defeated by some 15,000 votes to 6,500, a majority based on the reformist stronghold in Milan, but this was the first discussion of the *ordinovista* scheme within a national union, and it was assiduously propagated by Andrea Viglongo, the most active of the council spokesmen.[6]

Union resistance was sharper within Turin itself. The union leaders counter-attacked strongly as they lost their grip in factory after factory. In a number of conflicts with the official unions, assemblies of shop-stewards met more and more frequently to co-ordinate action. These 'technical' meetings were transformed into revolutionary agencies, as the new commissars and their internal commissions thrashed out theory and practice. During October they multiplied. After a conflict with the *camera* over a proposed anti-nationalist demonstration, *L'Ordine Nuovo* sponsored an assembly which was said to represent 15 plants and 30,000 workers. Within days another meeting representing 17 plants put the councils' relations with FIOM on the agenda. On 20 October, the automobile and metal-workers' commissars elected a *Study Committee for Factory Councils*, on which Matta and the abstentionist Boero served. This was the dynamo of the campaign, co-ordinating thought and action. It was instructed to prepare a programme for the movement and to tackle the thorny problem of the relations between councils and unions. On 26 October, according to Gramsci, a commissar assembly held at the *casa del popolo* represented 32 plants and 50,000 workers.[7] *L'Ordine Nuovo* and its men and women were ceaselessly active. Gramsci's articles register structural modifications in his theories as working-class practice came to a focus on the trade-union problem. The number for 25 October he filled with union issues. He blamed the unions for the collapse of the Hungarian soviet republic, published John Reed on workshop commissars in the Russian revolution, Carlo Petri (Pietro Mosso) on the Taylor system, essays by workers, clerks and technicians on white-collar problems and proletarian culture and Togliatti on organization. In the *chronicles*, he urged the commissars on. A meeting on these themes, to be addressed by Gramsci, was advertized for 30 October.

It was postponed. For the annual meeting of the Turin section of FIOM was scheduled for 1 November. The council movement, still essentially concentrated in the metal and engineering plants, came to a focus on it. On 31 October what the militants called the 'first quasi-general assembly' of workshop commissars in Turin met to decide on action. The *Study Committee* presented its report. It was, without doubt, a product of commissar discussions. It departed, in some important particulars, from Gramsci's argument and from some of his permanent attitudes. But it was also without doubt steeped in Gramsci's style and spirit. It was adopted by the assembly and became the standard with which the council movement advanced to the conquest of Turin. For the Study Committee's report was *The Programme of the Workshop Commissars*.[8]

The Programme of the Workshop Commissars

Prologue

This programme has been adopted by the first quasi-general assembly of the factory commissars of Turin. It is more than a programme; it is meant to be an exposition of the concepts which inform the rise of the new form of proletarian power. The exposition is propagandist in intention and is designed to establish a basis for discussion with the proletarian organizations which emerged earlier in time.

This first assembly, therefore, does not arrogate to itself the right to formulate a definitive programme, because this is a programme of revolutionary labour and ought therefore to be open, on-going and a radical innovation. Its purpose, rather, is to set in train in Italy a practical exercise in the realization of communist society.

The arrogation of all rights to oneself is the style of first-comers; it is the style of some of those men who want to embody the life of the trade unions in their own persons and who would have everyone believe that the trade union and its agencies fills the whole of social life.

We, in the reality of our power and functions, are a first negation of this theory. It is not a theoretical negation, not an artificial construct of the human mind. Our power has arisen from the spontaneous will of the factory proletariat, weary of having to submit, in a full spate of democratic preaching, to a discipline and a formation of guiding concepts in which it has had no voice; weary of having to live, in constant suspicion, with the fear that, because of the tendencies or weaknesses of individual men, it will be carried along a road which is not the revolutionary road.

It is from this response of the spirit that commissars are arising throughout the nations. The rise of the commissars demonstrates that the manipulation of prices in the field of bourgeois competition and the administration of the means of production and masses of men are two distinct functions. The first has an objective which can be called commercial: on a given bourgeois market, to enhance the value of the labour of a category (craft/trade) so as to sell it at a better price (a function exercised by the trade unions); while the second has the potential objective of preparing men, organizations and ideas, in a continuous pre-revolutionary control operation, so that they are ready to replace employer authority in the enterprise and impose a new discipline on social life. This is the function of the commissars, who because of the very mechanism of their formation, represent the most democratic of authorities. With the precise objective of fixing the exact limits and competence of these two functions, the programme is preceded by a declaration of fundamental principles.

The example of the fatal conflict between trade-union leaders and council authorities in Hungary has compelled us to try to prevent its repetition in the Italian revolution by defining the relations between the two functions and allotting to each function those duties which its constitution, its informing principle and its daily practice assign to it.

The principle of the democratic mandate must prevail in every authority. The elected must be nothing but executors of the will of the mass. This principle has been truly realized in the commissars.

The suffrage in this system is not yet universal, for contingent reasons. There still exists a bourgeoisie with numerous agents, there still exist proletarians without consciousness and organization, who can and must have the right to vote, to exercise their will, but who must not have the right of candidature: they cannot be invested with authority over trade unions of which they have no consciousness, over social life which they do not understand.

But the commissars, precisely because they are elected by all the proletarians, are a social power, and because they are union men elected by all proletarians (and as conscious workers will without doubt win authority over the mass) can represent the will of the union men themselves within the organizations.

The programme, we repeat, cannot be and will never be definitive. Successive regional and even national assemblies must continuously revise it and develop the ideas it expresses.

Meanwhile, to secure its diffusion and discussion, the assembly of commissars has voted the following motions.

1. The factory commissars of Turin, in an assembly held on 31 October 1919, have drawn up the enclosed programme on the powers of commissars and councils, deciding further

(a) to request its publication in every proletarian daily and journal.

(b) to broadcast it in all the factories of Italy.

(c) to form industrial commissions composed of the former internal commissions, to study its application in different industries.

(d) to have it discussed and eventually accepted by every organization and co-operative which maintains itself on the terrain of class struggle.

2. The assembly of factory commissars of Turin undertakes to summon a regional assembly as soon as commissars have appeared in the region, to review the programme and to prepare a first regional or national congress.

Declaration of Principles

1. Factory commissars are the only, true social (economic-plus-political) representatives of the proletarian class, because they are elected, in universal suffrage, by all workers at their workplace. At the different levels of their constitution, the commissars represent the union of all workers which realizes itself in

the organization of production (work-team, workshop, factory, union of the factories of a determinate industry, union of the productive establishments of a city, union of the productive organizations of the mechanical and agricultural industry of a district, a province, a region, the nation, the world) of which union the councils and the system of councils represent the power and the social leadership.

2. The workers united in the council system recognize the utility of unions of craft and industry in the history of the class struggle and the necessity for them to continue in their function of organizing individual categories of workers to obtain improvements in wages and working hours, as long as the competitive labour market as constituted in the capitalist regime survives. They recognize in the trade unions an indispensable form of organization, because they represent a higher union of workers having equal individual interests stemming from the exercise of similar functions in the order of capitalist production. They maintain that all workers should be organized in trade unions.

3. Directives to the workers' movement must arise directly from union workers at their own workplace and must be transmitted through the factory commissars.

Unions of craft and industry must continue in their present function, which is to negotiate for the collectivity with employers' organizations to obtain good conditions, in wages, working hours, labour regulations, for whole categories, devoting the competence acquired in the struggles of the past to the preparation of clear and effective agreements which will truly take account of the current needs of labour and of the psychology of the factory workers.

The councils, on the other hand, incarnate the power of the working class organized by factory in antithesis to the employer authority exercised in that factory; socially, they incarnate the action of the whole proletariat in solidarity in the struggle for the conquest of public power and the suppression of private property.

4. The union workers in the councils accept without question that discipline and order in economic movements, partial or collective, be decided by the trade unions, provided, however, that instructions to the unions are given by factory commissars as representatives of the working mass. They reject as artificial, parliamentary and false every other system which the trade unions want to use to discover the will of the organized masses. Workers' democracy does not base itself on the bourgeois concept of the citizen, it bases itself on the functions of labour, on the order which the labouring class naturally assumes in the process of professional industrial production and in the factories.

5. The factory commissars declare themselves ready to confront

any resistance whatever which seeks to deny to their specific organizations the right of control (surveillance) over the internal life of professional proletarian organizations in the factories.

6. The commissars pledge themselves to direct all their propagandist activities towards the fusion into one single national union of all category organizations which are not confederal, but which act on the lines of the class struggle to achieve the aims of the communist revolution.

All the unions of craft and industry of the Italian proletariat should join the General Confederation of Labour. The commissars appeal to all the labour comrades who voted for them in communist consciousness, to use all their powers of personal persuasion to reinforce the organizations of which they are members. If workers, as they claim, have really achieved a full maturity of class consciousness, they must be convinced of the need to build one single, great union of all the proletarian forces of Italy. They must devote maximum activity to the life of the unions, carrying into them the ideas which govern the system of councils, and must work to eliminate all the difficulties which today obstruct proletarian unity. When into the various organizations which are today dissident, the workers have carried that will to victory, that will to self-government and proletarian power which animate the system of councils, the fusion of these organizations will be nothing more than a simple act of ordinary administration. On the other hand, the commissars call upon labour comrades to break away from those organizations which are built on religious or nationalist principles wholly alien to the functions and duties of workers' organizations.[9]

7. The assembly of all the factory commissars of Turin proclaim with assurance and pride that their election and the establishment of the council system is the first affirmation of the communist revolution in Italy. They pledge themselves to use all the means available to individual commissars and to the council system to see to it that the system of workers' councils, based on commissars elected by workshop and work-team, advances irresistibly throughout Italy, so that in the shortest possible time, it will be possible to summon a national congress of worker and peasant delegates from all Italy.

General Regulations:
Selection and powers of commissars

1. Commissars are chosen in each workshop of the factory, by work-team; their number, at present provisionally fixed by the internal commissions, will be established firmly by the factory council, which will make an exact survey of work operations. Council assemblies will establish the proportion between numbers of workers and numbers of candidates.

Administrative and directive personnel will be divided into the following categories: engineers, technician *capi*, designers, department secretaries, the clerical staff of internal administration, sales, accounts and auxiliary services. The exact survey of the specialisms in this sector of productive activity will be made by factory assemblies.

2. The electors are all the proletarians of the factory, manual and intellectual.

3. Eligible as candidates are union men, members of any union which is committed to the class struggle. A commissar whose mandate is revoked is ineligible for three successive assemblies; his right of candidature is thus suspended for one election.

4. The first elections will be arranged by the old-style internal commissions. The commissions elected will normally remain in office for six months: during this period, they can be renewed in part (in some workshops) or in their entirety throughout the factory, through the resignation of commissars. To the assembly of retiring commissars falls the duty of arranging the new elections, subject to the general principles which are unalterable.

5. The commissar must constantly enjoy the trust of the electors: he is, therefore, subject to instant recall. If he is disowned by one half plus one of his electors or by a majority of the factory assembly, the commissar is obliged to submit his mandate for renewal. The factory assembly will withdraw his right as representative from a commissar who, in these circumstances, does not secure a confirmation of his mandate.

6. Voting must be by secret ballot in working hours. The scrutiny must be immediate and public, with immediate announcement of result. The name of the candidate on the ballot must be written by hand. During the voting no worker from another shop must enter the workshop. If the result and its validity are in doubt, the voting must be repeated in the presence of the secretary of the council.

7. The factory council must meet at least two days after the elections. Temporarily, the council will meet in the room of the nearest socialist circle. When councils have been established in the factory, the assembly must meet within the factory itself. The method of convening the council will be fixed by the council itself.

8. The commissar has a double duty (a) he is the commissar of the union men of his workshop, exercising surveillance over the category organization of which he is a member. (b) he is the commissar of all the workers in his workshop, responsible for their economic defence and social action.

9. In the factory council, commissars, therefore, represent the whole proletariat of the factory. They elect from their midst the executive committee of the factory, to which they give an execu-

tive mandate within the factory itself and a representative mandate in assemblies of councils.

10. In a general assembly of all local commissars, on the other hand, commissars represent the interests of their category and of local production.

11. In assemblies of all the executive committees of the place, however, delegates represent the interests of the whole factory proletariat and of production in social life.

12. The commissars of a whole district who are members of the same union of craft or industry will meet in assemblies of craft or industry. The assemblies will elect from their midst the executive committee of the local section of the union.

Commissars and unions

13. Category assemblies are called on the initiative of commissars representing a tenth of the membership or by the section council. They must be called automatically for every category movement (agitation).

14. Secretaries of union administrative and propaganda sections must be men of proven capacity, able to conduct negotiations with employers' organizations, and must be considered executors of the will of the organized workers which expresses itself in the union and in the factory council. They are responsible to the executive committees.

15. The drawing up of agreements and negotiations with employers' organizations are tasks delegated to these secretaries, assisted by representatives of the executive committees.

The ratification of economic agreements touching the category is effected by the category assembly. No ratification is valid without.

16. Before the agreement is submitted to the assembly, a copy of it must be sent to every factory involved.

17. Agreements will thus be discussed in the assembly of commissars and the right to vote on the agreement will also be enjoyed by commissars who are members of an organization other than that which led the agitation. In the category assemblies, however, commissars do not have the right to criticise men and methods of a union which is not their own.

18. All the commissars gathered in category assembly, on the other hand, have the right to discuss and criticise the methods of those unions which are not committed to the class struggle.

The duties of factory commissars

1. The most important and most delicate of the commissars' duties is within the factory. He must always be the faithful interpreter of the sentiments of his comrades before the representatives of employer authority and in the heart of the council.

It is from the workshop that he derives his power, which resides in the solidarity with which his comrades support his actions and stand disciplined to his advice. Solidarity and discipline are genuine only when his electors recognize in him a sincere representative of their sentiments.

2. Commissars work. The assertion of their power within the factory must be limited in this sense, in that they can suspend work only in determinate circumstances which demand their presence outside the workshop.

3. The function of the commissar during working hours can be summed up as control. He must exercise control (surveillance)

a. over the exact application of existing labour agreements and must resolve any disputes which may arise between the workforce of the workshop and representatives of management.

b. in defence of the interests and the personal feelings of workers in cases of abuse of power by foremen, their incapacity or unfairness in assessing labour and in the event of a change in the labour process or a crisis of production on the market.

c. to maintain the order of labour against employer provocation and the misdeeds of dissidents from the majority will.

d. to obtain precise intelligence on i. the value of the capital invested in his own workshop ii. the production of his shop in relation to all known costs iii. the increase in production which could be achieved.

e. to prevent any alienation by the capitalists of capital invested in factory plant.

4. The commissar must study and urge comrades to study bourgeois systems of production and labour processes and call for criticisms and suggestions of improvements to ease labour and speed up production. He must try to root in the spirit of everyone the conviction that communist equality can be won only through intensive production, that well-being will be achieved not by disorder in production or a weakening of labour discipline, but rather by a better and more equal distribution of social duties and rewards, through obligatory labour and the equality of goods.

5. For similar reasons, the commissars must study internal technical innovations proposed by management and not decide about them until they have discussed them with the comrades, inviting them to agree and making sure, if temporary damage to the workers results, that similar sacrifices are made by the industrialist and that the results are helpful to the processes of production. They must further put pressure on the management for a full application of the laws on safety, health and workshop facilities.

For workers' schools

6. To the council falls the duty of organizing a school in the heart of the factory for all workers who want to perfect their professional skills. They must find capable teachers within the factory itself and obtain places and equipment from the management.

7. It is the council's duty, further, to compel management to create an integrated system of education for apprentices and to be vigilant in defence of their interests.

8. The council must intervene in appointments of workers to supervisory jobs, to unmask favouritism and denounce it as an employer's weapon in the class struggle.

9. Indifferent or backward workshop commissars must be shaken up by frequent elections and referendum (sic.). All commissars are under obligation to hold frequent referendum in their workshop on social and technical questions, and to call frequent meetings to explain the principles and advice propagated by proletarian organizations.

10. No council has the right to break a labour agreement without having first obtained the approval of an assembly of category commissars and hence of the executive committee of the section.

11. When disputes between a workshop and the management have been settled by the commissar, or when they become a matter of principle, or are caused by a conflict of interests between workshops, the commissar must report the case at once to the office of the commissariat. Throughout the dispute, he is excused work.

Executive Commissariat of the Factory
Selection, duties, powers

1. For the execution of its decisions and for negotiation with management, the factory council will choose a proportionate number of commissars who will form the executive commissariat of the factory. This will replace the former internal commission wherever the latter has been recognized by management.

2. Ratios and election methods will be fixed by individual councils and the assembly of commissars.

3. A fixed number of delegate members of the commissariat will be excused work for their period of office and delegated in permanence to the appropriate office of the executive commissariat, to receive complaints from commissars, examine them, reject or accept them and to support them with the power which the force of the entire factory concentrates in them.

4. Delegates of the commissariat must exercise surveillance over conversations between union secretaries and employers' agents in the factory.

5. Every evening members of the commissariat are called upon to assess the situation in the factory and the work done by their comrades.

6. Delegates of the EC must give all possible support to the commissars' work of control, study and propaganda, whipping on and driving the slow and denouncing the inept and the incapable to the council.

7. Members of the EC can remain in office continuously for the duration of the council; they remain in office during the elections and the period immediately following, to instruct the incoming commissariat in their powers and practices.

Members who lose the trust of the commissars in a council vote automatically lose their mandate.

8. The EC and the management have equal rights in the posting of notices in the factory.

9. The EC must ensure the free distribution of newspapers inside the factory during work-breaks.

10. The EC must try to publish a fortnightly factory bulletin which will print statistics designed to deepen the workers' knowledge of the life of the factory, explain the work done by the EC and the factory council, reprint information touching the factory from category journals etc.

If the factory is too small, it will join with others in the same industry.

11. The EC must try to create a social and savings fund, to establish a co-operative and a factory canteen linked to the local co-operative alliance.

12. The EC must keep a daily logbook of its work and submit it weekly for the approval of the council.

13. The EC will distribute the duties of propaganda and study between its members and the commissars.

14. The factory council must be summoned by the EC if possible every week (English Saturday) to hear the EC's report, examine the state and spirit of the factory, to make recommendations to the EC on matters concerning the external interests of the factory or the category.

In exceptional cases the council can meet daily.

Publications, notices, reports, meetings

1. The assembly of commissars of Turin resolves to recognize the newspaper *Avanti* as the only political daily of the region and to ask it to publish its notices, reports, advertisements of commissar meetings. It has no confidence in other dailies which squander the social substance.

2. It resolves, moreover, to call for the publication of articles propagating new ideas from all proletarian periodicals. The periodicals' replies to the commissars' request will be read at the next assembly.

The first point to note about this remarkable manifesto is its

earnest and resolutely *communist* tone and language. The (by definition!) fine Italian hand of Antonio Gramsci can be detected throughout. This is a 'subjective' fact of 'objective' significance. Among council militants, the council movement, viewed as an *international* phenomenon (for commissars arise throughout the nations), was consciously perceived and preached as 'the first affirmation of the communist revolution in Italy'. Since the movement on the ground ran
into multiple contradictions, it is important to establish and *possess*
this elementary but elemental truth : the Turin council movement, at
its climax, was *consciously communist* in spirit, and Gramscian-
communist at that.

On the other hand, when one turns from 'spirit' to 'content',
particularly in the 'constitutional' detail of the proposals, what is no
less striking is how much of the *Programme* is simply an exhortation
to good, democratic, trade-union practice : an exemplary biography
of the Ideal Shop-Steward. Equally arresting is the overpowering
emphasis on *production*, with its heavy, Sorelian, 'morality-of-the-
producers' overtones. In places it produces recommendations which
must have been (as they surely still must be) disconcerting to many,
if not most militants on the left. This 'productivist criterion' (much
talked of at the time, not least among fascists) was of course very
characteristic of Gramsci – though hardly less so of Marx and Engels
before him. That this attitude was self-defeating and ultimately
'petty-bourgeois' would no doubt be a commonplace of criticism on
the left. That the attitude was characteristic of working men and
women who not only called themselves, but acted like communists
and revolutionaries, even under fascist terror, should also become a
commonplace of such criticism.

Certainly, this was one ground for the opposition of Amadeo
Bordiga (though not of his supporters in Turin). This massive 'self-
improvement', even if it took class and collective form, was irre-
deemably destined for reformism. One takes the point, but a more
essential point, surely, is less the 'programme' of October 1919 than
the communist spirit which informed it, which demanded continuous
qualitative growth. In an 'exalted' moment, when theory and practice
momentarily fuse – and Turin in the council winter of 1919-20 *was*
such a moment – doctrines blur in action. The council movement, in
its *Programme*, was anchored in the theoretical *ordinovista* distinction between council and union. The driving force in mass reality,

however, was clearly widespread working-class disgust at and revolt against the union leadership. The result, in practice, was a drive, from the councils, immersed among the un-organized and in the syndicalist campaign for a united revolutionary front, a drive loud with 'communism', to take over the unions and turn them 'communist'. Bordiga denounced a council 'reform' of inescapably anti-revolutionary unions as itself reformist. His answer? – form communist groups within the unions, to turn them 'communist' in agency. No doubt, ample theory, or at any rate vocabulary, can be marshalled to make a critical distinction between two varieties of 'communism'. The Bordighists Boero and Parodi in the heart of council Turin at its climax might be forgiven for failing fully to appreciate the distinction. A distant and inadequately theological observer cannot help experiencing this particular debate in Turin in early 1920 as a dialogue of the doctrinally deaf.

Similarly, the intensive effort to take possession of the factories would obviously appeal to anarcho-syndicalists. Every variety of libertarian and syndicalist welcomed the councils. The *Programme* itself was openly friendly to the syndicalist federation USI (a 'dissident' union committed to the class struggle as opposed to the nationalist UIL and the catholic CIL). It was clearly responsive to calls for a 'united front' though it interpreted them in terms of a council 'fusion'. In truth, a central feature of the council movement, particularly after it failed to transform the socialist party after its own image, was the rising power of syndicalism within it.

The distinction between 'spirit' and 'content' is, of course, merely academic ; without the former, the latter would not have existed. The motives of ordinary workers in the movement, as distinct from its militants, have as usual to be sought in what they *did* : the customary half-blind groping of the historian after the minds of men who do not write, even to *L'Ordine Nuovo*. The council was certainly another, and very effective instrument, in the visceral struggle for immediate objectives. Agitations were endemic. The sharp intensification of the council movement early in 1920 was powered by wage claims. Nevertheless, Gramsci's sense of hitherto inarticulate people struggling, instinctively, for 'historical autonomy' seems to have been correct. The commitment of ordinary workers to a *principle* was massive. In April 1920, the workers of Turin fought a battle which was specifically *not* over wages or hours, but over their new independence, power and dignity, 'their house'. It was a struggle which, for tenacity, courage and endurance, ranks with some of the epic struggles of British miners. Working-class Turin in its council climax lived one of those exemplary moments in working-class history which illumine generations.

Nevertheless their movement ran into contradiction. The *Programme* drew a distinction between council and union which was entirely Gramsci's. In fact, it seems to be a *direct* reflection of Gramsci's article *Unions and Councils* of 11 October and his piece *Unions and the Dictatorship* of 25 October.[10] The union's function was 'commercial', the manipulation of prices on a given bourgeois market. The commissars were the only true *social* (i.e. economic *and* political) representatives of the proletariat. They were rooted in the unity of the working class 'organized by factory in antithesis to the employer authority exercised in that factory ; socially they incarnate the action of the whole proletariat in solidarity in the struggle for the conquest of public power and the suppression of private property'. This is straight Gramscian-communism.

But in translating these principles into action, all the bewildering problems of linking unions and councils arise. The Brevetti-Fiat solution of the open vote but the restricted commissariat is justified and the most elaborate instructions laid down for the interaction of the two institutions. All this certainly had some 'warrant' in the shift in emphasis of *ordinovista* thinking during October, but in *practice*, the movement often acted in ways remote from Gramscian theory. The *Programme* clearly intended to subordinate unions to councils, but it urged everyone to join the CGL. The two institutions were qualitatively distinct, but unions ought to be built on the councils. Throwing open the councils to the un-unionized was one way to displace union leadership but appalled good union men who were no less 'communist' ; what would letting in the syndicalists mean? What about the unemployed, the non-factory proletariat? Gramsci had attempted to deal with all these problems in his writing since 21 June. The absorption of the *ordinovisti* into the council movement, however, also implied an 'absorption' and distortion of their own argument. Through November and December Gramsci and his comrades had repeatedly to re-assert that profound distinction between councils and unions which was central to their argument, even as they had to rebut attacks from all sectors of the socialist movement on their 'inaccurate' equation of councils with 'soviets' – attacks which often employed against *L'Ordine Nuovo* actions by the council movement which were in fact contrary to the journal's own concepts.

One feature certainly united the *ordinovisti* and the council militants. Deep suspicion of and hostility towards the union leadership permeates the *Programme,* reflected even in practical detail: 'Delegates of the commissariat must exercise surveillance over conversations between union secretaries and employers' agents in the factory'! The core of the movement was not the 'constitutional' detail but the simple, brute fact that the CGL and the union leadership were the very stronghold of reformism in the socialist movement, the major obstacle to communist advance. Action against them, however unitedly 'communist' in spirit, could severely strain the connection between factory councils and Gramscian theory.

What was essential was dynamism, *qualitative* growth which could transcend these problems in a 'communist' solution. Industrial unionism, for example, was a logical corollary. For if the council movement came to a stop, it was finished. It would in truth slump into 'reformism' or more likely into stagnation and collapse. For it to remain 'communist', it had to achieve qualitative expansion. At some stage it would run into the *political* problem: the problem of power, the state, the party. Gramsci's own theorizing registers the dialectic. In October, it was already absorbing and making into something of a 'principle' the council swoop on the unions. In December it made a significant shift on the *party* even before the writhing dialogue with the abstentionists began.

The council movement was to find no political, party *translation.* As a distinctive movement, it ceased to exist as a centrality in Italian communism. But its militants, with wide mass support, certainly responded to the logic of their situation. The movement *was* 'open, on-going and a radical innovation'; it *did* express a 'will to power, a will to self-government, a will to victory'. Its brief but vivid history was a continuous thrust for qualitative expansion.

A Working-class Movement: Climax and Crisis

In July 1920, Antonio Gramsci wrote a report on the factory council movement for the Communist International. From the beginning, he said, the council movement ran into 'fierce resistance from trade-union officials, the leadership of the socialist party and *Avanti*'. The aim of the councils, he said in July, was 'to win the trade unions to the cause of communism, to shift trade-union struggle from the narrowly corporative and reformist field to the terrain of revolutionary struggle, the control of production and the dictatorship of the proletariat'.

He added, 'the question of factory councils was also placed on the agenda'!

Also!

Even for a reader accustomed to Gramsci's incurable habit of continuously rewriting and refurbishing his own past, this stops the breath![11]

The detail of his report in July in fact reflects the position he had reached or been driven to by the summer of 1920. That he felt it necessary to present the council movement then as a movement *to transform trade unions*, in terms much less nuanced than his articles of October 1919, is one of the more painful ironies of a movement rich in paradox. For as the council movement moved to its remarkable climax in Turin, much *ordinovista* energy was expended precisely to *prevent* it acquiring such a character.

Even at the point of take-off, in October, a struggle had to be fought. One of its major combatants was Palmiro Togliatti. It is itself symptomatic that as the council movement grew in opposition to the unions, and took possession of *L'Ordine Nuovo*, Tasca tended to withdraw from the forefront. It was Togliatti who took on more and more of the journalistic polemic. On 1 November, he went into action against Gino Castagno, who levelled some of the most powerful trade-union criticisms against the council movement in the pages of the CGL journal *Battaglie Sindacali*. Castagno was rooted in the perspective which had developed in CGL since 1918: a commitment to a 'labour parliament' and union control over industry, set in the context of the democratic remaking of Italy, which would make use of internal commissions, subjected to strict union control. Some of his criticisms of the council movement were 'technical'; some indeed would have been accepted by the *ordinovisti*. He singled out the threat of factory particularism, the weaker position of individual units as against a union-enforced collective agreement. But he concentrated on a defence of old-style internal commissions which could have achieved 'worker control', denounced the threat from the un-organized and opposed any attempt at a council takeover of unions which would, further, destroy the CGL's link with the PSI.[12]

Togliatti, in response, re-asserted the supreme revolutionary value of the councils, dismissed the old-style commissions as a union oligarchy operating in the apathy of the 'amorphous masses'. The workshop commissar system in fact created the unity and the articulation of the working class *as such*, as a unity of 'all producers'. He re-affirmed, in short, the *revolutionary* character of the councils. Within a week, however, in defence of precisely the same concept, he had to attack on another front. For that same assembly of commissars which had adopted the *Programme of the Workshop Commissars* decided to take over the local section of FIOM and, in a stormy meeting on 1 November, did so.

The union leadership resisted. It was prepared to have commissars elected and enjoy consultative status, but it would not permit them to elect the section executive and it fought to the death against giving the vote to non-union men. The commissars of Fiat-Centro presented a scheme of their own, inevitably nicknamed 'centrist'; this was based on their own system – commissars with powers of decision on the council model, but with the vote restricted to union members. The council movement's onslaught on the union, led appropriately by the abstentionist Boero and the libertarian Maurizio Garino, demanded the full conciliar programme. The Fiat-Centro proposals were acceptable, under duress, to the union leadership, as the limit of 'democratization' to which they were prepared to go. Fiat-Centro was in fact divided; *L'Ordine Nuovo* published a letter from some of its militants which hailed the granting of the vote to non-union men as 'a principle of the greatest historical and political value'. In the event, 'centrists' and 'conservatives' came together in the face of the council-communist attack, which, however, carried the day by a large majority and displaced the section executive.[13]

Whatever the ultimate motives of the council communists, the debate in the FIOM section had been conducted entirely in terms of union reform and on 8 and 15 November, *L'Ordine Nuovo* attacked this deviation. On 8 November Togliatti, in a powerful piece, said there could be two interpretations of the council movement as it was developing: that which saw it as a programme of 'concrete revolutionary preparation' and that which regarded it as a 'democratization' of union structure. The latter he dismissed as merely a mirror image of the trade-union bureaucracy, locked inescapably into bourgeois society. It was a 'denaturing' of the councils. He re-asserted the essentially qualitative difference between councils and unions and denounced any attempt to use the former to 'democratize' the latter.[14] A week later Mario Montagnana took the same line and located the argument effectively in two radically different assessments of the Italian situation. He said that many were crying, 'You are dreamers. You talk as if the Revolution had already happened! We reply – We will prove the contrary! What's certain is that you talk as if the Revolution must never happen!' On no account, said Montagnana, must the councils try to absorb or abolish craft unions. The councils were the cells of the new communist order: their aim was the dictatorship of the proletariat not the dictatorship of the unions. Togliatti followed up with a supporting essay denouncing talk of 'democratization' as 'confusionism'. The councils must be a *class* organization aimed not at changing the face of society but at achieving the revolution. In effect the position taken by Viglongo and Gramsci in August was powerfully re-affirmed.[15]

As they wrestled with this problem, the *ordinovisti*'s main pre-occupation was the widespread popular revulsion against giving the vote to non-union men. This proved to be the major obstacle to council growth at the rank-and-file militant level (union leaderships proved to be more flexible, provided their ultimate control was ensured). Much of the correspondence which the journal received was on this problem. It could be resolved only by the acceptance of the *revolutionary* perspective to which the group was committed. One way ahead and out of the dilemma was industrial unionism, and a deal of the paper's space was given over to the minute exploration of achieving such unity in widely diverse contexts. A whole series of essays tackling this problem were published, many of them reports for the *Study Committee for Factory Councils*. Central was the problem of technicians, on which Pietro Mosso and Pietro Borghi wrote at length, while Andrea Viglongo appeared to be everywhere, searching in town and country for anything which could be turned into a council or an industrial union.[16] *L'Ordine Nuovo* encouraged an attempt to create such a union in the metal sector and by 5 December in fact, technicians in the industry voted to support the council movement and called for detailed study of its possibilities.[17]

The *ordinovisti* were stretched to the limit, then, as the

council movement surged forward after the capture of FIOM. It staged its first successful strike and battled through the engineering industry in the teeth of intensifying union resistance. The *Study Committee* was active and *L'Ordine Nuovo* packed its pages with information, propaganda and debate. As late as 1 November, its print was little over 3,500, its subscribers had climbed to over 600. After the brilliant success of its 8 November number, the print jumped to over 5,000 and subscriptions crossed the 1,000 line.[18] 'Make your council active, make it *yours*!' called Pietro Mosso on 22 November. Montagnana had already launched educational-propaganda courses and on 30 November, following a summons to *Create a School*! from Togliatti, the journal opened a School of Propaganda with intensive lecture and discussion courses, serviced by four-page summaries and a promised series of *L'Ordine Nuovo* supplements. Zino Zini set the tone with the inaugural lecture *From Citizen to Producer*. The theoretical bases were laid by Zini on historical materialism, Tasca on anarchism, Togliatti on the economy and Gramsci on trade unionism. The historical series deployed Gramsci, Tasca, Togliatti and Terracini on revolutionary history. The crucial course was that on the Council State, in which Gramsci lectured on unions and soviets and the dictatorship of the proletariat, Terracini on factory councils, Togliatti on economic councils and Tasca on councils of soldiers and peasants. Polemic focused on religion, education, co-operation, local government, morality and art. The School was a great success; the youth movement took it up and gave it national publicity.[19]

The movement drove forward through and out of the metal industry, into chemicals, tyre plants; it evoked echoes even in the traditional textile trade, among printers, all manner of crafts.[20] In *L'Ordine Nuovo*, 6-13 December, Gramsci struck a triumphant note. The theme of council communism had become the 'patrimony' of the working class and a new phase was at hand. The Turin section of the PSI was to discuss the *political* meaning of the movement; in the provinces of Piedmont, extraordinary sessions of leagues and sections were raising the issue of councils, the whole socialist press was echoing with it. What he was heralding was the climax to this first phase of council growth, the invasion of the central institutions of the Turin working class.

The Turin section of the PSI was easily won. The section

voted overwhelmingly to support the new system. It passed under the leadership of the abstentionist-*ordinovisti* alliance; it sponsored a new *Study Committee*, presided over by Togliatti, with Viglongo as secretary, and on which Boero, Matta, Tasca and Montagnana served; it issued a resonant proclamation to the Turin working class, hailing its creative power and historical initiative.[21]

The *camera del lavoro*, summoned into special session on 14-15 December, was a tougher nut. By now the movement had been attacked by Serrati and other maximalists not only on the usual grounds but with the charge that it had falsely equated factory councils with soviets. Gramsci, in fact, was hard pressed, given the actual practice of the movement in working-class reality. He re-affirmed the absolutely original character of the councils and their essentially *political* nature, but admitted that in present circumstances their action could represent only an extension of trade-union activities which would nevertheless radically alter their significance. But the council-communist argument, ably supported by the anarchist Garino, carried the day and won over even a majority of the delegates of Fiat-Centro. A telegram from Serrati, urging the *camera* to leave the problem of votes for the un-unionized to the leading organizations of the PSI and the CGL, was overriden and an *ordinovista* motion won by 38,000 votes to 26,000.[22]

The victory in the *camera*, whose decisions were in theory binding on all working-class organizations and which had called for the formation of councils throughout Italy, spurred on the council drive. By-passing the unions and their agreements with employers, the councils colonized the Turin complex. *L'Ordine Nuovo* devoted the whole of its 3 January 1920 number to workers' control, with a strong article by Togliatti on *Class Control*: 'The formation of councils has value only if it is seen as the conscious beginning of a revolutionary process . . . Between a bourgeois organization and an organization of workers there can be no compromise. There is no power to be shared between them. There is a power to be conquered.' In February 1920, the circulation of the journal reached its maximum. And as the first re-elections of workshop commissars went through, it was estimated that 150,000 workers had been organized in the council system.[23]

It was at that moment of triumph, however, that *L'Ordine Nuovo* began to reflect an awareness that its position was precarious.

A series of articles examined the situation in Milan, capital of the socialist movement, in terms of unrelieved pessimism. An *ordinovista* mission had been directed to the city in January 1920 but had achieved little. The scattered, disparate nature of the city's working class was emphasized, the strength of reformism, the power of banking and commercial as opposed to industrial interests. There was widespread popular militancy but maximalism was loudly empty and un-organized. In consequence, the syndicalists were capturing the militants. In truth, syndicalism increased in strength throughout the summer ; the journals of the movement moved to Milan, home of *Avanti*, Serrati and the major centres of socialist power. Gramsci was driven to such frustrated rage that he wrote an article, *The Historical Function of the City* which claimed that this situation – Milan as a merely nominal capital, Turin as a real centre – had existed in the time of the *Risorgimento*! [24]

What happened at Milan was symptomatic. The Turin council movement failed to extend itself outside Turin and its hinterland in Piedmont. There were all sorts of 'council' and 'soviet' schemes mooted elsewhere, but the CGL, backed by the PSI, held the line against the Turin infection. It was prepared to countenance, indeed create 'commissars' ; even, in the last resort, to tolerate some extension to non-union men, but union control had to be firmly maintained. By and large, it succeeded in winning the bulk of militants. Even within FIOM, Turin was isolated. [25] The union leaders were powerfully supported by the conscious action of the maximalists of the PSI and the confusion generated by the party's own commitment to the creation of 'soviets' at the Bologna congress. With a whole series of academic 'soviet' schemes being mooted within the party and with the Comintern representative supporting party charges that the Turin councils were in no sense true 'soviets', the council-communist advance ran into sheer confusion, as Togliatti had predicted. [26] Given this major maximalist effort to embrace 'councils', the distinctive character of the Turin region condemned it to isolation.

The consequences were serious. It was the syndicalists who moved to the head of such council movements as developed elsewhere, notably in Liguria and later in Milan, and essentially these were combat organizations. Already in November 1919 the Turin industrialists had begun to concert action against the councils and the threat of an employer offensive grew. [27] With the Turin movement isolated and struggling to advance under a blizzard of attacks from all sections of the socialist movement, its 'communist' character was insecure. Unless it could break out of Turin and into the socialist movement it was threatened with destruction, reformist or syndicalist take-over.

And by the turn of the year, relations between the *ordinovisti* and the CGL had become poisonous. The public campaign against the councils was supplemented by what Gramsci called 'café gossip', directed against the young Turin leaders as 'arrivistes', jumped-up and arrogant intellectuals. The Mussolinian and allegedly 'interventionist' past of some of them was dredged up, the old sneers at Gramsci rehearsed. The council communists were awarded all the time-honoured epithets common to fraternal discourse on the left.

In *L'Ordine Nuovo* for 6-13 December 1919, Gramsci replied to comrades who had asked why the journal did not answer the 'tide of nonsense and untruth flowing from the columns of *Battaglie Sindacali*' (the CGL organ). His reply:

> *L'Ordine Nuovo* and *Battaglie Sindacali* are two organs of totally different culture. *L'Ordine Nuovo* is a free force (disciplined to the doctrine and tactics of international socialism as defined by the First Congress of the Third International and the recent Bologna congress of the PSI). It proposes to develop out of the masses of workers and peasants a disciplined revolutionary vanguard, conscious of the tremendous responsibilities incumbent upon the proletarian class in the present historical period, capable of managing communist society with energy and wisdom. *L'Ordine Nuovo*, in sum, seeks to mould into living shape the socialist and revolutionary slogan: 'The emancipation of the workers will be the work of the workers themselves.' *Battaglie Sindacali* claims to be the official organ of the CGL (although its editorial staff are not an expression of any confederal congress, although the theses it argues in its articles are not theses developed and promulgated in any confederal congress and therefore *Battaglie Sindacali* ought to consider itself only the officious organ of the leadership circles of the CGL): it proposes, out of the editorial staffs of capitalist newspapers, the management offices of factories, banks, chambers of commerce, banking and industrial consortia, the ministries, the corridors of Montecitorio [parliament] and the senate . . . a democratic vanguard.

It thought the time had come to install a species of *mezzadria* (share-cropping) in industrial production and to create a senate, to give full force to the irresistible and ineluctable law-making capacities of the *Leaders* (in English) of the Italian trade-union movement. 'Any systematic and deep dialogue between *L'Ordine Nuovo* and *Battaglie Sindicali* is organically impossible.'

Despite this tone, however, it was not until late January 1920 that *L'Ordine Nuovo* effected another shift in its argument, towards industrial unionism and the formation of 'communist groups' in the factories, in a tortuous dialogue with the Bordiga communists, which itself threatened to disrupt the *ordinovista* fraternity. What came between was the national council of the Socialist Party in Florence in mid-January.

The *political* choice was inescapable.

6. Council Communism and the Socialist Party

On 28 January 1924, Antonio Gramsci, in a letter to Alfonso Leonetti said, 'During 1919-20, we committed very serious errors which we are now paying for in full. For fear of being called arrivistes and careerists, we did not form a fraction and try to organize it throughout Italy. We did not want to make the Turin factory councils into an independent directive centre which could have exercised an immense influence on the whole country, for fear of splitting the trade unions and of being prematurely expelled from the Socialist Party.'[1]

As is customary in Gramsci's letters of 1923-24, it is very difficult to distinguish historical truth from the 'knowledge' of hindsight. Scandalous attacks on the Turin council communists there certainly were, but the isolation of their movement derived from less contingent factors – the distinctive character of their region and the powerful political counter-attack on the council movement by the PSI and the CGL, particularly from November 1919. Evidence from 1919-20 itself strongly suggests that, once the council communists recognized their predicament, they made every effort to create a national fraction in their support.

The Gramscian Party: into a Maximalist Prison

The first overtly party-political comment in *L'Ordine Nuovo* was an essay by Alfonso Leonetti on 9 August 1919 on the coming elections, in which he dismissed the abstentionism preached by *Il Soviet* and the followers of Bordiga. Giovanni Boero, secretary of the Turin socialist section had in March denounced the party leadership for failing to live up to their 'splendid assertions' of November 1918, raised an alarm against the 'electoral idyll' in which the party was living and called for participation in the election campaign only to 'unmask capitalism'. Boero further asserted that unless soviets were created, a split in the party was inevitable. He was at once called to

heel by *Avanti* ; in August his move to win the Turin section to abstentionism was defeated by Leonetti, but a minority of the most dedicated militants in Turin joined the *abstentionist communist* fraction
of Bordiga.[2]

When Gramsci had first seriously entered national politics
in 1917, he had rallied to the *intransigent revolutionary* fraction. He
had been the only delegate to support Bordiga at the clandestine meeting in Florence in November 1917.[3] He fully shared Bordiga's detesta-
tion of parliamentary democracy, his commitment to 'communism'.
His thinking on the *party*, however, was unclear. He had welcomed
the Rome congress in 1918 and had committed himself to the *L'Ordine
Nuovo* enterprise. In May he was elected to the Turin section executive as its only intellectual. Bordiga's men were active in the council
movement ; indeed Boero was the only delegate to speak of the Turin
councils at the Bologna congress of the party.[4]

On abstentionism, Gramsci took a straight Leninist line. It
was needless sectarian folly. Elections were useful as propaganda
exercises, socialist deputies could sabotage the bourgeois machine. As
he told Sylvia Pankhurst, recalling his 1913 experiences in Sardinia,
the electoral process itself might be the occasion for an explosive
mobilization of the masses.[5] But, in truth, he discounted the election-
ist-abstentionist argument as a diversion. In August, on the executive
committee of the section, he said: 'For me, the elections have no im-
portance. Abstentionism is an exteriority which will strike no reson-
ance in the country. The important thing is to work to build workers'
and peasants' councils.'[6]

At that point, Gramsci saw no immediate prospect of revolution. On the eve of the elections in November, he said the reformists were correct to say that the objective conditions for revolution
did not exist in Italy – but only if Italy were thought of as an entity
independent of the rest of the world. It was primarily for international
reasons that Italy must be propelled towards revolution. In this,
however, he did not differ from Bordiga, for whom the revolution
was also something of a long haul.[7]

But Gramsci's response to the burning of *Avanti* in May and
even to the food rebellion of June-July was almost schoolmasterly.
The PSI leadership he congratulated for *not* taking retaliatory street
action in May ; the hunger revolts were further proof of the futility
of the streets and the desperate need for *institutions.* This from a man

who in 1921-22 was calling for armed insurrection against fascism (though 'well-prepared' of course!). No wonder Bordiga smelled reformism in 'cultural revolution' in 1919.[8]

On the PSI itself, before the winter of 1919-20, Gramsci was almost inconsequential. Reformist corruption was to be expunged, but there was no specific demand for expulsions. The emphasis was on 'renewal'. At that point, Bordiga, too, was hoping for a conversion of maximalists. Gramsci's whole effort, however, was directed to a 'molecular' mobilization of the mass base. To the party itself, he devoted only fitful interest. Thus, on 21 August 1919, according to Gramsci, the 1892 programme of the party needed no change except for a clause on the councils. By 13 September, the councils were requiring 'fundamental innovations' in the party programme.[9] In his conciliar writings, the 'party' which was to preside over the council movement was now the socialist party, now the communist party, now the communist fraction within the socialist party. Just as the development of the immanent crisis in the capitalist mode of production was incorporating all workers, whatever their ideology, into the dictatorship of the proletariat, so apparently, Gramsci's 'party' would be a socialist party going communist in response to its historical commitments. Bordiga's 'party', if rigid, was at least consistent.

In September, Tasca won a striking political victory in the Turin section. In elections to the executive, when Gramsci and Terracini headed the poll, the abstentionists were out-numbered two to one.[10] It was Tasca who dominated the party congress number of *L'Ordine Nuovo* on 4 October. That issue published the *ordinovisti*'s *Programme of Work*. The defeat of abstentionists and reformists at the congress was now clearly inevitable and the council communists of Turin were anxious to infuse their spirit into the maximalist majority. Their programme is an almost painful symptom of their political situation at that time.[11]

The puritanical and head-prefect tone of much *ordinovista* writing (particularly Gramsci's) which often maddened comrades, is very apparent. Seven sectors of action were indicated. Strong and conscious nuclei of militants should be created everywhere, ready to direct mindless movements into socialist channels. Systematic research must identify areas of weakness and equally systematic work must eliminate them. And this was to be something serious, not 'the usual choreography' . . . 'The greatest care must be taken, however, that comrade orators do not become obsessed with applause at any price . . . It is necessary that comrades realize that to hold a meeting is a serious thing'; they had the duty to conduct a meeting so that it 'becomes an efficient moment of revolutionary education for the masses'.

Co-operatives were to be grouped into socialist consortia, linked up with consortia of rural producers, in order to initiate the small proprietors into the collectivist regime. Communes were to be won not in the name of 'the people' but in that of the working class. The internal commissions and the factory councils were to be supported and craft unions trained as technical organs for the co-ordination of the experience of the councils; Gramsci's article of 13 September on *The development of the revolution* was quoted – the rise of the councils would lead to a violent clash between the two great classes and 'if the foundations of the revolutionary process are not laid in the intimacy of productive life, the revolution will remain a sterile appeal to the will, a nebulous myth, a fallacious Morgana: and chaos, disorder, unemployment, hunger, will engulf and crush the best and most vigorous proletarian energies.'[12]

Economic councils to plan the action of the workers' state must be created in every province; associations of ex-servicemen must be encouraged in order to penetrate the countryside and set the fear of war against the smug complacency of peasant proprietors. These associations should form the nucleus of the 'red guards' who would defend the socialist republic. Finally, while the *ordinovisti* did not want the Directorate to be transformed into 'the thinking head of a subject body', it was essential that it cease to be 'an essentially administrative organ' and become 'a technical organ of revolutionary preparation'.

In every instance, there was a minute concentration on the *mass base*, its organization and its incorporation into new institutions which were to be the nuclei of the proletarian state. On the central problems which were racking the party *as a party*, the journal was diffident and neutral, indeed rather superior. Now that the abstentionist 'prejudice' had been ovecome, the maximalists who had won 'perhaps too complete a victory' were lectured. This nonsense must be cleared away so that institutions could be built. What was essential was to give maximalism 'a concrete content'. The only specific party recommendation was the call to turn the Directorate into a technical organ of revolutionary preparation.

'Preparation' is the key word. In it, echo both the 'amorphous masses' and all those Stentorellos pullulating in Italian socialism, not least in that maximalism which was such a sanctuary for 'big mouths and little brains'. Bordiga was moved by the same revulsion. His solution was a rigid and purist communist party based on a narrowly-defined proletariat, shunning alliances with other parties and groups, drilling the masses in a schematic form of 'communism'. Gramsci, from similar motives, was obsessed with the 'molecular' creation of communist consciousness. Without that, Bordiga's revolution would be mere manipulation: 'If the revolution comes by decree from above and the worker simply changes his boss . . . the factory will remain alien and work a slavery . . .' Similarly, while Bordiga in a few months was ready to break away, with a small minority if necessary, Gramsci four years later called the Livorno schism which created the communist party (minority and 'to the left') reaction's greatest victory, because it detached the masses from communism.

These are eloquent testimony to the difference in quality between the two movements. When one recollects the despair of comrade Lenin at the end of his life, the Bordiga-Gramsci tension (so much more than a simple opposition: more a seizure upon different aspects of a complex whole which, in its tense dialectical unity, constitutes Marxist-Leninism) assumes centrality in the permanent dialogue within the revolutionary workers' movement.

Gramsci did not get to grips with the PSI in actuality until he had to. Probably there is some quality in a marxism which is brilliant, perceptive and nuanced in its concentration on building communism, the communist state and communist consciousness which inhibits a command over the blunter exigencies of the dialectic. Capitalism cripples us all. For revolutionaries moving towards the crunch, it is the identity of the crippled member that counts.

If the Bordiga-Gramsci duality was a local reflection of the permanent schizophrenia which afflicts a revolutionary socialist movement in bourgeois society, the practical consequences were no less disastrous. The council movement reached a strictly localized but still extraordinarily intense maturity during the winter of 1919-20 when it was confronted with the urgent necessity, under fierce counter-attack, to break out, to lodge itself in and if possible convert the Italian socialist movement. It ran against what had become the frozen blocks of maximalism and the CGL on one hand, Bordiga's abstentionism on the other. It was broken. Its surviving spokesmen, Gramsci in particular, having been tributaries of maximalism, became tributaries of Bordiga.

In the autumn of 1919, its lack of specificity in a party sense simply exposed it to the power of Angelo Tasca and the forces he represented, which were, ultimately, social-democratic. In the nullism of abstentionism and the party-political formlessness of *ordinovism*, Tasca and the thinking he represented won the day. It was Tasca who dominated the congress numbers of *L'Ordine Nuovo* and who, in effect, represented the *ordinovisti* at the Bologna congress. There, while the maximalists won easily, hardly any voice sounded an *ordinovista* note, even though the air was thick with fashionable talk of 'soviets'. Tasca joined Serrati's committee and helped to soften their motion in the hope of catching some centrists. On 18 October, *L'Ordine Nuovo* carried an article by Tasca in defence of 'party unity'. Bordiga was to use all this against Gramsci, and Lenin's praise of him at the Second Congress of the Third International in 1920. If the council movement was politically present at all[13] in October 1919, it was as an eccentric fringe of the maximalists. In substance it was absent.

While the maximalists drove into the electoral campaign, it was the swelling power of the council movement which filled the pages of *L'Ordine Nuovo*, through the October articles which reshaped conciliar theory, to climax in the brilliant success of the 8 November number, with its *Programme of the Workshop Commissars*. But the general election of November forced the more general political issue on Gramsci's attention, even as he got to grips with Giolittian wooing of the reformist socialists.

His attitude was governed by two factors: fear of an increase in the parliamentarianism of the party on the one hand and, on the other, an appreciation of the possibilities opened up by electoral success. He wrote a tough note *Revolutionaries and the elections* for the 15 November number of *L'Ordine Nuovo*. What could revolutionaries expect from an electoral system which masked the bourgeois dictatorship? A group of socialist militants in parliament strong and combative enough 'to make it impossible for any *leader* of the bourgeoisie to form a strong and stable government, to force the bourgeoisie as a result to drop the democratic act, to drop legality and to drive the widest and deepest masses of the working class into revolt against the oligarchy of exploiters.' Conscious revolutionaries, believers in 'the proletarian dictatorship incarnated in a system of workers' and peasants' councils', had struggled to get socialist deputies into a bourgeois parliament for specific reasons.

'The communist revolution cannot be achieved by a *coup de main*. If a revolutionary minority managed to seize power by violence, that minority would be overthrown the next day by the mercenary forces of capitalism, because the un-absorbed majority would stand by and let the flower of revolutionary power be massacred, would let all the evil passions and barbarism born of capitalist gold and corruption flood over them. It is necessary, then, that the proletarian vanguard materially and spiritually organize this inert and cowardly majority ; it is necessary that the revolutionary vanguard, with its own methods and systems, create the material and spiritual conditions in which the proprietor class can no longer go on peacefully ruling over great masses of men, but is forced, through the intransigence of socialist deputies controlled and disciplined by the party, to terrorize the masses and bludgeon them blindly into revolt.' Only in this sense was parliamentary action acceptable – 'to paralyze parliament, to strip the democratic mask from the double-face of the bourgeois dictatorship, to expose it in all its horror and repulsive ugliness.'

He rehearsed his argument that it was international, rather than purely national conditions which called for revolution in Italy, and stressed the complexity of the task which therefore fell to the communist minority. The revolution finds the mass of the Italian population 'shapeless, still pulverized into an animal horde of individuals without discipline and culture, obedient only to the stimuli of the belly and the barbaric passions'. This was why revolutionaries had undertaken the electoral struggle 'to shape this multitude into some unity and primitive form', to tie it to the socialist party, 'to put some meaning and a glimmer of political consciousness into its instincts and passions'.

But it was also necessary not to delude these masses into reformism. It was necessary to make the bourgeoisie themselves prove that they could not satisfy the basic needs of the masses. It was necessary that the latter be forced in practical terms to confront the dilemma: 'Either death by hunger, the slavery of a foreign heel on the neck driving the worker and peasant to break himself on a machine and a clod of earth, or an heroic effort, a superhuman effort by the workers and peasants of Italy to create a proletarian order, to suppress the proprietor class and with it, every source of waste, barrenness, indiscipline and disorder.'[14]

This is a distinctly unpleasant document, harsh with the repulsive arrogance which tends to inform Gramsci's more savagely unbridled writing. As happens frequently in his work, it seems to reflect an uncertainty and a lack of secure belief in his own argument. He, with his Sorelian contempt for democracy, was certainly treading a tightrope here, as taut as that between his barbaric belly-slaves of the cowardly and the inert who are to be transformed by the whip and the wonder-workers of the proletarian vanguard into heroes of productive creation. It was this kind of thinking, however, that informed the article in which, virtually for the first time, he confronted the practical problems of the party and power – *The Problem of Power* of 29 November, following the decisive electoral success of the PSI, which won over 30 per cent of the vote and 156 seats in the Chamber.[15]

The Problem of Power begins with a global survey of the forces and powers of 'the class of the exploited in Italy': the corporative forces, the vanguard industrial workers and rural workers of the region of intensive cultivation mobilized in the CGL, the restless and indisciplined because backward workers who 'camp in the nomad tents of USI'; the railwaymen's union, 'an amorphous mass of vanguard industrial workers, petty-bourgeois clerks, couldn't-care-less technicians and a vague and uncertain number of wage and salary earners clinging limpet-like to the coffers of the state as only the petty-bourgeoisie and small peasantry can'; catholic peasant unions who introduce 'alien and contradictory principles into trade unionism (religion: vague and chaotic libertarian aspirations)'; scattered peasant leagues who are a symptom of the lack of cohesion in the national economy, and ex-servicemen's associations. This movement has concentrated a mass of 6 million workers representing about 25 million of the national population. 'It has banished the "free" labourer from the economic scene and has paralyzed the capitalist labour market ... The capitalist order of production has been rocked to its foundations, the "freedom" to exploit, the freedom to extract surplus value from labour-power . . . has been limited, in however indirect a manner, by proletarian control. The economic bases of capitalist organization, which reaches its summit in the highest association in capitalism, the parliamentary-bureaucratic state, has been dislocated, by sabotage at the very source of capitalist power: the freedom to extract surplus value.'

For the political movement of the class of the exploited, 'the Italian class of producers who do not own the instruments of labour, the means of production and exchange' has achieved a concentration of power, three and a half million workers, peasants and white-collars, representing some 15 million of the population, who have elected 156 socialist deputies, a concentration which 'brings parliament to a full stop'. The electoral victory is a simple reflection of 'the fundamental, primordial economic phenomenon', the paralysis of the capitalist labour market. These workers and peasants 'have done all they can do in a democratic society, in a society which is defined politically'; they have chosen the Socialist Party as their instrument. They have committed themselves, in however inchoate a manner, to the dictatorship of the proletariat.

This schematic but striking survey is rooted in the crisis in the mode of production; paralysis in parliament reflects paralysis in the labour market. And in terms of the 'illusion of the epoch' instilled into men's minds by bourgeois hegemony, the democratic illusion, workers have done all they can do by indicating the PSI as their agency and the proletarian dictatorship as their aspiration. That dictatorship is immanent in the developing crisis, just as consciousness of their historical mission is implicit in the action of the workers. From this firm, if elementary marxist base, Gramsci moves to the Socialist Party and its realization of this potential.

How to organize this mass of 25 million people, potentially a 'stable and secure base for the proletarian apparatus', but differentiated sharply in its technical and political capacities? 'It is the problem of the modes and forms which will make it possible to organize the whole mass of Italian workers in a hierarchy which organically culminates in the party.' This means the 'construction of a state apparatus which, internally, will function democratically, that is, will guarantee freedom to all anti-capitalist tendencies, the possibility of becoming parties of proletarian government, but externally, will be like an implacable machine which crushes the organizations of the industrial and political power of capitalism.'

The key force is the party 'and, within the party, the revolutionary communist tendency, which represents the mature form of the present historical consciousness of the proletarian mass'. For these revolutionaries, then, the central problems are:

> 1. To fix the great mass of working people in a social configuration which is adapted to the process of industrial and agricultural production (formation of factory and village councils with the vote given to all workers).
> 2. To make sure that within the councils, the majority is represented by party comrades, workers' organizations and sympathetic comrades, but without excluding the possibility that temporarily, in the first moments of uncertainty and immaturity, it may fall to *popolari*, anarcho-syndicalists, reformists, in so far as they are wage workers who have been elected at their workplace and adhere to the workers' state.

In the higher ranges of this hierarchy not only producers as such, but party organizations, unions, co-operatives will be represented. Hence a socialist majority will be notable in those districts ; in the heart-centres of capitalism which grip the whole nation in their tentacles, in those regions where 'the workers' state will be truly a proletarian dictatorship (of the factory workers)', the socialist majority will be overwhelming.

The key here is evidently the socialist 'state apparatus', already existing in bourgeois society, which culminates in the party and is to embrace the multiform mass, as that mass is being propelled by the crisis into the dictatorship of the proletariat. This 'apparatus', completely libertarian in its internal life, completely ruthless in its external operation, is strikingly reminiscent of Daniel de Leon and the SLP. Its essence is the council, though the party would *have to accept* that in the initial phases of the transition, those councils might well fall to *popolari*, syndicalists, reformists. The interaction of the communist will and the crisis in the mode of production would in the end secure a communist majority. Further, there is a safeguard in the insertion of socialist organizations in the higher centres and particularly the great cities.

While a simple and elementary sketch, the essay does catch something of the process of incorporating and marshalling in a communist array inchoate and divergent movements of workers and peasants in a continuing mode-of-production crisis. The operation called for, however – a toughly centralized and communist party, operating in a *completely libertarian* manner in the heart of the whole mass of the working population – was to say the least, dialectically delicate! It flows naturally enough from Gramsci's own argument, but the relationship between party and masses in this, as in other projects of similar temper (Rosa Luxemburg's concept of leadership, for example) reads like an attempt to square the circle. One notes that an 'inevitable' socialist majority is carefully inserted where it matters – at the top – as a 'long-stop'.

What is completely absent is any discussion of how the organic culmination of this apparatus, the party, is to *act* ; how the state apparatus' is actually to get 'state power' in vulgar reality. For, to Gramsci, the 'problem of power' is the problem of the 'modes and forms' in which the whole mass of Italian workers is to be organized into a hierarchy ; it is to 'fix' the mass in a 'configuration' adapted to the realities of production and then to win a majority within. One sees the muscle. Where's the punch? This is worlds removed from Bordiga's communist party, which would surely find it, at the least, utopian.

More immediately serious, it was irrelevant to the PSI in reality. For, as Gramsci was writing this article, the council communist movement was coming under attack, not only from the CGL, but from the party centre itself.

The Councils and the Party

In May 1926, Gramsci wrote the obituary of Giacinto Menotti Serrati, who died of a heart attack while returning from a clandestine meeting of the communist party in the mountains above Comasco. Talking of the war years, Gramsci said, 'It is certain that Serrati was then loved as no party leader had ever been loved in our country.' After the crisis of 1911-12, Serrati had done more than anyone to re-establish the marxist revolutionary movement, to hold it through the shock of the defection of its charismatic leader Benito Mussolini in 1914, to keep it alive during the war. 'In this sense,' said Gramsci in his obituary, 'Serrati has been the highest and most noble representative of Italian revolutionary socialism. He embodied

everything that was most generous and disinterested in that generation. If one does not take account of that, one cannot understand the
drama of the post-war years and the full historical significance of
Serrati's adherence to the Communist Party.' He added, 'Perhaps we
of the younger generation did not fully appreciate the drama which
the older generation then experienced. We were therefore cruel, perhaps beyond measure, in our attack on what seemed useless senti-
mentalism and a sterile love for old formulae and old symbols.'[1]
Cruel he certainly was ; the conflict between Gramsci and Serrati was
one of the most vicious to stain the history of the working-class
movement. Understandably, for Serrati did more than anyone on the
left to destroy the council movement.

A sincere and committed revolutionary, he responded immediately to the October revolution. He led the PSI into the Third
International and to a commitment to the dictatorship of the proletariat. But he was acutely aware, firstly of the real strength still
remaining in bourgeois society despite the paralysis of its state ; and
more importantly of the essentially fragmented and disparate nature
of the popular revolt in 1919-20. He was particularly alive to the problem of rural Italy, where the *popolari* were making the pace and
where the socialists had achieved and were achieving little lodgment.
In his celebrated correspondence with Lenin, he was acute and powerful on the differences between the peasant crises in Russia and Italy
and his arguments generally can in no sense be ignored. He thought
in terms of 'realities', feared that the millions of new members and
supporters would unhinge what he saw as the 'great tradition' of
Italian socialism, which had after all, been born, under Turati's guidance, in a schism with anarchists. He doubted the possibility of immediate revolution, and fully shared the 'fatalism' of the PSI in the
sense that he thought a revolution could not be forced or even 'prepared' ; in the crisis of capitalism the revolutionary moment would
come. It was essential to keep the party and the entire movement
united, so that they could ride the revolutionary tide to victory and
then administer the dictatorship of the proletariat in what he foresaw
as appalling difficulties. So, this man of incomparable prestige and
influence, representative of the maximalist mass of the party, clung
to the Third International but refused to obey its directives, refused
to expel the reformists – 'Do you really think that Turati and
D'Aragona, new Joshuas, can stop the revolutionary sun from rising?

– and refused to countenance anything which might imperil unity. Driven along this road by his increasing reliance on the CGL, and the difficult job of managing a massive new parliamentary party which could paralyze the state, he was intransigent in his opposition to Bordiga's demand for an expulsion of the reformists and the creation of a monolithic party, as well as to the council movement's attack on the trade-union bureaucracy.[17]

In November 1919, he launched a blistering attack on the council movement in Turin. 'This is the realm of aberration!' he said, speaking of the council communists' advocacy of the vote for the unorganized; he denounced their 'proclamation of the revolutionary capacity of the amorphous mass' and their setting aside of 'that organized movement which is the nucleus of the future society'. In the new theoretical journal, *Comunismo*, he pressed the attack home, accusing the Turin comrades of 'a curious confusion between soviets, political organs and instruments of government of a triumphant revolution, and factory committees, *technical* organs of production and industrial regulation'. In practice he threw the weight of the maximalists, bubbling with all sorts of academic 'soviet' schemes, behind the resistance of the CGL.[18]

Decisive was the support of the Comintern representative, Nicolai Ljubarsky, who wrote under the name of Carlo Niccolini. With all the weight of Comintern and Russia behind him, he dismissed factory committees, pointed to the undoubted fact that this form of 'workers' control' had been short-lived in Russia, hammered home the primacy of the unions and denied that any factory organization could be a *political* power.[19]

On this particular point, the maximalists were in fact in accord with Bordiga. This, coupled with the more earthy campaign on the ground waged by the CGL, without doubt helped to hold the line against a spread of the Turin contamination, and it certainly rocked the *ordinovisti* back on their heels. They had from the first construed the Russian revolution as a *soviet* revolution; it took some time for the role of the *party* to register. There was considerable ignorance about the actual course of events. *L'Ordine Nuovo* certainly had a good theoretical case for its translation of soviets into factory councils, at least as an initial stage, but given the immense prestige of the Bolsheviks, they were without doubt thrown on the defensive. The process registers in Gramsci's writings. He had always kept the distinction clear in his own mind, but in practice, during the growth of the council movement, it had been blurred. In his writings into January-February 1920, Gramsci in a sense re-affirms his original position of June 1919 and, in the manner which one comes to recognize as characteristic, presents factory councils as a stage *towards* soviets, technically no 'withdrawal' but in practice, certainly, a change in *tone* from his articles of October and November. He turned the argument against the maximalists by using it to dismiss any attempt to create 'soviets' out of the blue by party fiat.

But blow followed blow. On 29 October, Lenin addressed his first serious programmatic letter to Serrati. It was published on 6 December 1919 and disconcerted *ordinovisti* and Bordighists alike. Lenin whole-heartedly supported the decision to contest the November elections, put Italian 'communists' (the party had confirmed the affiliation to Comintern with acclamation) on guard against premature rebellion, advised them to watch for the proper moment and generally hailed the advance of 'communism' in Italy. The letter was exploited in the interests of the maximalist centre.[20]

In December 1919, therefore, the council communist movement was running into a labyrinth of contradictions and an intensifying party crisis. At the very moment when it was winning an overwhelming, if strictly localized, success in Turin, it was becoming increasingly isolated within the socialist movement and subjected to attack from all sides. It was in December that the first signs of dislocation appeared among the *ordinovisti*. They all responded sharply to attacks, whether from Serrati, Bordiga or the CGL, Gramsci in particular taking issue with Serrati's assertion that the 'dictatorship of the proletariat is the conscious dictatorship of the Socialist Party'. But Angelo Tasca, who had long enjoyed close relations with the trade-union leaders in Turin, began to distinguish his position from that of his colleagues.

Writing ten years later, he asserted that the main purpose of his activity on *L'Ordine Nuovo* had been to 'link up and co-ordinate the *new forms* with which the vanguard proletariat (though practically only in Turin) advanced towards the *organization of the revolution* with the *old forms* which still held the allegiance of the great majority of the workers in town and country who were influenced by the socialist party – that is, with the trade unions and particularly with the *camere del lavoro*.' The *camere* he urged in 1929 were, in the climate of 1919, full of 'sovietist elements' as the food troubles had shown and were the principal centres for the mobilization of the Italian working masses.[21] On 20 December, 1919, in *L'Ordine Nuovo*, in an article on the problem of the un-unionized, he struck quite a different note from Gramsci, Togliatti and their friends. He talked of a 'mixed system' of councils, argued for the creation of economic councils with representation of factory councils, craft federations and the party. His writing registered some scepticism on the discovery of a 'soviet' tradition in the Italian working class and a subtle but sensible shift towards the trade unions.[22]

The December malaise took root in an atmosphere of deepening uneasiness. The socialist deputies certainly dislocated parliament; outside, state authority and the economic situation remained parlous. 'Subversive' and nationalist agitations were intensifying; USI was claiming 300,000 members and rapid growth. *La Stampa* and democratic radicals were calling for a return of Giolitti and hinting at alliances with Turati and parliamentary socialists. The PSI, thundering out its maximalist rhetoric to hold its people (and frighten the bourgeoisie) in practice yielded more and more to the functional centrism of the greatly re-inforced parliamentary group. The elections, far from effecting a breakthrough, confirmed the immobilism of the Directorate. A sense of urgency, even desperation, began to take hold of communists. It was now that Bordiga began to address Lenin direct.

In *L'Ordine Nuovo* there was a visible increase in tension. At the opening of parliament, the socialist deputies walked out as the monarch entered, and were promptly attacked by crowds of nationalists. During the general strike called in response, Gramsci claimed that the councils in Turin, without any preparation, mobilized 120,000 workers in an hour. 'An hour later the proletarian army swept like an avalanche into the city centre and cleared the streets and squares of all the nationalist and militarist rabble.'

Gramsci's own response was an extraordinary explosion of hatred. In *The Events of 2-3 December* in *L'Ordine Nuovo* for 6-13 December, he said the battle in the streets had not been between proletarians and capitalists but between proletarians and the petty and middle bourgeoisie, who had come out in defence of that liberal democracy which guaranteed them their corrupt and useless parasitic privileges. In an onslaught which anticipates his later analysis of fascism he raked them, the petty bourgeoisie in particular, with virulent abuse of an almost hypnotic intensity. 'The petty and middle bourgeoisie is in fact the barrier of corrupt, dissolute, rotten humanity with which capitalism defends its economic and political power; a servile, abject humanity, a humanity of hirelings and cowards, today become the 'slave mistress' who sucks a ransom from production larger not only than the total of wages paid to the working class, but than the booty grabbed by the capitalists themselves.' The war had given these creatures power, especially the particularly horrible species from the South: 'flocking from the depths of villages and townships in the South, from street-corner shops run by papa, from the warmed-to-no-purpose benches of the middle and high schools, from the editors' chairs of blackmailing rags, from the trash of city suburbs, from all those ghettoes where there rot and decompose all the villainy, vileness and arrogance of the social rubbish and debris deposited by centuries of servility and the domination of the Italian nation by foreigners and priests. They were given the wages of indispensable and irreplaceable men and they were given power over masses of men, in factories, cities, barracks, the trenches at the front. Well armed, well fed, subject to no control, in a position to satisfy the three passions which pessimists claim are inherent and unsuppressable in human nature: the passion for absolute power over other men, dominion over the life and death of other men, the passion to possess many women, the passion to possess much money to buy pleasure and luxury – these tens and tens of thousands of the corrupt, the crooked, the dissolute, bound themselves to the monstrous military-bureaucratic apparatus built during the war. They want to go on governing masses of men, to be invested with absolute authority over the life and death of masses of men; they organize *pogroms* against proletarians, against socialists, they hold the streets and squares in a reign of terror.' And the answer? – 'expel it from society as one expels a swarm of locusts from a half-devastated field.'[23]

On 20 December, Gramsci got to grips with Serrati's exploitation of Lenin's letter and registered another advance in his thinking on the party. *La Stampa*, he said, had managed to use the letter to 'prove' that Lenin was a Giolittian! Serrati's exercise was similar. Maximalists completely failed to grasp the instrumental statecraft of the letter. This was because Italian 'communists' did not know what a 'professional revolutionary' was, and had done little to train themselves. 'They move among the giant cogwheels of history like a yokel in a factory, treading timid, face now bold, now fearful, amid the noise and the beat of the great machines.' (Good metaphor for a council communist!) They were abandoning the Italian masses to a stark choice between catastrophe and Constituent Assembly.

But 'Italian communists are finally groping their way out of the dark. They are mastering the "machine" of revolution.' There followed a concise statement of Gramsci's views of the functions of the party at that date:

'For the Third International, to "make" the revolution means to "give" power to the soviets, means to fight to win communist majority in the soviets.' But the process of 'giving' this power?

'For the Third International, to be revolutionaries means to escape from the dominion of union corporatism and party sectarianism.' This, no doubt ruled out both the CGL-reformists and the Bordighists. But the argument does not in fact come to a climax. *Because it comes full circle.*

'For the Third International, to be revolutionaries means to perceive the movement of human masses seeking a form, and to work so that that form shall be the system of councils.' For the 'machine' of revolution, (of course) is 'the system of factory councils'.[24]

However sweeping the perspective, the scenario is Hamlet without the Prince. On the party and its complex and delicate relationship with these wide-open councils – which were yet subject to the iron discipline of reality, the inexorable emergence of the dictatorship of the proletariat from the crisis in the mode of production – Gramsci was now clearer, at least in intention. For the party to 'take' power meant to 'give' power to the councils. Realization was a different matter. And in this comment, for the first time, criticism is directed overtly not only at the reformists but at the so-called 'communists' of the maximalist majority who had formally adhered to the Third International.

And on 27 December, Gramsci moved to an attack on Serati's identification of the proletarian dictatorship with the dictatorship of the socialist party, in an article *The Party and the Revolution,* which represents his first serious attempt to confront the problem.[25]

This essay, while schematic, is a brilliant, terse and powerful statement, which begins from an essentially marxist base, but then gets lost.

Gramsci begins by rejecting any identification of the dictatorship of the proletariat with the dictatorship of the socialist party. After describing the party as an 'apparatus of proletarian democracy', he identifies it as the model of a 'libertarian' society, voluntarily disciplined by an explicit act of consciousness. 'To imagine the whole of human society as a colossal socialist party, with its applications for admission and its resignations, can only intensify the contractual prejudices of many subversive minds reared on J.-J. Rousseau and anarchist pamphlets rather than on the historical and economic doctrines of marxism.'

This identification had been the fatal error of the German party:

> German Social-Democracy . . . has created a paradox; it violently forced the process of the German revolution into the forms of its own organization and believed it had mastered history. It has created its own councils, by order, with a safe majority of its own men; it has shackled the revolution, domesticated it. Today, it has lost all contact with historical reality, except for that of Noske's fist on the nape of the workers' neck, and the revolutionary process follows its own uncontrolled, still mysterious course, to boil up again from unknown depths of violence and pain.

Where then to locate this autonomous revolution? This is the first crunch: 'Communist society can be conceived only as a "natural" formation inherent in the means of production and exchange ; and the revolution can be conceived as the act of historical recognition of the "naturalness" of this formation.'

This concentration on the *mode of production* as the determinant in the last instance and on the 'involuntary' character of the ultimate communist society is rooted in the very heart of marxism and can indeed be employed as a touchstone to differentiate false from genuine marxism. Reaction against the determinism and fatalism of the Second International, response to the liberation-fulfilment of marxism by Leninist action, have tended to blur the utterly essential and irreplaceable character of this first principle.[26] The only acts which can be considered communist are those which advance the *communist mode of production* which creates the lived-in 'superstructure'. Gramsci *lived* this. He looked *through* the future to the ultimate communist society; *every* act of the workers' movement must have the building of that future in mind. *Any* act, however 'revolutionary', which did not contribute to it was un-marxist and hence ideological, petty-bourgeois and unreal. This, at least, was the model and it must remain the model for any communist. Not merely the communist 'revolution' in an immediate sense, but communist 'revolution' in its real sense, which has no time-limit, communist 'society' must be implicit in every communist's acts here and now.

But in Gramsci's writing, this was in no sense a crudely 'determinist' conception – not from a 'Bergsonian' and 'voluntarist'! The essay goes on: 'The revolutionary process identifies itself, therefore, only in a spontaneous movement of the labouring masses, caused by the clash of the contradictions inherent in human society in a regime of capitalist property. Trapped in the pincers of capitalist conflicts, menaced by a condemnation, without appeal, to the loss of civil and spiritual rights, the masses break away from the forms of bourgeois democracy, break out from the legality of the bourgeois constitution.'

The masses break out of bourgeois order and thus order itself. This means a *collapse into barbarism* unless the implicit new order – the order implicit in their actions and in the crisis – is realized by *human action in communist will*. 'Society disintegrates, all production of useful wealth slumps, men plunge into a black pit of poverty, barbarism and death, unless there is a reaction from the historical consciousness of the popular masses, who discover a new structural form, who realize a new order in the process of the production and distribution of wealth.'

In the 'discovery' of the new order implicit in the crisis of the mode of production, the fighting organizations of the proletariat are 'agents'. While the socialist party cannot be conceived as the *form* of the revolutionary process, it is without doubt the major 'agent'. In its intransigence, it achieves the same result as the trade unions in the economic field: 'it puts an end to free competition'. It achieves this by acting as an 'incorporeal government' . . . 'The socialist party, with its revolutionary programme, pulls out from under the bourgeois state apparatus its democratic base in the consent of the governed.' It identifies itself with the historical consciousness of the popular masses and governs their movement – 'This government is incorporeal; it functions through a myriad spiritual links, it is an irradiation of prestige, which can become an effective government only at moments of climax: a call to the streets, a physical array of militant forces, ready to fight to beat off a threat, disperse a cloud of reactionary violence.'

When the action of the bourgeois government has been paralyzed, the more delicate and difficult task of positive action begins. Through its influence over the masses implicitly groping towards a new order immanent in the crisis, it generates 'new social configurations . . . organizations which function by their own inner laws, embryonic apparatuses of power, in which the mass realizes its government, in which the mass acquires consciousness of its historical responsibility and of its definite mission to create the conditions for a regenerating communism. The party, as a compact and militant formation of an idea, influences this intimate elaboration of new structures'. But its influence is organic, in an 'apparatus of spiritual government' in which the masses recognize the historical consciousness which moves them.

The party then 'remains the superior hierarchy of this irresistible mass movement. The party exercises the most effective of dictatorships, that born of prestige, which is a conscious and spontaneous acceptance of an authority perceived as indispensable.' But woe betide if the party follows the German model – 'Woe betide, if out of a sectarian concept of the party's role in the revolution, there is an attempt to make this hierarchy material, to freeze in mechanical forms of immediate power the government apparatus of the masses in movement, to force the revolutionary process into the form of the party: the result would be to divert a number of men, to "master" history; but the real revolutionary process would escape from the control and the influence of the party, which would unconsciously become an organ of conservatism.'

Note that 'agent' in his description of the party is put in quotation marks. The key here is the second crunch, the notion of *historical consciousness*.

Begin with his earlier article *The Problem of Power* of 29 November. Among the forces arrayed there are – 'the socialist party and within the socialist party, the revolutionary communist tendency, which represents the mature form of the present historical consciousness of the proletarian mass'. In this December article, the crisis in the capitalist mode of production expressed in the mass break from order will plunge men and society into the 'black pit' unless there is a reaction from the historical consciousness of the masses. This can be only that consciousness which is instinctive, immanent, implicit in their actions. The 'embodiment' of this consciousness is the socialist party – 'millions and millions of workers, establishing new hierarchies and founding new orders, know that the historical consciousness which moves them finds its living embodiment in the socialist party'. In acting as an 'incorporeal government' the party, as it influences the masses, is 'identifying itself with the historical consciousness of the popular masses'. BUT it is the 'new social configurations . . . organizations which function by their own inner laws . . . embryonic apparatuses of power' generated by this interaction between the party's action and the *mass living* of an historical consciousness implicit in the crisis in the mode of production, which are the crucial element. For it is in these new configurations that 'the mass acquires consciousness of its historical responsibilities and of its definite mission'. It is the *councils* then which are the crucial *areas of translation*.

But how does this 'agent . . . incorporeal government' effect its positive action? : – 'The concepts which the party disseminates operate autonomously in the consciousness of individuals and determine new social configurations . . .'

This is an idealist statement and an un-marxist deviation from his effort to conceive the emergence of communist organization as an interaction between the process of the crisis in the mode of production and an equally historically conditioned 'communist will' which realizes an implicit historical consciousness. It is probably some indication of the 'imposed' character of Gramscian communism in the Turin council movement, whose growth it clearly echoes. On the other hand, of course, Bordigan communism would find it difficult to answer a similar charge.

The conclusion leads on remorselessly to the reshaping of the masses into the communist 'natural' formation through the councils, the allocation of functions between council, party and union, the rejection of any attempt by the party to impose its own forms on the councils, an attempt to elucidate how the party 'makes' the revolution by 'giving' power to the councils.

A brilliant essay which *does* get lost. The loss occurs precisely in the area of interaction between the party and the *conquest* of self-consciousness by producers. The loss occurs precisely in the area of the 'influence' the party exercises to imprint consciousness on workers 'set loose' by the crisis, who are yet to conquer consciousness themselves. This would be a totally idealist concept *were it not* for the assumption that the dictatorship of the proletariat is *immanent* in the crisis, that the 'influence' in fact consists of a 'discovery' or as he said elsewhere, the 'recognition' of an objective reality. Implicit in this particular argument, then, *is* a form of 'determinism', despite the author's 'voluntarism'. Indeed, the 'determinism' is a *condition* of his 'voluntarism'.

It is probably for this reason that the actual vulgar *seizure of power* is largely absent from his work.

The problem, of course, remains central to a marxist revolutionary party. Gramsci spent the rest of his life exploring it. Why should the consciousness of the masses groping towards an unrealized and immanent communism, tend, even under guidance, even tendentially, towards the form of 'communism' propagated by an *equally historically conditioned socialist party itself an element in the superstructure of bourgeois society*? (in the 29 November article, he was more precise in locating the 'mature' form of the historical consciousness of the masses not in the socialist party but in the communist tendency within it). In practice, of course, it frequently did not. Hence the *need*, in Gramsci's courageous phrase, for the disciplined, monolithic party to be ready, if need be, for councils full of syndicalists, reformists, *popolari* and Stentorellos 'in the initial stages'.

But hence the focus, too, on the work of communists within the councils, which approximated to Bordiga's concept of 'communist groups'. Gramsci's visible shift towards 'communist groups' in the winter of 1919-20 was by no means simply an accommodation to Bordigan communism. It was implicit in his own conciliar thinking. It soon became explicit. For the thrust of the whole article was to warn off the PSI from creating its own 'councils' in the style of the German party. But this is precisely what it did. A crucial moment for communism in Italy, whether Bordigan or Gramscian, was the national council of the PSI held at Florence in mid-January 1920.

The action of the CGL and the PSI had been successful in holding the line against the Turin councils, but as popular discontent intensified over the winter, it became necessary to present a positive alternative. At the Bologna congress in October 1919, there had been much enthusiasm for 'soviets' and Enrico Leone had won support for his proposal that soviets be created to embrace all revolutionaries and energize the unions. In January 1920, Bordiga began to publish *Il Soviet* again and the local triumph of the factory councils in Turin was consummated. The maximalists exerted themselves to contain the threat. On 9 January, Egidio Gennari proposed that socialist-controlled communes should set up soviets and hand over power to them ; he developed this later into a complicated scheme, which tried to embrace factory councils while sterilizing them. This was offered in support of a motion brought forward by Nicola Bombacci, counted an 'extremist', at the PSI's national council meeting at Florence in mid-January.[27]

Bombacci like Gennari, was at pains to distinguish between factory councils and workers' councils or 'soviets'. He proposed structures of separate 'soviets' for workers, peasants and white-collar workers and general councils to embrace all categories. Some provision was made for the incorporation of existing factory councils into the scheme, but all such councils were to be strictly controlled by the party. In fact, the entire project, hastily cobbled together, was to be run by committees of the party who were to 'create' councils. The motion was easily carried in an assembly which rejected or ignored *both* the *ordinovista* and the Bordighist arguments and was transparently pre-occupied with suppressing the challenge from Turin. Serrati himself was very dubious about the whole project, while Gennari said baldly, 'it is essential to answer the demands of the masses somehow'.

The Florence meeting, held as it was in the context of continuing socialist immobilism, a new wave of popular discontent and syndicalist growth, and a visible strengthening of both government power and reformist weight, had a devastating effect on the communist wings of the socialist movement. Bordiga resolved on a break. He renewed his efforts to contact Lenin direct, talked freely of the failure of revolution and began to look for support in the creation of a communist party.

In Turin, the disgust was hardly less strong. Togliatti in *L'Ordine Nuovo* moved to a sustained attack on the Bombacci proposals, supported by Viglongo who savaged the whole concept of a 'labour parliament'. The executive of the Turin section, in the throes of renewing itself, reacted violently and began to demand a radical change in party policy. In response to the national council meeting, there was something of a convulsion in Turin, which carried the section swiftly in a communist direction, carried the *ordinovisti* into their first disruption and carried Gramsci's thinking into a new phase.

7.   The Critical Choice

The party has shown itself incapable of giving a firm and precise leadership to the class struggle being fought by Italian working people: the activity of the party has been confused with the action of the parliamentary group, with an action, that is, either openly reformist and opportunist or absolutely void of any concrete content. . . . This state of atrophy and lethargy was exposed in a striking manner at the discussions during the national council in Florence . . . from which it became obvious:

1. that the leading organizations of the party are more than ever manipulated by opportunists and reformists.

2. that the weakness of maximalist action stems from the absence of a firm and concrete conception of the moment through which the class struggle is passing . . .

To escape from this state of atrophy and disorientation, it is necessary that the party begin a positive action in the midst of the masses, to realize the theses of the Third International . . . The Turin socialist section must assume the responsibility . . .

The Turin section of the PSI responded to the Florence meeting of the national council with an assertion of its claim to lead communists in a campaign to 'renew' the party.

The section executive had resigned early in January. An election committee was preparing a list of candidates, designed to renew and develop the alliance between abstentionists and *ordinovisti*, when the dismal news came through from Florence. There was a spasm of impatient reaction. The electoral committee instead prepared an *Action Programme* and Gramsci wrote an indictment to accompany it: *First: Renew the Party. L'Ordine Nuovo* published both on 31 January.[1]

What is to be done?

First: Renew the Party was a passionate denunciation of the PSI, 'party of the workers and poor peasants' for failing abysmally in its duty. The party, like the trade union, is now unequivocally located within bourgeois society: 'born in the field of liberal democracy (field of political competition, projection of the development process of capitalism)'; its transcendence, like that of the trade unions, is implied.

> Its mission is to organize the workers and poor peasants into a ruling class.

It had fulfilled the first duty, to win the masses, but it was failing totally in the second, to organize the masses into an apparatus which could take power. So it was falling to pieces.

> The party daily loses contact with the great masses in movement; events unfold and the party is absent; the country shudders in spasms of fever . . . and the party does not intervene . . . The party which had become the most powerful of the historical energies of the Italian nation has fallen into a crisis of political infantilism and is today the most crippling of the social weaknesses of the Italian nation.

All Europe was lurching towards revolution, disintegrating in its own contradictions and under the hammer blows of the Red Army. The bourgeois Italian state was crumbling in the collapse of its policies and in great strikes in the public services. 'The sufficient and necessary conditions for the proletarian revolution are becoming reality in both the international and the national fields. And look! the socialist party fades away from itself and its mission.'

The root cause was the stranglehold of trade-union officials and parliamentary deputies, who were eroding and degrading the party. The union membership, 'permanent army' of the revolution, was left under the control of opportunists who systematically sabotaged every revolutionary action. In consequence, the bewildered masses were exposed to the twin germs of dissolution, 'reformist nullism and anarchist pseudo-revolutionary rhetoric (two aspects of a single petty-bourgeois tendency)' – and the two most serious threats to the Turin council movement.

During the two great strikes in the postal and railway services which had rocked the state in the early days of 1920 the party had done nothing but repeat the 'stale and worn-out cliché' of the Second International: the distinction between a political and an economic strike. As the state neared collapse, as the bourgeoisie, 'armed and full of hate', prepared a military coup, the party abandoned the workers to their own devices. The anarchists would be the gainers.

And the communist wing was doing nothing. It was doing

nothing to 'disinfect' the party, to organize it into a homogeneous bloc and a section of the Third International, firmly integrated into the world system of revolutionary forces. The communist workers must rally to their duty. It was they who must 'renew the party, give it precise form and precise direction ; they must stop petty-bourgeois opportunists reducing it to the level of so many parties in this Land of Pulcinella . . . The Socialist Party must be renewed if it does not want to be overthrown . . . it must be renewed because its defeat would mean the defeat of the revolution.'

This article signals Gramsci's breach with the PSI as constituted. The Pact of Alliance with the CGL and the grip of the reformists are singled out as essential targets. A purge – a 'disinfection' of the party – is implied. Moreover, there is a new note of breathless urgency, talk of a militarist coup, clear alarm at anarcho-syndicalist growth. The conclusion is not, however, a break-away to form a new party such as Bordiga was now contemplating. It is still 'renewal'. Reformists must go, the 'agitators, nay-sayers, apostles of elementary theories' be overcome, but the answer still lay in overcoming the 'mental laziness which is proper to the workers as to all other Italians' and which was prevalent in what Gramsci still called the 'communist, the revolutionary wing': the maximalists.

What is radically new, of course, is the priority : *first*, renew the party. In a very real sense it represents a belated agreement with Bordiga's long re-iterated insistence on the need for a party of a new type.

The *Action Programme* was the programme of 'renewal'. Its provisions may be summarized :

1. The Turin section must drive the party to promote the creation of councils throughout Italy, first as an extension of trade-union action directed at control, then to build the higher institutions of soviets. On no account must councils be subjected to the bourgeois state or drawn into class collaboration.

2. In Turin, since a powerful council system already exists, the section must move immediately to the second phase and create an urban workers' council, as the local organ of future proletarian power. In the interim, the urban council will serve to criticize parliament and the bourgeois state and to exercise control over the municipality, Communists must win control of the urban council and propagate communism.

3. The section must put an end to the ambiguity of the Pact of Alliance. It must therefore 'promote the formation of permanently constituted communist groups within every union and every league'.

4. These communist groups will 'promote the creation of industrial unions' which will work with the councils to realize in practice 'the transcendence of the present phase of struggle over hours and wages'.

5. The Turin *Avanti* must be brought under strict control.

6. The co-operative movement must be made an effective instrument of class struggle and must submit 'a moral report' every six months.

7. 'The working mass must be called frequently to assizes, so that we do not lose that profitable concord with it which has been so rich in results in the past and which constitutes our greatest strength now and in the days to come.'

8. 'We must agitate in the midst of the masses on every problem which touches a real class interest, in order to preserve and intensify the political sensibility of the proletariat and direct it towards communism.'

9. 'Because we believe that the bourgeoisie cannot escape the fate that awaits it unless it resorts to a reactionary and military dictatorship, and that sooner or later, it will so resort, it is imperative that the party take action to safeguard its own organization and the proletariat its own gains'; the section must therefore organize red guards.

10. Along this axis, the section must organize all its activity, directed towards

'1. solving the problem of the arming of the proletariat.

2. creating in the province a strong class movement of poor peasants and small-owners in solidarity with the industrial movement.'

An urban soviet and red guards had figured in Gramsci's earlier writings, just as he was to be the only man seriously to call for them during the Occupation of the Factories in September 1920, when he was more 'insurrectionary' in an institutional sense than even the syndicalists. The maximalist onslaught on factory councils as 'false' soviets had obviously struck home. The attack was absorbed and turned back on the attackers, on Bordiga no less than Bombacci. No soviets could be created by party fiat; they would grow out of the councils. Nevertheless, the new priority of renewing the party had enforced a radical shift in emphasis. Moreover, the incorporation of 'communist groups' into the wide-open council scheme, while perfectly valid in terms of Gramsci's theory, obviously posed problems both practical and theoretical. Moreover, it seemed to imply a shift towards Bordiga's abstentionists, who had been preaching them for some time. The Bordighists were not relenting in their rejection of the councils and their leader, abandoning 'renewal', was seeking support for a secession to form a communist party.

This was the crux. The council communists of Turin and the Turin left generally were now in full revolt against the PSI leadership, in the name of communism. They were presenting themselves as leaders in a campaign to make the PSI communist. But a communist fraction in permanent revolt and with a brutally clear-cut policy for the formation of a communist party had long existed. How were the two movements to relate? It was on this question that crisis broke on the *ordinovisti*.

In the *Chronicles* of the 14 February number of *L'Ordine Nuovo*, Gramsci wrote a very personal and enigmatic note. He talked of strain and difficulty. He talked of a mere handful of men and women running a journal which represented a great mass movement. He appealed for spiritual support. He said, 'It is useless to deny it, we are passing through a period of crisis. It is a crisis partly determined by internal conditions . . .'[2] Four years later in January 1924, in a private letter, he talked of Angelo Tasca's having 'separated from' the *ordinovisti* in January 1920. At that time he was recalling his own isolation during the summer of 1920. There was a public breach and a prolonged polemic with Tasca from May 1920 and in July-August, in the crisis which preceded the Occupation of the Factories, Togliatti and Terracini had also broken with Gramsci and, as he put it in 1924, 'joined Tasca.'[3]

Gramsci was to elaborate on his differences with Tasca during the summer of 1920, particularly in a long article *The Programme of L'Ordine Nuovo* (14-28 August 1920). Tasca treated council, party and union on the same plane: he had not understood that for the journal, the council was 'a form of "historical" association, comparable say to the bourgeois state, not to the "voluntary" organizations of the party and the union . . . 'the factory council is an institution of "public" character, while the party and the trade union are associations of "private" character'. Tasca, a very 'inattentive' reader of *L'Ordine Nuovo* had not shared the theoretical formation of the group which was 'for that matter nothing but a translation into historical Italian reality of the conceptions expounded by comrade Lenin in some writings published by *L'Ordine Nuovo* itself and of the conceptions of the American theorist of the revolutionary syndicalist association, the IWW, the marxist Daniel de Leon'. Gramsci referred to the number of 5 June 1920 as exemplary. This published not only an attack on Tasca, but the article *The Factory Council*, a polemic between Romain Rolland and Max Eastman on intellectuals and an extract from Marx on the Paris Commune. And he stated baldly that the fundamental bases of the *ordinovista* position were 'the works of Marx, De Leon and Lenin' of which Tasca evidently had no grasp.[4]

It is important not to succumb to that 'posthumous' rationalization to which Gramsci himself was prone, but it is quite clear that Tasca's attitudes differed profoundly from Gramsci's. The difference had begun to register in *L'Ordine Nuovo* as early as Tasca's article on the un-unionized of 20 December 1919. The immediate occasion of the break was the election of a new executive committee of the Turin socialist section.

An election committee had been chosen to select the names after the old committee's resignation on 6 January. This was the committee which produced the *Action Programme*. It clearly intended to turn the ad hoc alliance between council communists and abstentionist communists into an effective force, adopting the *Action Programme*, blurring abstentionism itself a little, but toughening it up with calls for military preparation, the mobilization of rural support, expulsion of the reformists. A rival list was entered however and Gramsci thought that Tasca was the moving force behind it. In early January and again in February, Bordiga had resumed his criticism of the councils in *Il Soviet* and it was Tasca who wrote a major reply in *Gradualism and Revolutionism in the Factory Councils*, on 17 January. Bordiga himself spoke in Turin before the elections and *Il Soviet* made a point of stating in February that Gramsci's ideas on the councils were quite different from Tasca's. The elections were won by an alliance of abstentionists with *ordinovisti* – Gramsci, Togliatti and Matta were elected as well as abstentionists who were active in the council movement like Parodi and Boero. The incident is in fact obscure. Terracini, who had been co-opted by the Directorate of the PSI even though he was waspishly criticizing official policy, figured on the rival list. To the public, Tasca remained in some sense a 'political' spokesman for *L'Ordine Nuovo* through to May. It was all very typical of the distinctly muddled 'political' character of the group.[5]

But what is clear is that in reaction to the Florence meeting, the *ordinovisti* and Gramsci in particular, moved in a direction which dislocated their unity and made a dialogue with Bordiga's communists imperative.

Bordiga and Gramsci

On 15 February 1920, Bordiga's journal *Il Soviet* published an article by Francesco Misiano, a comrade much respected for his heroism during the war, which argued against a premature split in the PSI, in reply to a piece which had called for an immediate break with *both* reformists and maximalists. This was a powerful instinct among the Bordigans, anxious to *define* communism and have done with the muddle of the PSI. 'Nothing's better than a good split', said *Il Soviet* on 1 February, 'Above all, everyone in his right place . . . We'd know just who is a communist and who isn't ; no more muddle . . . A good split lets the light in. Communists here, all the shower of opportunists over there . . .'[6]

Bordiga published Misiano quite freely. With his decision to break away, he was looking for support in the electionist left. And while he repeatedly asserted the necessity for abstentionism in his comments on Misiano's article, he praised him as the only socialist, not an abstentionist, who had called for an expulsion of reformists from the PSI. In fact, a similar call was coming from Turin at that moment.

The originally *instrumental* character of abstentionism is clear from Bordiga's comments on Misiano. The need was to create a communist party in *total* opposition to all bourgeois institutions ; to clean out reformism, it was necessary to break with parliament. But in the course of 1920, abstentionism was hardening into something approximating a fundamental principle. By the time the fraction held its national conference in May, it was calling for an anti-electoral fraction within the International itself, despite Bordiga's earlier and crucial distinction between German and Italian realities. Abstentionism was to prove a tough obstacle to a fusion of Bordighists and council communists ; less perhaps in itself than as a symptom of qualitatively different marxist sensibilities.

From January 1920, three themes were central to *Il Soviet:*
a split in the party
abstentionism
a critique of factory councils.

The three themes formed an integral unity, a total and totalizing perspective.

Central was the overpowering need to *define* communism, to cut it absolutely free from the bourgeois world. The core of the conception was a very precisely defined proletariat. Bordiga frequently cited Russian electoral law on the point, with its exclusion of anyone who 'lived on the labour of others'. In reply to Viglongo's article in *L'Ordine Nuovo* for 30 August 1919, Bordiga on 14 September commented on the argument over union and non-union men: 'some workers, even union men, could be excluded from the electoral lists of the civic political soviet, if, in addition to their labour in the factory, they lived from the proceeds of a small monetary or landed capital. Such cases are not infrequent among us' and he referred to the Russian constitution, article 65, clause 1.[7]

This clearly ruled out workers of 'mixed' status and, further, any element of the *artisan* from the proletariat; given Italian conditions, a serious decision. Over and above his hostility to trade unions as reformist and essentially bourgeois institutions, there seems to have been a suspicion of the element of 'property' in an organized trade or craft. This difference from Gramsci no doubt stems in part from his experience of Naples, with its vast and inchoate sub-proletariat as opposed to Turin's advanced industrial workers, but in fact it runs strictly parallel to his fierce exclusion of every 'bourgeois' contamination by the guillotine of abstention.

From this strictly proletarian base, a *class* instrument had to be created. And this instrument was built on an *individual commitment* to marxism which transcended all *residues* of bourgeois experience. This stress on *individual conversion* is very striking and was to inform his entire management of the Italian communist party 1921-23 and to lodge in the *Rome Theses* of 1922 which codified it. The revolutionary movement of the proletariat, he wrote early in 1920,

> finds its true instrument in a representation of the proletarian class in which every individual enters as a member of that class committed to a radical transformation of social relations and not as a component element of a professional category, a factory or any local group whatever.
>
> As long as political power remains in the hands of the capitalist class, a representation of the general revolutionary interests of the proletariat can be achieved only on the *political* terrain, in a class party which gathers in the personal allegiances of those

who, by committing themselves to the revolutionary cause, have transcended egoist interest, craft or trade interest, and sometimes even class interest, in the sense that the party will admit deserters from the bourgeois class who support the communist programme.[8]

There is, in truth, a powerful feeling of *conversion* about this, a commitment to communism which means a *total rupture* with the bourgeois world, a total commitment to *living communist.*

In view of later developments, it is important to stress now that Gramsci arrived at a similar intensity, a similar stress on the imperative of *living communist* in total, though in no sense insulated, differentiation from the bourgeois world. The centrality of Bordiga's scheme was therefore the *party*, built strictly on Bolshevik principles, the concentration of individual conversions to living communist in the service of a class. Gramsci, as we are seeing, was much slower to arrive at this point (which Bordiga had reached, in fact, by 1912). *But arrive at it he did.* Later history and even later historiography has masked the essential fact that there was, on the central issue of the *historical definition* of communism in Italy, a *fundamental consonance* between Bordiga and Gramsci. The leadership of the Bordigan communist party in 1921 was in fact varied in original provenance. Even in conflict with Comintern, they proved intransigently 'Bordighist'; at the Imola congress which formed the communist party, it was precisely Gramsci who defeated a critical movement which would have *blurred* this definition. It was on this ground of 'historical responsibility' that Gramsci, with the others, for long stood by the party against Comintern.

The basic *differences* stem from the form this definition takes in terms of the interaction of party and masses, the relationship of theory and practice. Bordiga's stress on individual conversion to the service of a class in an uncontaminated class party reflects a perhaps clumsy but strong sense of marxism as a *science*. The threat is that the 'science' will be perceived as a once-for-all acquisition and become paralyzing sectarian dogma. Gramsci was much more historicist, committed to 'creative intervention' and alive to the play of historically conditioned *social forces*. The threat in him is of a total historicism which will submerge communism in the reality it strives to master. It is symptomatic that Bordiga saw Lenin as the 'restorer' of marxism; Gramsci saw him as a creative innovator. Bordiga's communist party assumed the 'orthodoxy' which he had been seeking to re-assert since the 1912 crisis. Gramsci's *Lyons Theses* of 1925-26, in which he shaped *his* communist party, rejected the whole socialist tradition of Italy.

There was, or to be more exact, there developed as Gramsci developed, a fundamental consonance, but there was also a crucial divergence between the two marxisms in the area of the relationship between theory and practice. From the divergence arose more contingent differences in both strategy and tactics. These were very real and in fact prevented any 'fusion' of Bordighist and council-communist movements. But they have also been distorted and exaggerated both by the play of political 'events' and by the play of 'history' upon them. The political incoherence of the *ordinovista* group meant that this deformation set in very early. In February 1920, after Bordiga's visit to Turin, *Il Soviet* announced the 'discovery' that Tasca's views on the councils were in fact not Gramsci's. Neo-Bordighist historians have actually asserted that the council opinions 'traditionally' attributed to Gramsci were really Tasca's. This is a surprising comment on 'tradition' unless it is further proof that 'classics' are great books which are never read.[9]

This is not to say that the differences between the two men and the two movements were not profound. They were, and they shaped radically different movements in *action*. The divergences on the theory-practice dialectic, on 'science' and 'historicism', register profound differences in the quality of the marxist sensibilities at work. But the divergence was from what became, with Gramsci's development, a *common base* in a commitment to a total and totalizing historical definition of communism in Italy, and it is therefore necessary to try to distinguish the fundamental differences from the contingent. For Bordiga and Gramsci were not the Gog and Magog of Italian communism which 'history' has made them. They were twin if tautly dialectical polarities of Marxist-Leninism.

By early 1920, the Turin council movement with its Gramscian-communist tonality, had created one of Bordiga's 'historical situations'. But it was one which he failed to recognize and accept, a rejection probably stemming from a defect in his communist perception of the unity of theory and practice, inherent in the quality of his perception of marxism as a science. On the other hand the slowness with which Gramsci arrived at communist definition *in a party*

and his apparent failure to perceive the limitations of the Turin movement as structural rather than contingent, probably stem from a defect in his communist perception of marxism as science, inherent in
the quality of his perception of marxism as history.

It is difficult to see how an effective communist movement
can be built on one to the exclusion of the other.[10]

Bordiga had criticized the council movement as early as
September 1919. The party and political action were central; council
action was a diversion. The basis in craft and workplace set particular
interests within the class against the interests of the class itself. These
had to find expression in forms which transcended particular interests;
soviets therefore were *territorial* units, not units based on the productive processes of capitalism, and only soviets could be *political*.
He was prepared to allow factory councils some technical role in the
process of socialization, but little more.

On 21 September 1919, he stressed the absolute priority of
the party. To try to create organs of workers' power in factory
councils, while the bourgeoisie were still in power, was to make 'a
formal imitation of a future institution, but one which lacks its fundamentally revolutionary character. Those who can, today, represent
the proletariat which will assume power *tomorrow*, are the workers
who are fully conscious of this historical perspective, that is to say,
workers inscribed in the communist party. The proletariat which
struggles against bourgeois power is represented by its *class party*,
even if this is only an audacious minority. The soviets of tomorrow
must have their genesis in the local sections of the communist party'.
And a communist party could assume such responsibilities only if it
abandoned the practice of electing representatives to the organizations
of bourgeois democracy.[11]

From January 1920, with his commitment to a split, Bordiga
committed himself to the formation of communist groups within the
unions and other working-class organizations. While in the interests
of building a communist fraction, he was ready to make speeches giving some recognition to the value of councils, his general attitude
towards them in fact hardened. Under bourgeois society, they could
only serve reformist or syndicalist ends. With the rise in syndicalist
power and influence, he hammered the argument, and through January
and February, devoted much space in *Il Soviet* to a sustained critique
of *ordinovism* as, objectively, a surrender to maximalism. It invested

the council with a soviet political character, it subordinated the party to a network of councils. *L'Ordine Nuovo* was becoming estranged from marxism in that the revolution could never be the product of education, culture or the technical capacity of the proletariat but only of an inner crisis in capitalism (the latter an odd criticism to level at Gramsci who repeats the point ad nauseam!).

It was an error of the *ordinovisti* to lay such stress on the 'formal coincidence between the representation of the working class and the diverse aggregates of the technical-economic system of production'; this coincidence would register only at a more advanced stage of the communist revolution, as production was socialized. It was an error to 'transport into the world of the proletariat as it actually exists, the wage-slaves of capitalism', the formal structures which it was assumed communist management of production would take and then to invest those structures with some revolutionary virtue intrinsic to themselves. The *ordinovisti* were, in short, putting the cart before the horse. 'At the point where we now are, when the state of the proletariat is a programmatic aspiration, the fundamental problem is that of the conquest of power by the proletariat, better still by the communist proletariat, that is, the workers organized in a class political party, resolute to achieve the historical form of revolutionary power, the dictatorship of the proletariat'.[12]

While many of these points are shrewd, anyone confronting these criticisms fresh from a reading of articles specifically written by Gramsci, tends to be thrown into confusion. Many of the points Bordiga makes, Gramsci of course makes. Even on the party – the need for a strongly organized and centralized nucleus of disciplined militants in full awareness – the language is frequently identical. The 'criticisms' of *Il Soviet* are in the majority of cases the 'principles' of Gramsci.

There were of course some functional and contingent factors which exposed the *ordinovisti* to distortion. The concentration during much of 1919 on building factory councils in Turin *did* lead to an obsession with the enterprise which produced an apparent blur over the notion of 'soviets'. After the Florence national council meeting, with its 'soviet' projects, *L'Ordine Nuovo* was at pains to clarify its attitude. 'No! No! comrade Niccolini has no right . . .' exploded Gramsci in April in response to another attack on these lines.[13] Nor had he. The distinction between councils and full-blooded political soviets was in fact clear in Gramsci's writing if not always in *ordinovista* practice. The fact, however, that the Turin position could be so easily, and so effectively deformed, is itself one indication of its ambiguity *in practice*.

More central was the problem of the party. It is true that the *assumption* of a strong, coherent, homogeneous, centralized 'communist' party is central to Gramsci's schema ; the grand design is meaningless without it. It is no less true that before the turn of the year, the party was absent from Gramsci's writings except in the most global and grandiose terms. Moreover this meant in practice an utterly ambiguous position on the PSI in cold and brute actuality.

The Bordighists referred directly to the role of Turin spokesmen at party gatherings, where they were embedded in maximalism (Tasca at Bologna was one obvious example).

Gramsci's concertina use of 'communist' and 'socialist' on the PSI finds a parallel in the vocabulary of Ljubarsky-Niccolini at Serrati's elbow, and indeed of Lenin's comments on Italy in the distance ; at that moment, they were *all* locked into an essentially *centrist maximalism*.

It is symptomatic that when Gramsci began to get to grips with the party problem in January 1920, he had to shift a certain distance *towards* Bordiga – expulsion of the reformists, denunciation of maximalists, formation of communist groups. And as soon as he did so, the *Ordine Nuovo* group began to break up. *Il Soviet* itself in February began to distinguish Gramsci's position from Tasca's. Gramsci differentiated political activity from the councils and saw a network of councils as subordinate to the party, its essential mass base. There was nothing new about all this. What *is* confusing is the loose and *politically* incoherent character of the *Ordine Nuovo* group. While Tasca opposed the Gramsci-abstentionist list in Turin and worked closely with union leaders in the city, he was until May still regarded as a spokesman for the *Ordine Nuovo* line, indeed as its leading 'political' spokesman. Terracini not only joined Tasca's list in February, he was admitted to the executive of the PSI. After Tasca's first partial recession in January–February, it was Togliatti who became the major commentator in *L'Ordine Nuovo* alongside Gramsci. But after the April strike, Tasca, Terracini and Togliatti all abandoned Gramsci and lodged securely, if not comfortably, in maximalism. This incoherence justifies Bordiga's criticism that the *ordinovista* problematic, whatever its *theoretical* aspirations, was a tributary of centrism.

Bordiga was also probably correct in that his line of attack, which often seems so *tangential* to Gramsci's own *theory*, was directed primarily not only at Tasca's line, but at the Turin movement itself *in its working-class reality*. The emergence of that reality in Turin had led to some structural changes in Gramsci's *theory*, which were in some respects a withdrawal from his original perception – for example, council take-over of unions – which had then to be presented as a *stage* in development towards the original objective. The *theory* was in fact *successful* in absorbing and 'recuperating' these adjustments, because of its innate marxist validity, but it is noticeable that Gramsci's shift towards a more precise conception of the party as a political instrument was a response to events *outside* Turin. The identification of the Turin council movement with Gramscian communism was in fact historically contingent. That communism certainly impregnated the movement; without Gramscian communism it is doubtful whether the movement would have been anything like the remarkable and remarkably distinctive movement it was. But the communism itself stemmed from the peculiar character of Turin. Even Bordiga was disposed to concede that, given the character of Turin, the council movement had revolutionary value and validity *in Turin*. Probably the *basic* reason for the failure of the council movement in its Gramscian mode to lodge securely outside Turin was precisely the distinctiveness of the city. But unless the movement could penetrate outside, achieve a party translation, Gramscian communism would be in stasis. Its function within Turin had been, in essence, one of mobilization; in its exalted, global, visionary, semi-utopian style, it *had* acted as a Sorelian myth. Without *achievement*, there was no *grip*. The movement could (as it did) shed the communism in an instant, slip to reformism, maximalist 'intransigence', anarcho-syndicalism. In April–May this is exactly what it did and there were signs of disruption earlier. One reason for Gramsci's advocacy of communist groups was the councils' tendency to slip away from 'communism'.

Bordiga was also correct, probably, to sense a surrender to bourgeois values in the 'productivist' criterion which informed Gramsci's conciliarism. This demon drive for *production* certainly had some basis in marxism, but its preaching in practice, no matter how Hegelian or Sorelian, could not escape the threat of 'raising' workers into a petty-bourgeois prison. *The Programme of Workshop Commissars* is itself pregnant with it. Gramsci's most creative and distinctive development of marxism, was his exploration of the *essential* problem of breaking the bourgeois hegemony over workers' minds, the need for workers and the workers' party to *think* themselves into *historical autonomy*, without which no permanent revolution is possible. It is customary to date this from his rethinking after the fascist victory. In fact, Gramsci begins to talk about 'historical autonomy' and workers thinking 'like a ruling class' precisely in this winter-spring of 1919-20. Then his advocacy of 'communist groups' pinpointed the problems of 'organizing' councils with a disciplined, minority party which had to operate in conditions of total workers' liberty ; a situation in which all of them were drenched in, pinned to the ground by, the omnipresent bourgeois hegemony, the 'corpses of the dead generations'. The shift in the spring of 1920 is a confession of the inadequacy of his first presentation of the problem of production (the problem itself of course remained, and for marxists remains, central). It is some justification of Bordiga's suspicion.

Paradoxically, however, this was also Bordiga's greatest and crippling weakness. For Bordiga's solution to the problem of breaking the bourgeois hegemony was mechanical, manipulative and ultimately primitive. Unlike Gramsci, who entered Italian working-class socialism from a rude, kindred-based pre-industrial society and a complex intellectual world both essentially external to it, Bordiga, whom no one ever accused of deviation towards culture, was rooted in an intransigent re-assertion of marxist 'orthodoxy' dating from the 1912 crisis. Both men faced an invertebrate and pluralist Italy ranging from the mass industry of Turin through a wide variety of rural modes of production to the swollen non-industrial urban centres of the south. The endemic 'diseases' of Italian socialism were reformism and species of anarchist and anarchic revolt. The permanent threat was petty-bourgeois contamination. Bordiga's solution was a Gideon's Army of the pure ; total opposition to every bourgeois symptom. His definition of 'proletariat' was very narrow and much more 'orthodox' than Marx's! The strict application of 'living only by selling one's labour' ruled out whole sectors of plebeian Italy, indeed whole sectors of the trade union membership. Sometimes Bordiga's analysis of trade unions anticipates current analyses of entrenched trade-union workers' elites in Latin America; this has been used to endow him with a Leninist perception of the realities of the imperialist phase of capitalism. But this tight, narrow 'proletarian' party was to marshal against bourgeois society all the hosts of workers. It would marshal them by seizing on grievance and rebellion and mobilizing them in a 'perhaps schematic and dogmatic' form of communism.

This is remote from Gramsci's communist party in its intense, delicate and continuous dialectic with the masses; his communist party 'must always live in the heart of the working mass'; his communists must move among the masses in a continuous process of reciprocal education (an 'education', one has to repeat, which can include armed insurrection); his communists have to tolerate, work with and convert councils overrun by *'popolari*, anarcho-syndicalists, reformists' even the un-organized and unaware; they *have* to, because this *is* communism as workers begin to *live* communist in response to the application of the communist will to the ineluctable processes of the mode of production of capitalism in crisis. This is *not* the 'mass party' of his latter-day reformist exploiters, but it is not the party of Bordiga. Parties like Bordiga's are probably better equipped to seize power (though, in point of fact, none has yet done so in Europe). But after power? When a schematic and dogmatic populist 'communism' will not suffice? The despair of Lenin in his last years calling for instant cultural revolution? And Gramsci's 'molecular' construction of a communist working class? How are they to act, as well as think, like a ruling class? How do Gramscians *take* power?

Problems of this order faced him as soon as he took up the creation of communist groups in unions and councils. How precisely were they to act? There was no answer of any substance. Probably there cannot be, since it is a matter of 'describing' the quality of communist leadership.

A Governing Party for the Working Class

It was in these circumstances that Gramsci began to develop and enrich his argument on the party and the councils. In the process, there is a certain absorption of Bordighist styles and he begins to confront issues which were to dominate his thinking for the rest of his life. In *The Instrument of Labour* of 14 February, he repeated the statement that the communist revolution is 'the historical recognition of pre-existing economic facts' which it 'reveals', defends and 'makes become law'. 'This is why the construction of *communist* (Gramsci's italics) political soviets can only follow historically a flowering and a first systematization of factory councils', which reveal and test the new positions of the working class. 'The working class draws the conclusions from the sum of positive experiences which single individuals live through personally, acquires the psychology and the character of a ruling class and organizes itself as such'. This is a tall order from the taking over of a single factory, and Gramsci in fact relates this process to the *system* of factory councils, where once again, the political role of communist agents must be decisive.[14]

And it was in the article *Governing Party and Governing Class* of 6 March that Gramsci made the first serious advance in his theory of the party since December.[15] The core section of the article ran:

> The socialist party is a governing party (party of government); it is a party dedicated to the exercise of political power. The socialist party is the expression of the interests of the proletarian class, the class of factory workers, who have no property and who will never become property-owners. Upon these interests, the socialist party bases its real action, upon the interests of those who have no property and are mathematically certain never to have any. The labouring class is not a class of industrial workers alone; but the whole labouring class is destined to become like the factory proletariat, to become a class which has no property and is mathematically certain never to have any. The socialist party, therefore, directs itself to the whole labouring class, to the clerks, the poor peasants, the small proprietors; it vulgarizes its doctrine, marxism, and it demonstrates how all working people, manual and intellectual, will be reduced to the condition of the working class, how all democratic illusions on the possibility of any of them becoming owners of property are precisely illusions, puerilities, petty-bourgeois dreams.
>
> The liberal party, the party of the industrialists, the party of economic competition, is the party typical of capitalist society; it is the governing party of the capitalist class. Through competition, it tends to industrialize the whole organized labour of society, it tends to reduce the whole proprietor class to the type of its economic client, the capitalist industrialist.
>
> The communist party, the party of the proletarians, the party of the socialized and internationalized economy, is the party typical of proletarian society; it is the governing party of the working class. Through a central council of the national econ-

omy, which co-ordinates and unifies production initiatives, it tends to socialize all labour which the capitalists have industrialized and to industrialize socialistically all other sectors of labour not yet absorbed into capitalist industrialism. It tends to reduce all men in society to the type of the proletarian, but an emancipated and regenerated proletarian, the proletarian who possesses no private wealth, but administers the common wealth and who draws from it only that enjoyment and security of life which is due to him because of the labour he devotes to production.

This historical posture imposes precise duties on the socialist party. It is a governing party in so far as it essentially represents the proletariat, the class of industrial workers. Private property threatens to strangle the proletariat, threatens it with death from hunger and cold. The economic competition characteristic of capitalist property, having led to over-production, has led to national monopoly, to imperialism, to the savage shock of imperialist states in conflict, to an immeasurable destruction of wealth, to famine, to unemployment, to death from hunger and cold. The class of the property-less, of those who can never become proprietors, has a vital and a permanently vital interest in socialization, in the advent of communism.

The other sectors of the labouring people, however, could spawn a new capitalism; those forms of production which capitalism has not yet industrialized could spew up new growths of property and the exploitation of man by man. With the breaking of the bourgeois state, the breaking of the apparatus which finance capitalism exploits to monopolize all labour and all production in its own interests, the artisan could try to exploit the socialist government to develop his business, to employ wage workers, to become an industrialist. If the proletarian government will not permit him, the artisan could become a rebel, call himself an anarchist, an individualist or God wot, and form the political base of a party in opposition to the proletarian government. The small proprietor or the poor peasant of the agrarian regime of the great estate based on extensive cultivation (latifundio) could exploit the fact that, temporarily, while the supply conditions created by the war persist, a kilo of potatoes is worth more than a motorcar wheel, a loaf of bread is worth more than a cubic metre of masons' work, to demand in exchange for his non-industrialized and therefore economically impoverished labour, a tenfold labour from the proletarian. And if the proletarian government will not permit the peasant to replace the capitalist as an exploiter of the worker, the peasant is a rebel, too, and finds among the agents of the bourgeoisie a group to form a political party of the peasants in opposition to the proletarians. All these sectors of labour, which cannot be denied political rights in the workers' state, these sectors of labour in which capitalist industrialism has not yet created the conditions of proletarian labour, of the labour which owns no property and is mathematically certain never to own any, could give birth, after the revolution, to anti-proletarian political forces, political forces working for the rebirth of capitalist property and the exploitation of the working class.

The socialist party, in so far as it represents the economic interests of the working class threatened with death by the private property of capital, will be mandated by the working class to the revolutionary government of the nation. But the socialist party will be a governing party (party of government) only in so far as it succeeds in overcoming all these difficulties for the class, only in so far as it succeeds in reducing all men in society to the fundamental type of the proletarian emancipated and regenerated from wage slavery, only in so far as it succeeds in founding the communist society, that is, the International of nations without a state. The socialist party will become a party of revolutionary government only when it postulates concrete aims for the revolution, when it says: the proletarian revolution will solve in such-and-such a manner such-and-such problems of modern life which assail masses of human beings and drive them to despair.

The revolution as such is today the maximum programme of the socialist party; it must become the minimum programme. The maximum programme must be that which indicates the forms and modes in which the working class, in its organization and methodical proletarian labour, suppresses every antagonism and every conflict which could emerge from the conditions in which capitalism leaves society, and establishes the communist society. To prepare the working class, which has a vital interest in the establishment of communism, to reach its historical goal, means precisely to organize the working class into a ruling class. The working class must make for itself a psychology similar to that of the present bourgeois class, similar in the art of governing, the art of carrying an initiative, a general action of the workers' state, through to a good conclusion, certainly not similar in the art of exploitation. Besides, even if he wanted to, the proletarian could not acquire the psychology of the exploiter. The proletarian cannot become a proprietor, unless he destroys the factories and the machines to become the proprietor of useless scrap metal and die of it the next day. Precisely because, given the technical conditions of industrial production, he cannot become a proprietor and an exploiter, the proletarian is summoned by history to establish communism, to liberate all the oppressed and exploited . . . A workers' government cannot exist if the working class is not capable of becoming, in its totality, the executive power of the workers' state. The laws of the workers' state must be executed by the workers themselves:

only thus will the workers' state avoid the danger of falling into the hands of adventurers and politicians, of becoming a counterfeit of the bourgeois state. Therefore the working class must train itself, must educate itself in social management, must acquire the culture and the psychology of a ruling class, must acquire them by its own methods and systems, through meetings, congresses, discussions, mutual education. The factory councils have been a first form of this historical experience for the Italian working class as it moves towards self-government in the workers' state.

This essay was perhaps the most successful Gramsci had yet achieved in its integration of his governing concepts:

the determinance of the mode of production,
the exercise of communist will in creative intervention,
the centrality of cultural and 'superstructural' factors,
the role of the party.

It is, in essence, an application of Lenin's *State and Revolution*. There is internal evidence from other writings of Gramsci's that *State and Revolution registered* fully in his thinking during this period.

There is further, a *clear infusion of Bordiga's style*, of his style of talking if not thinking. The 'proletariat' is more precisely defined than before – people with no property and mathematically certain never to have any – and is sharply distinguished from other plebeian sectors ; artisans, small peasants, who are in fact identified as possible sources of capitalist restoration. The proletariat, more strictly defined, is made central and in other writings of this period, Gramsci repeats that the party represents *solely* this class. In view of later distortions of his thinking, it is important to stress that this acquisition became permanent. Moreover he says the socialist party 'vulgarizes' its doctrine in appealing to the masses, an echo of Bordiga's simplified, schematic, dogmatic form of 'communism'.

This proletarian party concept, however, is located in a complex class and group pattern. It was during this period that Gramsci, always alert to the problems of the South and the peasantry, returned frequently in his writings to the peasants, the *popolari* and the Giolittians and began to elaborate his concept of the proletariat as a 'leading class' in a hegemonic coalition of forces against capitalism. The particular quality of his thinking, *which had little in common with later presentations of his thought as an argument for a 'mass party'* and a *'popular front'*, begins to emerge in this precise period.

It is rooted in the mode-of-production problematic. Parties are identified by their 'type-figures'. The socialist party 'represents' the proletariat but can address itself to the whole labouring class because the whole labouring class 'is destined to become like the factory proletariat'. The *communist* party is the party *of* the proletariat (rather than simply representing its interests). It is the party of 'the socialized and internationalized economy . . . it tends to socialize all labour which the capitalists have industrialized and to industrialize socialistically all other sectors . . . to reduce all men in society to the type of the proletarian . . .'

In this striking presentation the communist party is the state-building party ; it is the party that realizes communism by realizing, in human emancipation, the immanent mode of production. *The communist party is not the party that 'takes' power ; it is the party that exercises it after the transition.*

Even more remarkable is the long vision. The duty of the socialist party is not merely the moment which obsesses most communists, the seizure of power ; it is the anchoring of the revolution in permanence *by wiping out all sources of possible capitalist restoration*. The council movement is, precisely, central to *this* process. 'To prepare the working class . . . to reach its historical goal, means precisely to organize the working class into a ruling class. The working class must make for itself a psychology similar to that of the present bourgeois class.' Moreover, the working class must become '*in its totality* [my italics-GAW] the executive power of the workers' state'. The council movement is the first step in this process of achieving self-government in a workers' state.

This process and the role of the party within it, was further elaborated in an accompanying article *Proletarian Unity*. This was directed primarily against the two major threats to the council-communist movement – the reformists and the anarcho-syndicalists. It is something of a 'classic' statement of his case.

The present period was revolutionary, said Gramsci, because the traditional institutions of government of human society, product of the old mode of production, had lost all meaning and function. The centre of gravity of society had shifted ; institutions remained 'mere exteriority, pure form, without historical substance, without animating spirit'. The bourgeois class pursued its vital interests outside parliament, the workers sought the institution of their government outside the unions and found it in the system of factory councils. Because competition had been abrogated in the imperialist phase of world capitalism, 'the national parliament has exhausted its historical mission'.

But the institutions of the working class had also collapsed with the old mode of production ; hence the vain thrashing about of union leaders, not only the reformists, but the revolutionary syndicalists. All syndicalism had done, with its handfuls of revolutionaries, was to multiply the number of proletarian parties and worsen formal disunity. But 'Proletarian unity exists in fact. The epidemic form which every local and corporative movement assumes proves it. Proletarian unity exists because capitalist unity exists ; it is the consequence of the new phase which the economic and political relations of bourgeois society have entered'.

The workers find their new institutions outside the unions, in the factory councils. It is the duty of the socialist party to ensure the realization of this will.

> For communists, the will of the mass, the historical and revolutionary will, is that which realizes itself daily when the worker mass is mobilized around the technical necessities of industrial production, when every individual feels himself bound to his comrades in the functions of labour and of production, when the working class feels the thrusts of immanent historical necessity within its specific world of activity. The will of the mass is that which asserts itself in an organic and permanent manner, building every day a new cell of the new workers' psychology, of the new social organization which will develop into the communist International, supreme regulator of the life of the world.

This strong argument, escaping from the idealist trap of his December thinking, thrusts to the forefront the problem of the party's action in this process. Every day the duty of 'the proletarian vanguard which constitutes the socialist party' becomes clearer. The proletarian state will guarantee the development of these new workers' institutions. The socialist party today must act as a model of this state. 'The party today guarantees the liberty necessary for the working mass to find itself again in its specific domain, production ; the party, through its action of culture and clarification, helps the working class to acquire consciousness of its historical position, helps it to give concrete and organic expression to the sentiments and passions which arise from the urgent necessities revealed by the new material conditions of existence of men'.

All its efforts therefore, must go into the building of the council system and into clearing the political path for it. The whole power of the mass must be concentrated in the system of councils 'responsible to the mass, constituted of delegates subject to instant recall, constituted of delegates who if they belong to the socialist party as well as to union organizations, are also controlled by the party, itself subjected to a discipline established by congresses in which the revolutionary vanguard of the whole nation participates'.

This was the clearest statement Gramsci had yet made on the role of the party and its relationship to the council movement; an essentially socio-*cultural* enterprise (but a cultural training which could embrace armed action) linked to a mode-of-production argument. Evidently, the socialist party (equally evidently a 'renewed' party) in the process would 'transmute' into the communist party. One central problem, however, is absent. The party as an instrument for 'taking' power is absent from Lenin's *State and Revolution*; it is absent from *Governing Party and Governing Class*. All that Gramsci says is this: 'The socialist party, in so far as it represents the economic interests of the working class threatened with death by the private property of capital, will be mandated by the working class to the revolutionary governing of the nation'.

The word 'proletariat' is not used and it is employed quite precisely throughout this essay. The sentence implies, then, a move to power at the head of a coalition of threatened interests. We know from his other writings that Gramsci at this time was concerned with the threat of a military coup, the need to arm the workers, the immobilism of the PSI and the growing threat from anarcho-syndicalism. The only assumption possible is that he shared something of the maximalists' 'fatalism' to the extent of seeing the coming to power as a 'mandate' from the workers in crisis. His phraseology is economistic. Further, while committed to the expulsion of the reformists now, he evidently still believed in the possibility of a 'renewal' of the socialist party.

There had clearly been an infusion of Bordiga's style. It was in fact in response to this particular challenge that Gramsci began to elaborate some of the master-concepts of his life's work. But despite his alliance with the Turin abstentionists and his shift towards them, he maintained the council-communist position. His position was still distinct from Bordiga's.

The concluding section of the essay, however, was a programmatic statement. The formation of factory councils was the first step towards workers' self-government. The second was to be the first *national* congress of factory councils. 'To it all the factories of Italy will be summoned: the congress will be a congress of the whole proletarian class of Italy, represented by delegates elected directly and not by trade-union officials'. This brought to a logical climax the process begun by the publication of the *Action Programme* of the Turin section. During February and March, the *Study Committee for Factory Councils* had been active, even as the first re-elections of workshop commissars went through in a two-weeks' fever of discussion. It tried to re-organize the councils, to create a central commissariat; it called repeatedly for a national congress of councils as the party section called for a special congress of the PSI. The council movement was shaping itself into a national fraction.

There was an urgency about the action, however, a certain desperation. Because the situation in Turin was becoming explosive. The day after Gramsci's article appeared, Olivetti, director of *Confindustria*, declared war on 'dual power' in the factory. The climax of the council movement was also its crisis. For it was precisely at this point that the *communist* shell of the movement began to crack.

8. The April Struggle

The Anarcho-syndicalist Challenge

When Gramsci wrote his report on the Turin movement of factory councils for the Executive Committee of the Third International in July 1920, in which history was suitably adjusted to the taste of communists immersed in Lenin's *Left-wing Communism: an Infantile Disorder*, one insistent note ran as a descant throughout.

Hailing the April struggle as an event unique in the history of the working class, when a whole city proletariat fought for a month, not over wages or hours, but in a struggle for control over production, he said: 'At the head of the movement to form factory councils were the communists belonging to the socialist section and the trade-union organizations.' He added 'The anarchists also took part and tried to oppose their bombastic rhetoric to the clear and precise language of the marxist communists'.

The grudging admission turned into stronger language elsewhere in the report: 'The propaganda of the anarchists and syndicalists against party discipline and the dictatorship of the proletariat had no influence on the masses even when the strike ended in defeat because of the treachery of the leaders'.

It would perhaps be uncomradely to remind the shade of Antonio of his ringing statement a year earlier – 'To tell the truth is a communist and revolutionary act.' In that same report he said the Turin movement, betrayed and abandoned by the whole socialist movement, still found popular support during the April struggle: railwaymen in Pisa, Livorno and Florence had refused to transport troops; the workers and sailors of Livorno and Genoa sabotaged the ports, the proletariat in several cities broke into strikes against the orders of their unions. He omitted to mention that these actions were either directly led or indirectly inspired by anarcho-syndicalists. He refrained from making the point that the council movement outside Turin was essentially anarcho-syndicalist. And when he said of Turin

'Anarchist and syndicalist groups have hardly any influence on the working mass', he could perhaps be forgiven for not reporting that these un-influential groups were in March-April threatening to cut the council movement out from under him.[1]

Anarchists and revolutionary syndicalists were the most consistently and totally revolutionary group on the left.[2] Anarchists were probably few in number, but they were certainly 'contagious individuals'. Their great hero Errico Malatesta, smuggled back to Italy at the end of 1919, was an almost legendary figure, with a popularity which transcended party lines. News of his mere presence sent shudders through the prefectures of the kingdom. All over Italy crowds listened to his preaching of direct action and hailed him as Italy's Lenin (which could hardly have pleased him: 'Lenin is dead. Long live Liberty!').

Ancona, headquarters with Bologna of the anarchist union, the UAI, had ignited the insurrection of Red Week and was to provoke another against the expedition to Albania in the summer of 1920. Parma lives for ever in the history of the working class. Through the dismal collapse of the left before the fascists, Parma's great victory over the massed *squadristi* shines like a beacon. In February 1920, the UAI moved its operative headquarters to Milan and brought out its journal *Umanità Nova*.[3] It claimed a circulation of 50,000. Anna Kuliscioff, Turati's companion, thought it might have reached 100,000 by the summer of 1920 and in her letters to Turati said gloomily that 'anarchism rules the piazza'.[4]

For by March 1920 the anarcho-syndicalist union federation USI with its journal *Guerra di Classe* had also transferred to Milan.[5] This move into the capital of Lombardy and of socialist reformism was a striking symptom of the most obvious feature of the history of syndicalism and anarchism in 1919-20: rapid and virtually uninterrupted growth. The libertarians were strong in their traditional areas, among rural workers in Parma and Ferrara, building workers in Bologna and Rome, railwaymen, dockers, seamen and some engineering plants in Lombardy. The independent railway and maritime unions were heavily influenced. The most powerful libertarian-communist force was the union federation USI under its anarchist secretary Armando Borghi. And while several union leaders were flamboyant and unpredictable – the seamen's leader Giulietti was renowned for his exploits – USI was strong, professional and growing continuously. From its strongholds in Romagna and the Marches and its footholds in Liguria, it expanded rapidly from the end of the war. A particular conquest was the small-shop metal industry of Liguria in the Genoa complex. FIOM could hardly get off the ground there. There were said to be 30,000 in the syndicalist federation's metal-workers' union. The *camera* at Sestri Ponente, with 14,000 members, was in the hands of the syndicalists under Antonio Negro, who ran a journal *La Lotta Operaia*; Savona and La Spezia were also strong-holds. By 1919 USI was claiming 300,000. Its growth through 1920 was so rapid that there was talk of 800,000.[6]

The syndicalists above all captured militant working-class opinion which the socialist movement was utterly failing to channel. For the second striking feature of the movement was its revolutionary commitment to working-class unity, often despite its own prejudices. In April 1919, Borghi called for a united revolutionary front, to embrace the PSI, the CGL, USI and the UAI together with the railwaymen. The CGL was totally opposed. The rivalry between FIOM and USI, dating from pre-war days was deadly. In the first heady days after the war, however, there was considerable support within FIOM for united action. The settlement won by FIOM in the spring of 1919 directly hit syndicalist workers in Liguria who lost their newly-won 'English Saturday' and offended militants everywhere; a brief flicker of response in the PSI leadership soon died. To the CGL and the PSI, 'syndicalism', associated with mindless and anarchic revolt which could bring disaster upon painfully-constructed working-class institutions, was a standard term of abuse.

USI however remained committed to the united front and was often surprisingly ready tactically to subordinate itself to FIOM in the cause, though given the near-paralysis of the socialist forces, it could certainly be confident of winning militant recruits. In Turin, there was no USI branch until the summer of 1920; libertarians worked within FIOM. They were heavily involved in the *Ordine Nuovo* campaign from the beginning. Pietro Mosso, a libertarian engineer, was a prominent contributor, the journal evoked a response in such circles. More important, it harnessed the energies of some of the best worker militants, like Maurizio Garino and Pietro Ferrero with their Turin Libertarian Group.

In December 1919, the Parma congress of USI heard Matta as a guest delegate. Alibrando Giovanetti, secretary of the syndicalist metal-workers, urged support for the Turin councils because they represented anti-bureaucratic direct action, aimed at control of the factory and could be the first cells of syndicalist industrial unions. The inner structure of the councils was congenial. The *Programme of the Workshop Commissars* was openly friendly. The syndicalist congress voted to support the councils. Although Malatesta was full of reservations, he supported them as a form of direct action guaranteed to generate rebelliousness and most anarchists had fewer scruples. *Umanità Nova* and *Guerra di Classe* became almost as committed to the councils as *L'Ordine Nuovo* and the Turin edition of *Avanti*.[7]

With the intensification of discontent in the early weeks of 1920, the outbreak of the 'strike frenzy' in northern Italy, the shattering struggles on the railways and the postal network, the continuing travail of the socialist movement, the syndicalist unions entered another phase of growth. This ran head-on into the Turin left's campaign to renew the PSI in the style of the *Action Programme*. Potential support outside Turin, particularly in Milan, was slipping to the syndicalists. There was an outbreak of factory occupations in characteristically syndicalist style. Within Turin itself, industrialists began to complain loudly of 'indiscipline', and commissars to call for factory occupation. Luigi Galleani, an anarchist veteran, restarted his journal *Cronaca sovversiva* in the city at the end of January.[8] *Ordinovista* spokesmen found themselves having to confront an upsurge in syndicalist *styles* within their own bailiwick. And through February and March, Gramsci, Togliatti, Viglongo had to return time and time again to anarchism and syndicalism in the pages of *L'Ordine Nuovo*.

Gramsci's view was clear-cut in theory, less easy to sustain in practice. Anarchism and syndicalism offended his state-building instincts; how could his 'communist' language stretch to their aspirations? In *practice*, he was probably closer to anarcho-syndicalist militants than to anybody else; so many of them after all were living examples of his model 'communist'! The operation of his councils was in theory and in practice entirely libertarian. On the other hand, the principles of anarchism and syndicalism were anathema and the jibe of syndicalism a powerful weapon in the hands of his enemies. Besides, so many of those loud-mouths of the streets, whom he detested, loudly proclaimed themselves 'anarchist'.

His theoretical position was essentially Lenin's. Anarchism was anathema but anarchists, particularly working-class syndicalist militants, were magnificent revolutionaries and comrades. He related this distinction directly to the mode-of-production argument which buttressed his developing theory of the communist party.

In an *Address to the Anarchists* of 10 April 1920 he argued that 'Every determinate class has had a determinate conception, its own, belonging to no other class. Marxist communism is the determinate conception of the modern working class and of no other.' Anarchism on the other hand was 'the elementary subversive conception of every oppressed class and it is the diffuse conception of every ruling class. Since every class oppression has taken form in a state, anarchism is the elementary subversive conception which identifies the state, in itself and by itself, as the cause of all the miseries of the oppressed class. But every class which has become a ruling class has realized its own anarchist conception because it has realized its own liberty' and he cited the bourgeoisie as an example. But the conception proper to the bourgeoisie was liberalism, just as marxist communism was to the proletariat.

Could agreement be reached between anarchists and communists? It could for anarchist groups of class-conscious workers, but not for anarchist intellectuals, 'professionals of ideology'. For workers' anarchism is really a struggle against the *bourgeois* state, not the state itself. The realization of communism, immanent in the crisis of the mode of production, would create the communist state which, because it means freedom for the workers, will mean freedom for anarchist workers. Because the communist society 'cannot be built as an empire, with laws and decrees: it springs forth spontaneously from the historical activity of the labouring class which has acquired the power of initiative'.

With the creation of the communist state, 'the anarchist worker will appreciate then the existence of a centralized power which guarantees to him in permanence the liberty that has been won'.[9]

In August 1920 his two comrades and friends, the libertarians Ferrero and Garino responded very sharply to his attacks on anarchist 'pseudo-revolutionary rhetoric'. Gramsci wrote in reply: 'Individually Garino and Ferrero are two workers, two fine and good workers, two sincere and loyal militants of the proletarian class ; it is unimportant to us that they are anarchists, if their activity is real and concrete. In historical creation, all workers are "libertarians".' The basic argument was the same. In creating communism workers act in a libertarian manner. He cited the communist free work-Saturdays of the *subbotnik* movement in Russia. 'Marxist communists do not believe in historic creation by administrative and legislative means ; the workers' state is the Committee of Public Safety of the proletarian revolution, it is the guarantee to the working class that it can work to build its city.' The anarchist makes liberty into a programme, when it can be liberty only if it is not reduced to a programme ; he thus confounds himself ideologically with the Christian or the bourgeois liberal. 'The marxist communist is a historical materialist. Liberty for him means the organization of conditions in which liberty can be realized'. Ferrero and Garino are workers, so 'we believe and hope that historical "determinism" in a given moment will act upon the superficial veneer of their political "demagogy" and induce them (spontaneously, by inner conviction, in a libertarian manner) to support the workers' state'.[10]

This was not likely to convince Ferrero and Garino ; like Gramsci's argument on the party, it rests entirely on the *organic* state realizing itself in the crisis of the mode of production, carrying all workers, whatever their personal ideology, into the proletarian dictatorship ; and while the distinction between the essentially libertarian mass institutions of the emerging state on the one hand, and the disciplined party on the other offers scope for 'freedom', it is less clear how this 'freedom' is to be realized after the transition into his communism managed by his communist party – except of course in terms of the kind of libertarianism inherent in Lenin's *State and Revolution*. In terms of brute and vulgar reality, this argument makes anarchist comrades in the movement into sick men, whom 'History' is curing, at best subordinate comrades on probation.

And on anarchist rhetoric in general, particularly the intellectual variety, Gramsci lavished his considerable gifts of invective. During the spring of 1920 he had to resort increasingly to attack, argument, persuasion. For the syndicalist drive was in fact the most dangerous to his conception of the conciliar movement. Nothing better illustrates the *instrumental* character of Gramscian communism in that movement. The syndicalists, with their opposition to the state in theory and to parliamentary democracy in everyday practice, their scorn for 'parties', their concentration on the economic terrain, the terrain of class, their acceptance of the democratic structure of the councils and its inner industrial-unionist logic, were council leaders born. Once the Gramscian-communist grip began to slip, the movement was wide open to the seductive themes of factory seizure and the expropriating general strike. Indeed, despite the thunder of Gramsci's *discipline* rhetoric, one may even suspect that his system, if put into practice, would have resulted in something not unlike the achievements of the Spanish CNT as it tried to rebuild itself after its 'defeat' in May 1937. This is speculation ; the *consonance* between the council movement and the anarcho-syndicalists was fact. And by March 1920, the 'communist' discipline of the Turin movement was breaking down.

The Closing of the Trap

Through February and into March 1920, with its circulation at a peak, *L'Ordine Nuovo* pressed on with the campaign outlined in the *Action Programme*. Togliatti and Viglongo subjected the Bombacci project and the 'labour parliament' to prolonged attack ; reports of councils in Bologna and Milan were seized upon, the problems of technicians, clerks and industrial unionism were explored. But they were making heavy weather of it. The power of the state and the bourgeoisie, in royal guards, a strengthening of police and governmental action, in pressure on parliamentary socialists to join in a Giolittian political situation, was visibly recovering. Industrialists were regaining their nerve and many were impatiently militant. In the communist international, the ultra-left was coming under attack from Moscow. Bordiga's faction was locked in angry debate over a split and its temper was hardening. At its congress in May, it was to announce its intention of forming a communist party as soon as the delegates returned from the Second Congress of the International, which was casting its shadow. The *ordinovista* movement achieved no advance.

And in late February a rash of factory occupations broke out in Liguria, Piedmont and Naples. On 17 February, after the breakdown of pay talks, workers occupied the metal and shipbuilding plants in Sestri Ponente, Cornigliano and Campi in Liguria. They had acted to forestall a lockout. For up to four days, under syndicalist leadership, they ran the plants through factory councils. On 28

February, two Mazzonis cotton mills near Turin were occupied after a strike. These were actually a manoeuvre by the textile union to force a government requisition to break the deadlock. The Mazzonis action, in which union-controlled councils were set up, was supported by the CGL, which, however, denounced the Sestri syndicalists, and stood by while a harsh police action expelled them.[11]

The occupations were an alarm signal, to industrialists, the CGL and the *ordinovisti*. To the latter, they were a classic illustration of the double pressure, reformist and syndicalist, which was now grinding on the Turin movement. Togliatti and Viglongo analyzed the occupations in depth and talked of an 'opportunism of revolt'. The occupations were a disaster ; the seizure of individual factories could never overthrow the state. At best they would be exploited by reformist unions. At worst, they would bring down massive repression.[12] But early in March, in a strong syndicalist campaign to establish councils in Milan, Armando Borghi called for mass factory occupations. In Turin the re-election of workshop commissars was just ending a two-week orgy of passionate discussion and workers caught the fever. Commissars began to call for occupations.[13]

This upsurge of militancy ran into the beginnings of a sustained and organized counter-offensive by employers. On 7 March, when a re-organized *Confindustria* held its inaugural meeting, Olivetti singled out the factory councils and denounced them as an intolerable invasion of employer authority. He showed himself fully aware of their revolutionary potential, explicitly attacked 'dual power', and called for a mobilization against them.[14] A few days later, the executive committee of Fiat-Centro presented an alarming report. The directors of the firm had challenged the very principle of the factory council, had tried to stop the activity of commissars during working hours and had refused to recognize the new system. A strike had brought them temporarily to heel. But the precedent was ominous.[15] Employers began to complain of a rising tide of 'indiscipline' in the factories and on 20 March, Olivetti, Agnelli of Fiat and De Benedetti of the Turin Industrial League went to see the prefect of Turin. Indiscipline in the factories was now intolerable and they had resolved on a mass and immediate lock-out. They won a promise of state support for the enforcement of existing industrial regulations, to which the councils, of course, were alien. *The Study Committee for Factory*

Councils called the workers to vigilance and meetings passed defiant resolutions.[16]

It was at this point, when crisis was about to break, that the council movement made its most serious effort to achieve a party *translation*. The national council of the PSI was scheduled to meet in Turin in April and the council communists moved to create what was in effect a revolutionary fraction with mass support. The *Study Committee* had sponsored the creation of a central commissariat for the councils and was proposing reforms designed to centralize and toughen their action. On 27 March, *L'Ordine Nuovo* splashed over its front page the long-awaited summons to a national congress of factory councils in Turin, to break trade-union bureaucracy and mobilize the proletariat: it was signed by the journal, the *Study Committee*, the Turin Libertarian Group and the Turin party section.[17] And, as conflict was breaking out in the factories, Gramsci wrote a manifesto for the Turin section, which was to be taken to the national council of the PSI and to the congress of the International. It was one of the more celebrated of the *ordinovista* documents – *For a Renewal of the Socialist Party*.[18]

In a sense, the manifesto drives the January call *First: Renew the Party* to its logical conclusion. 'The present phase of the class struggle in Italy,' it asserted, 'is the phase which precedes: either the conquest of political power by the revolutionary proletariat . . . or a tremendous reaction by the proprietor class and the government caste.' The latter would spare no violence to break the socialist party and swallow up the unions, 'to subject the industrial and agricultural proletariat to slave labour'.

The manifesto pointed to the 'maximum concentration of class power and discipline' achieved by the industrialists, who were at that moment applying it to the destruction of the Turin working class. In contrast, the working-class forces lacked all co-ordination and revolutionary consciousness. The leadership of the PSI had shown that it understood 'absolutely nothing of the phase of development which national and international history is passing through at this moment'. The complaints of *First: Renew the Party* were rehearsed and amplified. The party was a spectator of events. 'It never has an opinion of its own to express which derives from the revolutionary theses of marxism and the Communist International'. That 'sector of the proletarian class which . . . has succeeded in preserving its own autonomy, its conscious and disciplined spirit of initiative, must incarnate the vigilant revolutionary consciousness of the whole exploited class'. It had to concentrate the whole mass around itself 'so as to become its guide and thinking head'. Therefore the party must 'live always immersed in the effective reality of the class struggle'. It must 'root in the mind of multitudes the conviction that there is an order immanent in the present terrible disorder'.

But the PSI could never do this. It had stayed immobilized within the narrow limits of bourgeois democracy ; it had not acquired the independent character of a party of the revolutionary proletariat 'and only of the revolutionary proletariat'. There followed the long catalogue of its sins. It had not made itself a party of the Third International, it was absent from the international scene, it reported nothing of that scene, it did not even translate essential works – Lenin's *State and Revolution* was singled out. It had remained a party of the Second International and a prisoner of the reformists.

The solution presented now, unlike that in the January document, was clear-cut. 'Those who are not communist revolutionaries must be eliminated from the party' ; there must be an end to a search for 'unity' among the tendencies. The party must cease to be a 'petty-bourgeois parliamentary party' and become a party of the revolutionary proletariat. A cohesive party must organize its nuclei in every field of working-class life. Any attempt to create 'soviets' before this was done was 'absurd'. It must prepare a revolutionary programme as a party which founds its power *solely* on 'the class of industrial and agricultural workers who have no property whatever, and considers the other strata of the working population as auxiliaries of the class which is strictly proletarian'.

On the basis of this argument, strongly reminiscent not only of *First: Renew the Party* but of Gramsci's 6 March article *Governing Party and Governing Class*, immediate and radical action was called for. All communists must immediately come together into an organized alliance which would exercise surveillance over the party leadership until an emergency congress could expel non-communists and turn the PSI into a communist party.

This was the document which, at the climax of the desperate struggle in Turin, Togliatti was to carry to the socialist party council, where it was ignored. Lenin at the congress of the International did not ignore it, but singled it out for praise. Whereupon the whole

Italian delegation protested. The fate of *For a Renewal of the Social-ist Party* is ironic. For the council movement and the Turin left reached the logical climax of their movement at the point where, in virtually total isolation, it was about to be destroyed.

And, after the first bitter and confused week of the struggle, Gramsci noted in his pained address to the anarchists that they at least would always be able 'to rinse the satisfied mouth . . . with an I told you so'.

The April Strike[19]

It was in his *Address to the Anarchists* written in the first phase of the April struggle that Gramsci first used in *L'Ordine Nuovo* the slogan which was to become the motto of his life: 'The socialist conception of the revolutionary process is characterized by two traits which Romain Rolland has summarized in his motto: *pessimism of the intelligence, optimism of the will*.'

About the conflict in April, he was certainly pessimistic. At the end of the first week of the strike he wrote, 'The Turin proletariat in these days is living its Passion Week'. 90,000 were then on strike, 50,000 of them, the metalworkers, in more or less clear awareness that this was a decisive moment in the history of their class. The indus-trialists, in collusion with the government, were on the attack. As many as 50,000 troops with tanks and machine-guns were investing the city. Why? Because this 'localized' struggle was in fact critical for the whole proletariat. The revolutionary energy concentrated in Turin was seeking an outlet which had to be national.

But he was stoic on the probable outcome. Hold to the will to conquer, he urged, even if Turin is completely abandoned. 'Even lost hope, disillusion, the rage in our hearts when we go back into the factories, even that will be a weapon for our victory'.[20]

His pessimism is explicable. The industrialists had carefully prepared for the conflict. They seized an opportunity presented to them by clumsy and ill-considered action by some workers. They struck while Turin was still isolated. The extra-legal character of the councils, which operated outside the terms of union contracts, pro-vided a justification for supporting action by the state and its armed forces in defence of 'legality'.

The issue of 'legality' in the relations between union and

council was to occupy Gramsci's mind in a classic essay on the councils he wrote in June.[21] More immediately significant are some comments he made in retrospect in an essay on the communist groups written in July. 'In the metal strike which preceded the massive action of last April, communist groups were no sooner formed than they took over the leadership of the workers because of the ineptitude of the councils of workshop commissars, preventing the breakdown of revolutionary discipline and halting all dissoluteness at a stroke.'[22] Whatever the meaning of 'dissoluteness' or 'depravity' in this context, it is quite clear from this evidence, from a significant change in the *tonality* of Gramsci's writing during the summer and from the angry debate which followed defeat, that the councils had fallen short of 'communist' coherence in the first conflicts.

The very day after Olivetti, Agnelli and De Benedetti had seen the prefect of Turin to warn him of a planned lock-out in the immediate future, legal summer time was introduced. Reminiscent of the forced labour of wartime, it was unpopular. The Turin *camera* actually denounced it as a badge of servitude and called for action against it. On the other hand, Mario Montagnana maintained that hostility to legal time was simply the obsession of a few old maximalists.[23] At one plant owned by Fiat, the internal commission set back the hands of a clock on their own initiative. They were dismissed and the workers staged a sit-in. At the same time there was conflict over the powers of commissars at another Fiat plant, where they enjoyed fewer rights than their comrades elsewhere. The employers made the powers of these commissars and their 'indiscipline' the subject of the dispute.

Police and troops expelled the workers from the clock-hands factory. Troops had in fact been arriving in Turin for some little time, in such numbers that a leading Rome newspaper sent a correspondent to find out what was going on.[24] Workers were handicapped in negotiations by the fact that the internal commissions in both cases had been high-handed. It was a period when in some areas, strikes could flare up on apparently trivial issues or issues which involved anything which could be called a 'principle'. In one steelworks, the workers struck because of a rumour that the brother of one of them had volunteered for the royal guards.[25] In the Fiat plant, worker support was at first somewhat ragged, but when the employers demanded that the 'guilty' commissars be excluded for a year, there was a sharp revulsion at this invasion of proletarian independence, what Gramsci called 'proletarian civil rights'. A general assembly of commissars decided to call for sit-in strikes throughout the metal industry of Turin. For this, they were severely criticized later and there is some evidence that it was meant as a ritual gesture. The response was a shock. The industrialists proclaimed a general lockout. Troops flooded into the factories, ringed them with barbed wire, mounted machine-gun posts. *Avanti* said there were enough troops in Turin to quell a whole region in revolt. The commissars were confronted with the power of the state and of a united and fully mobilized *Confindustria*, as it became clear in the long negotiations that the employers were bent on dismantling the councils.

According to Gramsci, 'The employers handled the workers' delegates like puppets, knew they did, knew the workers knew they did'. He claimed that the commissars intended to drag in the national union officials in order to extend the conflict.[26] It may be true that some militants took this view; it would run parallel to the *Study Committee*'s call for a national congress and the Turin section's *For a Renewal*. But the workers' delegates, probably because of the confused beginnings of the conflict, proved fairly amenable and with the intervention of FIOM, seemed ready to concede. After a fortnight in which privation had begun to bite, and amid disagreement, they decided to surrender on the immediate issues. Whereupon the employers presented a series of demands which amounted to a castration of the commissar system, which restricted the operation of commissars to hours after work and which re-imposed managerial control.[27]

The response this time was immediate and massive. On 13 April, the Turin *camera* called a general strike in defence of the factory councils. The alliance of abstentionists and *ordinovisti* which ran the socialist section moved to effective leadership. The Turin *Avanti* became a strike bulletin and the only newspaper in the city. *L'Ordine Nuovo* shut up shop for the duration and its men and women went to their posts. Some 80,000 workers were out already on sectional issues. The response to the strike call was colossal. All factories closed. The tram workers struck, the railway and post workers, even the municipal guards and customs officers. According to Mario Montagnana, 'For eleven days the life of the city and province remained completely paralyzed. Tramways, railways, public services and many commercial businesses stopped work, in addition to the whole of industry. There were absolutely no blacklegs.'[28] Peasant strikes had broken out in parts of Piedmont in defence of their labour exchanges. The Turin committee immediately embraced these as parallel institutions. Within a few days, the general strike was called in Piedmont. It was complete throughout the provinces of Turin, Novara, Alessandria and Pavia. The *ordinovisti* made the rural districts their particular parish. Gramsci was proud of the network of proletarian institutions they built there, in the teeth of a vicious campaign of slander by union officials accusing them of secret negotiations with the employers, misusing a motor-car and all manner of other 'dilettante and intellectualist' practices.[29] At its peak, the strike brought out 500,000 workers and involved four million people.

Riccardo Bachi called it 'certainly the most notable movement of solidarity one can recall in Italy'. It was probably the most remarkable moment in Italian working-class history, perhaps the major event in the post-war history of the European working class. Togliatti came to think of it as the climax of the post-war revolutionary wave. Mario Montagnana thought the Occupation of the Factories in September merely a dramatic aftermath.[30]

With four million people facing *Confindustria* and the armed power of the state in defence of the factory councils and the autonomy of the working class, the fear of revolution gripped parliament, ministry and bourgeoisie. The Turin committee called for a vast national movement. Fear of revolution gripped the socialist movement no less. All its leaders immediately warned against a general strike. The Turin men were accused of indiscipline. They had acted without consultation and had suddenly confronted the movement with a stark choice. As Serrati put it harshly later – 'We are not bound to accept battle every time the enemy, feeling himself strong and prepared, provokes it.' He accused the Turin leaders of using inflammatory language and then scurrying to the prefecture, running for help to those less strong than themselves, to 'burden the capacious shoulders of the party Directorate'.[31] He was supported by D'Aragona for the CGL, Bombacci and a whole range of leaders. Even where there was sympathy for the Turin workers, there was anger and fear over their leaders' 'precipitation' of a struggle for which the movement as a whole was not prepared. The response was harsh and cold.

The Milan *Avanti* even refused to print the Turin strike bulletin. The national council meeting was moved to Milan. 'A city in the grip of a general strike,' acidly commented Gramsci, 'was not a suitable theatre for socialist debate.'³² The PSI and CGL pledged themselves to call a general strike if the government used force against the Turin workers, but the socialist movement as a whole turned a face of brass.

The syndicalists were the only ones to move. Railwaymen in Pisa and Florence refused to transport troops to Turin, dockers in Genoa and Livorno struck in the same cause. Liguria was convulsed. Genoa in particular was militant. Men came out in Sampierdarena, Cornigliano, Sestri and Rivarolo. The Genoa syndicalists called for a general strike throughout Italy. A delegation of the socialist sections and the *camere* of Genoa and Sampierdarena left for Milan, only to be told that the strike was being satisfactorily settled.³³

The Turin committee and the *Study Committee for Factory Councils* issued call after call. 'Class war declared!' proclaimed the *Study Committee*, 'all Piedmont is on the move . . . at stake is a revolutionary institution, the workshop commissars and the factory councils, the interest not only of a local category but of the whole communist proletariat of Italy . . .' The battle could not be won unless the whole worker and peasant class joined the struggle. 'Vibrant sympathy throughout Italy' reported the strike committee. But the organizations of the socialist movement held firm and aloof against 'localism' and 'indiscipline'.³⁴

The critical meeting of the national council of the PSI at Milan ran from 19 to 21 April.³⁵ From Turin went Tasca and Terracini. In face of the alliance of capitalists and the state, said Tasca, the CGL and the party must move. The general strike had united workers and peasants in Piedmont; this was an opportunity which must not be lost. He called for a general strike. Terracini went much further. A general strike was no longer enough. The party must annul the Pact of Alliance and take over the struggle. On the night of 20-21 April, he said that in three months all Italy would be in Turin's situation. 'We say, prepare for insurrection!'

Not a voice was raised in support. Reformists like Modigliani used the Turin crisis to argue for an agreement with the government. Radicals like Bombacci expressed sympathy but pressed for time to prepare. The Bombacci soviet project was the principal item on the agenda and the council spent interminable hours discussing its feasibility. They went on chattering about soviets and councils, snarled Gramsci, while in Piedmont and Turin half a million workers starved to defend the councils which already existed.

The workers in Turin were in truth near the end of their tether. Togliatti went to Milan and presented *For a Renewal of the Socialist Party* to the council. It was ignored. It was at this point that Bordiga demonstrated the limits of his doctrine and his imagination. He attacked the leadership for its irresolute behaviour but to Turin offered nothing but principled doctrinal criticism. The experience was confirming all his deepest suspicions of 'involvement'. The Turin men, in despair, withdrew their own motion. The leadership proposed a motion which, rich in maximalist rhetoric, called for more time to instill communist principle and prepare a 'proletarian armed force'. A motion from Misiano, equally empty but rather more urgent in tone, was entered in contest. The Directorate's motion was carried by 61,000 votes to 26,000. Bordiga's group, controlling some 7,500 votes, characteristically abstained. The socialist movement was summoned to hold fast to the leadership, avoid localized action and maintain discipline. It was a disavowal of Turin.

In Turin, the *Study Committee* issued a last, despairing call for an Italian general strike and the strike leaders approached Malatesta. But D'Aragona of the CGL moved remorselessly in to settle it. By 24 April, it was all over. The defeat was not total. The councils survived. But they were emasculated. In particular, they were not to operate during working hours. They remained as shadows, their power merely potential. Employer authority was re-established, union influence restored. The Gramscian-communist perspective was eliminated. The council movement itself, to a degree, was discredited.

A terrible gulf of hatred opened between the Turin left, the *ordinovisti* in particular, and the CGL leadership, with which the party Directorate was associated. The union men ruthlessly uprooted the organization which the *ordinovisti* had built in the rural areas and did it with such effect that during the September struggle, not a word the Turin men said was believed there. There was an outbreak of recrimination in Turin and the communist movement suffered a serious recession. All that was left was the still unbroken spirit of the Turin workers. 'A battle is lost. The war continues!' said the *Study Committee* and on May Day, the workers staged a massive demonstration in defiance, losing two of their men to police bullets. Gramsci saluted them in *L'Ordine Nuovo* as living proof of the vitality of the communist revolution : 'The working people, raw material for the history of the privileged classes, have at last become capable of creating their own history, of building their own city.'[36]

In the building of that city, however, Antonio Gramsci was apparently to have no part.

9. The Angry Summer

During the summer of 1920, there was an important shift in the balance of power against both wings of the communist movement in Italy.[1] April had been a heavy defeat. Observers noted a check in the advance of 'subversion', a strengthening of nerve among police and employers. In Turin, industrialists began to inch forward against militancy. The distant but visible prospect of a recession encouraged them. The parliamentary state was still largely ineffective, but the radical and democratic forces began to rally and in June, Giolitti returned to office, at first with the support of *Confindustria*, even though his programme was anti-plutocratic and demagogic in tone.

Reformists within the socialist party took the initiative, in Turati's celebrated speech *Rifare l'Italia* (Remaking Italy) and in the equally celebrated *Critica Sociale* article, 'Shorten the range!' During August-September a *socialist concentration* fraction was organized, with its directive centre among the co-operatives of Emilia ; it argued for an explicit abandonment of revolution and a commitment to structural reform.

The maximalist centre around Serrati were content enough with the defeat of the Turin radicals, but were anxious to retain and strengthen their Comintern connection. They tried to re-integrate the left, which was itself disorientated and trying to find a new cohesion. In the International, Lenin moved decisively against the left's nascent organization in the Amsterdam bureau. The Second Congress was looming. This would be, in effect, the real founding congress, at which communism would define itself. The purpose of Comintern was to create genuine communist parties by expelling reformists, while retaining as strong a mass base for such parties as possible. The anti-parliamentary and anti-union 'ultra-left' was to be curbed and convinced of error. The Amsterdam bureau was suppressed and Lenin wrote *Left-wing Communism: an Infantile Disorder*, a copy of which was presented to every delegate at the congress.

In these circumstances, there was a marked recession of communist strength in Italy.

Pessimism of the Intelligence: Defeat

After the April disaster, the council communists of Turin looked for a way out of their disarray. *L'Ordine Nuovo* published *For a Renewal of the Socialist Party* when it resumed on 8 May; shortly afterwards they brought it out as a pamphlet. The need was to create the revolutionary fraction which *For a Renewal* called for.

On 8 May Bordiga's abstentionists held their congress at Florence. Gramsci was invited as an observer, together with Gennari for the party leadership, Capitta for the youth section, and Misiano. The congress had its own problems. Comintern's hostility to abstentionism was now patent. The western secretariat of the International urged communists to remain within the PSI, to capture a majority for communism. The Bordighists were unabashed. The Florence congress announced that it would summon a congress to form the communist party of Italy as soon as the delegates had returned from the congress of Comintern. Moreover, despite Bordiga's earlier and critical distinction between German and Italian realities, it called for the formation of an anti-parliamentary fraction within the International itself.

The fraction failed to extend itself. Gennari was opposed to a split, but supported a purge; Misiano was for a purge but against abstentionism. In *Il Soviet* on 2 May, Bordiga severely criticized the Turin movement of April. It was an error 'to make the question of power in the factory rather than political power central'. In the theses of the fraction published in June, the attack on the *ordinovisti* was repeated. Gramsci argued at Florence that abstentionism was too narrow a base for a political party. 'There has to be broad contact with the masses, which we can get through new forms of economic organization.' He failed to persuade the Bordighists to abandon or modify their policy. He stressed, however, that in Turin, abstentionists and council communists had always worked closely together. There was some shuffling into alliance, but no real meeting of minds. Gramsci, unlike most of his comrades on *L'Ordine Nuovo*, took pains to maintain his alliance with the left, but during the summer, his thinking moved away from that of the abstentionists.[2]

He returned from one wing of the communist movement shrinking into purism to a Turin where the other wing was in full retreat. The union campaign to absorb the councils acquired new impetus in May, when the directive council of the CGL discussed a project of Gino Baldesi's. He denied that the factory council could be a revolutionary body but granted it some 'contingent functions' in defence of the workers and in technical preparation for control over the means of production. He outlined a scheme to integrate such councils into union structure.[3] No decision was taken at the meeting, but the Baldesi project was the signal for an advance in Turin.

The congress of the Turin *camera* met on 23-26 May. After a spate of recrimination over April, it turned to discuss the councils. Angelo Tasca spoke for three hours and completely captured the meeting. The experience of the lock-out had evidently brought to fruition the kind of unitary thinking he had displayed in his 20 December essay on the un-organized. Tasca was at this point still generally regarded as a spokesman for *L'Ordine Nuovo*, whose work was praised in a motion carried unanimously. But the scheme he now proposed in effect overthrew its position. April had shown, said Tasca, that councils and unions could not be separated ; they were a single body with a single aim, 'the liberation of the proletariat'. They should therefore be fused. The essential need was to transform craft into industrial unions and the councils would be a vital element in this process. The industrial-union cell was to include technicians and clerks as well as workers. But these councils which were to democratize the unions, were to operate under strict union control. Workshop commissars were no longer to take decisions or to elect the local executive of FIOM. A new general council of commissars was to have the final say in internal union disputes. This was to consist of all the internal commissions from plants where union members were more than 75 per cent of the work force. Where they were not, committees were to be elected by union members only.

In the psychological aftermath of April, Tasca's plan offered a focus for unity. Reformists and previous opponents of the councils rallied en masse and pledged themselves to work enthusiastically for the creation of such councils throughout Italy. The Tasca motion was carried by an overwhelming majority ; only seven anarcho-syndicalists voted against. Tasca was elected secretary to the *camera* and Enea Matta joined him.

L'Ordine Nuovo was thrown into a state of shock. Its whole *raison d'être* had been demolished. As councils went into eclipse and Tasca's industrial-union plan vanished into limbo, Gramsci exploded in anger. Tasca had sold the pass for a union job. He was preaching like a bishop in infidel parts. His surprise action was fully in the rotten tradition of Italian individualism and Bonapartism. He had supported a policy in the *camera* directly opposed to the policy of the Turin party section. He had opened the way to a revival of trade-union bureaucracy and opportunism within the socialist section. Above all, he was subjecting the crippled councils to unions still under the control of reformists. He had betrayed everything *L'Ordine Nuovo* had stood for.[4]

Gramsci printed Tasca's speech in the journal and raked it. Tasca sent in a long reply and opened a polemic on the whole programme of *L'Ordine Nuovo* which occupied much of the summer. Given the recession of councils into a shadowland of half-life, Tasca's defection was a deadly blow. The paper retained the affection of most militants. Its subscriptions settled at around 1,000 and its print-run oscillated between 4,000 and 4,500, though there were increasing delays in publication, probably because of shortage of active staff. It was still a powerful journal, full of detailed analyses. But its material was now almost wholly Russian or European. It went on preaching the councils, but the change from the autumn-winter of 1919-20 is striking. The journal was no longer part of the living tissue of the Turin working class. Gramsci went arguing on with Tasca like a man shouting at his echo in an empty hall.

He still felt a desperate need to *clarify*. In *The Factory Council* of 5 June, he rehearsed the arguments. 'The proletarian revolution is not the arbitrary act of an organization which calls itself revolutionary or a system of organizations which call themselves revolutionary. The proletarian revolution is a very long historical process which manifests itself in the rise and development of determinate forces of production (which we sum up in the expression "proletariat") in a determinate historical context (which we sum up in the expressions "private property ... capitalist mode of production ... factory system ... organization of society in a democratic-parliamentary state"). In a determinate phase of this process, the new productive forces can no longer develop and organize themselves autonomously within the official framework within which human community is evolving. In that determinate phase, the revolutionary act occurs: a direct effort violently to break this framework . . .'

The real revolutionary process could not be identified with organizations of a 'voluntary' or 'contractual' type like the union or the party, which were 'organizations born on the terrain of bourgeois democracy' . . . The actual unfolding of the revolutionary process takes place 'underground, in the obscurity of the factory and of the consciousness of the countless multitudes that capitalism subjects to its laws . . . where the relations are those of oppressor and oppressed. of exploiter and exploited ; where for the worker liberty does not exist, democracy does not exist ; the revolutionary process realizes itself there where the worker is nothing and wants to be everything, where the power of the proprietor is unlimited and is the power of life and death over the worker, over the worker's wife, over the worker's children.'

The workers become revolutionary, then, when they cease to resist the employer within the framework of democracy and launch a movement that must debouch in the building of a workers' state. 'We say the present period is revolutionary because the working class tends with all its power, all its will, to found its own state. That is why we say that the birth of the workers' factory councils is a great historical event, is the opening of a new era in the history of the human race.' Upon this process, the voluntary, contractual organizations of the party and the trade union must not impose themselves 'as wardens or as a ready-made superstructure for the new institution, in which the historical process of the revolution assumes controllable historical form. They must be the conscious agents of its liberation from the forces which imprison it, which are concentrated in the bourgeois state . . .'[5]

And it was in this defiant assertion of what had become the doctrine of a small and isolated minority that Gramsci got to grips with yet another working of the union-council relationship. In that same number, he was able to print the address of the Comintern representative to the Milan council of the PSI, which pointed to the April struggle as the first sign of the bourgeois offensive and called for the creation of factory councils as a matter of urgency. The next week, Gramsci published *Unions and Councils*.

The article is drenched in memories of the opening of the April struggle. Gramsci begins: 'The trade union is not this or that definition of a trade union. The trade union becomes a determinate definition, that is, assumes a definite historical character in so far as the strength and will of the workers who constitute it imprint upon it that direction . . . that objective, which are affirmed in the definition.' Thus while the trade union is the 'form which the labour-commodity assumes and can only assume in a capitalist regime when it organizes itself to dominate the market', it remains malleable to the workers' will.

This represented a subtle shift in the quality of Gramsci's more recent thinking. His locking of the trade union firmly into bourgeois society had enabled him to enforce the critical distinction between council and union, but had co-existed uneasily with his attitude to the Socialist Party, which, while equally 'bourgeois', was apparently much more *plastic* and susceptible to the communist will. Now, in this essay, nothing is immune to creative communist intervention in the process of history.

The great achievement of this organized labour-commodity, the union, has been the establishment of 'an industrial legality'. This had been a great gain, since it had improved the material conditions of the working class. But it was no more than a compromise, which it was necessary to support only so long as the balance of force remained unfavourable to the working class. If trade-union officers were to look upon this legality as necessary, but only as a stage towards the development of revolutionary action, then the union would become a revolutionary instrument.

Relations between council and union had to be considered in this light. For the factory council 'is the negation of industrial legality. It tends to annihilate it at any moment, tends continuously to lead the working class towards the conquest of industrial power, to make the working class the source of industrial power . . . therefore it tends to universalize every rebellion, to give value and decisive meaning to every one of its acts of power.' The trade union, on the other hand, tends to 'universalize and perpetuate legality'. 'The council tends, because of its revolutionary spontaneity, to unleash the class war at any moment ; the union, because of its bureaucratic form, tends not to permit the class war ever to break out.'

Relations between the two, said Gramsci, with April obviously in his mind, must be such as to ensure that 'a capricious impulse' of the council did not result in a defeat for the working class.

Here, the *discipline* of the union is vital. The council must accept and assimilate the discipline of the union, while its own revolutionary energy dissolves the 'bureaucracy and the bureaucratism of the union'. 'For that reason, communists cannot want the union to lose any of its disciplinary energy and its systematic concentration.'

The only way effectively to link union and council is that a majority or 'a conspicuous number' of council electors should be union members. Any attempt, like Tasca's, to link them in a relationship of hierarchical dependence can only lead to the destruction of both. If the council is subjected to the union, it is sterilized. If however the unions 'were to lean directly on the councils, not to dominate them but to become their superior form, the tendency proper to the councils to break out from legality at any moment . . . would be reflected within the union.' The union would cease to be a regulatory force over the working class and would become a revolutionary instrument.

At first glance there seems to have been a notable withdrawal on the union ; its discipline is essential, communists cannot want it diminished. As the argument proceeds, however, it is clear there has been no basic shift. The original primacy of the councils is maintained. There has *been* a shift, however towards the *logic of discipline*. 'Communists, since they want the revolutionary act to be as far as possible conscious and responsible, want the choice of the moment . . . to rest with the most conscious and responsible sector of the working class.' Therefore, communist groups must be formed which 'must carry into the unions and the factories the conceptions, the theses, the tactics of the Third International. They must influence union discipline and determine its ends. They must influence the decisions of factory councils and transform into revolutionary consciousness and creativity the rebellious impulses which surge up out of the situation which capitalism has created for the working class.'[6]

From January 1920 onwards, the essential and creative role of the *party* is increasingly stressed in Gramsci's writings. In this essay, it is becoming central even *within* the councils. The role of the party, implicit in his earlier writings, moves further and further centre stage. The party is in fact beginning to assume some of the functions which he once assigned to the councils themselves.

The formation of that party had now become the first

priority. Circumstances, however, had changed dramatically for the worse.

Pessimism of the Intelligence: Dissociation

It was in August 1920 that Anna Kuliscioff warned Turati that the morning trams of Milan were filling with workers reading *Umanità Nova*. Already in July, the Turin socialists were alert to groups of anarchists and syndicalists working intensively within their trade union sections. In that month a branch of USI was founded in Turin.

By June 1920, food prices were 20 per cent higher than they had been in April 1919. From January to September 1920, essential expenditure for a working-class family rose by a third. Employers began to exploit the April victory. There were sackings at Fiat and workers felt the bite of restored managerial authority. The syndicalist tide rose through the summer and the PSI decided to accept an invitation from USI to a joint conference.[7]

But at the end of June there was a war scare. The Russo-Polish campaign was at a critical moment. And on 26 June Italian troops massed at Ancona for a proposed, and disputed, expedition to Albania, mutinied. Once again, Ancona sparked a popular rising. Troubles rippled across Italy and a campaign developed against the production of arms which might be used against Soviet Russia. Syndicalists swept to the head of the movement. In the Romeo works in Milan, workers refused to work on war materials and were locked out. Comrades seized an arms factory in protest. The PSI hurriedly broke off the talks with USI and worked out a joint policy with the CGL. They were full of talk of a revolution, if Italy went to war with Russia, but in private agreed to abandon the general strike as a weapon which had become far too dangerous. In Turin, a revolt by shop-floor militants against FIOM's hesitancy was exploited by syndicalists who revived the movement for factory councils. Boero, the abstentionist secretary of the Turin socialist section, was involved.[8]

All this was torture to Gramsci. 'Where is the Socialist Party going?' he shouted on 10 July. The direct action of the masses was bound to be destructive ; it was revolutionary 'precisely because it is eminently destructive'. An alienated and voiceless working class in factory, army, state apparatus, would mean complete destruction. *Communists* know this and do not fear it. They must master reality and direct its potency to the will to reconstruct. But the socialist movement? – the CGL had 'an English gardener's conception of workers' control'. If the PSI lost control over the masses, the latter would be reduced to a worse state than their brothers in Austria and Germany. Only the communist groups could do the job. 'Since the April movement, we of *L'Ordine Nuovo* and the Turin socialists generally have been presented to the proletariat as a rabble of uncontrollables, frenetics and hot-heads.' The leaders of what Gramsci called 'the official party' did not see reality. 'They see history unfolding through the operation of ideological abstractions (classes in general, party in general, humanity in general) and not through the actions of real men called Peter, Paul and John.'[9]

'Many events in working-class life in the present period,' Gramsci wrote in an article *The Communist Groups*, on 17 July, 'mass indiscipline towards institutions, pronunciamentos in individual factories in favour of anarchist and syndicalist theories, periods of discouragement and acute prostration, ephemeral and noisy triumphs of sundry Masaniellos pullulating in the streets – would be incomprehensible if they were not interpreted in the context of the decomposition of the traditional institutions of government.' They were symptoms of an oppressed class trying to escape from slavery and establish a new order. The Socialist Party and the trade unions were decomposing with the bourgeois society to which they belonged. And in an analysis brimming with a Sorelian contempt for democracy, he pointed to the communist groups as the key to a 'crisis of organic transformation'.[10]

There is a kind of despair in Gramsci's writing this summer. The communist groups either did not get off the ground or were drowned in the syndicalist and populist tide. During the Occupation of the Factories in September, communist groups were said to have been 'reconstituted'. The Bordiga fraction was locked into 'sectarianism' and pressing for an immediate breakaway. The councils were eclipsed or reviving as syndicalist-inspired 'impulses'. The *ordinovista* thematic was discounted. There was an absence of leadership which became physical as major figures like Serrati, Bordiga, Borghi gathered in Russia for the Comintern congress. It was natural to feel despair.

It was also correct. For in July the syndicalist crisis rolled over the Turin party section and the *ordinovista* group disintegrated.

Policy towards the approaching local elections provided the occasion for the split. The Bordighists, working to the decisions of their May congress, tried to force the pace. Some of them had been caught up in the syndicalist campaign, which touched an old nerve of revulsion among many PSI members. The section executive resigned and the rival forces marshalled their strength.

The *abstentionist communist* fraction adopted their national programme. They demanded an immediate purge and the formation of a communist party. They called for communist groups, but said little about factory councils. In reaction there was a strong rally against them led by Tasca and Terracini. An *electionist communist* group was formed. It advocated participation in the local elections to win positions of power. It was opposed to a break from the PSI, proposing instead to win a majority within it and to isolate the right wing. It, too, urged the formation of communist groups and supported the factory councils, though in ambiguous terms – in the form already approved by the majority of Turin socialists. It deplored the strength of syndicalism.

Gramsci took the crucial decision to stand apart. He refused to follow Terracini. In practice, as he reminded his friends four years later, he took a stand alongside, but independent of, the Bordighists, in opposition to any rally to maximalism. He was abandoned. Among the leading men of *L'Ordine Nuovo* only Andrea Viglongo stayed with him. There was a stampede of former *ordinovisti* into the *electionist communist* ranks: Togliatti and Terracini went over, 'joined Tasca' as Gramsci put it later, so did Montagnana and Matta. This marked the end of any recognizable *ordinovista* group.

In the angry summer of 1920, communists closed back on their basic instincts. The Gramscians, characteristically, formed a *communist education group*. They were to be Marx's Old Mole of the Revolution, burrowing beneath the surface through to and beyond the as-yet unsuspected 18th Brumaire of Benito Mussolini.

Only 17 comrades joined Gramsci, all workers, including Viglongo and Battista Santhia. They published their declaration:

> Our group has decided to stand apart from the two fractions to try to break the magic circle within which the best energies of the proletariat are being dissipated. We will continue to stand

apart. We will not take part in the contest for the section executive. We mean to initiate organizational work by a disinterested group which does not offer the proletariat emancipation through municipal councils or trade-union leaders, but intends to work in the field of mass action: for communist groups in factory and union, for the workers' council, for that proletarian unity now threatened in its very heart. To attain this objective of clarity and recovery, there can be only one method:

1. to insist, with indefatigable and patient energy, that the section discuss the fundamental problems of the working class and the communist revolution.

2. to make sure that the choice of section leaders is not made on the swampy and pestilential terrain of fictitious programmes ...

3. to see to it that the section does useful work in preparing the cadres of the revolution and of the social organization which must be its concrete expression and thus, through the thrust of the masses, give a precise direction to the unions and the **camera del lavoro** ...

The election issue Gramsci dismissed as 'illusory', a measure of the 'mediocre' level of political education in the party, which was throwing the masses to the 'empty demagogic rhetoric' of the syndicalists.

In the July of 1920, the attitude of the *communist education group*, markedly more hostile to the electionists than the abstentionists, was a confession of immediate irrelevance. The group was overwhelmed. The *electionist communists* won by an average 450 votes to the abstentionists' average 185. Togliatti displaced Boero as section secretary. Gramsci had called on comrades to return blank ballots: 31 did so. Gramsci and his tiny group were reduced to total political isolation.[11]

Optimism of the Will: Towards the City of Man

It was out of his defeat and isolation that Gramsci began to build his city. During the bitter summer of 1920 he pulled the threads of his thinking and his experience together. On 3 July, at the onset of the crisis of the Turin section, he wrote an article *Two Revolutions*, directed at the abstentionists, which developed some of the themes of his March essay *Governing Party and Governing Class*. After several weeks of growing tension and of argument within the Communist International, he wrote *The Communist Party* and published it on 4 September, as the Occupation of the Factories was beginning. This did not materially advance the argument on the party but located it in a richer and fuller context. Moreover it registered an important shift in his thinking on the councils.

Taken together, the two articles effectively summarize Gramsci's thinking on the party, the councils and the working class on the eve of his entry into the new communist party of Italy. Moreover they establish some of the basic lines of argument he was to develop during his period of leadership of that communist party in 1924-26 and, in some significant senses, during his years in prison. They are worth reproducing in full.[12]

Two Revolutions (3 July 1920).
Every form of political power can be conceived and explained historically only as the juridical apparatus of a real economic power. It can be conceived and explained only as the defensive organization and condition of development of a determinate order in the relations of production and distribution of wealth. This fundamental (and elementary) canon of historical materialism sums up all the arguments we have tried organically to develop around the problem of the factory councils; it sums up the reasons why, in handling the real problems of the proletarian class, we have posited as central and pre-eminent the positive experience achieved by the profound movement of the working masses in the creation, development and co-ordination of the councils. We have therefore maintained:
1. the revolution is not necessarily proletarian and communist if it proposes and secures the overthrow of the political government of the bourgeois state.
2. it is not even communist if it proposes and secures the destruction of the representative institutions and the administrative machine through which the central government exercises the political power of the bourgeoisie.
3. it is not even communist and proletarian if the wave of popular insurrection thrusts power into the hands of men who call themselves (and sincerely are) communists.
The revolution is proletarian and communist only in so far as it is a liberation of the proletarian and communist productive forces which have been developing in the very heart of the society ruled by the capitalist class.
It is proletarian and communist to the extent that it advances and promotes the growth and systematization of proletarian and communist forces capable of initiating the patient and methodical labour required to build a new order in the relations of production and distribution; a new order which will make it im-

possible for a society divided into classes to exist, whose systematic development, therefore, will tend to coincide with a process of withering-away of state power, with a systematic dissolution of the political defence organization of the proletarian class which will itself dissolve as a class to become mankind.

The revolution which realizes itself in the destruction of the bourgeois state apparatus and the construction of a new state apparatus interests and involves all the classes oppressed by capitalism. Its immediate cause is the brute fact that, in the conditions left by the imperialist war, the great majority of the population (made up of artisans, small landowners, petty-bourgeois intellectuals, masses of desperately poor peasants and also backward proletarian masses) no longer has any security in the elementary necessities of daily life. This revolution tends to have a predominantly anarchic and destructive character and to manifest itself as a blind explosion of anger, a tremendous explosion of fury without concrete objective, which will take shape in a new state power only if weariness, disillusion and hunger force a recognition of the need for a constituted order and for a power which can really enforce respect for it.

This revolution can take shape in a constituent assembly pure and simple, which tries to heal the wounds inflicted on the bourgeois state apparatus by popular anger.

It can go as far as soviets, the autonomous political organization of the proletariat and the other oppressed classes, which however do not dare go beyond organization, do not dare touch economic relations and are therefore thrown back in the reaction of the propertied classes.

It can go as far as the complete destruction of the bourgeois state machine and the establishment of a condition of permanent disorder in which the existing wealth and population dissolve crushed by the impossibility of achieving any autonomous organization.

It can go as far as the establishment of a proletarian and communist power which wears itself out in repeated and desperate attempts to create, by act of authority, the economic conditions for its survival and growth, and in the end is overthrown by capitalist reaction.

In Germany, Austria, Bavaria, the Ukraine, Hungary, these historical processes have happened. The revolution as a destructive act has not been followed by the revolution as a process of reconstruction in communism. The existence of external conditions: a communist party, destruction of the bourgeois state strong trade union organizations, the arming of the proletariat – has not been enough to compensate for the absence of this condition: the existence of productive forces tending towards development and expansion, a conscious movement of the prolet arian masses to buttress political with economic power, the will of the proletarian masses to introduce proletarian order into the factory, to make the factory a cell of the new state, to build the new state as a reflection of the industrial relations of the factory system.

This is why we have always maintained that the duty of the communist nuclei which exist in the party is not to fall into particularist hallucination (the problem of electoral abstentionism, the problem of creating a 'truly' communist party) but to work to create the mass conditions, in which it will be possible to solve all particular problems as problems in the organic development of the communist revolution. In fact, can a communist party exist (as a party of action, not an academy of purist doctrinaires and politicians who think 'well' and express themselves 'well' on the subject of communism) if there does not exist in the midst of the mass a spirit of historical initiative and an aspiration towards industrial autonomy which must find their reflection and their synthesis in the communist party? And since the formation of parties and the rise of real historical forces of which parties are a reflection, does not spring from nothing, at a stroke, but happens according to a dialectical process, is not the major duty of the communist forces precisely that of giving consciousness and organization to the productive forces, communist in essence, which must develop and in expanding, create the secure and permanent economic base for the political power of the proletariat?

In the same way: can the party abstain from participation in electoral struggles for the representative institutions of bourgeois democracy, if it has the duty politically to organize all the oppressed classes around the communist proletariat? To achieve this, is it not necessary that for these classes, it become the governing party (party of government) in a democratic sense, given that only for the communist proletariat can it be a party in a revolutionary sense?

In so far as it becomes the party of 'democratic' trust for all the oppressed classes, in so far as it keeps itself permanently in contact with all the sectors of the working people, the communist party leads all sectors of the people to recognize in the communist proletariat the ruling class which must replace the capitalist class in state power. It creates the conditions which make it possible for the revolution as a destruction of the bourgeois state to identify itself with the proletarian revolution, with the revolution which expropriates the expropriators, which must inaugurate the development of a new order in the relations of production and distribution.

Thus: in so far as it presents itself as the specific party of the industrial proletariat, in so far as it works to give consciousness and precise direction to the productive forces which capitalism has engendered in its development, the communist party creates the economic conditions for the state power of the communist proletariat, it creates the conditions in which it is possible for the proletarian revolution to identify itself with the popular revolt against the bourgeois state, in which this revolt becomes an act of liberation for the real productive forces which have accumulated in the heart of capitalist society.

These different series of historical events are not separate and independent. They are moments of a single dialectical process of development, in the course of which, the relations of cause and effect interlace, reverse themselves, interpenetrate. Experience of revolutions has shown, however, that after Russia, all the other two-stage revolutions failed and that the failure of the second revolution has plunged the working classes into a state of prostration and humiliation, which has allowed the bourgeois class to re-organize itself in strength and to begin the systematic extermination of the communist vanguards which are trying to reconstitute themselves.

For communists who are not content monotonously to chew over the basic elements of communism and historical materialism, but who live in the reality of struggle and grasp that reality, as it is, from the viewpoint of historical materialism and communism, the revolution as a conquest of political power by the proletariat can be conceived only as a dialectical process, in which political power makes possible industrial power and industrial power makes possible political power. The soviet is the instrument of revolutionary struggle which permits the autonomous development of the communist economic organization, which from the council, arrives at the central council of the economy, which creates plans for production and distribution and thus suppresses capitalist competition. The factory council as a form of the autonomy of the producer in the industrial field, and as the base of the communist economic organization, is the instrument of struggle which is mortal for the capitalist regime in that it creates the conditions in which a society divided into classes is suppressed and any new division by class is rendered 'materially' impossible.

But for communists who live in struggle, this conception does not remain an abstract thought: it becomes an incentive to struggle, the stimulus to a greater effort of organization and propaganda.

Industrial development has produced in the masses a certain degree of mental autonomy and a certain spirit of positive historical initiative. It is necessary to give an organization and a form to these elements of proletarian revolution, to create the psychological conditions for their development and their gener-

alization among all the labouring masses through the struggle
for control of production.

It is necessary to promote the organic constitution of a communist party which will not be a collection of doctrinaires or
little Machiavellis but a party of revolutionary communist action, a party which has an exact consciousness of the historical
mission of the proletariat and an ability to guide the proletariat
to the realization of its mission. It will therefore be the party of
the masses who want to free themselves by their own means,
autonomously, from industrial and political slavery through the
organization of the social economy; it will not be a party which
uses the masses to attempt heroic imitations of the French
Jacobins. To the extent that it is possible to achieve this by the
action of a party, it is necessary to create the conditions in which
there will not be two revolutions, but in which the popular revolt
against the bourgeois state will find organized forces capable of
beginning the transformation of the national apparatus of production from an instrument of plutocratic oppression into an
instrument of communist liberation.

The Communist Party (4 September 1920).
Since Sorel, it has become a commonplace to refer to the
primitive Christian community in assessing the modern proletarian movement. It must be said at once that Sorel is in no way
responsible for the pettiness and spiritual coarseness of his
Italian admirers, just as Karl Marx is not responsible for the
absurd ideological pretensions of the 'marxists'. In the field of
historical research, Sorel is an 'inventor'; he cannot be imitated;
he does not make available to his aspiring disciples a method
which can always be mechanically applied by everyone to achieve
intelligible results. For Sorel, as for marxist theory, Christianity
represents a revolution in the fullness of its development, that
is, a revolution which drove through to the ultimate ends implicit in it, to the creation of a new and original system of
human relations, moral, juridical, philosophical, artistic. To
assume these consequences as the ideological schema of every
revolution is a crude and un-intelligent betrayal of the Sorelian
historical intuition. That intuition can give rise only to a series of
historical researches into the 'germs' of a proletarian civilization
which must exist, if it is true (as it is true for Sorel) that the
proletarian revolution is immanent in the heart of modern industrial society and if it is true, further, that from it, an original
way of life will arise, an absolutely new system of human relations, characteristic of the revolutionary class.

What is the significance, then, of the assertion that, in contrast to the early Christians, the workers are not chaste, not
sober, not original in their way of life? Apart from the slipshod

generalization which makes the 'Turin metal workers' into a rabble of brutes, who eat a roast chicken every day, get drunk every night in brothels, neglect their families, seek the satisfaction of their ideals of beauty and moral life in the cinema and in a simian imitation of bourgeois habits – this puerile and dilettante generalization aside, the assertion cannot properly serve as the premise of an historical assessment. It would correspond, in the order of historical intelligence, to another: because modern Christians eat chickens, run after women, get drunk, bear false witness, are adulterers, etc, etc, therefore it is a myth that there ever were ascetics, martyrs and saints. Every historical phenomenon, in sum, must be studied in its characteristic peculiarity, in its real historical context, as a development of the liberty which manifests itself in a purpose, in institutions in forms which cannot be confused and compared in any absolute sense (other than metaphorically) with the purpose, the institutions, the forms of past historical phenomena.

Every revolution which, like the Christian and like the communist, realizes itself and can realize itself only in an upsurge of the most vast and deep popular masses, can do nothing but break and totally destroy the existing system of social organization. Who can imagine, who can foresee the consequences of the entry into the arena of historical destruction and creation of countless multitudes who today have no will, no power? These because they never have 'will' or 'power' think they see will and an achieved power materialized in every public and private act they find the whole of existence mysteriously hostile; they want to destroy it to its foundations. But precisely because of the immensity of the revolution, because of the quality of the unforeseeable in it, its limitless liberty, who can dare risk even one single definitive hypothesis on the sentiments, the passions, the initiatives, the merits which are being moulded in such an incandescent furnace? Everything which exists today, everything we see today, outside our own will and our own force of character – what transformations might they not undergo? Every mutation of individual consciousness, in so far as it is simultaneously effected throughout the whole popular mass – will this not have unimaginable creative results?

From present evidence, nothing can be foreseen in the order of moral life and the life of the sentiments. One solitary sentiment is today proven; become now a constant, so that it characterizes the working class: it is solidarity. But the intensity and the power of this sentiment can be counted as a sustenance of the will to resist and sacrifice only over a period of time which even the scant popular capacity for historical foresight can roughly estimate. It cannot be counted, and therefore taken for granted, as a sustenance of the historical will through the period of revolutionary creation and the foundation of a new society, when it will be impossible to assign any temporal limits to resistance and sacrifice, because the enemy to combat and overcome will no longer be outside the proletariat, will no longer be an external physical power which is controllable and limited, but will be the proletariat itself, in its ignorance, its sloth, its mountainous impenetrability to quick perception, when the dialectic of the class struggle will be interiorized and within every consciousness, the new man, in his every act, will have to combat the 'bourgeois' lying in ambush for him. Therefore the workers' trade union, an organization which realizes and disciplines proletarian solidarity, cannot serve as the ground and basis for forecasting the future of civilization. It lacks capacities for the development of liberty. It is destined to undergo radical changes as a consequence of the general developments; it is determined, not determining.

The proletarian movement, in its present phase, tends to effect a revolution in the organization of material things and physical forces; its characteristic traits cannot be the sentiments and diffuse passions of the mass which sustain the will of the mass. The characteristic traits of the proletarian revolution have to be sought only in the party of the working class, in the communist party which exists and grows in so far as it is the disciplined organization of the will to create a state, the will to impose a proletarian systematization upon the ordering of existing physical forces and to lay the foundations of popular liberty.

The communist party at the present time is the only institution which can seriously be compared with the religious community of primitive Christianity. Within the limits in which the party now operates, on the international scale one can attempt a comparison and establish an order of assessments between the militants of the City of God and the militants of the City of Man. The communist is certainly not inferior to the Christian of the catacombs. More! The ineffable end which Christianity holds out to its champions through its impressive mystery, is a justification full of heroism, of the thirst for martyrdom, of sanctity. The entry into play of the great human forces of character and will is not necessary to evoke the spirit of sacrifice in him who believes in the heavenly prize and eternal happiness. The communist worker who, week in, month in, year in, after eight hours' work in a factory, disinterestedly works more than eight hours for the party, the union, the co-operative is, from the viewpoint of the history of man, greater than the slave and the artisan who defies every danger to make his way to the secret conventicle of prayer. In the same way, Rosa Luxemburg and Karl Liebknecht are greater than the greatest saints of Christ. Precisely because the cause for which they fight is concrete, human, limited, the warriors of the working class are greater than the warriors of God.

This driving force the sentiments of the worker will never acquire: the worker, bent over his machine, endlessly repeating the ritual of his craft for eight hours a day, monotonous as the closed circle of clicking rosary beads – when will he become a 'master', when will he become the measure of social values? The very fact that the worker still manages to think, even when compelled to work without knowing the why and the wherefore of his practical activity – is this not a miracle? This miracle of the worker who daily conquers his own spiritual autonomy and his own liberty to build in the order of ideas, struggling against the weariness, the boredom, the physical monotony which tends to mechanize and even kill his inner life, this miracle organizes itself in the communist party, in the will to struggle, the will to revolutionary creation, which find their expression in the communist party.

The factory worker has truly executive duties. He does not move forward with the general process of labour and production. He is not a point which moves to create a line. He is a pin stuck in a determinate place and the line results from a succession of pins which an alien will has laid out for its own ends. The worker tends to carry this mode of being into every aspect of his life. He tends to adjust himself easily, everywhere, to the function of material executor, of a 'mass' guided by a will alien to his own. He is intellectually lazy, he does not know and will not see beyond the immediate, therefore he lacks any criterion in the choice of his leaders and he lets himself be easily deluded by promises. He wants to believe that he can get something without a great effort on his part and without having to think too much.

The communist party is the instrument and the historical form of the process of inner liberation by which the worker, from an *executor* becomes an *initiator* from a *mass* becomes a *leader* and a guide, from an *arm*, becomes a brain and a will. In the formation of the communist party are gathered the germs of liberty which will have their growth and full development after the workers' state has organized the necessary economic conditions. The slave or the artisan of the classical world 'knew himself', achieved his liberation by entering to form part of a Christian community where he felt concretely that he was an equal, a brother, because the son of a single Father. So the worker enters to form part of the communist party, where he collaborates to 'discover', to 'invent' original modes of life, where he collaborates 'voluntarily' in the activity of the world, where he thinks, foresees, has a responsibility, where he is an organizer rather than an organized, where he feels himself forming a vanguard which runs ahead, drawing after him the whole popular mass.

The communist party, even as a mere organization, is revealed as the particular form of the proletarian revolution. No previous revolution has known parties; they were born after the bourgeois revolution and are decomposing on the terrain of parliamentary democracy. Even in this field there is proof of the marxist idea that capitalism creates forces which it then cannot control. Democratic parties served to select political men of substance and to secure their success in political competition; today the men of government are imposed by banks, big newspapers, industrial associations; parties have disintegrated into a multiplicity of personal cliques. The communist party, rising from the ashes of the socialist parties, repudiates their democratic and parliamentary origins and reveals its essential characteristics, which are original in history. The Russian revolution was a revolution carried out by the organized men of the communist party who, in the party, made themselves a new personality, acquired new sentiments, realized a moral life which tends to become the universal consciousness and end for all men.

Two Revolutions is clearly directed at the abstentionist fraction. As against the maximalist centre and its left prisoners, Gramsci stood squarely with the 'purists' on the *historical definition* of communism in Italy, the imperative need to break with the traditions of the PSI. But he could not accept the mode of acting and thinking which the *quality* of Bordiga's commitment to abstentionism implied. After the basic mode-of-production argument, with its *State and Revolution* perspective, which opens the essay, he affirms the pluralist and destructive nature of the 'first' revolution and then lists possible outcomes if the 'constructive' phase is not achieved. These – i. a Constituent Assembly ; ii. toothless soviets ; iii. total collapse ; evidently reflect Gramsci's assessment of i. the reformists (dragging a large sector of the maximalists with them), ii. the maximalist left of the Tasca variety with its refashioned councils, and iii. the anarcho-syndicalists. The final possibility – 'a communist power which exhausts itself in repeated and desperate attempts to create, by act of authority, the economic conditions for its survival and growth and is in the end overthrown by capitalist reaction' – is clearly centred on the abstentionist communists, as, no doubt, are the references to *Jacobins*. The remarks about 'doctrinaires, Machiavellis' (ironic in view of his later definition of the party as the New Machiavel!) and those who talk and think 'well' about communism, would also no doubt embrace them.

The core of the essay is the rejection of the *two-stage* revolution, the identification of the *autonomous* development of communism through a council system as the essential 'missing link' and, in consequence, the cogent assertion of the need to work in and with the *non-proletarian* masses of plebein society. 'Can a communist party exist', he asks, unless a new spirit of historical initiative has already registered among the masses? And, in a pluralist society such as Italy, how can the communist party hope to succeed unless it mobilizes the non-proletarian masses *around* the proletariat and its party?

This is a subtle and complex argument which is *not* an argument for a 'mass party' as the concept is usually conceived, although it was to be distorted in precisely this sense. And while his argument that the 'missing link' in earlier, failed, two-stage revolutions had been the unformed but growing communist economy and the semi-conscious proletarian will of the factory councils is perhaps not fully adequate, the presentation of his case for a communist party which operates on a pluralist society is cogent and compelling.

His single, driving, dialectical revolution thrusts through the chaos of capitalist collapse like an elemental force of nature, but one controlled and directed by the communist will realizing the unity of theory and practice in the developing crisis of the mode of production. The party's action is to be geared to the realities of communist creation ; it is still to unlock the potential communism which can be located only in the factory councils (the force which capitalism finds truly 'mortal'). But it is also geared to the objective realities of pluralist Italy, in which the proletariat is a minority. It is as the party of the proletariat (which is the archetype to which all other plebeian groups are being reduced, as he argued in his earlier essay) that the party is 'revolutionary' ; to other sectors of the popular masses, it has to serve as a governing party in a 'democratic' sense. Its purpose (working dialectically with the on-going crisis in the mode of production and the on-going development of the communist society through the councils) is to mobilize these non-proletarian sectors around the proletariat, recognized as a ruling class. The party then, 'creates the conditions which make it possible for the revolution as a destruction of the bourgeois state to identify itself with the proletarian revolution'. The task is to identify popular revolt with the *specifically proletarian* revolution of which the communist party is the *specific* agent. Councils are central to the process.

It is important to stress that this is *not* the 'mass party' of later imaginings. Nor does it bear any resemblance to the Popular Front theses of the 1930s, though Gramsci's arguments were used to buttress both. It *does* bear considerable resemblance to the *more radical* interpretations of the *United Front theses* of the 1920s, which emphasized their revolutionary, 'from-below' implications (and a form of which Bordiga himself was to accept even at the height of his conflict with Comintern). The Gramscian party here was not a 'mass party', but a party becoming dialectically 'one' with the masses in a basically instrumental sense, as the proletariat was becoming 'one' with non-proletarian groups in revolt. The aim was not a 'mass party' but a party which worked to create 'the mass conditions' in which all particular problems are resolved in the development of *communist* revolution. The position he achieved here remained Gramsci's basic position on the party. It finds remarkable expression in the Lyons Theses of 1925-26 in which he tried to shape the Communist Party after he had replaced Bordiga (though without losing Bordiga's basic acquisitions) – and indeed, to some extent in his Prison Notebooks.[13]

Basic to the argument, of course, is Gramsci's Doomsday Machine – the crisis in the mode of production and the embryo of the new civilization in the councils. But one cannot help observing that in this essay the *tonality* of his writing on the councils has *altered significantly*. The councils themselves are still conceptually central, but the *emphasis* is almost entirely on 1. the anarchic, destructive, pluralist character of the mass upsurge and 2. the intensely *creative* role of the communist *party*. The latter must certainly have the embryonic new force to work on and with, but there is a much greater stress on the party's *creative* role even here. The powerful evocations of the councils in earlier writings give place to – 'industrial development has produced in the masses a certain degree of mental autonomy and a certain spirit of positive historical initiative'. *O what a dying fall is there!*

But it is in his September essay, *The Communist Party*, a powerful and remarkable piece of writing in its own right, that this change of tone becomes a decisive, indeed jolting, change of gear.

Central to *The Communist Party*, of course, is the Church-Communism dichotomy which was to become central to Gramsci's life-long effort in exploration of the process by which a revolutionary force becomes *hegemonic*, achieves total power and a transformation in human civilization. For the Church was obviously the most sensationally successful example in human history to date. This first approach through an equation of Communists-of-the-First-Hour with Early Christians was derived immediately from Sorel, though it was rooted in the pre-occupations of Gramsci's earliest writings.

He opens with the Sorelian evocation of the Christian 'revolution' and his own remarkable evocation of the 'oceanic' character of the popular revolution. The search for the new civilization taking shape in this incandescent mass stresses the brute fact of total unpredictability. Only one certainty is visible: workers' *solidarity*. But this is a sustenance for an immediate, popular will, limited in time. What about the *historical will*, which has no temporal limits, because the communist revolution in its true sense *has* no temporal limits? – 'because the enemy to combat and overcome will no longer be outside the proletariat . . . but will be the proletariat itself, in its ignorance, its sloth, its mountainous impenetrability to quick perception, when the dialectic of the class struggle will be interiorized and within every consciousness, the new man, in his every act, will have to combat the "bourgeois" lying in ambush for him'.

This 'future' man cannot be anything but the *communist* man who lives the future here and now. There follows the remarkable evocation of the communist as Early Christian and the *miracle* of the breaking of the bourgeois hegemony. But *where* is the miracle located? Certainly among the workers who begin to live communist as the basic crisis registers at the point of production. But *which* workers?

'This driving force [the Early-Christian commitment to communism – GAW] the sentiments of the worker will never acquire: the worker bent over his machine . . . when will he become a "master", when will he become the measure of social values? . . . He is not a point which moves to create a line. He is a pin stuck in a determinate place . . . He tends to adjust himself easily, everywhere, to the function of material executor, of a "mass" guided by a will alien to his own . . . He is intellectually lazy . . .'

In the midst of this infidel mass, the *miracle does* occur – 'The miracle of the worker who daily conquers his own spiritual autonomy and his own liberty to build in the order of ideas, struggling against the weariness, the boredom, the physical monotony which tends to mechanize and even kill his inner life . . .' BUT *'This miracle organizes itself in the communist party'* [my italics – GAW]. It is the *communist* worker who is evoked in the hypnotic hymn to the warriors and martyrs of the City of Man. It is the *communist party* which is 'the instrument and the historical form of the process of *inner* liberation [my italics – GAW] by which the worker, from an *executor* becomes an *initiator*, from a *mass* becomes a *leader* . . . from an arm becomes a brain . . .' [Gramsci's emphasis.]

Note that even *inner* liberation has become a function of the *party. What now* about the 'most backward of workers and the most "civil" of engineers' *ineluctably* becoming 'communist' through the unifying *process* of production in capitalist crisis? For the individual worker, the process has ceased to be *process*: he is a stuck pin.

The roots of the original conception are not lost. The communist party is still a 'voluntary' institution as opposed to the 'involuntary' character of the organization arising directly from the process of production. The crisis in the mode of production still generates 'a certain degree of mental autonomy and a certain spirit of positive historical initiative'. Moreover, the communist party must immerse itself in this mass and not contemplate its own purist navel. But *what a charge* do the words 'a certain . . .' bear! What an invasion of 'pessimism of the intelligence' after the experiences of the spring and summer of 1920! The production process of capitalism in crisis no longer generates *of itself* the 'inner liberation'. This is precisely the force of the communist party (though this itself, of course, also 'emerges' from the crisis).

This is not simply to 'shift the emphasis to the party'. Too many interpreters treat the party and the council in Gramsci as entities which are distinct in a manner alien to his thinking. Their interrelation in the unity of theory and practice is difficult to grasp, let alone operate. But that is the difficulty of all communist practice, and there are several million martyrs to prove it. What is significant about this essay is that the *party* is fully charged with many of the functions (notably those of 'cultural revolution') formerly allotted to the *council*. The precise translation into party practice and council creation had still to be worked out. Gramsci tried to work it out in practice in the Lyons Theses. His party, for this reason, remained qualitatively different from Bordiga's. BUT the Lyons Theses themselves are what they are only because their *ultimate base* is itself *'Bordighist'*. Because what is called *Bordighism* was in truth, for these first years at least, the first essential historical *definition* of communism in the historical reality of Italy. Gramsci's communist party is present here in these two essays, as is his life's work on the problem of *proletarian hegemony*. But present also is Gramsci's commitment to that basic definition of Italian communism which was, historically and essentially, Bordiga's.

The twin crises of Italian socialism and the Comintern, and Italian socialism and the Occupation of the Factories, made Gramsci's commitment to the Bordigan definition total. His own particular vision had already been made marginal ; it remained marginal through the early years of Italian communism. And it became central to Italian communism when he had to take action – to defend the *original historical definition* of communism in Italy against threats which arose from Comintern policy and the *negative* character of Bordiga's resistance to them.

Despite the obvious and striking differences between Gramsci and Bordiga in their marxist practice, any interpretation which severs them totally and obliterates the fundamental consensus which unites them, robs the early history of Italian communism of both meaning and reality.

The communist party in practice was created by two crises. The first was the Second Congress of Comintern, 15 July–7 August 1920, at Petrograd and Moscow. This was in effect the real founding congress and its purpose was to define the Communist International. The lack of coherence of the Italian delegation astonished even this heterogeneous assembly. It is a commonplace to say that the *ordinovista* group was not represented. This is true, but it reflects a specific reality, in that the *ordinovista* 'group' had in effect ceased to exist. The central problem was the definition of the communist party, and the central conflict that between Lenin and Serrati. Serrati played down the reformist presence in the party, dismissing *Critica Sociale* (with a print-run of 953) and claiming that there were no Noskes in the PSI. Serrati was prepared to accept the crucial Twenty-one Points, but asked for more time and more flexibility in their execution. The root problem was in fact, *national autonomy*, as Serrati made perfectly clear on his return to Italy and in his citation of the 'concessions' made by Comintern to the French. Serrati himself was elected to the Executive of the International, but in response to the challenge of Lenin, in practice asserted the national particularity of Italy, especially on the peasant revolution, and rallied to the 'tradition' of the Socialist Party, with all its 'schools'. Lenin's call to 'expel Turati and then ally with him' evoked no real response. What was at stake was the very nature of the Italian party, which Serrati tended to assess in 'quantitative' terms, despite its 'polychrome' character. The issue was in fact referred to a congress of the PSI which was to decide on the Twenty-one Points. The characteristic equivocation of the PSI continued.

Bordiga, on the other hand, as spokesman for the communist tendency, was subjected to attack along the lines of *Left-wing Communism: an Infantile Disorder*. While maintaining his general position warmly supporting the Twenty-one Points and moving the toughest of them, Bordiga in fact altered his stance. Abstentionism, he declared, was not the 'fundamental fulcrum' of communist action ; the need was to create a communist party with a clear policy, not one founded on 'a negative distinction'. The abstentionists back home were already straining at the leash and hard to control. The reality of Bordiga's affirmation could be questioned. For several years after the founding of the Communist Party of Italy, there were complaints that the former abstentionists were forming a party within the party. Nevertheless, at the Second Congress of Comintern, Bordiga formally abandoned abstentionism (except for local elections) and committed his fraction to the organization of a communist party on as wide a base as possible.[14]

During the discussions, Lenin sprang his surprise. He singled out *L'Ordine Nuovo* and its *For a Renewal* of 8 May for praise, said that the article 'fully corresponded' to the principles of the Third International and was correct. This brought a storm of criticism on his head from every section of the Italian delegation. Bordiga, who had in fact presented the *ordinovista* case objectively, asserted that their general line could in no sense be accepted. They had maintained the unity of the Socialist Party, he claimed, to the very eve of the Milan council during the April conflict. Lenin, and Bukharin who had supported him, withdrew to the extent of admitting that they did not know enough to pass final judgement, but repeated that the specific article they referred to, *For a Renewal*, took a position they approved of.[15]

In the autumn of 1920, then, Gramsci faced a situation in which he and his minuscule tendency were isolated within the PSI, even if it was warmed by Lenin's commendation. He faced a maximalist left apparently wedded to equivocation, unable or unwilling to form an authentic communist party ; a left which embraced Tasca, Togliatti, Terracini and many other comrades who had joined the council communist enterprise. He faced a communist fraction whose instincts, symbolized by abstentionism, were unchanged, but which had formally dropped abstentionism and was passionately committed to the creation of a communist party and a rejection of the traditions of the PSI. Hobson had more choice.

Gramsci's 4 September article *The Communist Party* talks of the party 'rising from the ashes' of the socialist party and prefigures the rupture.

Optimism of the Will: the Anarcho-syndicalist Climax

The delegates returned from Moscow to find Italy paralyzed, with half a million workers occupying their factories and raising red and black flags over them.

The Occupation of the Factories exploded out of an ordinary wage agitation. Central to the climate of the crisis was the rise of the syndicalists.[16] It was not a matter of initiative. As in April, the initiative lay with the employers. Strongly organized in *Confindustria* and regional consortia, powered by an aggressive and militant group symbolized by the Perrone brothers, alarmed by the anti-plutocratic tone of the Giolitti government and its tentative gestures towards the socialists, the industrialists struck, struck hard and fought with grim tenacity. The massive working-class action was essentially a *response*.

Nor was it a matter of numbers within the working-class movement, though the syndicalists had been growing rapidly. Neither was it a question of the qualitative tone of the movement, at first. The crisis arose out of FIOM's campaign, which was a normal trade-union action. The condition of the working class, in the grip of inflation, with a threat of unemployment looming, was anything but 'normal'. More significant, perhaps, was the general climate of working-class opinion. The great moment had been expected for nearly two years and nothing had happened. Feelings were a compound of anger, half-hope or expectancy turning sour, and frustration. In the summer of 1920, the socialist movement was moving further from revolution, its communist minority trapped in conflict and nullity. The hunger for action found expression in syndicalist *styles*. They were *there*, calling for intransigence, self-help, action; they had their device – the seizure of factories and the building of a militant anti-state. Whether many workers accepted the doctrine may be doubted, but many, in increasing number, liked the style. Working-class response was by now essentially defensive, but response there had to be. FIOM negotiators had forever to look over their shoulders: the syndicalists were a point of reference. And when the crunch came, there was nothing for it but their remedy: workers marched into the factories. The scale of the response shocked everyone and is some measure of the pent-up frustration. In this climacteric the syndicalists themselves, perhaps inevitably, were transcended. But it was, without doubt, their climax.

The FIOM campaign grew out of the previous year's struggle.[17] The national agreement of March 1919 had left minimum pay scales and cost-of-living bonuses to regional negotiation. Despite a hard struggle in Lombardy and Liguria in the summer of 1919, this question had still not been settled; USI also objected to the factory regulations fixed in the agreement (which had been by-passed during the rise of the councils in Turin) and dissatisfaction was peculiarly acute in Liguria, where the syndicalists were strong. In Milan, with the rise of syndicalist influence during the summer of 1920, a campaign to create factory councils in the metal industry got under way.

FIOM had to take up the challenge; by this time a working-class family could not even keep going unless at least two of its members were working. FIOM worked out its aims at a congress in Genoa in May; a whole series of demands centred on a 40 per cent wage increase. Its claim was presented to the employers in June and was flatly rejected. An 'over-production' crisis was looming; the Giolitti government was distrusted but could be pressured for concessions; intransigence coalesced around an aggressive group led by the Perrone brothers, militant owners of the Ansaldo complex.

Other union federations joined the campaign. USI drafted a claim which paralleled FIOM's on pay, but denounced the factory regulations and called for workers' control over production through councils. The catholic union demanded profit-sharing. Across this scene blew the storm from Ancona, the syndicalist-led agitation over arms production and the sharp revulsion of the PSI and the CGL. The employers exploited the situation and demanded that all the union claims be discussed together. FIOM refused, citing 'moral reasons' for its opposition to joint action with USI.

Production was falling ; workers (and the government) suspected that the industrialists were forcing a stoppage in their own interests. In a rash of troubles involving Ansaldo in Liguria, workers demanded the arrest of the Perrone brothers. When the industrialists repeated their refusal of negotiations on 22 July, FIOM ordered a ban on overtime and the contending parties came together on 29 July.

The industrialists simply elaborated on the causes of the economic crisis and said a wage increase would be insupportable. The answer of USI was a 'punch in the face'. It was not the business of workers to take account of such matters but to defend their wages ; if capitalists could not run production, let them step aside. FIOM went into the detail of the argument and controversy raged. FIOM demanded proof of the employers' inability to meet their demands. The union was trapped by this basilisk intransigence of the industrialists, which paralyzed normal dispute procedure.

Meetings of workers were full of inflammatory talk when a final meeting with the employers on 10-13 August broke down, with the FIOM memorandum unconsidered. The industrialists' representative, Rotigliano, later a fascist, said to Bruno Buozzi of FIOM – 'There will be no concessions. Since the end of the war, we've done nothing but drop our pants. Now it's our turn. Now we're going to start on you.'[18]

FIOM called an extraordinary meeting of its national council and invited delegates of the PSI and the CGL. The financial state of both union and industry ruled out a strike, so the council decided on a carefully-controlled go-slow. Article 8 of the go-slow instructions yielded to the pressure of militants. If management countered the go-slow with a lock-out, workers were at once to occupy the plant and resume production. If necessary they were to batter in the gates.

The USI metal-workers, meeting at La Spezia on 17 August, opposed the go-slow as an ineffectual weapon. They called for both unions to occupy the factories. 'The expropriation of the factories by the metal-workers of Italy must be simultaneous and speedy before a lock-out shuts them out, and must then be defended by all necessary measures. We are determined, further, to call the workers of other industries into battle.' However, for the time being, they fell into line with FIOM 'in order not to divide the forces of the working class'.

The go-slow was an immediate success, but in the last week of August began to develop into a sit-down strike. Prefects' reports were full of syndicalist agitation, the collection of arms and supplies, talk of negotiations with local co-operatives. On 25 August, the government tried to intervene but were coldly rebuffed by the employers. In sharp contrast to the policy of the Nitti government in the previous April, Giolitti decided on, and held rigidly to, a policy of strict non-intervention, which included a refusal to put armed forces at the disposal of the employers. He was in fact sympathetic to CGL schemes for union control and joint management and was prepared to ride out a quasi-revolutionary moment.

It was clear that the industrialists were determined to stage a lock-out. USI called for a preventive occupation. Tempers rose. Work came to a stop at the Romeo plant in Milan, which had been active in the campaign against arms production and which was a Perrone shop. On 30 August, while the local prefect was still desperately trying to keep all lines open, the Romeo management locked out its 2,000 workers. The response of the Milan section of FIOM was automatic. Workers moved in to occupy over 300 factories in the Milan area.

There was an agonizing moment of indecision. The FIOM central committee in Turin, by this time shambling along behind the syndicalists, tried hard to hold the line ; it praised the Milan workers, but ordered everyone else to maintain the go-slow. Once more the decision was made for it. On the night of 31 August–1 September, the employers' federation in the metal industry ordered a general lockout throughout Italy, to be effected by local consortia. In the next few days a tidal wave of factory occupations rolled across the country until half a million workers were in action.

In Turin, the movement swept forward without check on the morning of 1 September. Thousands of workers poured into the factories and moved in discipline to their workplaces. The factory councils rose out of the ground and took over. 'Workers!', said Giovanni Parodi, entering his moment of glory as secretary of the commissars at Fiat-Centro. 'Show that, even without the bosses, you know how to run this factory!' The factories were gripped, armed for defence, ringed with red guards. Turin lived its workers' triumph as the climax of the council movement. The first Sunday, 5 September, was sheer euphoria, with songs and speeches everywhere.

And from the sidelines, moving once again to the centre, came the voice of that marginal man Antonio Gramsci, who spoke to the workers in Garrone-Fiat and who addressed them in characteristic terms from the Turin *Avanti* as *L'Ordine Nuovo* closed down for the struggle:

> The social hierarchies are broken. Historic values are overthrown. The *executive* classes, the *instrumental* classes are become *directive* classes. They have taken possession of themselves, they have found among themselves representative men to invest with the power of government, men who will undertake all those tasks which will transform an elementary and mechanical human aggregate into an organic brotherhood, a living creation . . .
>
> Today, Red Sunday of the metal-workers, the workers themselves must build the first historic cell of the proletarian revolution which thrusts through the general crisis with the irresistible power of a force of nature.[19]

10. The September Crisis

In response to the lockout, the metal-workers of Italy occupied their factories throughout the peninsula.[1] Between 1 and 4 September, the occupations rolled forward through Italy, not only in the industrial heartland around Milan, Turin and Genoa, but in Rome, Florence, Naples, Palermo, in a forest of red and black flags and a fanfare of workers' bands. In some small centres, the employers caved in at once and accepted the FIOM memorandum. Venezia Giulia was already convulsed by the fascist offensive. Otherwise the occupation was total. There was shooting at the Odero dockyard in Liguria, where royal guards killed one of the workmen clambering in over the stocks. Government averted a general strike by arresting some of the guards. Everywhere else, the security forces, under strict orders, stood back and red guards took command of the factories and their environs. Outside the industrial belt, most clerks and technicians went on working under workers' control for some time. In the great northern cities, the occupations grew into a dramatic mass movement, disciplined but fierce, arming itself and building defences . . . 'Workers! if the security forces try to break in, take to sabotage!' (Ansaldo shop, Sestri Ponente) . . . 'Workers! Show that you can scorn weariness, suffering, danger, in the cause of the emancipation of the human race from capitalist gangs!' (Brevetti-Fiat, Turin) . . . 'We want not wealth but freedom' (Fatme plant, Rome). Within three days, 400,000 workers were in occupation. As the movement spread to other sectors, the total rose to half a million. Everyone was stunned by the response: as in May 1968 in France, the frontiers of 'the possible', 'the normal', were suddenly breached. 'Everything goes on *normally* [my italics – GAW],' reported the prefect of Milan on 4 September, 'the workers . . . continue to arm themselves and to reinforce the defences.' An awe-struck Benito Mussolini went to find Bruno Buozzi and promised him fascist support if the 'revolution' was 'constructive'.[2]

Proletarian Order:
The Occupation of the Factories

On 6 September, the Florence section of FIOM ordered the election of factory councils in the occupied plants of the city. Every workshop was to elect one commissar; disciplinary power was to be exercised jointly by the workshop commissars and the old internal commissions; the council was to consist of equal numbers of representatives of the commissars and the white-collar workers. This is very different from the council system which had grown in the Turin complex during 1919-20; it lacks, in particular, the latter's 'autonomist' spirit. In fact, outside Turin, the 'conciliar' system of management, which inevitably emerged to run the occupation, was largely the product of joint action between FIOM branches and old-style internal commissions and tended to focus on the traditional centre, the *camera del lavoro*.[3]

The secretary of the CGL, D'Aragona, summed up his experience of the occupation later: 'We had plants where workers demonstrated real maturity and consciousness; others where the workers knew how to run their firm as it had been run under a capitalist. But we had others where, for a multitude of reasons which had nothing to do with the workers' maturity but everything to do with the lack of raw materials, the absence of technicians, leading personnel etc., the running of the plants proved to be impossible. And we had other factories which were deserted by the workers. We had to switch workers from one plant to another, to get a little nucleus inside which would give the impression that there were still workers there, to rule and run it.' Adelchi Baratono, too, at the PSI congress in January 1921, spoke of workers, 'poorly educated, too utilitarian perhaps', who insisted, before everything else, that they had to be supplied with the means to live, day by day, if they were to stay in the factories.

These were reformists, with an interest in playing down the experience. Syndicalists like Armando Borghi (who did not return from Russia until 20 September, however) talked of order, enthusiasm, discipline, regular labour, systematic exchange of raw materials and products and a rapid extension of the movement.[4]

In fact, there was a wide variety of response. Workers were in occupation for three to four weeks, without wages. What is remarkable is not that there was some crumbling of morale after a while: in fact, morale did not seriously decline until after the decisive meetings of 10-11 September when the socialist movement rejected revolution. What is remarkable is that it remained high for so long. Under heavy pressure from employers and newspapers and gripped by an agonizing wait-and-see paralysis, many technicians and white-collar workers abandoned the plants. This defection, together with supply difficulties, made production problematic. FIOM wanted to maintain the go-slow under the occupation, but in many places there were demands for an intensification of production and the sale of products. In fact, in many plants production at first increased over pre-go-slow levels, and several local *camere* organized sporadic sales. This did not last and results were very patchy. FIOM, with the CGL behind it, was anxious to keep the movement, as far as was possible in the circumstances, on strict 'trade-union' lines. The consequence was *improvization*, both within the factory and between production units, which remained under FIOM and *camera* control. Immediate needs were met by 'communist kitchens', hundreds of gestures of spontaneous solidarity and, above all, by a massive loan which FIOM raised from the co-operative movement. Significantly, it was alleged by Angelo Tasca (who was in a position to know) that the loan was surreptitiously guaranteed by the *Banca Commerciale Italiana* whose directors 'assured FIOM of their benevolent neutrality, offered and asked for pledges in case the movement ended in revolution'! The bank was regarded as Giolittian ; its alleged attitude would certainly be in line with Giolitti's own. As the Mazzonis occupation in February had shown, the workers' action, however radical in spirit, lent itself to exploitation in a strictly reformist and 'trade-union' sense.[5]

The syndicalist alternative had its own limitations. 'For us anarchists,' said *Umanità Nova* on 4 September, 'the movement is very serious and we must do everything we can to channel it towards a massive extension. We must lay down a precise programme which can be realized, completed, perfected in radical action every day ; we must foresee today the difficulties and the obstacles of tomorrow, so that the movement does not run aground and break up on the rocks of reformism.'[6] The militants of USI were certainly in the forefront of the movement, but in their very success, they ran the risk of being by-passed and superseded as the practical problems of workers' management and daily survival increasingly obsessed internal commissions and *camere*.

Their persistent call was for an extension of the movement to the whole of industry to institute their 'expropriating general strike'. And it was the syndicalists, through the railwaymen they influenced, who achieved the only *qualitative* development of the movement which transcended localism. From the beginning, the railwaymen had given support to the movement, particularly in Turin. As lorries commandeered by workers shuttled supplies between the occupied plants, sometimes stopped but never requisitioned by *carabinieri* and royal guards, the Turin section of the railway union, on 3 September, instructed its men to assist metalworkers in the 'liberation' of trucks loaded with fuel and raw material from the depots. The rail men sent them along the tracks and sidings feeding the plants. On 6 September, the rail union at Turin ordered its members not to return trucks to their stations of origin but to direct them to the factory sidings instead. On the same day, Fiat-Lingotto got 21 truckloads; on the following day, 14 truckloads of vital material fed other plants. This action caused a panic on the state railway board. The Minister of War, Bonomi, prepared for the militarization of the railways. The government was more alarmed by this than by the arming of workers, for it threatened to make the 'anti-state' an operative reality.[7]

The syndicalists, however, paid little attention to the factory councils except as combat units and bases for an extension of the movement. They, like the reformists, could do little to transcend the 'factory egoism' and the *localism* which were the inevitable immediate consequences of the occupation. In the Genoa complex, for example, with 100,000 *metalos* dominated by Ansaldo, there were three *camere* at daggers drawn (a situation paralleled elsewhere). Nervi was controlled by reformists, Sampierdarena and Voltri by maximalists, with syndicalists making the running as a militant and influential minority. The syndicalists controlled the *camera* at Sestri Ponente: 14,000 workers under Antonio Negro and a journal *La Lotta Operaia*. They were also dominant in Savona and La Spezia. The occupation here, as at some other strongholds like Verona, was incendiary. But while their actions were flamboyant and 'exemplary', and while agents of the internal commissions took over warehouses and even ships and a workshop commissariat established effective relationships with the co-operatives and 'traditional' working-class shops in a lively spirit of fraternity, they were not sufficiently serious in their creation of councils. *Two weeks* after the occupation began, the Genoa committee of agitation was still vainly asking workers for lists of council members.[8]

In these circumstances, apart from the ripple on the railways, which authority was exerting itself to block, there was no real escape from the isolated localism of the 'proletarian republics', as Gramsci called the occupied factories. His voice was the clearest. As was its habit, *L'Ordine Nuovo* closed down for the struggle and Gramsci and his group toured the factories. In the Turin edition of *Avanti*, however, they developed the case for a qualitative extension of the struggle. On 2 September, Gramsci argued that a mere occupation of the factories would establish no new and decisive positions because 'power stays in capitalism's fist'. Occupation was *not* an experiment in direct communist management. 'The proletariat has no coercive means to overcome the sabotage of technicians and clerical staff. It cannot provision the factories with raw materials and it cannot sell the goods produced.' Giolitti's ihtention was to sit out the crisis, to wear down the proletariat to the point 'when it will itself fall to its knees'. He urged workers to create 'a loyal armed force, ready for anything'. The next day he called the occupation a 'symbol' of a situation which was so revolutionary that ordinary trade-union practice was no longer possible. It must not become a synonym for revolution ; the eventual disillusionment would prove catastrophic. On the 5th, when he spoke at one of the factories which were living a 'revolutionary' euphoria, he returned to the charge. The necessities of factories trying to operate in isolation would force attention on the concrete problems of creating an urban soviet with its organized military force. No solution was possible unless the focus of the struggle were shifted to the real centres of the capitalist system : the means of communication, the banks, the armed forces, the state. By the 7th, Piero Gobetti was telling his girl that Turin was in the midst of a real revolution – 'a tiny minority (basically *L'Ordine Nuovo*, not Gramsci or Togliatti so much as the workers who support them) has assumed authority, with a complete disregard for personal sacrifice.'[9]

For in a manner which since 1912 had become 'traditional', Turin was the outstanding exception.[10]

By 3 September, 185 factories in Turin had been occupied and over 100,000 workers were in action. On the first morning at Fiat-

Centro, the workshop commissars and their internal commission took over control of discipline and attendance, made an inventory of materials and work completed. The workers' and the technicians' commissions went into permanent session. Giovanni Parodi, secretary of the commissars, the abstentionist who had worked closely with *L'Ordine Nuovo*, reported that 35 vehicles were produced on the 3rd, as against 27 under the go-slow and 67 on a normal day. The factory council, under Parodi's leadership, assumed more and more functions ; it created special commissariats to handle defence, transport, raw materials. The council appointed the red guards and armed them (a deal of production everywhere in the early days was of 'arms' of some kind or other). The communist groups were re-activated, but worked strictly through the factory council. Fiat-Centro – *Fiat Soviet* to its telephone operator – became the pilot-plant of the entire movement, but Turin factories generally, with their integrated character and their year-long experience of the councils, were thoroughly organized along conciliar lines.

All the main vehicle and coach-building works had been occupied and FIOM, here largely under workshop commissar influence, set up a Directive Committee, with several technicians serving, to co-ordinate the exchange of products and raw materials. It is an interesting comment on the limitations even of the Turin movement that *exchanges between different branches of the same firm did not require Committee authorization, whereas exchanges between different firms did.*[11] The pre-existing capitalist structure was thus maintained under workers' control. There was nothing like the drastic re-organization and rationalization of industry under workers' control which the CNT-UGT committees effected in Barcelona during the Spanish Revolution of 1936. But of course, in Spain, *state power* had disintegrated.

But if the Turin system remained imprisoned within a capitalist *definition* of 'industry', its 'internal' life was thoroughly communist. The Directive Committee demanded an inventory of stocks and work in hand from every plant. Copies were to go to the factory council, the regional committee, and the technical section of the central committee of agitation at Milan. Fiat-Centro, it was found, had enough stocks to keep up production for two months. But individual centres were absolutely forbidden to sell goods themselves. 'Production is for the collectivity and as such ought to be adminis-

tered by superior organizations which represent the interests of all.'
What the Directive Committee had in mind was 'possible direct trade
with Soviet Russia which – it is not inconceivable – may supply the
means to consolidate the workers' gains'.[12]

Within the factory, full 'communist order' was maintained.
Alcohol was strictly forbidden ; no one could enter or leave without
permission. Workers were searched and thieves severely punished (as
they were generally throughout the occupation : concern with 'morality' was obsessive and, directed at winning outside approval,
thoroughly 'bourgeois'). Red guards maintained surveillance both
within and without the gates. Very soon, there were heavy defections
of technicians and clerical staff, under pressure. Persuasion gave way
to threats, which were also directed against worker absentees. 'The
factory council gives notice to all technicians, office personnel and
workers,' ran a communiqué from the factory council of Diatto
Frejus on 3 September, 'that, from tomorrow 4 September, anyone
absent without good cause will be considered dismissed. Great new
events are preparing for the proletarian future. In expectation of
victory – solidarity! solidarity! solidarity!'[13] In Turin, many technicians remained loyal to communist order. The engineer Romita was
a key figure in the co-ordinating committees. Absenteeism was low ;
it rarely rose above 10 per cent of the labour force. Production was
substantial and not only at Fiat. Even in steel, which in this context
was a subsidiary sector, the suspect testimony of Camurri, director of
the Piedmont *Ferrieri* and an assiduous propagandist against the
councils, indicates a total of 3,978 tons at the *Ferrieri* in July, 3,093 in
August and 1,895 in September. Given the exceptional situation and
the large-scale withdrawal of engineers and technicians, this was a
notable figure.[14]

Romita made his mark as an agent of the *camera*. For by 13
September, the *camera* had taken at least nominal control. The movement was moving out of the metal sector. The first extensions were
'technical'. To make sure of essential supplies, FIOM ordered the
occupation of the oxygen plant in Turin. *The gasworkers obeyed at
once.*[15] This seems to have encouraged a general movement of occupation. The Michelin tyre works were taken over on 10 September,
by which time, about 150,000 workers were occupying their plants in
the Turin region. The Turin *camera* proclaimed on 13 September that
no more factories should be occupied without its permission. The

executive commission of the local section of the PSI, under the control of the *electionist communist* fraction led by Togliatti, moved in, and a new Directive Committee was created with four sub-committees, for technical, legal, supply and propaganda service. A special Exchange and Production Committee was set up: delegates from FIOM and the technicians' union under a *camera* chairman. It was this *camera*-based organization which took over the running of 'communist kitchens' supplied by the Turin Co-operative Alliance. Money found in the factories – 250,000 lire at Fiat-Centro, 60,000 at Brevetti-Fiat – was distributed to workers' families. The *camera* issued 200,000 5-lire vouchers and the co-operative and the union of small shopkeepers agreed to respect them; FIOM followed suit. By mid-September, the Turin councils, co-ordinated through the *camera* committees and directed by the *electionist communist* PSI section, were moving rapidly towards Gramsci's 'urban soviet' in an atmosphere of high communist purpose.

But not even Turin could survive within its own private world. As with the original *Ordine Nuovo* councils; as with the syndicalist enterprise, there had to be a *translation* into wider and political action. When the oxygen plant was occupied, the council of the local Turin leagues passed a resolution promising action if other industrialists went to the assistance of their colleagues in metal. It added: 'The struggle of the metalworkers opens a new era in the class struggle which will close only with the establishment of workers' control over all production.'[16]

The first Red Sunday, 5 September, was a festival. But before the bands and speakers had fallen silent, the atmosphere was suddenly charged with tension.

The Week of the Great Fear

Giolitti did not budge from his holiday hide-away in Bardonecchia, which remained his Colombey-les-deux-églises throughout the crisis. As press clamour climbed into panic and the lira plummeted on the exchanges, he remained ostentatiously calm, pinning his faith in the 'good sense' of workers and the CGL, confident that experience would teach workers the need for collaboration, resolute against the industrialists' demand for military action. The scurrying of the Minister of Labour, Labriola, and Lusignoli, prefect of Milan, were beneath his official cognisance. The employers remained rigid in total intransigence. But at the end of the first week, a desperate Agnelli rushed to Bardonecchia to demand, once again, that troops be turned loose on the factories. Giolitti blandly offered to bombard Fiat with artillery and a spavined Agnelli collapsed.[17]

The president of the council was secure. Bruno Buozzi repeatedly affirmed that FIOM was ready to open talks the moment the industrialists shuffled out of intransigence and on 3 September, the union published in *Avanti* a specific denial of any revolutionary intentions: 'the factories are in the hands of the workers only to prevent a lengthy struggle; this dispute must be resolved within a few days, to spare the country any more agitation and the workers any more useless sacrifice'. On the same day, by fateful coincidence, the reformists' *socialist concentration* fraction published their manifesto calling for a realistic socialist concentration on practical reformist objectives, and announcing a fraction meeting in Reggio Emilia on the 19th. It was signed not only by Turati, but by Buozzi, Baldesi and other CGL stalwarts.[18]

But already the ground was moving under their feet. The very act of occupation transformed the climate in working-class districts. There was a sudden access of aspiration. The syndicalist agitation was eroding moderation in all the big centres. In any event, the occupation could not stand still. From every centre, rose a demand to extend the action. Treves and Turati were gripped with fear. The former went so far as to contact the government and warn them of a threat of insurrection from masses in fever, of maximalist incitement. Lusignoli, prefect of Milan, supported by Corradini at the Ministry of the Interior and Arturo Labriola, made desperate efforts to ward off an extension of the occupation. He got Buozzi to agree to a smaller wage increase provided the industrialists would finance co-operatives to cut the cost of living. But the employers, led by Rotigliano of Ilva, blankly refused any wage concession. They saw no reason to yield.

And in the next few days the occupations rolled inexorably forward out of the metal sector. Between 6 and 8 September, occupation extended to the Fratte foundry in Salerno, the lignite mines of Castelnuovo Magra, factories in Padua and all the engineering works of Reggio Emilia, Oneglia and Rapallo. In Turin, all the large, small and medium plants, cars, coaches, foundries, service plants, railway material, marine engines, machine tools, bolts, precision instruments and typewriters, were taken over and the movement drove into the rubber firms, Spiga, Michelin, Martiny, Tedeschi, Saiga. Footwear plants, the tannery, textiles, four wool-factories, four hosiery firms, the artificial silk plant, fell. In Milan, Pirelli was taken over, the Campari distillery, the Italia beer plant, the Hutchinson rubber firm. The *camera* was discussing a wholesale seizure of the chemical plants to make sure of supplies. In Liguria, all warehouses were menaced and three ships were taken over. At a workers' control launching, the ship-master hailed the collapse of joint-stock companies, 'the curse of Italy'. With every occupation, the temper of the occupying workers rose.

But by this time the CGL had clumped into action. An emergency session of the 'states-general' of the workers' movement was held at Milan on 4-5 September.[19] The directive council of the CGL met the PSI Directorate and delegates from the major *camere*. The national council of the CGL was to meet in Milan on 10 September. This was the crucial date. The meeting called the leadership of the socialist parliamentary group to join the CGL national council and announced that the party and union leaders would 'sit in permanence' until 10 September, when all the forces of the political and union movement would assemble to come to a more precise decision on the objective of the struggle and the means to be adopted. And meanwhile, to hold the line? The meeting announced that if no satisfactory solution to the dispute in the metal industry were achieved, thanks to the stubbornness of the employers or the partiality of the government, then the proletarian organizations would direct the struggle towards the establishment of 'control over industry, to achieve collective management and the socialization of the means of production'.

The press exploded in rage and panic. Was a dispute in one sector of industry to precipitate the final solution? 'Where do they want to go?' shouted Albertini in *Il Corriere della Sera*, front-runner of the conservative press, 'To the revolution? There is no one, not a reformist, not even a maximalist, who seriously believes in the possibility of a revolution in which a good third of the population of Italy would perish from hunger and poverty.' Giolitti sat tight. Not a single factory would he requisition.[20]

But the next day, news came through of land-occupations in

he South. Near Palermo, 300 peasants, near Potenza, 600 peasant ex-
servicemen, marched into estates under the leadership of *popolari*.
And the PSI Directorate, to hold its rank and file, responded in traditional manner. On 6 September in a full blaze of publicity and a full
flood of maximalist rhetoric, it published a manifesto to peasants and
soldiers. 'Proletarians in uniform' were urged to resist their officers,
to refuse to attack the factories ; peasants were called on to support
the metalworkers who would eliminate the 'sharks'' profits of the
owners and feed the countryside cheaper machines. 'If tomorrow the
hour of decisive struggle strikes, the battle against all the bosses, you,
too, rally! Take over the communes, the lands, disarm the *carabinieri,*
form your battalions in unity with the workers, march on the great
cities, take your stand with the people in arms against the hireling
thugs of the bourgeoisie! For the day of justice and liberty is perhaps
at hand!'[21] The 'perhaps' was characteristic, but however meaningless the words, they were strong. The fever rose visibly in the factories. On that same day, the syndicalists, meeting in Milan, were
discussing a simultaneous occupation of industries, mines, fields and
mansions and on the 7th, a regional convention of Ligurian unions
meeting in Sampierdarena agreed to occupy Genoa and all the ports
of Liguria and to follow up with an occupation of every branch of
production. They were stopped only by a speech from Maurizio
Garino, the metalworker from Turin, a libertarian and FIOM leader,
ally of the *ordinovisti*. He maintained that on the 10th, the CGL
would itself call for a general occupation and he persuaded them to
hold their hand for three days. On the same day, back in Turin, the
Study Committee for Factory Councils, now dominated by syndicalists, called on workers everywhere to form factory councils ready for
the day. The proclamation was vague, intolerably vague for a reader
of *L'Ordine Nuovo*, but the tone was dramatic : 'Be alert to the possibilities of the present dispute, which may reach a climax from one
moment to the next. Get ready to support the struggle in any way you
can. Let every workshop elect its representative, every work-unit its
commissar. Create factory councils everywhere and stand by for any
eventuality.'[22]

A police spy reported the next day that FIOM and the CGL
were desperately trying to avoid a general occupation, but would
have to satisfy the workers somehow, win *some* kind of victory, or
everything would 'fall to pieces'. A general occupation, he thought,

would surely provoke a violent right-wing reaction from the bour
geoisie.[23] On the 9th, in truth, 300 industrialists protested to the pre
fect of Turin against government inaction and threatened to organize
direct action themselves. On the same day, the workers at Fiat
Centro, maddened by the discovery of a black-list and espionage
reports in the Fiat offices, sent a telegram to the central committee
of agitation in Milan: 'The workers of Fiat-Centro intend to negoti
ate only in terms of the abolition of the ruling and exploiting class
Otherwise, immediate war to total victory.'[24]

     Three days earlier, cannon with guard-shields had been
wheeled into the Piazza Castello in front of the Turin prefecture and
machine-gun nests had sprouted in the streets, after a night when the
factory sirens suddenly howled and hundreds of women and children
had poured out of the working-class quarters to block the factory
gates. In Milan the next evening, the prefect mobilized the security
forces along the line of the Naviglio to protect the banks from a
rumoured sortie. In all the major centres, armed force was deployed
under strict instructions to stay calm, but menacing in their strength
Prefects' reports run to a crescendo: 'In the factories the most exalted
elements feel that the moment of triumph for their ideals approaches
. . . strong armed detachments make ready to invade the city . . . The
occupiers have machine-guns . . . They claim to have armed a tank
built at Fiat for the state.' On the 6th, two AVS aircraft took off from
Turin airport and showered the city with maximalist leaflets. By the
9th, Corradini and the military were planning the armed defence of
every major city.[25]

     'I retain a vivid memory of one scene in Turin during the
occupation of the factories', Gramsci wrote to his wife some years
later. 'The military committee were discussing the necessity, which
might arise at any moment, of a sortie of armed workers from the
factories. They all seemed to be drunk. They were on the point of
coming to blows. Responsibility crushed them, chewed them to a
pulp. One of them who got to his feet, who had lived through five
years of war as an aviator and had brushed death many times,
staggered and seemed about to collapse. With a tremendous effort of
will, I intervened and made them smile with a witticism, led them
back to normal and profitable work.'[26]

     Gramsci sounds, as he often does, like a marxist Head Pre-
fect. What sort of 'normal and profitable work' *was* a 'military com-

nittee' to undertake? What his anecdote illustrates, perhaps unconsciously, is the *unreality* of any talk of an insurrectionary solution.
Fiat-Centro had 5,000 rounds of machine-gun ammunition; 'ten
minutes of fire'. Are you comrades in Turin ready to attack? a delegate was asked on the 9th. 'If you are talking about a sortie from the
factories to fight in the streets,' he replied, 'we would be finished in
ten minutes.' Not even the syndicalists thought of action in this sense.
Unlike their comrades of the Spanish CNT, they no longer conceived of 'revolution' essentially in terms of 'fire-power'.

There certainly were arms in the factories and weapons of
some kind were made there. For the most part, they were revolvers,
pikes, 'sometimes model 91 rifles or cavalry muskets'. A police raid
on Fiat-Lingotto failed to seize some machine-guns which were distributed between occupied plants. But on the 9th, twelve military
trucks took away 60,000 explosive charges from a plant of the
Metalgraf at Lecco, *after talks between the sub-prefect and the
internal commission.*[27] Gramsci waxed sarcastic over this performance at the socialist 'capital' in Milan, but in fact, all the military
preparations of the workers were essentially *defensive.* Even the raids
and sorties, primarily against banks, which were without doubt discussed, were at base *supplements* to the occupation. Angelo Tasca
was accurate enough: 'Armed insurrection was impossible because
nothing was ready. The masses felt secure behind the walls of the factories not only because of their weapons, which were actually primitive and inadequate, but because they thought of the factories as
securities which the government would hesitate to destroy by artillery
fire in order to expel the occupiers. Between this defensive attitude
and open struggle in the streets, the difference is great, and the workers
sensed it in more or less confused manner. In Turin itself, even where
there was a bold vanguard better armed than elsewhere, communist
leaders refrained from every initiative of this type and restrained
those groups which at Fiat had prepared trucks for a sortie.'[28]

Moreover, a characteristic symptom of the movement, it
proved impossible to plan any *co-ordinated* defence. Every factory
looked to its own defences, like a *militia.* There was no co-ordination.
There was no communist party.

It is symptomatic that what finally brought Giolitti into
action was worry over the arms deposits which workers should have
found in the arms factories when they took over. What worried

Giolitti however, was the deep suspicion that industrialists knew all about the arms deposits, but were withholding the information in an effort to blackmail the government into taking armed action against the workers. Under these circumstances, said Giolitti, we have the right to *compel* the industrialists to come to terms. And he re-opened the lines to Buozzi. Buozzi, in turn, could say only that the conflict now concerned not merely the metalworkers but the whole Italian proletariat. He pointed to the 'assizes' of the socialist movement which were to assemble on 10 September.[29]

Of those 'assizes' Lenin was to say, 'During the occupation of the factories, did *one single* communist make an appearance in Italy?'[30] This was harsh and unfair. Communists there were in plenty. Communist *party* there was none. Its absence was painfully obvious in the military field. The essential weapon of the movement was a general occupation. The consequences of such action would have been unpredictable. But there *are* symptoms. On 15 September, Albertini of *Il Corriere della Sera*, spokesman for Italy's rooted and respectable conservatism, declared that there was only one way out of an intolerable situation: the government *must give power to the CGL*. Between 21 and 23 September he went to see Turati and 'offered' him power.[31]

Recollect the general strike of May-June 1968 in France and the similar absence of a party geared to the revolutionary assumption of power. At the meeting in Charléty stadium to create one on 26 May, it was Mendès-France and the PSU who appeared as the political *translation*. During the manic last two days, with de Gaulle's 'disappearance', when the unthinkable finally *had* to be thought, when 'normality' had to be either restored or qualitatively changed, when the Communist Party and the CGT finally sent their hundreds of thousands on to the streets 'alone' – 'Adieu, de Gaulle!' – the *only* 'practical political' solution, other than anarchic civil war, seemed a Mitterrand or Popular Front 'translation'. This would probably still have been true, even if the CGT *had* given the word for 'workers' control'. That the installation of such a government, even more the manner of its installation, might have initiated a revolutionary *process*, is conceivable. To quote St Just, from an earlier revolution – 'The Revolution only *begins* when the Tyrant *dies*.'

But the Tyrant did not die. Consider the rout which de Gaulle inflicted on the French Left in his 'master-stroke' – in fact a reading of the balance of *political* forces and the well-timed extraction of the maximum 'magic' from it: Giolitti's master-stroke in September 1920 had the same quality. The Old Fox of Colombey like the Old Fox of Dronero knew better than professed marxists that the relations of immediate 'political power' are *mediated* human relations and at the crunch *irrational*. In a total crisis of 'political' confidence they understood *power*'s quality of magic, of bluff, the black humour essential to its maintenance or overthrow (itself a 'superstructural' reflection of the revolutionary rupture, the transcending of 'normality'). They confronted professed marxist parties which could not conceive of 'magic', let alone black humour, as an element in the dialectic. Genuine leaders of the 'revolutionary moment' – Lenin, Trotsky in 1917, Mao – have never made this error. But genuine leaders of the 'revolutionary moment' – Lenin, Trotsky in 1917, Mao, have, of course, been marxist *historians*, not historical *rapporteurs* like Serrati or a-historical militants who substitute activism for analysis.

The basic, immediate, human obstacle to revolutionary action is the rooted *sense of the normal* (the return of which one senses and awaits even as the rubbish piles up in strike-bound streets and a torrent of unprecedented talk breaks over the paralysed city): the *normality* which is the ultimate mystification of the mode of production, the lubricant which makes tolerable an objectively insufferable situation. At the point when a crisis becomes 'intolerable', it *has* to be broken, by an exercise in 'magic' carefully inserted into a correctly-read balance of actual and potential force: a disappearance, a return from an invisible but 'present' army, a communiqué ribbed with an ancient authority, a well-staged spontaneous demonstration, a release of petrol to the pumps for a 'normal' Whitsun weekend. The Old Foxes had built careers out of creative bluff; fit saviours for capitalism. They even talked the same language – of 'participation', both a structural and a black-humorist necessity. Since the structure of their respective societies was in truth objectively changing, their victories proved a species of personal, and to differing degrees, 'political' suicide. But the 'marxists' simply lost and returned to the 'normality' of a licensed opposition.

By 10 September 1920, the situation in Italy was becoming 'intolerable'. The socialists of Italy, unable to take either the revolutionary or the reformist road, had no magic left in them. They had no bluff left, except the final one. They responded to their deepest instincts ; they reverted to 'normal'. *They put the issue to the vote.*

This, of course, was itself a 'decision'. One delegate in Milan commented, chauvinistically but accurately: 'You don't make a revolution by first calling a convention to decide whether there is going to be a revolution or not. This was Mexican stuff they were trying to import.'[32]

Three Days in Milan

The decision was in fact taken on the first of the three days which shook the Italian socialist movement.[33] On 9 September, the directive council of the CGL met, with some PSI representatives, to make a preliminary 'inventory' of the situation. Here, the delegates from Turin, Togliatti for the PSI section, Benso for the provincial federation, were subjected to interrogation. The CGL asked them : are you ready to move to the attack, yourselves in the van, where to attack means precisely to start a movement of armed insurrection?

Togliatti said no.

'If there is an attack on the factories, the defence is ready and should be effective ; not so an attack. The city is ringed by a non-socialist zone. To find proletarian forces which could help the city, we would have to go as far as Vercelli and Saluzzo. We want to know if you have decided on a violent insurrectionary attack. We want to know what your objectives are. You cannot count on an action launched by Turin alone. We will not attack on our own. It demands a simultaneous action in the countryside. Above all, it demands action on a national scale. We want assurance on this point. Otherwise we will not commit our proletariat.'

All the hatreds of the previous April bubbled to the surface. Did the CGL want to destroy the Turin movement? Was Turin to be exposed to the full force of government coercion as in April? Gramsci said that the countryside which had supported Turin in April, was hostile in September ; because of 'the vile campaign that trade-union officials and Serrati opportunists waged against the Turin communists, the whole organization created for the region from Turin had completely collapsed.'

Benso made the same points and thought a trade-union solution of the conflict the only way out. Togliatti favoured an extension of the occupation and an insurrection, if necessary, provided it were national in scope.

The CGL's purpose was to stamp out any threat of revolution. They told the Russians, in reply to criticism, that revolution would mean civil war and famine. Italy would be isolated in Europe, under American power and exposed to blockade. Turin was recognized as a 'communist vanguard' city. Its admission of insurrectionary incapacity was a powerful weapon.[34]

On 10 September the formal meetings began. They operated strictly within the terms of the Pact of Alliance. The PSI Directorate (many of its leading members, including Serrati, were absent, on their way home from Moscow) met in the morning and issued a formal declaration of intent. It would 'assume the responsibility and the leadership of the movement, to extend it to the whole country and the entire proletarian mass'. The movement was to embrace all industries and become a permanent expropriation. It would absorb all other movements in train and drive towards the seizure of the land.

'We had to expect and we did expect that the bourgeoisie . . . would resort to extreme defensive measures, while it kept its grip on political power and all the defensive force of the state', reported the Directorate in January 1921, 'We pressed for rapid and immediate preparation, to sustain momentum, to move to the attack, to seize political power. The expropriation could have become definitive, reconstruction in a communist sense possible, only with a victory of the proletariat in the political field.' The workers, strengthened by 'the security they held in their hands', would have mobilized maximum revolutionary audacity, confident that this was the final struggle.[35]

This imperious position was abandoned in a matter of hours. It is difficult to think of it as anything other than a ritual exercise.

The directive council of the CGL met on the same day and drew up a wholly contradictory resolution. It was the CGL which would assume leadership of the movement; 'the objective of the struggle shall be the recognition by employers of the principle of union control over companies. This will open the way to those major gains which will inevitably lead to collective management and socialization and thus organically solve the problem of production.'

The CGL, then, proposed its own 'political' solution ; no revolution but an extension of the campaign for 'union control' to all industries and increased financial support for FIOM. It was without doubt what Tasca called 'a retreat forward'; a way out. But it corresponded to basic CGL thinking, manifest since 1917 and the controversy over the Constituent as a Labour Parliament. The discovery of secret papers in the Fiat offices had stimulated demands for 'control'. Moreover, and this was perhaps the essential point, the union leaders, in constant touch with the prefects of Milan and Turin, knew that Giolitti's thinking was consonant with theirs. The CGL solution was 'possibilist', would evoke some response from, offer the prospect of 'victory' to, workers who were tense, strained, hungry and tired, with pinched wives and children, desperately anxious for a 'qualitative' change of some kind. Their unions would take over.

That evening, 10 September, the CGL leaders and the PSI men met in dramatic confrontation. D'Aragona, Baldesi, Dugoni presented the political leaders with a stark choice. 'You believe,' said D'Aragona, 'that this is the moment for the revolution. Very well, then. *You* assume responsibility. We who do not feel able to shoulder this responsibility – the responsibility for throwing the proletariat into suicide – we say we will withdraw. We submit our resignation. We feel that, at this moment, the sacrifice of our persons is called for. *You* take the leadership of the whole movement.' D'Aragona and the others told the party secretary Gennari that 'they were ready to face every risk, every danger', once it had been made clear that they no longer had any responsibility. Gennari later publicly acknowledged the honesty of their statement.

There is no reason to doubt their sincerity. It will be noted, however, that they posed the choice solely in terms of insurrection, just as on the international plane, they talked of nothing but isolation and blockade. They must have been aware of the immense power at their backs, in the unions and in the whole establishment of socialist communes, co-operatives and deputies. They must have been familiar with what had become the 'tradition' of maximalist practice. The real problem was 'the masses' pullulating in the factories. But to them, the PSI was even more 'external' than the CGL.

The response of the PSI leaders was probably inscribed in their history. Terracini (who was present) told Comintern later: 'When the comrades who led the CGL submitted their resignations, the party leadership could neither replace them nor hope to replace them. It was Dugoni, D'Aragona, Buozzi who led the CGL; they were at all times the representatives of the masses.' We could not accept so grave a responsibility, said Gennari to the socialist congress ('Because you were afraid', cried a voice). It was Gramsci's military committee: responsibility crushed them, chewed them to a pulp. The decision stands as its own comment not only on two years, but perhaps on twenty years of the history of the socialist party.[36]

The renunciation was followed by a more ambiguous decision. The representatives of the parliamentary group were present but, under the Pact of Alliance, had no say. If the party Directorate refused to accept the resignations of the CGL leaders and take over the movement at executive level, where was the decision to be made? The national council of the *party* was ruled out; its assembly, it was said, would take too long. But the national council of the *union federation* was present. The Directorate decided to refer the decision to the national council of the CGL, full of trade-union officers, delegates from reformist *camere*, the great mass of rural labour, many of them remote from the *political* implications of the struggle and from experience of the struggle itself.

The national council of the CGL on 10-11 September was faced with three motions.[37] The CGL called for the campaign for union control under CGL leadership. For the party, Schiavello of Milan and Bucco of Bologna moved a motion – 'The national council of the CGL requests the Directorate of the party to take over the direction of the movement and to lead it towards the maximum solution of the socialist programme, that is, the socialization of the means of production and exchange.' Buozzi of FIOM submitted his own motion, which took an intermediary position. It proposed to extend the movement to all industries with the aim of 'effecting all the political and economic reforms most insistently demanded by the socialist proletariat which are compatible with the condition of the country'. It is quite possible that the 'revolutionary reformism' of Buozzi's motion in fact most accurately reflected the temper of the masses of workers in occupation, as opposed to that of the committed militants, but its vagueness and ambiguity could not stand between the two more clearcut positions around which opinion swiftly polarized. Buozzi himself found the Schiavello-Bucco motion terrifying. 'How, I said (to Gennari) can you submit such a motion to public debate in a convention? To warn the whole Italian bourgeoisie that tomorrow we are going to extend the movement to all industries for an immediate overthrow of the bourgeois regime? And I said to Gennari: with this resolution you are inviting the most immediate and ruthless of reactions.' In the event, Buozzi withdrew his motion and the FIOM representatives largely abstained.

The debate rehearsed positions already assumed. D'Aragona expressly rejected the Russian model for the Italian revolution. Delegates should be absolutely clear that if they voted for the Schiavello-Bucco resolution, they were voting for communist revolution and the dictatorship of the proletariat. The CGL was working for 'that type of socialism which cannot be destroyed'. Its principle of trade-union control of industry would eventually lead to collective administration and socialization. Gennari expressly called for the occupation of all enterprises in order to realize the communist revolution. Tasca, who argued his own council-communist case for the metal industry, supported the Schiavello-Bucco motion.

The result was a clear but not overwhelming victory for the CGL.

CGL motion:	591,245
Schiavello-Bucco:	409,569
Abstentions (FIOM):	93,623

This voting pattern conceals one decisive fact of structural significance. By September 1920, the CGL was 1,930,000 strong. Voting in Milan, however, was on the 1919 figures totalling nearly 1,100,000. The report of the International Labour Office (which supported the CGL line) stressed the fact that the rural workers were thus only half represented, since during 1920 membership of the rural unions, of *Federterra*, had risen from 400,000 to 890,000. Had the rural workers polled in real strength, claimed the ILO, the CGL motion would have got a million votes.

The rural workers' delegates certainly voted for the CGL.[88] Mazzoni, leader of *Federterra*, recalled in 1949 that, at Milan, he had openly fought against any irrevocable actions which 'would have recoiled upon the most impoverished and weakest proletariat – the field workers'. At the moment of the Milan meeting, a ferocious struggle in Bologna province, which had raged since February, was reaching its climax. In October, socialists won a Pyrrhic victory which precipitated a major fascist offensive. What is striking about the rural socialist movement is not only its ferocity, but its isolated and often deeply corporate character. Government recognition of socialist-run labour exchanges had been the point of entry and in whole series of often violent campaigns, which enraged the local middle classes, throughout 1919-20, 'red baronies' had emerged, often in the midst of agrarian war and in deadly rivalry with all competitors in the struggle for work. During 1920, as the Bologna struggle mobilized *mezzadri* tenants as well as *braccianti* labourers, the socialist rural unions generally mushroomed from 400,000 towards the 900,000 mark, in the teeth of the rapid expansion of catholic unions, syndicalist campaigns and the strength of reformist co-operatives in regions like Emilia. Its chief characteristic was thus an intensely corporate spirit. Moreover, though the fascists had to fight to smash these socialist rural unions, once they had smashed them, they consolidated their control over the mass membership fairly easily. Indeed, when for tactical reasons, the fascist unions adopted a temporarily combative stance towards landowners and employers, they achieved an adequate popular mobilization. The upsurge of the socialist rural unions was certainly an element in the 'awakening' of an oppressed rural population, but it swiftly and increasingly developed a corporatist self-absorption and operated virtually in isolation from both other rural movements and the struggles of the industrial working class.

Apart from FIOM, the building workers, with 200,000 men in 1920 and the textile workers (155,000) were the largest groups in the CGL, followed by 60-70,000 contingents from the chemical, gas, public and private white-collar workers, with smaller 20-30,000 clusters of craft federations.[39] Many of the craft federations rallied to the CGL. The rural workers were totally opposed to any extension of the occupation movement. And the CGL majority was built on them. The militant railway and maritime unions were present at the convention, but had no vote. The syndicalists of USI, of course, were not there at all and at this time were claiming 800,000 members. If one follows the ILO's example and speculatively 'distributes' the 'missing' votes of the new 1920 members, the result would probably not affect the majority *within* the CGL except to strengthen it, but would surely intensify the polarization between the industrial proletariat and other workers. To put it at its lowest, the CGL majority was *not* based on the industrial working class, certainly not on the factory proletariat of the industrial heartland. Its majority was arithmetical and democratic, not organic and socialist.

This polarization has another face, of course. What the Turin workers had felt in April, the whole working class were feeling in September. Perhaps the most tragic and painful feature of the whole fascist offensive of 1921-22 was the *isolation* of the industrial working class. That isolation first registers on a national scale during the occupation of the factories. It registers first of all *within the union federation of the socialist movement itself*. The fragmented character of the Italian populist revolt, the failure of the PSI to transcend it in a communist spirit, struck home in September 1920 and struck to the heart of the socialist movement.

Not that the party Directorate would have welcomed a victory in the vote! As Nenni wrote in laconic summary: the convention of 10-11 September 'liquidated the political solution with the complicity of the party leadership itself, which wanted to lose'. After the vote, Gennari rose to make a formal statement. Under the Pact of Alliance, he said, the party had the power unilaterally to take over the movement. For the moment, the Directorate did not intend to avail itself of these powers. It reserved to itself 'the right to assume the leadership in the course of time, in a changed political situation'. No one was deceived. 'The party leaders heaved a sigh of relief', said Angelo Tasca. 'Liberated now from all responsibility, they could complain at the tops of their voices about the CGL's betrayal.'[40] On 11 September, by a democratic vote of rural workers and craft federations against the industrial working class and, in particular, against the factory proletariat of the dominant industrial complex, the socialist movement adjourned the revolution *sine die*.

The Old Fox and the Little Foxes

From 11 September 1920, it becomes essential to make the crude, often deceptive, but necessary distinction between 'militants' and 'masses'. We know what the former thought and did; they tell us, frequently and at length. The latter vote with their feet. The great virtue of the CGL motion was that it offered them a way to walk, towards economic gains, honour and a sense of victory, a justification for their enterprise, begun in a high tide of innovatory zeal, now beginning to ebb in suffering, bewilderment and confusion. 'Militants' and 'masses' moved in opposite directions after 11 September. In Turin during the desperate struggle against unemployment and fascism in 1921, there was a striking dichotomy in the metal industry. Militants at the workshop commissar, shop-steward level were generally communists, in opposition to a union leadership which was socialist and could command a majority among the rank and file. That pattern began to take shape throughout industrial Italy during the last fortnight of September.

The first to move was the Old Fox. On 11 September, before he knew the result of the Milan vote, Giolitti took steps to meet an extension of the occupation. They were entirely designed to avoid conflict. Troops of the line were to be confined to barracks; royal guards and *carabinieri* to be deployed only at street outlets to squares. If disorder broke out, the security forces were to withdraw behind a screen of machine-guns and, if necessary, light artillery. There was to be no use of individual fire-arms. The railways however were to be prepared for militarization. On the same day, the premier telegraphed the prefect of Milan: 'It is necessary to make the industrialists understand that no Italian government will resort to force and provoke a revolution simply to save them some money.'[41]

Government set to work to break up the industrialists' monolith. Prefects were sent hunting for Achille Pogliani, director of the *Banco di Sconto*, who might be able to influence Ansaldo. Yoked with him was Toeplitz, director of the *Banca Commerciale*. Toeplitz was later accused (though he denied it) of threatening to cut off credit from industrialists who refused to accept the CGL's terms. Nationalist capitalists frothily denounced him as an agent of German capital. This occult pressure through the banks was supplemented by bribery. On 14 September, the duty on foreign cars was raised to 40 per cent. Allowing for wage increases of some 40 million lire, this would bring in 120 million to Fiat, according to one liberal economist.[42]

And, ignoring a storm of abuse from the press and threats of resignation from his own ministers, Giolitti left the country to keep his appointment with the French premier Millerand on the 12th at Aix-les-Bains (which served as everybody's Colombey during these years). There he got Corradini's telegram informing him of the Milan vote. His response was instant agreement: 'Final solution of the industrial question lies in the integration of workers, if necessary as shareholders, into the structure of industry.' Very striking is the reply of Filippo Turati to questions about 'union control' from a puzzled Corradini because it reveals a precisely similar attitude. '. . . in other words, collaboration of labour with the enterprise (not antagonism and destructive political struggle) and collaboration of labour and the enterprise with the interest of the public and consumers, more or less represented by the state . . . a full development of trade unions, drawing them into a more intense collaboration and a wider vision of the national interest . . .' A classic reformist alignment was in the making here.[43]

On the 12th however, an 'inter-proletarian' convention, sponsored by USI, assembled delegates from the syndicalist federation, the rail and maritime unions and the anarchist Union. *Umanità Nova* was calling for peasants to occupy lands, sailors to take over ships, railwaymen to stop trains, postal workers to 'suppress the correspondence of the bourgeoisie'. The convention denounced the Milan vote as minoritarian, arbitrary and null ; it launched renewed and urgent, though vague appeals for action. After the convention, cotton mills in Verona and uncultivated lands in Puglia were occupied. But the convention recognized that it could not act alone, without the CGL, and it lamented the isolation of industrial workers, locked in their factories, from the countryside, the ex-servicemen, some elements of the petty bourgeoisie.[44]

The other stronghold of opposition was Turin. On 14 September, the communist groups of three leading factories demanded that the Turin section of the PSI fully take over the struggle locally, because it was now 'political'. On the next day, Boero the abstentionist and Ferrero and Garino (whose speech to the Ligurian union convention on the 7th had been given the lie), libertarians within FIOM, bitterly criticized the behaviour of Turin delegates in Milan as insufficiently militant. On 16 September, the workshop commissars from all the metal factories in Turin assembled and, with only four votes against, decided to send delegates to Milan to demand an immediate seizure of all public and private enterprises.[45]

During these days immediately following the Milan vote, however, the first serious recessions of morale registered among the workers. On the 13th, FIOM had to recall its members to discipline ; the Turin *camera* asked workers to stop carrying goods out of the workshops for private use or sale. That night there were outbursts of firing and an industrialist killed two workers. On the 14th, Fiat-Centro and Ansaldo San Giorgio effectively stopped an exodus by threatening absentees with dismissal. The line was beginning to break.[46]

But on 14 September the CGL translated its victory into

action. Having set up a central committee of agitation (the FIOM committee remained in being to hold the occupation firm for negotiations) it published its proposals for a solution of the conflict: the creation of a joint commission to work out the application of control, which would enable union leaders to learn the true state of industry and make wage bargaining effective. The unions would be able 'through their factory representatives, who are emanations of the trade union, to contribute to the observance of regulations, have a say in hiring and firing, and encourage the normal development of activity within the factory'. This proposal, which dismissed 'factory councils', offered a practical programme of action which evidently rallied considerable support among the workers in occupation.[47]

Giolitti responded at once. On the 14th a message reached the CGL and on the next day representatives of the CGL and *Confindustria* were invited to meet Giolitti in Turin, almost as he got off the train. The national council of the industrialists were meeting in Milan, ravaged by the prospect of the 'prison' of union control. Their first confusion – Perrone had asked Olivetti whether he should have his papers attack the government and the secretary of *Confindustria* had been too perplexed to answer – had yielded to an icy intransigence. Their newspapers were in full cry against 'surrender'. But the banks had been at work. A small minority began to emerge, ready not so much to concede as to ride the tide and redirect it. The directors of the *Banca Commerciale* were the core, together with Fiat and some of the smaller Turin men. Ettore Conti of the *Banca Commerciale* spoke up for conciliation, but he was overwhelmed. The delegates to the Turin meeting, Conti, Olivetti and an engineer consultant, were strictly mandated to resist union control.

They travelled on the same train as the CGL delegates, D'Aragona, Baldesi, Buozzi, Colombino and Bertero. 'You see that man?' said the prefect of Milan to Benedetti, who had shot two workers in Turin two nights earlier, 'He's the saviour of Italy.' He was pointing at D'Aragona.[48]

In the Hotel Boulogne, the two parties confronted each other. Conti went through the *Confindustria* ritual: immediate evacuation of the factories, punishment of workers guilty of violence, no negotiation until legality and hierarchical discipline were restored. D'Aragona said all further discussion was pointless and Giolitti intervened. It was no longer tolerable that in a great enterprise, one man should command and thousands obey. 'We must give the workers the right to know, to learn, to raise themselves, the right to share in the running of the firm, to assume some responsibility.' D'Aragona followed up. The workers needed control to learn what operations entered into production costs, what the state of profits actually was. How else could they know whether a wage claim was practical or not? He cited the example of big firms which ended up with heavy liabilities which were then cleared by the state with tax-payers' money, because they were essential to the armed forces. Ilva was a case in point. Its directors controlled subsidiaries in supply, transport, banking, as Max Bondi did. They reaped huge profits on the side. Union control would encompass all this. On the other hand, D'Aragona denounced any 'conciliar' interpretation. Not only was this potentially 'subversive'; it would breed craft and work-group egoism.

The debate exploded. Giolitti stopped it by confronting the nonplussed industrialists with a draft government decree setting up the CGL's proposed joint commission. They streamed back to Milan the next day to confront a national council in uproar. The Stefani agency had published news of the draft decree in the afternoon and someone ran with it into the meeting. There was outrage and panic. The meeting broke up in confusion. When they re-assembled in the evening, a bitter debate ground on into the 17th. Conti and Crespi, president of the *Banca Commerciale*, argued the case for compliance. It was a subtle one. They should accept the decree but only as a *diktat* from Giolitti, a forced surrender; they should then employ every means to postpone its application. A labour crisis was looming, unemployment lay ahead. Economic crisis would transform the climate and bury union control. Conti said: 'Since it is easy to foresee that a commission of this kind will never produce any reasonable plan, the matter will end without victors or vanquished. Unfortunately a labour crisis is imminent and there'll be no more talk of control.'

This was too subtle for Ilva and Ansaldo, for the Lombard consortium in engineering, for AMMA in Turin. Had they fought 'dual power' in the factories in Turin in April, on the urging of Olivetti, to give in to the liberal state? The industrialists' council, in a process which was repeated all over Italy, went through agonies of indecision, calls to resist to the death, furious threats of revenge. The fascist psychology was forming. But they were ground down by the pressure. Albertini, in the great journal of their order, was calling on the government to give power to the CGL. Any order, even socialist order, was better than this chaos. Agnelli of Fiat had lost all confidence. As he said a few days later when he offered to surrender Fiat to the workers – 'How can you build anything with 25,000 enemies?' Rotigliano led the last-ditch resistance. But a motion was finally carried by 21 votes to 14. It deplored the violence and illegality of workers and the supine conduct of the government, but continued: 'The general confederation of Italian industrialists agrees, if the other side is sincerely of the same opinion, to accept a control over industry based on legislative provision, provided that this does not establish a trade-union monopoly or predominance and that it means genuine collaboration and co-responsibility between the different factors of production.'[49]

When it first heard the news, even the Turin *Avanti* cried victory. A great hymn of praise for the genius of Giolitti rose from the liberal press, as conservatives went snarling into a black night of defeat and dreams of revenge. The *popolari*, whose congress was ending, hurried to associate themselves with the movement, to propose radical schemes of joint management and profit-sharing. Salvemini, discomfited by yet another successful Giolittian corruption, drew a direct parallel with his exploitation of universal suffrage in 1911 and talked a language similar to that of the equally discomfited *ordinovisti*. The socialist press oscillated wildly. Everywhere there was the firm belief that the transition to a socialized economy had begun.[50]

The effect on the workers in occupation was dramatic. That most of the popular classes, and the working class in particular, were seized by a passion for qualitative change in 1919-20 is clear. The very vote at Milan confirms it. By the summer of 1920, among the working class, it had turned sour and exasperated, ready to respond in an instrumental manner to the appeals of syndicalism. The scale and sweep of the occupation had transformed it into a highly-charged expectation of qualitative change – an innovatory spirit. It would be too precise to call it a revolutionary spirit, though it was certainly the stuff from which revolutions are made. The immediate result of the Milan vote was clearly a collapse of morale. It is possible that, if the councils had not reacted promptly and severely, there would have been a major secession between 11 and 14 September. News of the industrialists' surrender was an immediate fillip. The first reaction was clearly relief; their sufferings were nearly over. With it went a *sufficient* sense of 'victory' – a 'victory' after all being hailed or denounced on all sides.

There was immediately a shortening of perspective, with two significant consequences. First, the practical one: how to pick up the threads of living again. Workers had produced during the occupation; in Turin they had produced a lot. 'In Turin in all the factories, men have worked,' said the Turin *Avanti*, 'A little in the first days, a lot in the days which followed. In some factories, they surpassed the average level of production. For whom have they worked? The workers would rather destroy everything they have produced than work twenty days for the bosses.'[51] There was a near-total concentration on the problem of payment for the workdays of the occupation. Secondly the great confrontation shrank. It was a dispute in the metal industry again. Both factors, together with a vague but real sense of victory, directed the 'masses' away from the 'militants'. The long dragging process of settlement poisoned this early euphoria and injected confusion and bitterness, the first sense of disillusionment. Real disillusionment did not set in until the abrupt shocks and reversals which followed thick and fast from November, unemployment, fascist attacks, isolation, the schism in the Socialist Party. What followed was a rapid and catastrophic collapse in morale and a socialist retreat which rapidly degenerated into a rout. Only communists held out to any degree against this debacle and that by withdrawing into the deepest purist sectarianism. The first effect of the process, the process in which capitalist order in fact disengaged itself from the democratic state, was a recession of the revolutionary tide in September, leaving militants still struggling forward on the watermark.

But even in militant circles there was as yet no full sense of a revolutionary opportunity which had been irretrievably lost. On the contrary, there was a widespread expectation of renewal. Malatesta, as late as 20 September, was writing: 'The workers come out of the factories feeling betrayed. They will come out, but with anger in their hearts and revenge in their minds. They will come out this time, but they will profit from the lesson. They will not 'work more and consume less' so the crisis will not be resolved. The revolution remains both necessary and imminent.' The Milan *Avanti* said: 'Revolutionary action develops in waves. After one is thought to have failed, look here's another rising even stronger, perhaps decisively.' The USI journal said the game was not over yet.[52] For some time after the Milan decision, there was little sense *of decision*. The last slow week of settlement eroded this illusion and bred resentment.

The first sign of 'revolutionary' criticism had been an interview which the Turin *Avanti* published on the 15th with Paul Levi the president of the German Communist Party; it anticipated the criticisms of the International. Writing before the industrialists' surrender, Levi claimed that a great revolutionary class action was in train but that the masses lacked 'a clear revolutionary objective'. Was it time for the revolution? Even if the time had not yet come to establish the Italian soviet republic, it was certainly ripe for the slogan of the political councils, the creation of a national workers' power as a rival to the bourgeois state. 'It is my firm belief,' he added, 'that the party runs the risk of succumbing to general inertia if, at this moment, it does not seize the reins of the movement, master events and become a motor force.'[53]

It was too late for the PSI. But the discontent among the militants in Turin was rising to a paroxysm. On the 17th, the day *Confindustria* yielded, an extraordinary congress of FIOM met in Milan to take stock. The new strength of the councils after the occupation led Buozzi to distinguish carefully between the union control demanded by the CGL and control over individual workshops which remained the function of the councils, which would not be superseded. The attack on the settlement, which was imminent, was led by the Turin delegates, mandated by the workshop commissars of the city and delivered by the libertarians Ferrero and Garino. They put forward a motion on the 18th demanding that the agitation from that moment should be considered *political* 'and therefore entrusted to organizations competent to carry out the seizure of all industrial firms and public services, thus excluding all possibility of negotiations and agreements'. This drastic appeal was countered by a Buozzi motion demanding that industrialists accept all FIOM's terms. Buozzi won easily. But he won by proclaiming that if the industrialists did not grant all the concessions demanded, FIOM would call for a general occupation of all industries from 20 September.[54]

On that same day the Turin *Avanti* published a statement from the executive committee of the PSI section, controlled by Togliatti's *electionist communists*. 'Events have confirmed the belief that the destiny of the socialist revolution depends above all on the existence of a party which is truly a communist party.' The PSI's failure to carry through the revolution in favourable circumstances was throwing revolutionaries to the anarchists and syndicalists, abandoning the masses to the reformist leadership of existing socialist institutions. The section executive, which in August had taken a stand against the schismatic abstentionists, called on comrades to confront immediately the problems of forming a communist party.[55]

It was in a continuing state of high tension, therefore, that the negotiators of the CGL and *Confindustria* met Giolitti in Rome on 19 September to reach final agreement. Giolitti had D'Aragona sit by his side, but there was a hard six-hour wrangle. Individual cases brought by industrialists for the punishment of workers were referred to a joint commission. For the time being, all personnel were to 'remain at their posts'. FIOM secured a notable victory. There was an increase of 4 lire a day on effective global earnings, with a smaller increase in workshops which employed fewer than 75 workers (often strongholds of USI). This was supplemented by substantial improvements in minimum pay, cost-of-living bonuses, percentages for overtime. Allowances for dismissal were increased and there were to be six days' paid holiday. Wages were to be paid, though at nominal rates, without bonuses, for the go-slow period. Payment for work done during the occupation was referred to local settlement. FIOM was to submit this agreement, which was widely welcomed by workers, to a referendum. Finally, Giolitti signed the decree creating a joint commission of six men from each side to formulate proposals for union control which would be the basis of government legislation. The decree repeated the CGL pledge that 'given such control, the CGL undertakes to secure an improvement in disciplinary relations between the buyers and sellers of labour, and an increase in production'.[56]

The substantial gains won by FIOM powered the settlement. But payment for the occupation workdays had still to be settled and the last ten days of the conflict were in fact the worst. Militants dug in for a bitter last-ditch resistance and deepening disillusionment drove many workers into desperation. Battista Santhia, one of the *ordinovisti* workers, recorded the tension in a Turin factory during the 'turn'.

'16 September: great agitation among the workers. Lively discussion of yesterday's events and our failure to react. We saw defeat looming. In the factories, hardly anybody worked. Between us and the sector committee there were many contacts, discussions, meetings of workshop commissars. A sense of weariness everywhere now. On the 16th and 18th, the absence of many workers noted, about 60. The workers' discouragement grew. A hundred lire on account were given to every workman ; the exchange of production material continued. The guards had to be increased because the disappearance of tools had been spotted. On the 19th, the thieves were caught. Two workers who later turned out to be spies. The making of bombs was stopped. Great struggle between us and the reformists who wanted to withdraw the guards and take away their weapons. During the night several shots were fired.'[57]

That night a workman was killed outside a foundry. On the 22nd a *carabinieri* brigadier was fatally wounded outside Fiat-Centro and there was a regular street battle outside the Gilardini plant. Some workers that night brutally murdered a young nationalist and a prison warder. *Avanti* warned workers against succumbing to individualist 'anarchism' and employers' provocations. The atmosphere in the waiting factories was turning nasty.[58]

It was the abstentionists who responded to the appeal of the Turin PSI section, and with embarrassing speed. The fraction at Fiat-Centro, led by Parodi, met on the night of 20 September and bitterly denounced the trade-union and socialist leaders. It was no longer possible to remain in the same movement with 'those elements'. They decided to secede from the Socialist Party and called on all like-minded comrades to join in forming a communist party. The next day the abstentionist fraction of Turin as a whole approved of this resolution and called on the fraction's national committee 'to begin work towards the immediate creation of the communist party, Italian section of the Third International, and to convene a national congress of the fraction to set up the necessary executive organs'.

Bordiga, just back from Moscow, had that day told workers in Naples, 'For the moment, the proletarian class must strike the red flag and abandon the factories. We must postpone the struggle to overthrow the bourgeois regime to a more opportune moment.' He was acutely embarrassed by the Turin move, having returned pledged to create as wide a communist party as possible. He rejected the demand of the Turin abstentionists and he was powerfully supported by the Comintern representative – 'I recommend and entreat you, in the name of the Executive Committee of the Communist International, not to take any hasty steps . . . We must instead remain in the party for the time being and devote all our energies to winning control of it . . .' The *electionist communists* of the Turin PSI section also responded sharply. 'It is not a matter of playing the game of who can go the farthest. It is a question of making sure that the communist party shall be, from the start, the only major organization in which the proletariat can have faith.'[59]

Gramsci, however, was fully in agreement with the abstentionists on this point. He felt nothing but disgust for the behaviour of the CGL in Milan and his first statements indicated a radical shift in favour of an immediate break and towards an élite party. In an article on *Political Capacity* which appeared in the Turin *Avanti* for 24 September, he asserted that a truly revolutionary opportunity had existed and had been lost. 'A revolutionary movement can only be founded on a working-class avant-garde and it must be run without prior consultations and without the machinery of representative assemblies.' He denounced the FIOM referendum. 'The form of a referendum is intensely democratic and anti-revolutionary. It gives weight to, and exploits, the amorphous masses; it breaks the vanguards who direct and give a political consciousness to those masses.'

Gramsci once again was responding to immediate practical experience. That the experience had been shattering accounts for the starkly uncompromising, anti-democratic and vanguard tone of his writing, which for the moment at least was remote from his August style. The argument, however, pointed in the same direction: 'The proletarian vanguard, today disillusioned and on the point of disintegration, should ask itself: is the responsibility ours? It is a fact that within the CGL, there is no single organized opposition, concentrated at the centre and able to exercise control over the bureaucracy, in a position not only to substitute one man for another, but one method for another, one objective for another, one will for another.' He demanded 'tighter, more disciplined, better organized activity'. It was the Gramsci of Bordiga's communist party who wrote *Political Capacity*, as metalworkers were voting in the FIOM referendum.[60]

The referendum had been confirmed at the extraordinary FIOM congress which had resumed on 21 September after the Rome settlement. Once again the Turin delegates led by Ferrero resisted. They denounced the settlement, while Colombino had to remind his listeners that the occupation had originally been a preventive action against a lockout! The referendum was carried by delegate votes representing a majority of 148,740 to 42,140 with 5,059 abstentions.

It was resisted. 'Boys,' said the popular Ruggero Chiarini of the Muzzi plant in Florence, where they remembered his words fifty years later, 'we have to have a referendum. If we say yes, we move out of the factory. If we say no, they boot us out.'[61] The holding of the referendum seems to have brought all the seething and contradictory emotions of the last week of September to a sudden focus. There was widespread satisfaction with the gains of the settlement, still a vague sense of victory and of a new prospect opening up. But there was also a deepening disillusionment, a vague suspicion of trickery. The struggle over payment for occupation workdays was becoming a regular battle in many places and this inevitably turned workers' minds to the men who had deserted, the white-collar workers above all. There was an upsurge of bitterness, attempts to shut them out, a near-tribal excommunication. An awareness of isolation which had developed during the Milan meetings was intensified by the sheer anti-climax of it all. Some men were driven mad. There was more trouble during the last week than in the whole occupation period. And the militants, now in near-total hostility to the PSI and its maximalist leadership, were fighting hard against surrender.

The focus of resistance, as usual, was USI. When the syndicalist federation was invited by the prefect of Milan to recognize the agreement, it replied that it held itself free to take any action it liked. Not only did it not intend to subscribe to the agreement; it proclaimed its intention to sabotage 'in every way possible the application of control over the factories'. In Sestri Ponente on 21 September, a meeting presided over by Armando Borghi (a day after his return from Russia) and Negra, passed a resolution calling on workers not to abandon the factories under any circumstances. Disorder and violence broke out in Sestri between the 21st and the 24th. There were attacks on white-collar workers and a bomb was thrown at the *carabinieri* barracks. Borghi moved to Verona on the 22nd and there was more trouble there and at Brescia. USI called on all workers to boycott the referendum. But the tide of feeling was running against it. Amid spectacular gestures of solidarity in Genoa and elsewhere, the workers were ready to move out.

In Milan, where there was no strong communist current and

where the syndicalists had exhausted themselves during the occupation, resistance was weaker. Schiavello, however, a left maximalist, submitted a tough resolution to a meeting of the internal commissions. He did not attack the agreement, which was popular in Milan, but voiced distrust of the CGL leadership 'which no longer corresponds to the political and trade-union thinking of the masses themselves' and expressed regret because 'the movement in the metal trades could have and should have been exploited to the limit by a broad political movement which entirely corresponded to the aspirations of the proletariat'. The resolution was carried.[62]

Opposition to the referendum was most sustained in Turin. The prefect reported committees of 'communists and anarchists' moving resolutely about the factories. On 20 September, all work stopped as mass meetings were held, and votes went heavily against the agreement. Fiat-Centro called for a struggle to the bitter end. Liaison secretaries from 58 factories met at the *camera* and rejected the settlement. It was the workshop commissars and commissions who controlled everything ; delegates reported back to them and they, not the official FIOM branch, organized the referendum itself. Even in Turin, however, weariness and relief, together with a fear of renewed isolation, were pulling workers strongly towards peace.[63]

In these circumstances, the result of the referendum was certain.[64] The agreement was ratified by 127,904 votes to 44,531, with 3,006 blank ballot papers, a heavy majority. In the bigger centres, the majority was often overwhelming: Genoa: 2,944 against 47, with 222 blank papers ; Voltri: 2,477 against 23 ; Sampierdarena: 3,692 against 458. There were, however, some exceptions, largely because of difficulty in getting payment for occupation workdays. Rome was against ; so was Livorno. Small shops got a smaller pay increase and the closest vote was actually in the Tuscan region which had 13 of FIOM's 133 sections (the fourth province in order of strength). There the agreement was carried by 5,871 to 5,719 with 23 blank papers. Small shops were also USI strongholds and USI had preached abstention. In fact the abstention rate was generally high and in Milan and Turin massive. These cities were the centres of FIOM's major provinces.

> Lombardy (41 sections) 57,272 against 10,633.
> Piedmont   (39 sections) 30,839 against 19,645.
> The provincial vote was a good deal closer in Piedmont than

in Lombardy and in fact the great bulk of the 'no' votes came from Turin. As opposed to Milan, which registered 23,571 against 6,668 with 1,455 blank papers (107 factories for the agreement as it stood; 95 broadly for, but insisting on payment for occupation workdays, 28 for total intransigence, and all swathed in massive abstention), the Turin vote was 18,740 against 16,909 with 1,024 blank papers and a crippling abstention rate. In many of the smaller subsidiary factories, including Diatto Fiat, Brevetti-Fiat, Scat, Acciaierie Fiat and Industrie Metallurgiche, there was a substantial 'no' majority. No precise figures were given for Fiat-Centro, but they were summarized as 6,000 for and 4,000 against with very heavy abstentions.

What emerges most clearly from the voting is the distinctive quality of Turin and the utterly contradictory character of the workers' response to the settlement. What emerged most clearly of all to the men who lived through these days, however, was the massive resurgence of the factory councils and their recovery of the position lost in April.

When the results were known on 25 September, FIOM ordered all workers to stay in the factories until the 27th when they were to leave, to be recalled by the employers before 4 October. In fact, the evacuation was ragged, dependent on settlements for occupation workday payments, the local intensity of hostility to the 'deserters' and other factors. Generally speaking, the workers moved out between the 25th and the 30th. Very often there were ceremonies. Milan went in for farewell banquets. In Florence, the workers marched out with drums beating and red flags flying. There was, once again, the scent of victory, if an ambiguous one. For Bruno Buozzi was in one basic sense correct when he said several years later that 'the victory of the metalworkers had no parallel in the whole history of the international workers' movement'. Most of the local agreements surrendered to the workers' demands; the gains under their national agreement were striking, and they set a pattern for whole sectors of the working class.[65]

Nowhere were the evacuations so dramatic as in Turin. The employers' association bluntly refused to pay for any work done since 2 September. So the workers remained in occupation on the 27th, indeed, mobilized their forces once more. Only at the last minute, in negotiations at the prefecture on the 29th, did the employers cede the principle. Local agreements were worked out on the 30th –

and they were decided by the factory councils. Typically, two Ansaldo plants were the last to yield, on 4 October. FIOM authorized the negotiations, but in fact the factory councils went ahead without any reference to the union. At Fiat-Centro, the commissars were able to exclude 8,000 workers and foremen from the shops, because they had absented themselves during the occupation. Parodi presented Agnelli with a list of 'blacklegs and thieves' and warned him that if he re-employed the former he would have to re-employ the latter. The council refrained from indicating which was which. No wonder Agnelli, in a few days, offered to turn Fiat into a co-operative: the offer was refused, on principle. Above all, the factory councils were fully re-established. The April defeat had been avenged.[66]

Fiat-Centro was evacuated on 30 September.[67] Between eight and nine, the workers gathered in two large assemblies in the great workshops. The comrades of the council explained the terms of the agreement and elaborated its implications. 'They referred once more to the ultimate objective, which had not been achieved but had not been forgotten.' They were supposed to disperse at nine, but for more than two hours, the workers stayed in the inner courtyards and in the *corso Dante* outside the gates. 'They were waiting for the bosses to come to take over again. Around 11.30, a long angry whistle like an alarm signal, a howl of pain, announced the arrival of the blacklegs, returning to their posts with an escort of thugs. A great shout greeted them, a cry which was all protest, all promise – *Evviva i Soviet*! The bosses passed, livid, between two ranks of red guards, coming to a halt before the Council of the Factory in full assembly . . .'

1. Gideon's Army

It is the duty of the proletarian vanguard to keep the revolutionary spirit permanently alive in the masses, to create the conditions in which the masses will be ready for action, in which
the masses respond instantly to revolutionary orders. In the
same way, nationalists and imperialists, with their frenetic
preaching of patriotic vanities and hatred against foreigners, try
to create conditions in which the crowds will approve a war
already contrived by the army general staff and the foreign
office. No war would ever break out if the people were asked its
permission first . . .

This appalling statement, which seems to equate the proletarian 'mass' with the nationalist 'crowd' and to undo at a stroke
Gramsci's whole carefully-constructed universe of the molecular
building of communism, comes from his article *Political capacity* of
24 September, directed against the 'exquisitely democratic and anti-
revolutionary' FIOM referendum on the settlement.[1]

There was, without doubt, an invasion of grim realities into
utopian projection, a coming to terms with the grisly actualities of the
working class, the massively a-political character of proletarian existence. The article is full of vanguard 'elitist' calls and references to the
'amorphous masses'; it documents, without doubt, a powerful
emotional support to the positions he was already elaborating, for
example his radical revision of council theory in *The Communist
Party* of 4 September.

But too much should not be made of it. The very abruptness
and looseness of the writing (as so often in Gramsci's work) reveal it
for what it is: emotional revulsion. The meaning of the nationalist
crowd-proletarian mass analogy is in fact contradicted within the
same article. Today, it is the entrepreneurial class which has decom-
posed into Marx's 'sack of potatoes'; the young and virile proletariat
is the key to the future. It has proved itself capable of self-government, an 'elementary truth' for communists. It is a mass 'guided and
disciplined in the factory' but by its 'direct representatives': demo-

cratic centralism. There is even a touch of mistaken optimism – the middle class is coming over to the proletariat – probably a response to Giolitti's flexibility. The basic position is unchanged. Within weeks, Gramsci was identifying the formation of councils as the peculiar duty of the new communist party.

But the emphasis has switched entirely to that party. The whole essay is directed squarely at the 'vanguard' to bring them up to the level of their task. They must confront objective reality as it is, not in the light of wishful thinking. They must look upon events as 'an historical movement *susceptible to conscious extension and development*' [my italics – GAW]. Weaknesses, deriving from working-class professional organization, are in fact weaknesses which stem from capitalist conditioning, *mediated in particular through the socialist movement.* In the article, there is a much greater overt awareness of the strength of this old order and of the need for communists to be truly a vanguard. The enterprise is not one of little account or little men – 'only he who can keep his heart strong and his will as sharp as a sword when the general disillusionment is at its worst . . . can be called a revolutionary.' Before long, Gramsci was to be quoting Kipling's *If* at militants. It is a call to the Early Christians whose future is theirs if only they are Christian enough.

Along with other writings, however, the article does register a *revulsion*, which is a total revulsion of the spirit, not only from the Socialist Party, but from the *Italy* it reflected and represented.

The Land of Pulcinella

Italy holds the record for murders and killings. Italy is the country where mothers educate little kids with blows to the head from clogs. It is the country where the young generations are least respected and protected. In several regions of Italy it seemed natural up to a few years ago to gag vineyard workers so they would not eat the grapes; in several regions, landowners locked up their dependents in the stables after work so that they could not go to meetings and night school.

The class struggle has always assumed the bitterest character in Italy, because of the 'human' immaturity of whole strata of the population. Cruelty and the absence of human *simpatia* are two characteristics peculiar to the Italian people, which passes from puerile sentimentality to the most brutal and bloody ferocity, from impassioned rage to the cold contemplation of another's suffering.[2]

This ferocious piece, *Brute Force*, was written in response to the fascist attack on Turin in April 1921, but in fact, this style, this rage and despair at 'Italianity' itself (an echo of Lenin's despair at 'Russians' toward the end of his life) after some premonitory flickers during the summer, *invaded L'Ordine Nuovo* after the occupation of the factories and Serrati's clash with Comintern. It forced out of Gramsci some of the most ferocious polemic ever directed by a man against his own people : not merely against the 'Bandar-Log, Kipling's Monkey-People' of a petty-bourgeoisie and the 'Spanish-fly paroxysms of a bourgeoisie in senile impotence' but essentially against the Socialist Party and the Italianity it represented.

Gramsci's tirade against the Socialist Party from late 1920 into 1922 must rank, for contemptuous ferocity and sheer zoological inventiveness, with the *great hates* of all time. It is too often forgotten that the very *spearhead* of Bordiga's allegedly 'sectarian' onslaught on the socialists was *L'Ordine Nuovo*, become a daily, with a circulation of 45,000. Not only the 'cockroaches' of reformism, but above all the centrist, pseudo-communist, concealed social-democrats of maximalism, personified in Serrati, were the target: Serrati 'the parrot who wants to be an eagle' (as well as an infinity of other contemptible biological species). These creatures had to be *blotted out* of the working-class mind – men like Adelchi Baratono, a woolly maximalist who suffered rushes of the *Internationale* to the head but had dared to call the Livorno congress a 'carnival'. He became Baratono the 'brothel-keeper', his writings 'scribblings on lavatory walls . . . castrated fleas'. What human type did he represent: the pedagogic dunce? But they had some autonomy, some originality, some element of humanity. 'Moreover their asininity is monumental. Baratono is certainly an ass but his asininity is not monumental. Well, then, is he perhaps a poodle? But poodles are known to die on their masters' graves. There is not enough humanity in Baratono for that.' What characterized him was 'cerebral phosphorescence like fireflies in a cemetery'. He was really that unheard-of type, the Swedish match which ignites only when rubbed against a specific box. 'Is it possible to get angry with a Swedish match? *Ma si, ma si*, Baratono has written on Livorno.' Come then, a prize of 1,000 lire for the most spirited essay in *L'Ordine Nuovo* on the Swedish match.[8]

Gramsci savaged the 'glorious tradition' of Italian socialism, much in maximalist mouths in the conflict with Comintern, as 'glorious ignorance, glorious absence of all scruple in polemics, glorious irresponsibility, gloriously vile demagogy, glorious vanity, glorious charlatanism – behold the most glorious and most *Italian* of traditions.' The CGL's hostile report on Russia had said that few there seemed to go to brothels. The explosion from Turin was predictable. The 'sensual energy' of Italians was contrasted with the creative energy of Russians. The union bosses were living proof of democracy's failure to develop talent. 'The workers ask for engineers and they get ballet dancers.' The confusion of bureaucratic skill with technical capacity 'is an error wholly Italian'; in the unions' report, 'all the cowardice and all the vile fickleness of the Italian character coagulate'.[4]

But the real stronghold of this Italianity was the PSI which had to be destroyed, in order to rescue as much of the Italian working class as possible from the disaster into which it had been led. Gramsci was pillorying Serrati as early as 2 October (and already developing the notion that socialism and fascism were simply two faces of the same bourgeois reaction) in *The Land of Pulcinella*; the Socialist Party presented 'a stupefying spectacle . . . a spectacle wholly Italian, of the worst Italianism, of the Italianity which does not study, does not think, which does not bother to inform itself about events in its own country. Men who know nothing of the development of the agrarian movements in Puglia and Sicily . . . and have raised the flag against the theses on the agrarian question approved in Moscow which are the result of decades of study and three years of government experience'. Perhaps there is some truth in Serrati's claim of an Italian 'particularity'. How otherwise to explain how the PSI rallied to Zimmerwald without knowing what Zimmerwald meant? How the PSI joined the Third International two and a half years ago and only today concerns itself with what the decision means? How the change of name from socialist to communist causes such sentimental devastation in so many militants. '. . . the title of socialism has a glorious tradition, yes, but how much ignorance, how much fickleness, how much play-acting, how much big mouth and little brain in that glorious tradition . . .'[5] Serrati and the maximalists, of course, replied in kind. Where were the learned gentry of the New Order during the war – all these professors and lawyers, Their High and Mightinesses of the New Order? Gramsci returned with a blast against the Old Men who had failed, who had created only an academy of Roman senators who 'installed on their thrones, sceptre in hand, defend the Campidoglio against the barbarian Gauls solely with their statuary presence'. No wonder that today 'the party as a whole knows only how to catch fish . . .'

The ferocity is a symptom of the psychological impossibility of that united front, indeed fusion with the left socialists, which Comintern was to urge upon the new Communist Party almost as soon as it was born. It was a psychological, because *structural* impossibility. Communism in Italy defined itself in a total breach with socialism, much as the latter had defined itself in a breach with anarchism. The party's resistance to Comintern 1921-23 was not the resistance of a stubborn bunch of sectarians. It was a conflict between general Comintern policy and the *historical imperatives* of communism in Italy. That is why men of widely different provenance became 'Bordighists' to a man. After the September experience, even Tasca was through with the PSI ; so were Terracini and Togliatti. But there was only one alternative: the fraction of that Amadeo Bordiga who had foreseen the necessity as early as 1912. The communist party formed around the former abstentionist fraction, as groups and individual maximalists rallied to it in whole-hearted commitment to its *historical identification*. Terracini was counted more 'Bordighist' than Bordiga. It was not 'Bordighism', though Bordiga has the honour due to the first-comer. Bordiga had had to move, too. But it was around and behind Bordiga that the party formed, with Gramsci in the van.

His commitment was made public in an article *The Communist Party*, of 9 October.[6] Parties, said Gramsci were the 'nomenclature' of social classes and groups. They rose, disintegrated and declined as the groups and classes they represented formed and reformed in crisis. Even 'historically lazy' classes could not escape the dissolution of capitalist crisis. He cited the *popolari*, sprung into existence as an expression of the great revolt of the countryside and even then disintegrating as class struggle broke up the rural bloc. Capitalism itself, in terms of 'party' was in collapse.

> Capitalism . . . no longer has a political party whose ideology also embraces the petty-bourgeois strata in town and country and thus secures the continuance of a legal state on a broad base. Capitalism has been reduced to finding a political representation only in the great newspapers (400,000 circulation, a thousand electors) and in the Senate, immune as institutions to

the actions and reactions of the great popular masses, but without authority and prestige in the country; hence the political power of capitalism tends to identify itself ever more closely with the high military hierarchy, with the royal guards, and with the myriad adventurers who have pullulated since the armistice and who aspire, each against the other, to be the Kornilov and the Bonaparte of Italy; so the political power of capitalism today can realize itself only in a military coup d'état and the attempt to rivet an iron nationalist dictatorship which will drive the brutalized Italian masses to restore the economy by the armed plunder of neighbouring countries.

This chilling and half-prophetic statement climaxed an argument for the 'exhaustion' of the bourgeois class. Therefore 'the working class is called ineluctably by history to assume the responsibility of a ruling class. Only the working class can create a state, because only it has a programme – communism – which finds its necessary preconditions and premises in the phase of development reached by capitalism with the imperialist war of 1914-18'.

The major obstacle is the Socialist Party. The 'colossal historical error' of the party's leaders had been the belief that they could preserve the unity of the PSI from the dissolution of the order of which it was a part.

> . . . the Italian Socialist Party, in its traditions, in the historical origins of the various currents which constitute it, in the pact of alliance, tacit or explicit, with the CGL (a pact which in congresses, councils, every deliberative assembly, gives an unjustifiable power and influence to trade-union officials) in the limitless autonomy conceded to the parliamentary group (which also gives to the deputies in congresses, councils and in discussions of the greatest significance, a power and an influence similar to that of the union officials and equally without justification) . . . the Italian Socialist Party differs in nothing from the *English Labour Party* and is revolutionary only in the general assertions of its programme. It is a conglomeration of parties.

Hence the paradox that, in Italy, it was the masses who stimulated and 'educated' the party, not the party which guided and educated the masses. The Socialist Party 'is nothing but a poor notary who registers operations carried out spontaneously by the masses. This poor Socialist Party which proclaims itself the leader of the working class is nothing but the baggage train of the proletarian army'.

Disaster had been avoided only because of the communist groups, which needed only organization to become a communist party. The groups, therefore, must at once organize themselves, win over as much of the PSI membership as possible, and form a true communist party, as a section of the Third International. It was the duty of communists, having saved the metalworkers from disaster, 'to save the primordial structure of the party of the working class (and rebuild it) and give to the Italian proletariat that communist party which will be capable of organizing the workers' state and creating the conditions for the advent of communist society'.

The Beginning of the Communist Party

The process began with the meeting of the party Directorate of 28 September – 1 October, which assembled as the occupation of the factories was ending, to discuss the Twenty-one Points which defined membership of the Third International.[7] Of the Moscow delegation, Bombacci and Graziadei supported them, Serrati was against. He presented a motion asserting that the PSI was already committed in substance to the politics of the Points and rejecting mass expulsions. Expulsions were to be on an individual basis (he was prepared to throw out Turati). The rival motion agreed in principle to a mass purge, which was to be effected by the national congress to be held in Florence at the end of December. The radical motion was carried against Serrati and four others by a majority of seven, which included Terracini, Gennari and the youth leader Polano. Serrati offered to resign from *Avanti*. This was unanimously rejected. The Directorate decided not to publish the Moscow directive to Serrati, told him to contact Zinoviev on his visit to Berlin and more or less suspended action until the congress. In the aftermath of the Comintern congress and the occupation of the factories, the Socialist Party dissolved into fractions.

The first to act, as usual, were the reformists. They had been impressively strengthened by the outcome of the occupation of the factories, the Giolittian project of democratic reform, the local elections which were under way and which were winning over 2,000 communes for the PSI. The *socialist concentration* fraction met at its stronghold among the co-operatives in Reggio Emilia. They adopted a familiar leftist tone. They accepted the 'possible' need for violence and the dictatorship of the proletariat at some stage and as a temporary measure. They confirmed their adherence to the Third International, but demanded national autonomy within it. They reaffirmed the need to use all methods, including the parliamentary, to achieve socialism and, on a motion from D'Aragona and Baldesi the CGL leaders, rallied in defence of the name, the traditions and the unity of the party. They affirmed in particular the tradition of tolerating different 'schools' within the party, which was to remain pluralist. The tone of the discussions was virulently anti-Bolshevik, hostile to the 'cannibalism' and violence which would expose the movement to fascist destruction. Treves came very near to Serrati in his attacks on 'anarcho-dictatorial' tendencies. They immediately set about a febrile organization of support for the congress.[8]

The communists were slower to get together. The main difficulty lay in the rooted attitudes of the abstentionists. They were few in number but critically influential and they had a national organization which would inevitably be the skeleton of the new party. They had jumped the gun in Turin but had been restrained. Bordiga came back from Moscow, having renounced formal abstentionism, pledged to create as wide a party as possible. This went against the grain. In Turin it would require the abstentionists to work with the very men who had defeated them in the section elections in August. The sorry ending of the occupation of the factories had merely confirmed them in their suspicion of 'mass actions'. It is characteristic that, throughout September, *Il Soviet* managed *never even to mention* the occupation in its editorials.[9] Abstentionist coherence and rigour bred a certain tribalism.

This was sharpest in Turin. Revulsion against the performance of the PSI had in some ways brought the original *Ordine Nuovo* group together again, though it is incorrect to talk any more of an *ordinovista* tendency. Terracini had been repelled by his experiences at leadership level. Tasca himself now wanted a complete break with the PSI. He said later that he joined the Communist Party only with reluctance and with many reservations. He found his natural place almost immediately on its right wing. Togliatti oscillated between Tasca's and Gramsci's positions. But, in practice the group shuffled together again and most of the Turin section of the PSI followed them. Early in October, during the public discussions which the section had opened on the formation of the communist party, Gramsci's *communist education group* put forward a motion denouncing the

PSI leadership. Its tone was characteristically Gramscian. 'Trade-union independence and blind reformist tactics may drive the working class to armed insurrection and the seizure of political power *before* the technical and political preparation which would give the workers a guarantee of success in the struggle has been completed'. The motion directly linked the formation of the new party to the need to develop factory council activity (itself sufficient to refute any over-dramatic interpretation of Gramsci's article *Political Capacity* of 24 September).[10]

The motion was carried almost unanimously, but alongside the report of this decision in *Avanti* appeared a resolution from the Turin abstentionists welcoming all those who wished to see an implementation of the Twenty-one Points 'into the abstentionist fraction'. Bordiga firmly refused to build the Communist Party from the abstentionist sections only, but in fact charges of a party-within-a-party were not far from the mark. Bordiga himself informally maintained the fraction as an inner core within the new Communist Party and six months after its formation, the Turin people were still warning against the admission of 'opportunists'.[11]

But this was precisely their strength. Earlier than anybody else, they had called for a split, for rigorous discipline and a *very precise definition*, to break with all the 'schools', 'tendencies', the sheer *blur* of the PSI which was the major vehicle for bourgeois-democratic penetration. Gramsci was in total agreement; for both him and Bordiga, *Reaction began with the maximalists*. But they were still hopeful of winning a majority of the disorientated left maximalists. Zinoviev, early in November, was confident they could win over 75 to 90 per cent of the PSI. Bordiga in the last resort was ready to split with a handful, but throughout October and November there was a terrible rending and tearing at the maximalist mass.

Gramsci and Bordiga opened the attack on Serrati. The former's onslaught on the CGL leaders on 8 October was so savage that Serrati was forced hurriedly to call them into conference and publicly affirm a 'unitarian' position. The Milan *Avanti* returned the fire. The *Ordine Nuovo* group, in its youthful 'arrogance', its intellectual 'know-all' character, its 'Mussolinian, interventionist' past and its 'Bergsonian, voluntarist' tone, was the prime target. They were peculiarly vulnerable, in their total commitment to Comintern, in that they could be pilloried as a 'fifth column' in the service of alien, remote and uncomprehending powers. Serrati appealed above all to the experiences of the War, when the PSI, *including* Turati and his friends, had stood out alone against the nationalist frenzy, and had emerged as a rock of strength while the Second International collapsed around it. The PSI had driven out *its* Noskes in 1912 ; it needed no lessons in revolution from afar ; it understood the rural problem better than foreigners. It called on members to rally round the glorious old party, its name, its traditions, its pluralist character, which would hold all the 'schools' together and carry the party united through the revolution. This struck very deep into the spirit of Italian socialists. The Comintern representative who attacked Serrati at the Livorno congress was howled down.[12]

It is symptomatic that Gramsci was using the 'youth versus the failed old men' argument before the end of October. That is preeminently the line of a *minority*. For the Communist Party, as it took shape, formed around the existing, organized, 'traditionally' oppositionist abstentionist fraction, itself a small minority. Small groups, sometimes individual maximalists, joined and a constituency shaped among militants at the workshop-commissar level ; the local cadres of the occupation, from whom the mass had receded after 17 September, men who retained their prestige as fighters within the factories but did not register as political ideologues.

The decisive meeting for communists was a Milan gathering on 14 October. It published a manifesto three days later. This called for full adherence to the Third International, the change of party name, the expulsion of all anti-communists. The party was to become a strongly centralized and rigorously disciplined party (no 'schools'), was to aim at winning over all working-class institutions. There was to be a merely 'tactical' exploitation of elections and the ultimate goal was armed insurrection. Basically, this was the abstentionist programme, minus formal abstention itself. There was a certain softening of the Comintern and communist line on expulsions, evidently in the high hope of winning larger numbers. The manifesto was signed by Bordiga, Bombacci, the Milanese Fortichiari and Repossi, Gramsci, Misiano, Terracini, and Polano for the youth federation. Apart from the youth, only Misiano represented a 'tendency' ; he had often collaborated with Bordiga's group. Gramsci and Terracini represented 'Turin', rather than any *ordinovista* specificity. An official journal, *Il Comunista* was to be published from Bologna.

On the same day Pastore and Togliatti announced the independence of the Turin *Avanti* from the PSI. Serrati had resigned his (formal) editorship over Gramsci's attack on the CGL chiefs and the party 'suppressed' the paper. The Turin communists decided to fuse *Avanti* and *L'Ordine Nuovo* into a new daily which would come out on 1 January 1921 under the title *L'Ordine Nuovo. Il Soviet* became the party journal in the south. The Bologna paper never really got off the ground but another of the same name was to appear in Rome under the editorship of Togliatti.[18]

Serrati in response decided to form his own *unitarian communist* fraction. Gramsci was later to feel that this was a fatal decision which imprisoned many people who 'ought' to have been in the Communist Party within a PSI which was to agonize over the Twenty-one Points for another two years.

At this time, the critical Halle congress of the German Independent Socialists, the USPD, was being held. Its position was regarded as analogous to that of the PSI. Zinoviev himself spoke at the congress and after a tough fight, secured a majority for the Twenty-one Points of 236 to 156. As a consequence, some 300,000 members of the USPD joined the tiny Communist Party and made it a mass party; the USPD's deputies and journals stayed with what rapidly became a rump. In December, at Tours, the French Socialist Party congress voted three to one for the Third International. These were regarded as victories for the Twenty-one Points, but at the same time, Comintern and the Russians were very anxious to build *mass* support for the communist parties; the united front policy was in fact casting its shadow before. Comintern stretched points in favour of such as Marcel Cachin of the French party, who had been a 'social-patriot'. This ambiguity in search of mass support displeased the Comintern left, of which Bordiga was to be the major spokesman.

The dialectical character of Comintern's approach comes out most clearly in Lenin's dialogue with Serrati, which stressed the need *both* for a crystal-clear communist party *and* for a policy aimed at mass support. He suggested that the five members of the Directorate who had voted against the Twenty-one Points be expelled but then re-admitted, citing the example of Zineviev and Kamenev before the October Revolution. 'Expel Turati and then ally with him', became the catch-phrase. Serrati was adamant. He rejected Comintern agrarian policy in favour of the small peasant, which he denounced as 'reactionary' (extending the attack to the Italian communists) and evidence of Comintern's ignorance; hence the absolute necessity for every national party to be autonomous. This Lenin dismissed as a mere reversion to the Second International. Serrati denied that the Italian reformists were traitors, even objectively, cited their good international record and their defence of Russia in the Italian Chamber. They were no Noskes and they offered no obstacle to the Italian revolution. In any event, there had never been any insurrectionary moment in Italy; the occupation of the factories was not a revolutionary crisis. It was essential to keep all socialist institutions intact for the revolution. The party name, structure and tradition were necessary. Above all, there must be national autonomy. If Cachin could be treated as a 'special case', why not the Italian PSI, which had so much better a record? Serrati, member of the executive of the Third International, ignored Lenin's indication of the *socialist concentration* fraction as an intolerable element in a member party of the Third International. A planned meeting with Zinoviev fell through. The latter's letters moved from persuasion to threats. He was compelled finally to give up Serrati and to rally to the communist fraction. Serrati responded with a denunciation of foreign interference and a Red Freemasonry.

So the *unitarian communist* fraction held its own convention in Florence on 20-21 November. It accepted the Twenty-one Points (there was no fraction of the PSI which did *not*!) but 'saving the historical peculiarities of Italy'. It asserted that the PSI had already conquered an effective political power and had to remain united for the revolution. It supported the Third International, but claimed as much independence as the French and re-asserted the 'glorious' name and tradition.[14]

By this time, Serrati was fairly sure of a thumping majority. The exception was Turin. As ever. The provisional central committee of the communist fraction – Bordiga, Bombacci and Fortichiari, met in the city on 31 October and were able to win over the local abstentionists to full co-operation with the others. On 25 November, a regional federation was created for Piedmont; the executive committee consisted of Gramsci, Parodi and Terracini. The *absence* of an *ordinovista* tendency is demonstrated by the fact that Parodi represented the former abstentionists, Terracini the former electionists and Gramsci his still extant *communist education group* – the three fractions of the August elections. On the 27th, the decisive debate in the Turin PSI section resulted in a victory for the communists by 249 votes to 84. Turin was to become the stronghold of Italian communism.[15]

Elsewhere, however, there was frightful confusion. And when the communist fraction held its formal convention at Imola on 28-29 November, it was at once threatened with extinction – and in the most characteristically *Italian* manner. Graziadei and a colleague Marabini, appalled at the splitting of 'communists' between two suicidally rival fractions, desperately tried to form a 'bridge'. They sent out a circular in the Bologna district calling for a union of communists and left maximalists in a fraction which was, temporarily, to bear the name the *Communist Socialist Party of Italy*. This was perhaps the climax of the PSI's 'glorious tradition'! At the convention there was uproar. One delegate suddenly denounced abstentionists for forming a fraction within a fraction and the whole 'communist' movement was threatened with disruption.

It is important to note that it was a speech by Gramsci which saved the day. The *circular* group's action, of course, was precisely that style in Italian socialism which he rejected as violently as Bordiga. In a speech which achieved maximum impact, he stressed the *historic, long-term* significance of the meeting. It was essential to put a stop to all 'vain chatter' and to form a *party* which was distinct and clear, with its own programme, direction and its own particular connection with the masses. He was supported by Parodi and Berti from Turin and by Chaim Haller (Chiarini) the Comintern spokesman. The *circular* group were rebuffed. At their own meeting, after harangues from a communist and a unitarian, they joined the communists. Representatives of about 200 branches of the PSI were to take the Graziadei-Marabini line at the Livorno congress and those who joined the Communist Party were to form a rather uneasy right wing within it, of which Tasca became the natural leader.

At Imola the communist fraction's programme was toughened. They were aware now that they would not win a majority of PSI members and it was their *historical* significance which concerned them. They affirmed membership of the Third International and the change of name of the party. They adopted the Bologna programme of the PSI but pledged themselves to carry it through in a revolutionary manner. The criteria for expulsion were made much more rigorous. The whole *socialist concentration* fraction was to be expelled and, in accordance with the Twenty-one Points, anyone who had voted against the Points. The most stiffly centralized and disciplined party organization was envisaged. Bordiga faced a *minority* future squarely. Communists could not accept 'the arithmetical representation of the opinion of a party which was not a party'. The communist party was an historical phenomenon. It must be a *class* party acting like one man. With this, Gramsci was in perfect agreement. Much is sometimes made of the fact that 'factory councils' were not specifically mentioned in the programme and were in fact depreciated during the Bordiga regime. This is partly true. It is also sheer formalism. It overlooks the 'little local difficulty' that the Turin factory councils were destroyed in April 1921 by a combination of employer, state and fascist action ; that under fascism and the terror which preceded it, councils were a physical impossibility. Communist groups, however, were mentioned and the manifesto had spoken of the new party's particular connection with the masses. Even in the Rome Theses of 1922 which are often treated as profoundly 'non-Gramscian', the theses on trade unions were actually drafted by Gramsci and the *tonality* is unmistakable. There can be an excess of formalism in a search for 'factory councils' by name, reminiscent of the 'communist socialist party' of Graziadei! That many of the characteristically Gramscian themes went into eclipse under Bordiga cannot be denied. But the real differences between Gramsci and Bordiga are often incorrectly identified. They are not to be located in the presence or absence of specific references to 'factory councils'. What is certain, and what the conflict with Comintern for several years demonstrated, is that Gramsci was totally committed to the new party at Imola.[16]

And from Imola the fraction went into the Livorno congress on 15 January 1921, into a stormy and agonized debate which ended the 'glorious tradition', and in which Bombacci at one point drew a revolver.[17] And they marched out singing the Internationale, with a minority vote of 58,783 against 98,028 for the unitarians and 14,695 for the reformists. At the point of schism, the PSI had a paper membership of 210,000. After the schism, during the year which followed, over 100,000 people failed to renew their membership in either party. So the Communist Party of Italy entered life, to the intense satisfaction of most of its members, as a small, but compact, disciplined and fanatical Gideon's Army of some 40,000 'contagious individuals'.

Its first action after birth was to struggle desperately for life. Bombacci drew his revolver because somebody accused him of running away from fascists in Bologna. The congress had been moved to Livorno because the PSI could not stand, in Florence, against the fascist terror.

The End of Illusion

'Illusion is the most tenacious weed in the collective consciousness', wrote Gramsci in March 1921, 'History teaches but it has no pupils'.[18]

The Communist Party of Italy was born on a day of dupes. The first illusion to go was the 'victory' of union control.[19] The joint commission set up by Giolitti met on 21 October 1920 and broke up in total disagreement on 5 November. The CGL presented its own scheme. All industries were to be subjected to union control in the form of union representatives with full powers on boards of directors. They were to be elected by all workers over 18, but under union discipline. A higher commission elected from union controllers was to preside over each category of industry and to exercise negative planning powers in that they could 'discourage' new enterprises (exempted from control for two years) if it seemed necessary. Employment was to be channelled through exchanges under joint or union control and dismissals were to be subject to surveillance, though employers were to be permitted some measure of independence. Internal commissions were to be chosen under union direction and one of their members was allowed to work at his shop-steward job for one hour or more during working hours.

The catholic unions put forward a similar scheme, with profit-sharing. The employers, however, countered with a scheme for joint commissions for each category of industry, whose functions were essentially technical and educative. Internal commissions were to be extended if they seemed desirable but were not to operate during working hours. Employers' rights were safe-guarded in hiring and firing. In January 1921, to resolve the deadlock, Giolitti introduced his own scheme. Nine classes of industry were to be subjected to control. State enterprises and small-scale firms employing less than fifty, were excluded; so for four years, were new enterprises. Workers over 18 were to elect 6 representatives, technicians and clerks 3, from union lists, every three years, to serve on a commission for each class of industry. The commission in turn was to nominate two, preferably senior, workers within any plant as its delegates, for local control. Employers were to create parallel organizations and their delegates were to sit in, but not vote, at commission meetings. Employment was to be controlled by joint commissions and workers' political and union rights were protected.

This proposal, which failed to satisfy the CGL and was dismissed with scorn by the left, precipitated a violent campaign by industrialists. Alienated from the Giolitti government since September, they began to pour funds into the fascist offensive which from November 1920 began to mushroom into a mass movement, armed and violent, connived at and frequently supported by authority. Beginning in the rural areas of the north, spreading into Tuscany, it systematically destroyed working-class institutions, beginning with the reformists and *popolari*, widening into a general onslaught. During the first six months of 1921, the fascist squads, climbing through the year towards the 300,000 mark, mobile and well-equipped, destroyed 59 *case del popolo*, 119 *camere*, 107 co-operatives, 83 peasant leagues, 141 socialist centres ; they killed over a hundred, wounded thousands, and terrorized whole communities, forcing socialist municipalities out of office. Frequently, police and army followed up.

The offensive, which reduced all left and some centre movements to a state of semi-paralysis and even semi-'legality', mobilized essentially the middle class and the petty-bourgeoisie, full of two years' suppressed rancour, and was the most startling symptom of the disengagement of 'real' society from the legal and political structure which went on 'functioning' like a headless chicken. It rode the tide of economic depression against a working class already disarmed by political disillusionment after September, the disruption of the socialist movement, and the ravages of unemployment.[20]

The economic crisis, which broke immediately after the occupation of the factories, was a 'normal' one. Giolitti's policies in fact handled it 'successfully' in capitalist terms. Prices collapsed and some of the giants, Ilva, Ansaldo, the *Banca di Sconto*, came apart at the seams. In November, industry was making desperate appeals to government for assistance. By the spring of 1921, firms were sacking workers wholesale. But in a 'normal' manner, the system re-adjusted through 1922 and was able to resume growth from 1923. The price fall meant cheaper coal and food ; from February, Giolitti was able progressively to reduce the bread subsidy against socialist resistance. Foreign borrowing eased off. The lira which had fallen to 101.5 against the pound by December 1920, stabilized at just below 100 during 1921. Per capita income, supported by an agrarian recovery (wheat production climbed back to 51 million quintals) regained pre-war levels and it has been estimated that industrial real wages, for those in employment, rose sharply to an index level of 127 (1913 = 100).

This kind of characteristic capitalist crisis, quite apart from its psychological impact on workers emerging into the disillusionment of October, proved peculiarly divisive. The industrial working class, already politically isolated, was ravaged in particular by unemployment which in the official registers increased six-fold, from the 107,000 of 1920 to over 600,000 in early 1922. The tightening of US immigration regulations worsened the situation, which the official figures only palely reflect. There was a devastating crisis of unemployment, under-employment and insecurity which struck particularly at heavy industry, heart-land of militancy.[21] Militants, at the top of the list for dismissal, naturally, responded politically. On 19 October, the Turin section of FIOM formally warned metalworkers not to hunt for jobs in Turin and at the end of the month, the factory council of Fiat-Centro suddenly seized designs and other vital documents, when a director asked to take some of them home. They suspected that Agnelli and others meant to take their capital and knowledge abroad and destroy the industry. Agnelli offered his resignation, which was rejected by his fellows. But unemployment continued to increase, to reach a paroxysm in the April of 1921. Workers continued to suspect political motives behind the dismissals (they had plenty of reason to do so) but the increasing hostility between socialists and communists bedevilled the situation and among workers generally there was widespread fear.[22]

The local election results of November 1920 proved another delusion. The socialists won nearly 2,200 communes out of 8,300 and 25 provinces out of 69. This really registered the effects of their earlier growth. An anti-socialist bloc growing out of the experiences of September actually checked their advance. The conservative bloc won Turin by a narrow margin, helped by the split between communists and socialists. An instinctive rally to traditional socialist institutions was a natural mass response and helped to isolate the new Communist

Party still further. But it rapidly proved hollow. Most of the gains had been in Emilia and Tuscany and were immediately subjected to the fascist attack, which grew directly out of the elections.[23]

Through the winter of 1920-21, there was a massive moral recession among the working class. They never accepted fascism. They were conquered. There were heroic local stands against it. But the Socialist Party preached calm, non-violence, a bowing of heads before what was thought to be a temporary storm. Halted only by a pact of pacification between socialists and fascists in the summer of 1921, which confirmed communists in their belief that social-democracy and fascism were simply twin facets of bourgeois restoration (an argument Gramsci was beginning to develop as early as October 1920), the fascist offensive drove on without cease, feeding on its own success, to the taking of power in October 1922. During 1921, membership of the CGL fell from two million to one million and all socialist institutions fell with it. During 1922 the retreat became a rout and the socialist movement disintegrated.

The Turin factory councils were an early victim of this reaction.[24] Their restoration in September proved an illusion. By November 1920, their prime function had become a dogged resistance to unemployment. The divergence between 'militants' and 'masses' being ground into apathy and withdrawal by disillusionment, insecurity, unemployment, fear and disunity, was sharply illumined by the annual round of union and council elections in November-December 1920. The militants, enthused by the council experiences of September, held assemblies in which ordinary workers were more vocal than ever before and they proposed sweeping schemes for yet further democratization of the councils. But in elections of commissars and the FIOM section executive, scarcely 15 per cent of the workers voted, despite repeated efforts to whip out a full democratic vote. Fully two-thirds of the commissars were communist, but as an employers' offensive took shape during February 1921 in wholesale dismissals, short-time and attacks on commissars, the latter, lacking active mass support, could hold the line temporarily only because of a compromise patched up by the hostile FIOM leadership, which was socialist.

This first wave of conflict coincided with the introduction of Giolitti's bill on union control, which got nowhere. The congress of the CGL was scheduled for 26 February and the conjuncture brought Gramsci out on what was to prove his last campaign for factory councils. This was squarely centred in his newly-achieved perspective on the role of the working class, led by the Communist Party, in a coalition against capitalism: a policy given added urgency by the patent isolation of the industrial working class in the fascist offensive.

In an article of 10 February on Giolitti's bill, he dismissed all such programmes and called for 'control' to be the focus of a national campaign of the working class in full 'consciousness of its autonomy and its historical personality'. Control must be established outside parliament, by the working class itself, through factory councils, which must build up to a national council. The struggle had to be 'conducted so as to organize around the working class all the popular forces in revolt against the capitalist regime, to ensure that the working class effectively becomes a leading class and guides all the forces of production to self-emancipation through the realization of the communist programme'. Scoccimarro called on the central committee of the Communist Party to organize such a national council or congress to mobilize all workers, including miners, transport workers and peasants. With the failure of the Giolitti bill and the imminence of the CGL congress, the campaign was transformed into an effort to capture or at least make inroads upon the confederation.

'Does the CGL exist?' asked Gramsci on 15 February, comparing its leaders to Caporetto generals. He engaged in a fierce polemic with Buozzi ('I respect Buozzi as I would a dirty rag') and on the 25th, tackled the problem of how to break the vicious circle which imprisoned a revolutionary minority within a constitution it could not change. The CGL was not even a parliamentary state, he said, it was more like Assyria or Babylon or the warrior guilds of Mongolia and China; the PSI had become janissaries of its mandarins and condottiere. The only answer was to move outside its constitutional terrain, as with the bourgeois state. The CGL, like parliament, must become a major theatre of propaganda. 'The struggle for the formation and development of factory councils and workshop councils we believe to be the specific struggle of the Communist Party.' In November 1917 the Bolsheviks had been supported not by the unions but by the factory committees. 'It is important to have at the heart of the CGL an organized and centralized communist minority.' But more importantly historically and tactically was work to convene, immediately after the CGL congress, a congress of councils and internal commissions from all the factories of Italy. They were to create a central organization of their own. He apparently saw this anti-CGL helping to create a strength within the CGL itself.

At the CGL congress, which Togliatti attended, a communist motion proposed a radical reform of the Confederation's structure, an end to the connection with the PSI, a break with the Amsterdam International and adherence to Comintern's union international. It secured nearly 450,000 votes, but the report of the executive was carried by 1,400,000. Gramsci denounced the attacks made at the congress on *L'Ordine Nuovo* but admitted:

> This has been for us a formidable experience . . . Our pessimism has increased, but our will is not diminished . . . The CGL represents in the historical development of the proletariat what the absolute state represented in the historical development of the bourgeoisie. It will be replaced by the organization of councils, workers' parliaments which have the function of dissolving the sediment of bureaucracy and transforming old organizational relations. Our pessimism has increased but our motto is ever live and present: pessimism of the intelligence, optimism of the will.

This was whistling in the dark. After the congress, Gramsci was heckled in commissar meetings by PSI and CGL men. The trade-union committee created by the Communist Party a few days later included nobody from the council-communist tendency. Bordiga and the abstentionists had always been suspicious. And in the strict discipline upon which the new party prided itself, the council theme and the call for a national congress of councils disappeared.[25]

The councils themselves, struggling to hold on to life during the crisis of unemployment and morale, soon followed. The struggle was mounting to a climax in March. In the car industry, 10,000 were unemployed out of a labour force of 50,000. In the tyre plants, it was said that 1,200 had been dismissed out of 5,000. A new wave of sackings at Michelin, directed as usual against commissars and communists in particular, led to a sit-in strike. But troops promptly acted in support of a lock-out and the socialist-controlled union accepted the dismissals.

The collusion of government and employers took increasingly violent form and, inevitably, came to a focus on Fiat. The firm proposed to dismiss 1,500 of its motor-car labour force of 13,000; many commissars, notably Giovanni Parodi, were among the victims. When the commissars' representative, the libertarian Pietro Ferrero, met Agnelli's team of negotiators, he was confronted with a demand that workers implement the provisions of the national agreement with FIOM, which entailed the dismantling of the council system. The workers refused and early in April troops flooded into the Fiat plants in another lock-out.

Once more, Turin was convulsed in a bitter April conflict. This time, the council militants were isolated against employers, the state and their own union, in the worst possible conditions, with *camere* and *case del popolo* going up in flames all over northern Italy. They held out for three weeks ; some held out even longer. Fiat undertook to welcome back anyone who would abandon the councils and work on munitions. By 26 April, over half the labour force had accepted Agnelli's terms. Many were now reduced to abject poverty. The final blow fell on the 26th. Funds in support of the locked-out men had been collected by the *camera.* In the night of the 26th, a fascist 'punitive expedition' ransacked and burned the people's house. Workers who occupied some factories in protest had their leaders sacked. Early in May, the commissars gave in and ordered the men back.[26]

The councils were finished. The new internal commissions, with their drastically reduced powers, were largely socialist, though the worker electors were apathetic and recalcitrant. They lived an attenuated existence for another four years before being abolished by the fascist labour law. In the general election of May 1921, there was widespread apathy. The communists in Turin secured some 30,000 votes, the socialists 57,000. Two communists were elected, Misiano and Rabezzana. Gramsci, whom the Communist Party had put first on its preference list, came fourth in preference votes and was not elected.[27]

It was appropriate. By May 1921 no council-communist argument could get a purchase on reality. A combined offensive by employers, fascists and the state, in the context of a collapse of working-class morale, had driven the councils out of history.

Into Gideon's Army

In the early months of 1921, Gramsci slumped into one of his fits of nervous depression and breakdown. It is hardly surprising. The workers' movement was defeated and stumbling into rout. That particular Turin experience which had charged his writing and activity with originality and excitement, giving his rather bleak personal life some meaning, was spent and, in some senses, devalued. He had been drenched in abuse at Livorno and saddled with a 'voluntarist, interventionist, Crocean' personality he never quite succeeded in throwing off. He was on the central committee of the new Communist Party, but not on its executive. He must have been acutely aware of the *marginal* quality of his work and of himself, become tributary to the former abstentionists who shaped the new party in Bordiga's image.

The party which took shape in 1921 and which codified itself in the Rome Theses of March 1922 was, in many important senses, the logical terminus of an arc of marxist theorizing and socialist practice which stretches back to the crisis of 1911-12.[28] In a very real sense the Communist Party of Italy was the realization of the project of a party first outlined by Amadeo Bordiga in 1912. It was a logic which shaped men of very different derivation into one 'Bordighist' mould in 1921.

Gramsci defended the party hotly in Moscow in the summer of 1923: 'The present majority of the Communist Party intends to defend to the last its position and historical role in Italy, where the unified communist party must be constituted with an ideological centre which is neither the traditional socialist one nor a compromise with that. We are defending the future of the Italian revolution . . .' The obsession with 'organization' which members and observers noted during 1921-23, was in fact an obsession with the essential historical *definition* of the party, in total breach with Italian socialism.

The party was overwhelmingly working class. It was weak in Lombardy and the Veneto, only patchy in Emilia and Tuscany and hardly present at all in the Centre-South. It was concentrated in the north and dense in Piedmont-Liguria. Its great stronghold was Turin. At least 98 per cent of its membership was working class. The party counted its 'intellectuals' very carefully and suspiciously: 'Intellectuals . . . professors . . . lawyers . . .: Genoa 10:1:6 ; Milan 13:5:4 . . .' In 1922, it reported precisely 245 intellectuals in these three categories. This was the first party of the working class in Italy which *was* working class.

The party thought of itself as an organ of the international proletariat in the geographical sector called Italy. The name of the party was the Communist Party *of Italy* (not *Italian*) ; a stress on the territoriality not the nationality. The same principle applied in its internal organization. The party was a territorial organization. It rejected organization by factory cells as a possible source of corporative and sectional contamination. The party had to be a class instrument, transcending all lesser category relationships. The party was to be an *organ* of the proletariat. Therefore, while it was the correct political representation of the proletariat, it could not be immersed *in* it, because it had to consist of the consciously communist who had committed themselves to the service of the class.

The party considered itself an 'operative collectivity' realizing the historical objectives of the entire labouring class; it was the 'theoretical-critical' consciousness of the proletariat. Therefore, admission could only be individual; no parties or fractions of parties could join the PCd'I. There had to be total individual commitment to communism. As the consciousness of the class, the party could not admit that consciousness and will were individual attributes; they were attributes only of the party as an historical force. The party was rigidly centralized. Its discipline was military. It had constantly to be on guard against bourgeois contamination. Its action among the masses had therefore to be very closely scrutinized and controlled.

The basis of its action was the proletariat. Though in Italy, this class was small, it was strategically placed and the policy of the party must be the realization of the *proletarian* future. The party was therefore content to be a small and select cadre force. Through 1921-22, it numbered about 40,000. In the same period, the Socialist Party fell to 80,000 and went on falling. The Communist Party held its numbers through the fascist offensive, survived the first repression and began to grow again until the imposition of totalitarian fascism after the Matteotti crisis, in 1925-26. The party had a youth section, which numbered some 28,000 by 1922, well drilled, very committed and even more 'left' than the party itself. Within the CGL, the party in 1922 could rally some 290,000 votes among *camere* delegates against some 550,000 for its opponents, some 136,000 votes among delegates of the craft federations, against nearly 800,000 for the socialists. Communists were also permitted to enter the syndicalist federation USI, to work for affiliation to the communist trade-union international.

Given the total commitment to the realization of the historical mission of the proletariat, the party's axis was a permanent offensive against the socialists and the bourgeois left, in order to free the proletariat from the democratic delusion. Policy towards the rural population was conceived in terms of this primary objective. Immediate and total socialization of the land was rejected as absurd. Great estates were to be nationalized and farmed out to co-operatives, but there was to be no attack on small property. Rent was to be abolished and an effort was made to mobilize the small peasants and rural proletariat behind the industrial proletariat.

The party believed that fascism would prove a temporary phase of re-integration in a capitalist system which, in order to survive, would assume social-democratic form. The party's duty therefore was to look through fascism to the developing structure of capitalism underneath. Consequently socialism was the main target and Gramsci's *Ordine Nuovo* a major instrument of the attack. For these reasons, the party strongly resisted the call of Comintern for a 'united front' with the socialists from 1921. It was prepared to work within trade unions as organizations of advanced workers. The Rome theses on trade unions were written by Gramsci, though he was balanced by Tasca: they could in fact have appeared in *L'Ordine Nuovo* in late 1919 or 1920.

This attitude towards fascism and its twinning with social-democracy was in no sense sectarian lunacy. There are very strong arguments to support it, in a basic sense, and in the period 1921-25, there was certainly an abundance of empirical evidence in favour of it. But in translating this basic doctrine into everyday practice, the party without doubt under-valued fascism and mis-read it. Bordiga carried the identification of fascism and social-democracy so far that he denied the possibility of a fascist coup. Gramsci had to get the Rome theses modified on the point. This under-estimate of the *specificity* of fascism (which Gramsci was more alert to) had very serious consequences for the personnel of the party and resulted ultimately in its near-destruction as a human organization within Italy. On the other hand, this kind of thinking, which survived Bordiga's displacement from the leadership, made the party quite remarkably tough, resilient and ultimately indestructible. It was in part because of the character given to communism in Italy by its first definition, that the party survived the twenty years of fascist repression to become the largest and in some senses the most effective communist party in Europe.

The party which emerged in 1921, then, was clearly bound to lock into conflict with Comintern during the rise of fascism and the attempts to form united fronts. By 1930, its leadership had been decimated in such struggles. This party, however, in its first self-definition, proved strong and resilient in face of the collapse of the working-class movements. Until 1925-26 it was slowly but steadily growing, and within its own terms. The sheer persistence, in the face of Comintern pressure, of leaders whose formation was in no sense 'Bordighist' is further proof of its relevance. While it certainly suffered from the weaknesses of its self-definition, which were to prove crippling in terms of action, this first communist party of Italy *does* represent a cogent and valid marxist reading of the imperialist crisis of capitalism as it registered in Italy from 1911 to 1921.

This is why Gramsci along with others who had not been 'Bordighist' in formation remained so loyal to it so long, in the conflict with Comintern, whatever his inner doubts (and later rationalization and 'development' of these doubts). Nevertheless his commitment meant that many of the themes and practices most characteristic of Gramsci's thinking and action went into eclipse on the formation of the party.

Antonio Gramsci, his own thinking made marginal, fought in the second rank of the Bordighist leadership, but in the front line of the struggle against capitalism and its social-democracy, in the teeth of the fascist advance. He fought for fifteen months. After the March congress of 1922, the party transferred him to Moscow. On arrival, he collapsed into a serious illness. He was lucky to be in Moscow in December 1922. In that month, the fascists devastated working-class Turin and killed Pietro Ferrero, his old anarchist comrade of the councils.[29] And they finally destroyed the office of *L'Ordine Nuovo*. Characteristically, it was occupied by the police at the time.

Epilogue:
Patrimony: The Holy Ghost of Italian Communism

In March 1923, Ruggero Grieco, at that time Bordiga's 'right arm', wrote an essay in praise of their leader in the name of all the comrades who had been imprisoned. Towards Gramsci, its tone was slightly malicious.

> Bordiga is no philosopher, no scholar, no writer. He is a communist who reached communism through the study of its Masters. To the comfort of a family of ancient lineage and a profession in which he excelled, he preferred the life of a leader of the masses. It is interesting to compare the most characteristic minds of our movement, Gramsci and Bordiga. The first is by temperament a thinker, an indefatigable student, 'hungry for theory', inclined to analysis, the patient assembly of all the elements necessary to an analysis. The other, Bordiga, is a synthesizer who distrusts books, loves battle, bursting with life and strength. In the first, decision is slow to develop, because it demands research into all its elements. In the second, decision is prompt because of the speed with which he distinguishes the useful and the necessary from the useless and the superficial, to arrive at a solution. Gramsci leans towards exposition, teaching, the school. Bordiga prefers to command armed battalions; he is no great lover of the professorial chair or the perambulating seminars of the night streets. Bordiga has written no books and we fear that he never will write any. He has never seen the cover of a book by Croce . . . But what counts is the revolutionary education which he has given the party, the habits of study and discussion . . .[1]

During the travail of the Communist Party after 1923, however, Grieco quit Bordiga and rallied to Gramsci's new leadership. At one point, in October 1926, Gramsci addressed a celebrated letter of protest to the Russian Communist Party, asserting that its internal conflicts were undermining the International and the Russian comrades' leadership of that International. The letter caused considerable embarrassment and was, in practice, suppressed. At every future conflict with the Russians, it was recalled as evidence of the Italians' 'oscillation'. After one such attack during the Popular Front period it was, ironically, Grieco himself who attributed Gramsci's attitude in 1926 to 'Bordigan origins', to the residual *Bordighism* of the party and of Gramsci himself.[2]

History to the defeated may cry alas but cannot pardon. Both leaders, Bordiga and Gramsci, were defeated and that old bitch *History* has disfigured them both.[3]

When the Comintern, in 1921-22, shifted to a united front policy and called for the unification of the new PCd'I with the Serrati wing of a rump socialist movement which had finally expelled the reformists in October 1922, the Communist Party under Bordiga resisted in total intransigence and commitment to principle. In the course of the struggle, Bordiga moved to attack what he perceived as a degeneration in the Comintern, a sacrifice of both principle and the non-Russian communist movement to Russian necessities. He became a leader of the left opposition within the International and was ultimately 'identified' with Trotsky, despite desperate efforts by both the PCd'I and the Comintern to keep him within the movement.

A right-wing minority within the party, associated with Angelo Tasca, was prepared to accept both the united front and fusion with the Serrati socialists. It was the threat of a Comintern-imposed take-over by Tasca which first propelled Gramsci into action, after the party leadership had been disrupted by the first fascist repression of 1923. Gramsci finally adopted a version of the united front 'from below', which he charged with his own characteristic style of argument. In a very slow and painful 'molecular' process during 1923-24, which went very much against the Italian grain, he managed to construct a new leadership for the party and to maintain its allegiance to Comintern. This leadership, directed against both Bordiga and Tasca, was inevitably dubbed 'centrist', though Gramsci was at pains to explain that it was centrist only in a 'topographical' sense, consistently refused to accept it as a 'reconstitution' of the old *Ordine Nuovo* fraternity and frequently referred to his position in the summer of 1920 as a parallel. Gramsci secured his victory over the winter of 1925-26, assisted by a sharp increase and a degree of turnover in party membership during the Matteotti crisis which threatened to unhinge the fascist regime. He codified his victory in the Lyons Theses which displaced the Rome Theses. In October 1926, however, he was himself asserting the autonomy of member parties against the Comintern executive and his arrest by Mussolini in the following month put a stop to his active leadership, as he entered upon his long calvary in prison.

After 1928, the International switched its policy abruptly, dropping the united front, affirming an equivalence between fascism and social democracy and calling for an utterly intransigent and independent communist action. The leadership of the Italian party was disrupted. Tasca was expelled; so were three leading militants in charge of the party's clandestine operations. And despite the content of the policy change, Bordiga was expelled as well, as an unrepentant oppositionist. In prison, Gramsci opposed the new policy and, in practice, virtually withdrew from an active party life.

Leadership fell to Palmiro Togliatti, and the first attempt by the Italian Communist Party to write its own history was a note by him in the April 1930 number of the exile journal *Stato Operaio*, directed against Bordiga. He acknowledged Bordiga's strength and the role of his faction as a force destructive of the old Socialist Party. But he dismissed his thinking as abstract, mathematical, fatalist and mechanical. He attributed Bordiga's influence to the minority and un-developed character of the proletariat in Italy, the consequent prevalence of petty-bourgeois strata and styles and he identified Bordiga's intransigence as a petty-bourgeois reaction to the sterility of Second International socialism. The key symptom, according to Togliatti, was Bordiga's failure to grasp the meaning of the factory council movement in Turin and the enterprise of *L'Ordine Nuovo*.

In the same number of *Stato Operaio*, Mario Montagnana, who had also been one of the original *ordinovisti*, but who had also abandoned Gramsci in the summer of 1920, attacked the opposite wing of the opposition, in the person of Tasca. Once more, an erroneous assessment of the factory councils and *L'Ordine Nuovo* was made a touch-stone.

At the very beginning of its agony, therefore, the Communist Party under Togliatti, in support of a policy which Gramsci had actually rejected in prison, deployed the 'Gramscian' experience against both Tasca and Bordiga. The attack became particularly fierce against Bordiga. In effect, the historiography of the Communist Party tended increasingly to dismiss the entire period of Bordiga's preeminence and to write it out of history. The original nucleus of communism in Italy, the original Leninism of Italy, was located in the

Ordine Nuovo group. Almost as soon as he was imprisoned, Gramsci's writings and his past actions were deployed in an *instrumental* manner, and in a 'translation' which was at best ambiguous.

After Gramsci's death in 1937 the process created what was virtually a 'Gramscian' sub-culture. His writings were used to defend the Popular Front and communist policy under Stalin. During the partisan war, came Togliatti's decisive 'turn' in 1944: a renunciation of immediate revolution, a commitment to a 'mass party' and the presentation of the Communist Party as a *national* force, in a sense, the completion of the *Risorgimento*, the creation of the first *genuine* Italian 'nation'. There was plenty in Gramsci's writings, particularly the prison notebooks, to provide some warrant for the enterprise. The need for a common historiography of the party was made even more compelling by the influx of millions of passionate but ignorant new members and supporters, drawn in by the party's heroic role during the partisan struggle and the civil war. The 'Gramscian' tradition met the need.

The publication of Gramsci's writings assisted the process, in the context of the massive defensive struggle of the Cold War years. Gramsci's prison letters were published first, in 1947 and immediately won the Viareggio literary prize. All friendly references to Bordiga had been deleted from those letters and Gramsci at once registered as a major figure within Italian 'national culture'. And although the *Ordine Nuovo* writings were published fairly early, the writings of his central period as an active militant did not appear until very late. The 'official' collection of material from the critical 1923-26 period did not in fact appear until 1971.

The first serious *impact* of Gramsci was the impact of Gramsci of the prison notebooks, in which he explored virtually every facet of human experience. The consequence was a species of Gramsci cult of quite remarkable scope and intensity. The process was enormously accelerated by the 'de-Stalinization' of communism after 1956, the dislocation of the communist International, the advance of revisionism within the communist bloc, the bubbling up of a variety of 'liberated' and 'libertarian' marxisms. Gramsci in fact suffered an experience not unlike that which Marx had experienced from the 1890s, a process of absorption into bourgeois culture. He became an altogether congenial fellow who could be put to all manner of useful work.

There was, inevitably, a reaction. Quite early, a couple of dissident communist historians had tried to 'rehabilitate' Bordiga. Both Bordiga (who did not die until 1970) and Tasca (who died in 1960) were still around and, during the 1960s in particular, published their dissidence from the party's historiography. The Communist Party of Italy responded in a striking and virtually unique manner, a manner which one has come to expect from the party which is not only the strongest Communist Party in Europe, but also the most intelligent. It virtually opened its archives to sympathetic but independently minded historians and began to publish its material itself. One consequence has been the best history of a Communist Party to emerge from the movement itself ; another has been a magnificent historical enterprise which has successfully reconstructed the early history of the party but has thrown open the whole field to passionate, informed and principled controversy. The net effect of the process, associated with the revolt of a left against the reformist practice of the mass party marching up a 'national road to socialism', has been a quite massive rehabilitation of Bordiga and an equally massive diminution of Gramsci. It coincided with the efflorescence of anti-historicist philosophy, associated with such men as Colletti and della Volpe in Italy and Althusser in France, which subjected the marxism of Gramsci to destructive criticism. In some quarters, historians finally arrived at a virtual identification (*objective* of course) of Gramsci and Tasca! Others go so far as to deny that Gramsci was a marxist at all.

The transmission of this travail to the world outside Italy has been yet more grotesque. In the English-speaking world, in particular, Gramsci has been assimilated in a manner even more lop-sided than the manner in which Gramsci himself assimilated Lenin. There has been a scatter of writings associated with the council movement and with particular aspects of his thought and recently, a systematic presentation of the prison writings. His strictly 'political' writings from his activist period are still largely unavailable. The process of assimilation into English of the 'first' Gramsci has scarcely begun, though a form of 'Gramscianism' has been widely diffused, at least in terms of vocabulary and style. The impact of the succeeding three or four 'Gramscis' created by 'history' has yet to come. Bordiga's head has, as yet, hardly begun to inch over the horizon. One braces oneself uneasily for the oncoming explosion, a cultural shock of the first order, and the possible collapse of the Gramsci market.

Bourgeois intellectual hegemony, as Antonio would no doubt be the first to point out, weighs upon our brains in a veritably archaeological strata-hierarchy of corpses.

It is perhaps time to rescue Gramsci and Bordiga from their fellow-countrymen before they are frozen for ever into statuary presences on the Campidoglio.

History, that battered old whore, has erected them into Manichaean archetypes of early communism. In fact, on a preliminary reading at least, it is the tense dialectic between their polarities which constitutes marxist revolutionary practice. Without Bordiga's sense of marxism as a 'science', without his fundamental 'rupture' from the bourgeois world, without his strong, combative and thorough assertion of marxism, it is difficult to see how communism is possible. Without Gramsci's global and molecular marxist exploration of human experience, without his examination, in total human reality, of the *process* of Bordiga's 'conversion', it is difficult to see how communism is realizable.

That is why the work of both needs to become part of the patrimony of the British working class and British marxism. The enterprises of both Bordiga and Gramsci were attempts to translate Marxist-Leninism into terms which were relevant and effective in countries where capitalism was developed and its social structure complex and elaborate. Sylvia Pankhurst, Daniel de Leon, the Socialist Labour Party, were all, to a greater or lesser degree, elements in the council movement which first formed around an interpretation of 'the English system'. The assimilation of Gramsci, still more of Bordiga, into English-speaking experience has only begun. It must continue.

There is another, equally important, patrimony to inherit. It was not 'history' which created the council movement. It is men who do all this. It was Giovanni Parodi, Battista Santhia, Andrea Viglongo and thousands like them: ordinary workers and working women, who were extraordinary men and women, trying to live communist in a hard time. Their conduct is part of the memory of the working-class movement which needs all the memories it can get. It needs memory to defeat death. The British working class needs to remember our comrades in Italy, whom Gramsci memorably saluted during the last of their black Aprils: [4]

The workers of Fiat have gone back to work. Betrayal? Denial of the revolutionary ideal? The workers of Fiat are men of flesh and blood.

They held out for a month.

They knew that they fought and resisted not only for themselves, not only for the rest of the Turin working class, but for the whole working class of Italy.

They held out for a month.

They were physically exhausted because for many weeks, many months, their wages had been reduced and were no longer sufficient to keep their families alive.

Yet they held out for a month.

They were completely isolated from a nation sunk in weariness, indifference, hostility.

Yet they held out for a month.

They knew they could not hope for help from outside. They knew that for the Italian working class the tendons had been cut. They knew they were doomed to defeat.

Yet they held out for a month . . .

The Italian working class is flattened under the roller of capitalist reaction. For how long? Nothing has been lost if consciousness and faith remain intact, if bodies surrender but not souls. The workers of Fiat have struggled hard for years and years. They have bathed the streets in their blood. They have suffered hunger and cold. They remain, with their glorious past, the vanguard of the Italian proletariat. They remain faithful and devoted soldiers of the revolution. They have done as much as it is possible for men of flesh and blood to do.

We take off our hats before their humiliation, because to sincere and honest men, there is something of greatness in it.

Chronology

1889:

Foundation of Second International / Formation of first *camera del lavoro* in Italy / Birth of Amadeo Bordiga

1891:

Filippo Turati launches *Critica Sociale*, journal of reformist socialism / Milan convention decides to form Party of Italian Workers / Birth of Antonio Gramsci

1892:

Genoa congress of Party of Italian Workers adopts socialist programme

1893:

Rural unions of Po Valley join the Party which adopts the title Socialist

1895:

After temporary suppression, party re-forms itself on individual membership under the name Italian Socialist Party (PSI) / Leadership formed in 'Marxist decade': influence of Antonio Labriola

1899:

Foundation of Fiat company

1900:

Adoption of minimum and maximum programmes by PSI

1901:

Formation of FIOM, metal-workers' federation – Formation of *Federterra*, socialist land-workers' federation

1902:

Creation of 'resistance secretariat' at Milan, federating *camere* and craft federations

1904:

General strike / Rise of syndicalist influence

1906:

Formation of CGL, trade-union federation in close alliance with PSI / First recognition of internal commissions in Fiat-FIOM agreement

1907:

PSI and CGL define separate areas of jurisdiction according to decisions of Stuttgart Congress of the International

1908:

Exclusion and withdrawal of syndicalists from socialist movement

1909:

Angelo Tasca forms Turin section of socialist youth federation

1910:

Formation of *intransigent revolutionary* fraction of PSI / Formation of Turin Industrial League, model for the first *Confindustria*

1911:

June: Giolitti introduces bill for near-manhood suffrage

September: Outbreak of the Libyan War

October: Modena congress of the PSI / Split between revolutionaries and reformists / Rise of Mussolini

1912:

April: Formation of Karl Marx circle at Naples by Amadeo Bordiga

July: Reggio Emilia congress of PSI – Expulsion of the reformists

September: 'Culture' debate between Tasca and Bordiga at congress of youth federation / Great strike in Turin / Rise of syndicalist influence

November: Formation of syndicalist federation USI

December: Mussolini becomes editor of *Avanti*

1913:

Mussolini exercises hegemony over socialist movement; forces temporary resignation of leaders of CGL; quasi-insurrectionary campaigns

Sharp rise in socialist membership and circulation of *Avanti*; increase in working-class character of PSI; emergence of new generation / A. Gramsci, P.Togliatti, U. Terracini join Turin youth section

Great strike in Turin

Parliamentary elections: PSI gains 52 seats and over one million votes

1914:

June: Red Week insurrections

July: Ancona congress of PSI reinforces revolutionary character of party, while local elections and CGL strengthen position of reformists

August: Outbreak of World War and collapse of Second International

October: Mussolini's article, 'From an absolute to an active and operative neutrality'; Gramsci's article, 'An active and operative neutrality' in *Il Grido del Popolo* (Turin); Bordiga's article, 'For an active and operative anti-militarism' in *Il Socialista* (Naples)

November: Mussolini launches *Il Popolo d'Italia* and preaches interventionism / He is expelled from the PSI / Serrati takes over *Avanti*

December: Bordiga in *Il Socialista* advocates resistance to the war and the intensification of social discord

1915:

Growing interventionist campaign

February: Government takes action against socialist demonstrations

May: The 'radiant days of May' interventionist campaign / PSI split, maximalists urging no support for war, reformists urging no alienation from the nation / General strike for 19 May called off / Turin, bloody conflict with police during general strike 17-18 May / PSI adopts slogan 'Neither support nor sabotage' / Italy enters war on 24 May / PSI deputies vote against war credits

September: Zimmerwald conference of anti-war left / PSI active

1916:

April: Kienthal conference of anti-war left / Serrati and Balabanoff move left but Morgari contacts the Henry Ford peace mission

June: Salandra government falls; Orlando, personal contact of Turati, becomes Minister of Interior

Gramsci active in socialist journalism in *Il Grido del Popolo* and *Avanti* in Turin / Bordiga cultivates small group in Naples

1917:

February: Gramsci publishes *La Città Futura* for Turin youth section

Ad hoc convention of PSI in Rome / Conduct of Directorate approved by 24,000 votes to 6,000, but tough Bordiga motion defeated by 17,000 to 14,000 / Turin delegates disaffected

March: Outbreak of Russian revolution

April: Entry of USA into the war

Directorate issues statement by Turati supporting American-Russian democratic bloc against central powers / Bordiga protests /

The youth federation calls for revolution

May: Revolt against privation and war in Milan

Milan meeting of PSI Directorate publishes democratic programme of post-war reconstruction

Youth federation calls for general strike against the war

July: On initiative of Naples section under Bordiga, meeting in Florence revives the *intransigent revolutionary* fraction of the PSI

August: Visit of Russian delegation, hosted by Serrati, meets crowds shouting 'Viva Lenin!'

21-28 August: Revolt of the working class in Turin / Crushed by military force / Over 800 militants arrested / 200 sent to the front / Gramsci takes over temporary leadership of section

September: Congress of youth federation rejects leadership's advice, adopts intransigence and makes Bordiga editor of *Avanguardia*

October: Orlando government takes office / Relations with Turati and PSI deputies grow closer

24 October-4 November: military disaster of Caporetto / Massive rally to patriotism and national defence

18 November: Clandestine meeting in Florence of *intransigent revolutionary* fraction, dominated by Bordiga / Gramsci attends and is only delegate to support Bordiga's call for action / Meeting calmed by PSI leadership, Serrati and Lazzari / Official slogan of PSI re-affirmed / First news of Bolshevik revolution

December: Gramsci, 'The revolution against *Capital*', *Avanti*, response to Bolshevik revolution

1918:

Wave of repression against PSI militants, while parliamentary group enjoys some autonomy

Growth of internal commissions in industry, particularly in Turin and revolt against official policy of unions / Gramsci in *Il Grido del Popolo* begins to popularize British shop-steward movement

March: The Papacy approves Catholic Union Federation, CIL

July-August: Proposal to create commission to plan post-war reconstruction of Italy – *Commissionissima* / CGL and much of parliamentary group favour participation / Directorate forbids participation / Rigola, reformist secretary of the CGL, resigns / Ludovico D'Aragona, reformist, succeeds him

September: Pact of Alliance signed between PSI and CGL re-affirming Second International definition of areas of competence between the two organizations

Congress of PSI in Rome: condemns conduct of Turati, asserts party control over deputies, proclaims maximum programme, but rejects demands of the left

November: The CGL in its post-war programme, puts a Constituent Assembly at the head of the list

The PSI Directorate issues a statement committing the party to the dictatorship of the proletariat / But it directs attention to the democratic programme of May 1917 as a focus for unity

The FIOM congress at Rome disrupted by a revolt of the rank and file focusing on the internal commissions

December: Bordiga publishes *Il Soviet* in Naples, calls for the expulsion of reformists and creation of a communist party

Separate edition of *Avanti* created for Turin

1919:

Mushroom growth of CGL, PSI, USI, the catholic union federation CIL, peasant leagues and unions / All manner of direct action / First great strike wave breaks

January: Congress of USI rejects Constituent Assembly and calls for working-class unity for revolution

Meetings of PSI Directorate divided; call for structural reform in revolutionary spirit / CGL launches campaign for 8-hour day

February: *Il Soviet* develops themes of socialist abstention from parliamentary elections, in order to break decisively with bourgeois society / Calls for the creation of a new party as the class instrument of a strictly-defined proletariat

March: Foundation of Third International

18-22 March: Meeting of Directorate in Milan votes 10-3 to adhere to the Third International

FIOM wins 8-hour day in metal industry but agrees to curb the internal commissions and restrict strike action

Giovanni Boero, secretary of Turin socialist section, argues for abstentionism and a split in the party and is rebuked by *Avanti*

April: Failure of Woodrow Wilson initiatives in Europe, radicalization of attitudes in PSI

15 April: Nationalists and fascists burn the offices of Avanti

17 April: Armando Borghi, secretary of USI, calls for united revolutionary front of the PSI, CGL, USI, the anarchist Union and the railwaymen / Some response from Bombacci and other PSI leaders

Strong resistance to FIOM's agreement in Liguria and in Turin, where a technicians' strike focuses attention on the internal commissions and the problem of class solidarity

1 May: Publication of *L'Ordine Nuovo*, Turin

Gramsci elected to executive of Turin socialist section

June: Congress of Popular Party (PPI, *popolari*, catholic)

7 June: Gramsci, 'The ransom of history', *L'Ordine Nuovo*

21 June: Gramsci, 'Workers' Democracy', *L'Ordine Nuovo*: initiates factory council movement

Popular insurrections over food prices, collapse of authority in some regions

5 July: PSI warns against 'facile illusions'; fading of food troubles

6 July: Abstentionists led by Bordiga decide to form a communist fraction of PSI

13 July: PSI appoints commission to revise party programme which includes Bordiga

19 July: *L'Ordine Nuovo*, description of British shop-steward movement

20-21 July: International strike in support of Russian and Hungarian soviet republics / Partial success

26 June: *L'Ordine Nuovo* publishes programme of Bordiga's communist fraction

Youth Federation rejects abstentionism

L'Ordine Nuovo conducts campaign for factory councils in socialist circles and meetings of militants

9 August: *L'Ordine Nuovo*, Alfonso Leonetti criticises abstentionism

16 August: *L'Ordine Nuovo*, Ottavio Pastore, 'The problem of the internal commissions'

17 August: *Il Soviet* calls for PSI to make clear choice between being party of proletarian dictatorship or one more party of democracy: Bordiga quits the PSI programme commission

23 August: *L'Ordine Nuovo*, comments by Giovanni Giardina, abstentionist, and Gramsci on Pastore's article

Fiat-Centro workers elect workshop commissars; union members only having the franchise

30 August: Andrea Viglongo, 'Towards new institutions', *L'Ordine Nuovo*, with supporting comments by Gramsci

31 August: Brevetti-Fiat plant elects workshop commissars: all workers having the right to vote, union members only having the right of candidature / Hailed as triumph of its principles by *L'Ordine Nuovo*

3 September: Tasca defeats abstentionists in Turin socialist section; Gramsci and Terracini top poll for executive

13 September: Gramsci, 'To the workshop commissars of Fiat-Centro and Brevetti-Fiat' and 'The development of the revolution', *L'Ordine Nuovo*

14 September: Bordiga, 'The system of communist representation',

Il Soviet, criticises the *Ordine Nuovo* programme

Factories in the metal and engineering industries in Turin elect workshop commissars

21 September: Bordiga, 'Shall we form soviets?' *Il Soviet*, further criticism of *L'Ordine Nuovo* programme

4 October: 'A programme of work', *L'Ordine Nuovo*, for the Bologna congress of the PSI

5-8 October: Bologna congress of the PSI. Maximalist motion (Serrati) wins by some 48,000 votes against the reformists' 14,000 and the abstentionists' 3,300 / Tasca and *L'Ordine Nuovo* support Serrati / Adherence to Third International confirmed; Comintern representative received, journal *Comunismo* launched / In accordance with congress decisions, Bordiga suspends abstentionist propaganda and *Il Soviet*

11 October: Gramsci, 'Unions and councils', *L'Ordine Nuovo*

18 October: A.Tasca, 'The unity of the party', *L'Ordine Nuovo*: maximalist / Factory council movement advances rapidly through Turin complex: working alliance between council communists and abstentionist communists

Meetings of workshop commissars in Turin in conflict with union leaderships and the *camera*

20 October: Workshop commissars in metal and automobiles elect a *Study Committee for Factory Councils* to co-ordinate campaign

25 October: Gramsci, 'Unions and the dictatorship', *L'Ordine Nuovo*: whole issue devoted to the problem of the trade unions

26 October: Assembly of commissars at *casa del popolo* of Turin represents 32 plants and 50,000 workers

26-28 October: First congress of chemical workers at Milan discusses and rejects Turin commissar scheme; first impact of Turin movement outside the city

Fierce criticism of council movement by union spokesmen

31 October: First general assembly of workshop commissars of Turin / Accepts report of *Study Committee* and adopts *The Programme of the Workshop Commissars* / Assembly decides to capture the executive of the local section of FIOM

1 November: Annual assembly of local section of FIOM / Union leadership proposes to recognise commissars but only as consultative bodies / Fiat-Centro delegates propose to grant commissars deliberative powers but to restrict franchise to union members / Boero and libertarian Maurizio Garino propose full council scheme / Council communists win by a large majority and elect the FIOM section executive

1 November: *L'Ordine Nuovo*, Togliatti attacks union attitude and re-affirms revolutionary character of councils

8 November: *L'Ordine Nuovo*, hugely successful issue; print of 5,000 sold out and reprint ordered / Publishes the 'Programme of Workshop Commissars' and Gramsci, 'Syndicalism and councils' / Togliatti attacks concept of councils as democratization of unions

Battaglie Sindacali, organ of CSL, Serrati attacks council movement

10 November: Bordiga addresses his first letter to Lenin; seized by the police

15 November: *L'Ordine Nuovo*, Gramsci, 'Revolutionaries and the elections'; Montagnana continues attack on concept of councils as democratization of unions

Parliamentary elections: massive socialist success, 156 deputies, over 30 per cent of votes; *popolari* win over 100 seats

29 November: Gramsci, 'The problem of power', *L'Ordine Nuovo*

30 November: *L'Ordine Nuovo*: School of Propaganda created / Council movement sweeps through much of Turin industry / Employers co-ordinate resistance

2-3 December: Socialist deputies walk out on monarch at opening of Chamber, attacked by nationalists and fascists; general strike

6 December: *Avanti* (Milan): Serrati publishes letter of Lenin to 'communists' of Italy and uses it against abstentionists and council communists / *Avanti* and *Comunismo*, Serrati and Comintern representative Nicolai Ljubarsky-Carlo Niccolini attack Turin council movement

11 December: Turin socialist section votes heavily to support council movement / Alliance of abstentionist and council communists takes control / New *Study Committee* elected under presidency of Togliatti

6-13 December: *L'Ordine Nuovo*, Gramsci, 'The events of 2-3 December' and 'L'Ordine Nuovo and Battaglie Sindacali'

15-17 December: Extraordinary session of Turin *camera del lavoro* / Council-communist motion, presented by anarchist Garino, wins by 38,000 to 26,000 votes, despite opposition by CGL and Serrati / Victory of council movement within Turin area / by new year, estimated that 150,000 workers organized in councils

20 December: Gramsci, 'The professional revolutionary', *L'Ordine Nuovo*
A. Tasca, in 'The problem of the un-organized', registers a certain dissidence

27 December: Gramsci, 'The party and the revolution', *L'Ordine Nuovo*
Parma congress of USI votes to support factory councils

1920

January: 'Strike frenzy' hits northern Italy / CGL and PSI, with their own council and soviet schemes, contain the factory council movement and restrict it to Turin area

3 January: Togliatti, 'Class control', *L'Ordine Nuovo*: whole number devoted to workers' control

4 January: *Il Soviet* resumes publication / 4 and 11 January: Bordiga begins series of essays under the title 'For the constitution of workers' councils in Italy', in criticism of council movement

6 January: Executive of Turin section resigns / Electoral committee prepares list to entrench alliance of abstentionist and council communists

9 January: Gennari proposes that socialist-controlled communes create soviets

11 January: Bordiga addresses second letter to Lenin; seized by police

11-13 January: Florence: first meeting of national council of PSI since Bologna congress and November elections / Representation of parlia-

mentary group on Directorate strengthened / Bombacci presents scheme
for soviets and council rejects both Bordighist and council-communist
arguments

17 January: *L'Ordine Nuovo*, A.Tasca, 'Gradualism and revolutionism
in the factory councils', reply to Bordiga; Togliatti opens prolonged
attack on Bombacci proposals, the CGL plan for a labour parliament
and policy of PSI since Florence council meeting; Gramsci, 'The historical
function of the city', opens discussion on communist failure in Milan

24-31 January: 'Action programme of the Turin socialist section' and
Gramsci, 'First: renew the party', *L'Ordine Nuovo* / Joint list of
abstentionists and council communists stand for section executive on
Action Programme / Luigi Galleani, veteran anarchist, re-starts *Cronaca
sovversiva* in Turin

1-29 February: *Il Soviet* resumes critique of council movement / Bordiga,
resolved on a split, speaks at Turin before section elections / *Il Soviet*
begins to distinguish Gramsci's position from Tasca's / Rival list to *Action
Programme* candidates, supported by Tasca, defeated

4 February: *L'Ordine Nuovo*, Gramsci, 'The instrument of labour',
and 'chronicle' on crisis within the Ordine Nuovo group

17 February: Workers under syndicalist leadership occupy plants in
Sestri Ponente and elsewhere in Liguria

28 February: Workers occupy the Mazzoni's cotton mills near Turin/Out-
breaks of occupation elsewhere. *L'Ordine Nuovo* criticizes the occupations
Re-elections of workshop commissars occupy two weeks in Turin
Anarchist Union moves its headquarters to Milan and publishes
Umanità Nova

March: USI moves its headquarters and journal *Guerra di Classe* to
Milan / Its secretary, A.Borghi, starts campaign for factory councils in
Milan / Syndicalist-inspired motions passed by commissar meetings in
Turin

6 March: Gramsci, 'Governing party and governing class', *L'Ordine
Nuovo* / *L'Ordine Nuovo* much occupied with anarchism, syndicalism
and industrial unionism

7 March: Re-formation of *Confindustria*: Olivetti attacks factory councils
as dual power in the factory
Study Committee tries to re-organize commissar system, to establish a
central secretariat, and issues calls for vigilance

20 March: Olivetti, Agnelli of Fiat and de Benedetti of Industrial League
visit prefect of Turin and warn of impending lock-out against 'indiscipline'

26 March: Gramsci, 'The problem of force', *Avanti* (Turin)

27 March: *L'Ordine Nuovo,* 'For a national congress of factory councils',
and Gramsci, 'The end of a power'

28 March: As a result of conflict over legal time and the actions of
commissars, industrialists in the Turin metal industry proclaim a lock-out,
supported by massive troop movements, against factory councils

3 April: Gramsci, 'Turin and Italy', *Avanti* (Turin)

9-10 April: Gramsci, 'Address to the anarchists', *L'Ordine Nuovo* /

Gramsci writes 'For a renewal of the Socialist Party' for the Turin socialist section

13 April: General strike in Turin in defence of factory councils / Within a few days, extended to Piedmont and complete in provinces of Turin, Novara, Alessandria, and Pavia / Complete success; estimated 500,000 workers and four million people involved / Workers at Genoa, Pisa, Livorno and Florence, under syndicalist influence, act in support / The CGL and PSI hostile

19-21 April: National Council of PSI at Milan, transferred from Turin / Tasca, Terracini and Togliatti present 'For a Renewal of the Socialist Party' and call for a general strike / Call rejected; Turin movement left in isolation / D'Aragona, secretary of the CGL takes over negotiations

24 April: End of general strike in Piedmont and Turin / Defeat for workers / Council system survives but is emasculated

2 May: *Il Soviet*, Bordiga criticizes the Turin movement of April

8 May: *L'Ordine Nuovo*: Gramsci, 'Superstition and reality', and publishes 'For a renewal of the Socialist Party' which is later produced as a pamphlet

8-9 May: Conference of abstentionist fraction Florence, which decides to form a communist party after the Second Congress of Comintern, to create a national organization and to call for an anti-parliamentary fraction within the International / Gramsci attends as observer, establishes alliance with abstentionists but rejects abstentionism

Gino Baldesi proposes scheme to integrate factory councils into union structure to directive council of the CGL

23-26 May: Meeting of the *camera del lavoro* of Turin / Tasca proposes scheme to unify councils and unions which marks a breach with the *Ordine Nuovo* programme / Carried overwhelmingly / Breach between Tasca and Gramsci / 29 May-28 August: *L'Ordine Nuovo* devotes much space to polemic with Tasca over the programme of the council movement

5 June: Gramsci, 'The factory council', *L'Ordine Nuovo*

6 June: *Il Soviet* publishes 'Theses of the Abstentionist Communist Fraction of the PSI'

9 June: Fall of Nitti government, Giolitti takes office

12 June: Gramsci, 'Unions and councils', *L'Ordine Nuovo*

Rise of syndicalist numbers and influence / PSI tentatively accepts proposal for joint conference with USI

26 June: Turati's speech on 'Remaking Italy' which becomes theme of a reformist 'labourist' solution preached by *Critica Sociale*

Mutiny of troops at Ancona starts campaign against arms production under syndicalist leadership / Many factories convulsed / Revival of councils and *Study Committee*, under syndicalist influence / Repulsion by PSI

3 July: Gramsci, 'Two revolutions', *L'Ordine Nuovo*

10 July: Gramsci, 'Where is the Socialist Party going?' *L'Ordine Nuovo*

15 July: Opening of Second Congress of the Communist International, Petrograd. Pressure on Serrati to accept the Twenty-One Points, on

Bordiga to abandon abstentionism / Lenin singles out 'For a renewal of the Socialist Party' for praise, but is attacked on this score by every tendency within the Italian delegation

17 July: Gramsci, 'The communist groups', *L'Ordine Nuovo*

20 July: Gramsci writes report on council movement for Comintern

22 July: FIOM calls overtime ban in face of employers' refusal to discuss wage claim

Crisis in Turin socialist section / Clash between abstentionists and others over local elections, syndicalist campaign and formation of communist party / *Electionist communist* fraction forms and most supporters of *L'Ordine Nuovo* rally to it, including Terracini and Togliatti / Gramsci forms *Communist education group* and decides to stand aside from section executive elections

7 August: End of Second Congress of Communist International / Serrati resists full application of Twenty-One Points; congress of PSI to decide issue / Bordiga renounces abstentionism and pledges himself to create a communist party on as wide a base as possible

10-17 August: Breakdown in talks between FIOM and employers / FIOM calls a go-slow and makes provision for occupation of factories in the event of a lock-out / USI calls for immediate occupation but falls in line with FIOM

In Turin socialist section, major victory for *electionist communists*; Togliatti becomes secretary / *Communist education group* gets very few votes and Gramsci reduced to political isolation

25 August: Government attempt to intervene in dispute in metal industry rebuffed by employers

29 August: Gramsci, 'What do we mean by demagogy?', *Avanti* (Turin)

30 August: Lock-out in Romeo works, Milan / Workers occupy factories in Milan

31 August-1 September: Employers order lock-out throughout Italy

1 September: The Occupation of the Factories / By 4th September 400,000 workers in action / As movement spreads outside metal industry, total rises to half a million

3 September: *Socialist concentration* fraction (reformist) announces meeting to create national organization

4 September: Gramsci, 'The Communist Party', *L'Ordine Nuovo*

5 September: Gramsci, 'Red Sunday', *Avanti* (Turin)

CGL calls all socialist leaders to its national council on 10 September and proposes the socialization of industry

6 September: Land occupations in the south; PSI issues revolutionary proclamation

7 September: Regional convention of Ligurian unions proposes occupation of every branch of production

9-11 September: Decisive meetings of the CGL and PSI at Milan / Turin refuses to lead armed insurrection / CGL offers to resign in favour of PSI Directorate if latter proposes to make the revolution / PSI Directorate refuses the offer / The issue put to the national council of the CGL / PSI's proposal that the movement be directed to the revolution defeated by 590,000 votes to 409,000, in favour of CGL's proposal for union control of industry

12 September: Inter-proletarian convention led by USI calls for general occupation

14-16 September: Communists and anarchists in Turin demand general occupation

15 September: Giolitti imposes solution of joint commission of unions and employers to establish union control of industry

17 September: Employers yield / Extraordinary congress of FIOM rebuts attack on settlement by Turin delegates led by libertarians Garino and Ferrero / Turin socialist section calls for action to form a communist party

19 September: Final settlement at Rome

21 September: Extraordinary congress of FIOM calls for referendum on the settlement

24 September: Gramsci, 'Political capacity', *Avanti* (Turin)

25 September: Referendum results: 127,000 votes in favour of settlement to 44,000 against, with heavy abstention

25-30 September: End of occupation of factories

28 September-1 October: Meeting of PSI Directorate on Twenty-one Points / Division of opinion and fragmentation of movement into fractions

2 October: Gramsci, 'The land of Pulcinella', *L'Ordine Nuovo*

8 October: Gramsci, 'Cowardice and fickleness', *Avanti* (Turin)

9 October: Gramsci, 'The communist party', *L'Ordine Nuovo*

10-11 October: Reggio Emilia, convention of the (reformist) *socialist concentration* fraction

14 October: Milan, meeting of communists to form a fraction / Gramsci signs manifesto with Bordiga, Bombacci, Fortichiari, Repossi, Misiano, Terracini and Polano for the Youth Federation

17 October: The Turin *Avanti* declares its independence from the PSI

31 October: Communist fraction unites in Turin

5 November: Joint commission established in Giolitti's settlement of Occupation of Factories, breaks up in disagreement

Severe economic crisis, with heavy unemployment and sharp fall in working-class morale

Local elections: socialists win 2,200 communes and 25 provinces, but formation of anti-socialist bloc checks their advance / Fascist offensive begins in rural areas of north / Fascist terror forces transfer of congress of PSI from Florence to Livorno

20-21 November: Florence, convention of *unitarian communist* fraction, maximalist under Serrati

25 November: Communist regional federation for Piedmont formed; executive consists of the three factions of the August elections to the Turin section executive.

27 November: Communists win Turin section of PSI by 249 votes to 84

28-29 November: Imola, convention of *communist* fraction / Attempt to

form *communist-socialist* fraction as bridge to Serrati fraction rejected
December: Elections of workshop commissars and internal commissions in Turin secure only a 15 per cent vote among workers
24 December: Last number of the weekly *Ordine Nuovo* / Turin *Avanti* renamed as daily *L'Ordine Nuovo*

1921:

1 January: First number of the daily *Ordine Nuovo*, editor A.Gramsci
14 January: Formation of Institute of Proletarian Culture, section of Moscow Proletkult, by Gramsci and *L'Ordine Nuovo*
15-21 January: Livorno: congress of the PSI / Unitarian communist motion: 98,028 votes; reformist motion: 14,695 votes; communist motion: 58,783 votes
21 January: Communist fraction secedes and forms the Communist Party of Italy, section of the Third International / Executive: Bordiga, Fortichiari, Repossi, Grieco, Terracini / Gramsci on central committee Giolitti presents his own scheme for union control of industry / Deadlocked in committee / Employers finance fascists, whose offensive redoubles / Beginnings of collapse of socialist and working-class movements
10, 15 February: *L'Ordine Nuovo*, Gramsci calls for national congress of factory councils and creation of communist organizations within the CGL
Heavy dismissals and reprisals in Turin industry; conflict between communist commissars and socialist unions
26 February: Congress of the CGL / Communist motion gets 450,000 votes against 1,400,000 for the union leadership / Trade-union committee of PCd'I includes no council communists
March: Fascist offensive / Struggle over dismissals and commissars in Turin leads to lock-out and military occupation of plants
April: Fierce three-week struggle in Turin around Fiat / Lock-out, supported by troops, against factory councils / Commissars isolated
26 April: Fascist punitive expedition against Turin *casa del popolo* / Defeat of workers / End of the factory councils
8 May: Gramsci, 'Men of flesh and blood', *L'Ordine Nuovo*
15 May: General election / 15 communists elected, against 123 socialists / In Turin, communists, with 30,000 votes against socialists' 57,000, secure two deputies, Misiano and Rabezzana; Gramsci, though first on communists' preference list, fails to win a seat
June: New parliament, with 35 fascists and *popolari* restive, ends Giolitti's premiership; Bonomi takes office with policy of 'reconciliation'
July: First check to fascist advance; Mussolini makes overtures to CGL and political parties / Formation of *arditi del popolo*, anti-fascist squads / Gramsci sympathetic but PCd'I concentrates on its own para-military organization
August: Pact of pacification between socialists and fascists / The PSI and CGL disown the *arditi del popolo* / Internal crisis within fascism
November: Economic crisis intensifies / Pact of pacification breaks

down / Fascism resolves inner crisis, shifts dramatically to the right and resumes its offensive / Massive fall in membership of PSI, CGL and all working-class organizations except the communist ones

December: Gramsci takes part in Rome discussions on the Theses of the PCd'I which contradict the united front policy adopted by the Comintern

Fascism, now a mass movement, supported by important elements within the political state and bourgeois society, begins to assume hegemonic force

1922:

February: Bonomi government falls; 'ghost' government of Facta takes office / Labour Alliance formed by shrunken CGL, USI, UIL, rail and maritime unions. PCd'I remains aloof

20-24 March: Rome Congress of PCd'I / Rome Theses approved by 31,089 votes to 4,151 for an opposition led by Tasca / Beginnings of conflict with the Comintern

26 May: Gramsci, in bad health, leaves for Moscow as delegate of PCd'I / Becomes a member of the Comintern Executive, but illness forces his withdrawal to a sanatorium

June: Socialist reformists, led by Turati, decide to support any government which will restore order / Censured by the PSI Directorate, 60 deputies form a separate organization

July-August: Fascist violence reaches its paroxysm / Prolonged governmental crisis / Labour Alliance calls 'legalitarian general strike', broken by fascist violence / Fascists take over all former proletarian strongholds except Turin and Parma / Collapse of working-class movements

1-4 October: Rome congress of the PSI / The party splits / The reformists under Turati, with 29,000 votes, form the Unitary Socialist Party with 61 of the parliamentary deputies and the support of the CGL / The maximalists under Serrati, with some 32,000 votes, re-affirm their adherence to the Third International / Membership of the PSI falls to 25,000, that of the PCd'I, to 24,000

28 October: The March on Rome: fascists take power

Glossary

Labour Organizations

Camera del lavoro: Literally, chamber of labour. Founded in Milan in 1889 in imitation of French labour organizations of syndicalist inspiration. The centre and focus of the local unions and workers' organizations of a particular commune or district. In time, these came to embrace local unions, leagues, co-operatives, savings banks. The *camera* served initially as a worker-controlled labour exchange and information centre to improve the bargaining position of labour. It grew into the real centre of working-class life, far more significant locally than its formal British equivalent, the trades and labour council. Unions were often sketchily organized, numerically weak and insecurely based financially. The *camera* could organize the labour force of a whole district in support of a particular group and the local 'general strike' was a feature of Italian labour practice. While in time, craft and industrial union branches were heavily represented in the *camera* which was often minutely sub-divided by craft, the organization was frequently more immediately responsive to popular feeling than craft or industrial federations and was a natural theatre of radical action. It could generate a populist, sometimes a class, rather than a trade or craft mentality.

Casa del popolo: Literally, people's house/home. The centre and headquarters of the *camera*. A hiring hall, labour exchange, educational and recreational centre, club, meeting-place. A prime target for the fascist squads during 1921-22, its destruction could cripple the local movement.

Internal commissions: Factory grievance committees: a small number of workers elected by union men within a factory to handle everyday problems of discipline and arbitration. First officially recognized in the Fiat-FIOM agreement of 1906, enjoyed a sporadic existence before the 1914-18 War and multiplied during that War. Forms of election varied greatly. In the Turin area, the commissions often numbered five workers elected for fixed periods to handle everyday problems in a shop-steward style. They were usually dominated by the metal-workers' union FIOM, were often chosen by union officials and/or dues-collectors, with election by union members a mere formality. They became genuine centres of autonomous shop-floor action during the war, often in opposition to union leaderships, and served as the focus for the factory council campaign. *The Programme of the Workshop Commissars* called for their election by workshop commissars, themselves elected by universal suffrage of workers at their workplace by workshops. These revolutionized internal commissions were the leading organizations in the council movement.

FIOM: Federazione Italiana Operai Metallurgici Italian federation of metal-workers, founded in 1901, with its headquarters in Turin. Most powerful of the industrial union federations, led by the able Bruno Buozzi. Claimed about 160,000 members at its postwar peak.

CGL: Confederazione Generale del Lavoro General confederation of labour. The nearest equivalent to the British TUC. Founded in 1906 in reaction against syndicalism. A federation of craft and industrial unions and *camere*. Complicated confederal structure, with much local autonomy, rising to a national council and a small directive council. Nominally controlled by representative congresses, which did not, however directly elect the directive council, which was recruited from the major unions. Allied with the Socialist Party, but claimed exclusive control over 'economic' as opposed to 'political' strikes, as defined by the Stuttgart congress of the Second International 1907 and confirmed in the Pact of Alliance signed with the socialist party in September 1918. Easily the strongest of the union federations, it approached two million in 1920. The strongest single grouping within it was the *Federterra*: *Federazione Italiana Lavoratori della Terra*, Italian federation of land-workers, whether landless or not, which reached the 900,000 mark in 1920. Other strong groups were the 200,000 or so building workers, the metal-workers, the 155,000 textile workers. There were blocs of 60-70,000 from the gas, chemical, public and private white-collar workers, the railwaymen (subject to the threat of militarization on the state railways) and maritime workers had autonomous unions which could send non-voting representatives to CGL congresses.

The leaders of CGL were generally reformist socialists; its journal was *Battaglie Sindacali* (Union Struggle).

USI: Unione Sindacale Italiana: Italian syndicalist union. Founded 1912 by revolutionary syndicalists, the most militant rival of the CGL. Its leadership was committed to revolutionary action in syndicalist terms. Its post-war secretary, Armando Borghi, was an anarchist. Scorned politics and political parties, believed the class war should be fought on class terrain, i.e. within industry or on the land. Committed to the building of industrial unions which would construct an 'anti-state' and take over industry in the 'expropriating general strike'. Placed a high premium on spontaneity, distrusted bureaucracy and union organization, strove to build a 'horizontal' alliance of *camere*.

It was strong in particular areas like Liguria, Emilia and the Marches and grew very rapidly after the War. In 1920 was claiming 800,000 members. Its journal was *Guerra di Classe* (Class War) and it transferred its headquarters from Parma to Milan in March 1920. Syndicalist influence was very strong also in the railway and maritime unions.

CIL: Confederazione Italiana del Lavoro: Italian confederation of labour. A catholic union federation which, after its official recognition by the Papacy, in March 1918, grew very rapidly well over the million mark after the end of the War. It was essentially a rural organization, though it was represented among women textile workers. Could be militant in trade-union terms, but politically ambiguous; considerable emphasis on profit-sharing and co-operatives.

UIL: Unione Italiana del Lavoro: Italian union of labour. A politically motivated federation formed in part by a breakaway from syndicalist USI during the War crisis 1914-15. Run by nationalist syndicalists, republicans, radicals, who supported Italy's intervention in the War. A much smaller organization than the other federations, its left nationalism supplied recruits to fascism.

Political Organizations: The socialist movement

PSI: Partito Socialista Italiano: Italian socialist party. Originally the Party of Italian Workers, 1891, which adopted a socialist programme at the Genoa congress of 1892 and took the name socialist in 1893. Revived in 1895, after a temporary suppression, as a party based upon individual membership. Modelled on the Second International pattern and the Erfurt programme of the German socialists. Complicated federal structure, based on urban sections with their ward circles, provincial federations, rising to a national council and a Directorate elected by party congress. The parliamentary deputies, the GPS, *Gruppo Parlamentare Socialista*, while nominally subject to the party Directorate under the 1913 regulations, enjoyed an autonomous existence, as did, for example, the League of Socialist Communes (socialist local authorities) formed during the war. The youth federation, *Federazione Giovanile Socialista*, FGS, was also autonomous and had its own journal *Avanguardia* (Vanguard). The PSI worked closely with the CGL, but claimed the right to call a general strike if workers were killed by the security forces, to take over the leadership of strikes which could be considered political, and to associate itself with movements of popular rebellion if it seemed appropriate. The PSI had a secretary, but the real leader of the mass party was generally the editor of its journal *Avanti*, founded 1896, moved to Milan, 1912. *Avanti* (Forward) allotted a separate page to Turin and in December 1918, created a separate Turin edition. There were also many local journals like *Il Grido del Popolo* (The Cry of the People) of Turin and *Il Socialista* (The Socialist) of Naples.

The PSI lacked ideological and organizational unity. The function of the Directorate was to preserve the *maximum* programme of the party, i.e. the socialist revolution (a minimum democratic programme was defined in 1900 and again in May 1917); in practice it was trapped in a permanent functional centrism.

In the general election of November 1919, the PSI emerged as the largest single party, with over 30 per cent of the popular vote and 156 deputies. During 1920, its paper membership reached 210,000.

The fractions of the PSI

All the radical fractions of the PSI intended to re-affirm its maximum programme against reformist or other deviation; they were all, therefore, *maximalist*. The term acquired a particular meaning in the post-war period, however, to signify an (often violent) *verbal* commitment to the socialist revolution and, after the PSI's adherence to the Third International, to the dictatorship of the proletariat and the soviet system and a rigid refusal of formal compromise in the sense of participation in bourgeois governments, respect for monarchical and parliamentary ritual etc. The term was often equated with Bolshevik, translated as 'majoritarian' or 'maximal'. In reality, the practice of many sectors of the party, especially the parliamentary group and the union leadership was reformist or else void of any revolutionary content *except* the verbal, and the word *maximalist* tended to acquire that meaning as well.

In such a fissiparous party, 'fractions' were frequent, particularly at congresses, where there was much manoeuvre around key motions. But organized fractions which attempted to organize themselves on a national basis and often around a journal (frequently a local paper) were common and recognized in a PSI which rather prided itself on its 'schools'.

intransigent revolutionary:

a. Founded in October 1910 to resist the surrender of the PSI to Giolittian reformism. In May 1911 launched a journal *La Soffitta* (The Attic) in response to Giolitti's jibe that Marxism had been banished to the attic. Was effective in the congresses of 1912-14 in expelling reformists and Freemasons, rejecting electoral alliances and re-asserting the maximum programme. Its major spokesman in this period was Benito Mussolini who, after his editorship of *Avanti* had been subjected to discipline, launched his own journal *Utopia*.

b. The title of the fraction was revived in July 1917, at a clandestine meeting in Florence, which formed a revolutionary movement intending to end the war by revolution. The moving spirit was Amadeo Bordiga, to whose circular from Naples about 100 sections of the PSI responded. It had strength in Naples Florence, Milan and Turin and a journal in *Difesa* (Defence) of Florence, ed. Egidio Gennari. Bordiga also was elected editor of its journal *Avanguardia* by the youth federation. The fraction held a further meeting in Florence in November 1917, when Gramsci rallied to Bordiga, but the Turin rising of August 1917 had dislocated any plans it had and it never succeeded in making itself effective.

abstentionist communist:

The major fraction, led by Amadeo Bordiga, which formed the core of the communist party. Its organ was Bordiga's journal *Il Soviet* of Naples, launched in December 1918. It called for an expulsion of reformists and, from February 1919, for abstention from parliamentary elections, to break completely with bourgeois society. It adopted the full communist programme and its anti-parliamentary and, to a degree, anti-union stance aligned i' with forces in Germany, Holland, France, Britain and the USA which tended to group around the Amsterdam Bureau of the Third International and which were attacked by Lenin in his pamphlet on *Left-wing Communism: an Infantile Disorder*.

The group decided to form an organised fraction in July 1919 published a rival programme to that of the PSI's Directorate and put forward a motion at the Bologna congress in October 1919 It then suspended abstentionist propaganda and *Il Soviet* in accordance with congress decisions, but Bordiga resumed publication of *Il Soviet* in January 1920, after attempts to contact Lenin direct. The fraction held a national conference in Florence in May 1920 and published its Theses in June. It decided to form a communist party after the second congress of Comintern and to try to form an anti-parliamentary fraction within the International itself.

At the Second Congress of Comintern however, Bordiga, at Lenin's prompting, dropped a rigid adherence to abstention from elections and committed himself to forming a broad-based communist party.

After the Occupation of the Factories and Serrati's clash with Comintern, Bordiga joined with other individual communists including Gramsci, to form the *communist fraction* on 14 Octo ber 1920. The fraction could command the Turin *Avanti* and *L'Ordine Nuovo* as well as other local journals. It held its final formation convention at Imola on 28-29 November, when the former abstentionists emerged as its hard core. On the defeat of its motion at the Livorno congress of the PSI in January 1921, it seceded to form the communist party.

electionist communist:

A Turin fraction formed in 1920 to contest the elections to the section executive in opposition to the abstentionists. Its formation broke up an alliance of abstentionists and council communists which had run the section. The leading spirits, former supporters of *L'Ordine Nuovo*, Togliatti, Terracini and Tasca, objected to the Bordighists' refusal to take part in forthcoming local elections, to their participation in a syndicalist campaign of the summer of 1920 and to their intention to seek an immediate schism in the PSI. They ultimately fused with their opponents and with the *communist education group* (below) to form the Communist Party in Turin, and merged themselves with the communist fraction of Bordiga.

communist education group:

A tiny Turin fraction formed by Gramsci in response to the crisis in the Turin section of July-August 1920. The group which numbered 17 workers, refused to join the electionists against the abstentionists but rejected the argument over elections as illusory. It took its stand on the formation of communist groups and factory councils and the raising of the level of political education of comrades. It called upon comrades to return blank ballots during the election. Only 31 did so, while the electionist communists won an average 450 votes to the abstentionists' 185. It merged with the other two fractions to form the Communist Party in Turin.

socialist concentration:

A fraction formed by reformists during August-September 1920. Reformists, with their strength in parliament, the unions, the communes, many local papers and Turati's journal *Critica Sociale,* had little need of fractions. But in the summer of 1920 and in response to the Giolitti government, the reformists decided to force a break with maximalism and verbal commitment to revolution, in favour of a commitment to radical structural reform. The strongholds of the fraction were Milan and Reggio Emilia. After the multiplication of fractions in response to Serrati's conflict with Comintern, the fraction directed its efforts to the Livorno congress. It organized itself formally on 10-11 October 1920 and secured some 14,000 votes at Livorno. Its members were to be the core of the Unitary Socialist Party formed in secession from the PSI in October 1922.

unitarian communist:
>A fraction formed by Serrati to support his claim for national autonomy within the Third International and rejection of immediate application of the Twenty-One Points in full rigour. The fraction organized itself formally on 20-21 November 1920 and won a heavy majority at the Livorno congress.

communist-socialist:
>An abortive fraction formed in desperation by Graziadei and Marabini, after they had sent a circular around the Bologna region protesting at the division of 'communists' into two rival fractions before Livorno. It sought to bridge the gap between Bordiga and Serrati. They attended the Imola convention of the communist fraction but were defeated, Gramsci being particularly active against them. They won support from some 200 sections at Livorno. Most of them joined the Communist Party, where their leaders formed a right wing.

L'Ordine Nuovo:
>Gramsci denied that the council communists around this journal – nicknamed *ordinovisti* – formed a fraction. The journal was certainly open to a range of supporters from anarchists to abstentionists. But from January 1920 the *ordinovisti* did have a programme for the renewal of the PSI, plans for calling a national congress of factory councils and for organizing a fraction around the statement of the Turin left, *For a Renewal of the Socialist Party*, published 8 May 1920 and singled out for praise by Lenin. The group however was closely involved with the abstentionists. The defection, first of Tasca in May 1920, then of a considerable number to the electionist communist Turin fraction in July 1920, reduced the Gramscian council communists to the small *communist education group*, which merged into the communist party.

Other politico-social organizations

PPI: Partito Popolare Italiano: popolari:
>Catholic party founded by Luigi Sturzo in 1919; held its congress in June 1919, absorbing many local groups. Catholic, largely rural but with much support among 'small men' in urban centres. Won over 100 seats in elections of November 1919, but lacked inner cohesion. Allied with the CIL.

UAI: Unione Anarchica Italiana:
>Anarchist organization revived after the War. Moved its headquarters from Ancona-Bologna to Milan in February 1920 and published *Umanità Nova* (Mankind Anew). Celebrated anarchist militant Errico Malatesta was its leading spirit in 1920 and it

won much influence among working classes during the summer of 1920.

Confindustria:

General Confederation of Italian industry. First formed 1910, in imitation of Turin Industrial League. Revived in March 1920, to embrace a number of regional and sectional consortia like AMMA, the organization of employers in the metal industry. A very powerful and aggressive organization.

Individuals

Bombacci, Nicola (1879-1945): Leading revolutionary maximalist, imprisoned during the War. On PSI commission to revise programme 1919; favourable to alliance with syndicalists. January 1920 proposed soviet scheme to national council of PSI; opposed Turin action during April strike 1920. Rallied to communist fraction October 1920. Leading member of communist party. Attached to Soviet Russian embassy and moved to position of sympathy with Mussolini. Expelled from communist party 1927. Ran a 'left-fascist' journal under Mussolini. Surfaced during Salò Republic 1943-45, acted as adviser to Mussolini in his last days. Reputed author of the 18 Points of Mussolini's testament, foundation for fascist revival. Shot with Mussolini in 1945.

Bordiga, Amadeo (1889-1970): Joined PSI 1910. Active in youth federation. April 1912, formed Karl Marx circle, Naples. Defeated Tasca in 'culture' debate in youth congress September 1912. Took over Naples Il Socialista 1914; opposed the war. Tried to revive intransigent revolutionary fraction July-November 1917; called up. December 1918, launched Il Soviet; formed abstentionist communist fraction 1919. Took lead in formation of communist fraction October 1920. First leader of communist party 1921-23. Arrested February 1923, acquitted October. The Rome Theses of his communist party in conflict with policy of Comintern; refused to rejoin executive of PCd'I in December 1923. In 1924 refused to serve as vice-president of Comintern. During 1924-26 displaced from leadership of PCd'I, which adopted Gramsci's Lyons Theses; accused of 'Trotskyism'. Suffered fascist imprisonment and deportation 1926-30. Expelled from the communist party 1930. Remained active until death with small Bordighist groups who now form the International Communist Party.

Borghi, Armando (1882-1968): Anarchist; involved in action from youth. Edited journal and founded builders' union in Ravenna-Bologna 1906-7. In 1912 joined USI and was one of the leaders of Red Week 1914. Defeated interventionist syndicalist de Ambris in 1914 and became secretary of USI. Under arrest through most of the war. In April 1919 called for a united revolutionary front of socialists and syndicalists and supported council movement. Visited Russia at time of second congress of Comintern and was active in last stages of Occupation of Factories. Arrested 1923; went into exile 1926. Returned to Italy in 1953 to edit *Umanità Nova*.

Buozzi, Bruno (1881-1944): Secretary of metal-workers' federation FIOM. Involved in conflict with rank-and-file militants 1918-19; prominent during Occupation of Factories. Opposed PSI motion for revolution at CGL national council meeting September 1920; submitted own 'revolutionary-reformist' motion but withdrew it and abstained. Engaged in polemic with Gramsci 1921. Consistent and courageous social democrat. After exile, helped to reform CGL in 1943 during civil war after collapse of fascism.

D'Aragona, Ludovico (1876-1961): Secretary of the CGL, August 1918, after the resignation of Rigola. Right-wing socialist, opposed to Soviet Russia and maximalism; pillar of strength of reformists. Hostile to Turin action in April 1920 and major CGL figure during the Occupation of the Factories. Committed CGL to Turati's Unitary Socialist party in October 1922. Tried to come to terms with fascism; declared the CGL independent of the socialist party and negotiated with Mussolini. In 1927 founded journal in attempt to influence fascist unions. Prominent in Saragat's social democratic movement after 1947.

Ferrero, Pietro (1892-1922): Anarchist. Metal-worker; frequented the socialist study circles in Turin pre-war. Became leader of Turin council movement and secretary of the Turin section of FIOM. Signed the manifesto calling for a national congress of factory councils on 27 March 1920. Polemic with Gramsci over anarchism. Leading figure during the Occupation of the Factories, September 1920. Led the resistance to the settlement. Led the final struggle of the factory councils in April 1921. On 18 December 1922 during the fascist attack on Turin, he was killed in the heart of the city.

Giolitti, Giovanni (1842-1928): Major political figure in pre-war regime. First became premier 1892; dominated the pre-war decade; perfected system of *trasformismo* and incorporation of socialism into parliamentary system. Rode out general strike of 1904; introduced near-manhood suffrage and launched Libyan War in 1911. Withdrew from office early 1914 and opposed Italy's entry into the war. Threat of his return to power precipitated 'radiant days of May' 1915. Returned to power June 1920. Very skilful handling of Occupation of Factories, September 1920. Scheme for joint employer-union management of industry. Tolerated and fostered fascist movement in belief he could manipulate it. Tried to negotiate with fascist regime, but final political act was to oppose Mussolini's electoral law of 1928.

Gramsci, Antonio (1891-1937): Born Sardinia, educated Turin university. Joined Turin youth section 1913-14; formed 'club of moral life'; first political article in Turin journal in half-support of Mussolini in October 1914; withdrew from active politics until late 1915 when resumed socialist journalism in Turin. Joined Turin section executive after rising of August 1917; allied with Bordiga's revolutionary fraction. Launched *L'Ordine Nuovo* 1919, leader of council movement. Prominent in effort to renew the PSI in early 1920 but politically isolated after April 1920. Joined Bordiga's communist party and served on central committee. Sent as delegate to Moscow May 1922. During 1923-24 constructed new leadership for PCd'I. Defeated Bordiga 1924-26 and reshaped communist party in his Lyons Theses. Arrested November 1926. Opposed change in communist policy 1929-30 and virtually withdrew. Wrote prison notebooks in appalling conditions. Conditional liberty 1934 in severe ill-health. Died 1937.

Lazzari, Costantino (1857-1927): Founder of Workers' Party in 1882 in Milan, tough self-educated printer. Joined with Turati to form PSI. Allied to intransigents during 1912-14 crisis. Became secretary of PSI and close ally of Serrati throughout the war and afterwards. Opposed expulsion of reformists and fought to maintain unity of party, displaying all his party medals going back to 1882 at Livorno congress 1921. Remained in PSI after schism, but went as delegate to Comintern. Archetypical maximalist.

Rigola, Rinaldo: First secretary of CGL 1906; reformist whose ideal was the British Labour Party. Forced to resign temporarily by Mussolini. Prominent in collaboration during war. August 1918, resigned when PSI forbade participation in Commissionissima. Tried to collaborate with Mussolini and joined D'Aragona in effort to influence fascist unions.

Serrati, Giacinto Menotti (1876-1926): Rose to prominence as intransigent during 1912-14, with companion Angelica Balabanoff. After Mussolini's defection became editor of *Avanti* and virtual leader of PSI. Remarkable record during the war. Rallied to Third International but refused to purge and reform PSI. Polemic with Lenin, Bordiga and Gramsci. Remained leader of PSI after communist schism 1921 but tried to retain Comintern allegiance and effect reconciliation. October 1922 expelled reformists from PSI, but defeated in his project to re-unify communists and left socialists by Nenni. He and his fraction joined PCd'I in 1924 and he died of a heart attack after clandestine meeting of communist party.

Tasca, Angelo (1892-1960): Son of Turin worker, founded Turin youth section 1909; defeated by Bordiga in 'culture' debate in youth congress 1912; heavily involved in union struggles 1912-13. Initiated Gramsci into PSI. Founder member of *L'Ordine Nuovo*

1919. Began to distance himself from Gramsci January 1920; broke with Gramsci's programme May 1920; member of electionist communist fraction July-August 1920. Founder-member of communist party 1921. Opposed Rome Theses March 1922. Member of opposition group within PCd'I which Gramsci acted to forestall. After Gramsci's arrest, shared leadership of PCd'I with Togliatti. Expelled as a right-winger 1929. In exile, joined socialist movement and wrote much history under name of A. Rossi. Contributed to a Pétainist journal and forced to clear himself after the war. Entered the debate on history of the communist party, in opposition to Togliatti, in the 1950s.

Terracini, Umberto (born 1895): Law student Turin university, secretary of Piedmont youth section, colleague of Tasca and Gramsci. Arrested for anti-war activities and sent to the front. Founder member of *L'Ordine Nuovo*. Joined Directorate of PSI 1920. Joined electionist communist fraction in July-August 1920. On executive of PCd'I; counted more 'Bordighist' than Bordiga. Polemic with Lenin at third congress of Comintern. Rallied to Gramsci, became delegate to Moscow. Arrested in Italy 1926, jailed for many years. In 1943 joined the Resistance and was secretary general of free government of Ossola. President of National Assembly and communist senator. Counted the best lawyer in Italy.

Togliatti, Palmiro (1893-1964): Joined Tasca's youth section in Turin 1914 while student at Turin. Supported intervention and served in war. Rejoined movement 1919, co-founder of *L'Ordine Nuovo*; very active late 1919 and early 1920. Took *For a Renewal of the Socialist Party* to Milan national council during April struggle. Formed electionist communist fraction in Turin July-August 1920 and became section secretary. Founder-member of PCd'I. Strong supporter of Bordiga, last leader to rally to Gramsci. After arrest of Gramsci, shared leadership of party with Tasca. After 1930 major leader of the Italian communist party and major figure in International. Served in the Spanish civil war. During Liberation and partisan war, directed the communist party into the 'Salerno turn' of 1944, towards the mass party and immediate post-war collaboration with democratic parties. Served as minister in several governments; led the PCI through the Cold War. After death of Stalin, leading figure in movement for 'polycentrism' and liberalization. During controversy over PCI's history, advocated and secured liberal and open attitude towards publication of sources. Died in the Soviet Union.

Turati, Filippo (1857-1932): Virtual founder of PSI. Converted from Milan democracy to socialism in company with Anna Kuliscioff; son of a prefect; interest in criminology. Joined first Party of Italian Workers. Created *Critica Sociale* in 1891; author of the Workers' Hymn. The personification of reformist socialism; worked with

Giolitti. Opposed the war but collaborated with Orlando government in particular. Rallied to the nation after Caporetto. Adopted Wilsonian perspective. Resisted communism. During 1920, created the socialist concentration fraction and favoured a social-democratic policy of alliance with liberal forces. In summer of 1922 defied party to advocate support of anti-fascist bourgeois government. October 1922, formed the Unitary Socialist Party in secession from PSI. Joined the Aventine opposition during Matteotti crisis. Fled into exile 1926.

Some Books

Coverage in English is necessarily incomplete. Hardly anything is communist in perspective. There are a number of works of a general character.

D.Mack Smith, *Italy*, University of Michigan, Ann Arbor 1959 is an elegant essay and Christopher Seton-Watson, *Italy from Liberalism to Fascism*, Methuen 1967 is full and vivid. Shepard B.Clough, *The Economic History of Modern Italy*, Columbia University Press, New York 1964 conveys a lot of information.

Adrian Lyttelton, *The Seizure of Power*, Weidenfeld and Nicolson, 1973 is a marvellous book: a very detailed study of fascism in its early years. It is not directly relevant to our theme but is extremely informative and stimulating. Similarly, F.W.Deakin, *The Brutal Friendship*, Weidenfeld and Nicolson 1962, while actually about Mussolini's last years, is often quite extraordinarily revealing on the past; read, in particular, the pages on the internal policy of the Salò republic and the attempt to revive the fascist squads in a kind of 'replay' of 1921-22. H.Stuart Hughes, *Consciousness and Society*, London 1959 is a good introduction to the intellectual styles of the period and E.Nolte, *Three Faces of Fascism*, London 1965, has a long essay on the ideology of the fascist movement. Several elements in this ideology were in fact shared by the left and I find some of the older books more useful on this aspect. Tasca's own study of the rise of fascism, available in English as A.Rossi, *The Rise of Italian Fascism*, London 1938 is still one of the best books on the subject, handling a sight more than fascism itself and I think G.Megaro, *Mussolini in the Making*, London 1938 still unsurpassed.

On the Italian left, we are hard pressed. W.Hilton Young, *The Italian Left*, London 1949, is a short and often blistering essay; R.Hostetter, *The Italian Socialist Movement, Origins 1860-1882*, Princeton 1958, is a scholarly study of its 'pre-history'; A.W.Salomone, *Italy in the Giolittian Era*, Philadelphia, 2nd ed. 1960, has material from the PSI congresses pre-war.

John M. Cammett, *Antonio Gramsci and the Origins of Italian Communism*, Stanford University Press 1967, is a full and scholarly coverage of Gramsci's career up to his imprisonment, with an examination of three central themes from the prison notebooks; it is full on the Turin background and is the best attempt yet to set him in immediate context. John Cammett sees Gramsci as a 'liberal' marxist. In his analysis of the Lyons Theses, for example, he distinguishes between the 'more specifically Gramscian ideas' and those which were no more than a 'translation' of Comintern instructions and is clearly unhappy with Gramsci's characterization of the maximalist socialists as 'reactionary'. The perspective which this comment implies governs the argument of the book, which is certainly the fullest treatment in English of Gramsci as a political activist. A similar outlook is visible in another essential text, G. Fiori, *Antonio Gramsci: Life of a Revolutionary*, translated (and very well) by Tom Nairn, New Left Books 1970. This is essentially the life of an individual. It stresses the Sardinian side of Gramsci's life (which as a Welshman I find thoroughly commendable!) and it is probably the best biography in any language. It is a very moving book and has lost none of its power in the translation. He, too, however stresses the 'liberalism' of Gramsci's marxism and seems to be rather loose in his handling of communist concepts and practice: he apparently thinks the united-front and the popular-front tactics are basically similar. Taken together, Fiori and Cammett certainly provide a good entry into Gramsci, from a particular point of view which represents a major current of opinion on the left.

I made a contribution to this current myself in an article on Gramsci's concept of *hegemony* in *Journal of the History of Ideas*, xxi, 1960. I now regard this article as itself a *symptom* of the kind of impact Gramsci made on the English-speaking world in the late 1950s and 1960s. I still nurse the illusion that there are some points worth making in the article, but now find the whole perspective which informs it wrong-headed and in a sense irrelevant; the piece should be consigned to the memory-hole.

The best introduction to Gramsci's political practice is, I think, the admirable introduction by Quintin Hoare and Geoffrey Nowell Smith to their anthology, *Antonio Gramsci: Selections from the Prison Notebooks*, Lawrence and Wishart 1971. Written from a communist standpoint, this seems to me very good, even on the nuances. You might also derive benefit from a perhaps unexpected source: Helmut Gruber(ed), *International Communism in the Era of Lenin*, Doubleday-Anchor, New York 1972: a collection of texts, necessarily selective, but one which *does* convey something of the feel and bite of early European communism and, rare among such compilations, actually quotes from those 'un-persons', the 'ultra-left', including Bordiga's manifesto of 1923. (If you have Italian, you should also read in this area Andreina de Clementi, *Amadeo Bordiga*, Einaudi, Turin 1971, which carries the attack on Gramsci and the rehabilitation of Bordiga to extreme lengths, but which is strong on the 'ultra-left' and presents a rigorous argument which has to be faced. The book ought to be translated as soon as possible ; the experience is akin to taking a cold shower while eating a lemon.)

Alastair Davidson, 'Antonio Gramsci', *Australian Left Review*, 1968 prefaces some translations from the prison notebooks with an interesting essay stressing the Hegelianism of Gramsci's marxism and printing a useful bibliography which includes attempts to 'apply' Gramscianism ; the author has counter-attacked Althusser's critique of Gramsci in an essay on the latter's handling of Machiavelli, in *Science and Society* xxxvii, 1973 ; his work, while significant, has an indirect relevance for the 1919-21 period. A.Pozzolini, *Antonio Gramsci*, translated by Anne F.Showstack, Pluto Press 1970, does handle the earlier period, but takes individual themes right through Gramsci's life, which while sometimes stimulating, is not always very satisfactory. The book is full of material uncommon elsewhere and has a valuable critical bibliography. Its tone seems a little quirky and the author takes a veiled gamin delight in occasionally exposing the more 'square' of Antonio's opinions and prejudices, for example on blacks or on education (the latter certainly would bring students out in a boiling rash in St David's College Lampeter let alone the university of Essex). John Merrington has a dense analysis of the quality of Gramsci's marxism in 'Theory and practice in Gramsci's Marxism', *Socialist Register 1968*, Merlin Press 1968, and V.G.Kiernan a more discursive commentary on the prison writings in 'Gramsci and Marxism', *Socialist Register 1972*, Merlin Press 1972.

It is the later writings of Gramsci which have also loomed large in translation. L.Marks (translation and introduction) *The Modern Prince and Other Writings*, Lawrence and Wishart, 1st ed. 1957, has been enormously reinforced by the first volume in that firm's projected Gramsci series, Q.Hoare and G.Nowell Smith, *Selections from the Prison Notebooks*, 1971. Individual pieces have appeared but the fullest collection of earlier writings is 'Soviets in Italy', from the 1919-20 period, in *New Left Review*, 51, 1968, reprinted as a pamphlet no.11 by the Institute of Workers' Control, and *Turin 1920*, translations from the 1920 period, published by Moulinavent Press 1970. The *New Edinburgh Review*, special Gramsci numbers, three volumes, 1974 (ed. C.K.Maisels), print a full translation of the 1947 edition of the Prison Letters (*Lettere dal carcere*, Einaudi, Turin 1947) by Hamish Henderson and some additional translations from the 1919-20 period. A selection from the 1965 edition of the letters (*Lettere dal carcere*, ed. S.Caprioglio and E.Fubini, Einaudi, Turin 1965) by Lynn Lawner, is promised by Jonathan Cape.

For this book, the most useful work in English has been an unpublished thesis, 'Factory councils and the Italian labour movement', PhD London 1966, by Martin N.Clark. This presents, for the first time in English, a full, detailed and accurate narrative of the development of working-class movements during and after the war, in which the growth of the council movement on the ground has been related to other sectors of the Italian labour movement. The study is not particularly concerned with the problems of communism in western Europe but it is invaluable in establishing the real and practical context. It has enabled my work to take the form it has and it ought to be made available in book form. A deal of its material appears in a wider context in the author's pamphlet, M.N.Clark, *The Failure of Revolution in Italy 1919-20*, University of Reading, Reading 1973.

The essential guide to the voluminous material on Gramsci and the period is the major bibliography (to 1967) by Elsa Fubini in vol.2 of *Gramsci e la cultura contemporanea, Atti* of the international convention at Cagliari 1967: Riuniti-Istituto Gramsci, 1970.

For this study I have used the Feltrinelli, Milan photographic facsimile of the journal *L'Ordine Nuovo*, 1966, together with the relevant volumes of the collected *Opere* of Gramsci published by Einaudi, Turin: *L'Ordine Nuovo*, 1954, 3rd ed. 1970 ; *Socialismo e fascismo*, 1966, 4th ed. 1971, and *La costruzione del partito comunista*, 1971 with some reference to *Scritti giovanili*, 1958, 3rd ed. 1972 ; and other anthologies, e.g., *2000 pagine di Gramsci*, ed. G.Ferrata and N.Gallo, 2 vols, *Il Saggiatore*, Milan 1964, 2nd ed. 1971 ; and Sergio

Caprioglio(ed) *Scritti 1915-21*, Il Corpo, Milan 1968. Most important have been Paolo Spriano's anthology, with valuable essay, *L'Ordine Nuovo e i consigli di fabbrica*, Einaudi, Turin 1971 ; P.Togliatti(ed), *La formazione del gruppo dirigente del partito comunista italiano nel 1923-24*, Riuniti, 3rd ed. 1971 ; L.Cortesi, (ed. and intro.) Angelo Tasca, *I primi dieci anni del PCI*, Laterza, Bari 1971 ; Alfonso Leonetti (intro.) *Bordiga-Gramsci: dibattito sui consigli di fabbrica*, Savelli, la nuova sinistra, 1973 ; and F.Platone(ed) Paolo Spriano (intro.) *Lenin sul movimento operaio italiano*, Riuniti, 1970. *Storia della sinistra comunista*, i, International Communist Party, Milan 1964 has something of the character of a Bordiga anthology and the party is producing a series of valuable anthologies from the period. People interested in Gramsci who have Italian should certainly immerse themselves in the magnificent edition by Sergio Caprioglio and Elsa Fubini of *Lettere dal carcere*, Einaudi, Turin 1965, which is a splendid monument to scholarship in its own right. Valentino Gerratana has been working for some years on the full critical edition of the Prison Notebooks ; its publication is now imminent. Its appearance will obviously be a vital moment in Gramsci studies.

Into the enormous output on Gramsci and the period in Italian, one entry is through the historiography of the communist party itself. There is now an excellent essay on this in Rosa Alcara, *La formazione e i primi anni del partito comunista italiano nella storiografia marxista*, Jaca book, Milan 1970. I have summarized the gist of this study in 'The making and unmaking of Antonio Gramsci', *New Edinburgh Review*, Gramsci-III, 1975 and made some comments on it. Note that, while the study is very valuable and scholarly, comrade Alcara is obviously a spiritual affiliate of the group of historians who have contributed valuable studies in particular to the *Rivista storica del socialismo* (available in the library of the London School of Economics) whose net effect has been to 'rehabilitate' Bordiga and to diminish, sometimes seriously, the work of Gramsci. Comrade Alcara ends her study with her own assessment of the Bordiga-Gramsci debate before Livorno. This is again very scholarly, save for one intriguing particular. As with many of her affiliates her 'Gramsci' seems to *stop* somewhere just after April 1920. The 'Gramsci' of the summer of 1920 is frequently an absentee from such studies. From the point of view of the marxism they represent, this is carefully to paint in Cromwell's warts while omitting his face.

There is similar historiographical strength in the introduction by Luigi Cortesi to Angelo Tasca, *I primi dieci anni del PCI* (above). Cortesi has himself been a major contributor to this important historical process. He and Stefano Merli were directors of the *Rivista storica del socialismo* and secured the publication of a wealth of essential material. Three pieces of major significance to the controversy are: S.Merli, 'Le origini della direzione centrista del PCI', 23, Sept-Dec 1964; L.Cortesi, 'Alcuni problemi della storia del PCI', 24, Jan-Apr 1965; Andreina de Clementi, 'La politica del PCd'I nel 1921-22 e il rapporto Bordiga-Gramsci', 28-29, May-August, Sept-Dec 1966. Luigi Cortesi, in *Le origini del PCI*, Laterza, Bari 1972 offers a cogent, rigorous and powerful synthesis on the period 1911-21 which I consider very effective and essential, while Andreina de Clementi, *Amadeo Bordiga*, Einaudi, Turin 1971 presents the first serious political biography of the founder of the PCd'I, which while in some senses patchy in coverage and extreme in its rigour and perspective, seems to me to be a major work.

The intelligent and liberal response of the PCI under Togliatti to the onslaughts on the 'official' historiography in the 1960s has meant, in effect, that the party's archives have been largely opened to sympathetic but independent historians. Consequently the work of the admirable Paolo Spriano towers over the field. His studies on Turin and the working-class movement are essential: *Socialismo e classe operaia a Torino dal 1892 and 1913*, Einaudi Turin 1958; *Torino operaia nelle grande guerra*, Einaudi, Turin 1960; *L'occupazione delle fabbriche*, Einaudi, Turin 1964 (my translation of the latter was published by Pluto Press, 1975), as well as the *Ordine Nuovo* anthology listed above. He is writing what is clearly the best history of a communist party to emerge from the vicinity of the movement anywhere on earth, which has now reached four volumes. The volumes relevant to this study are: *Storia del partito comunista italiano*, i, *Da Bordiga a Gramsci*, Einaudi, Turin 1967 and ii, *Gli anni della clandestinità*, Einaudi, Turin 1969. Spriano and Cortesi may stand as two polarities fixing the historical problematic at this time. They may be supplemented by an interesting, also 'dissident' history, which appeared relatively early: F.Bellini and G.Galli, *Storia del PCI*, Schwarz, Milan 1954; later edition by Galli alone, Schwartz, Milan 1958.

Further bibliographical references are provided in these works and the commentary by Rosa Alcara in her book is very useful.

Some more specific reference in individual cases in the present study is provided in my footnotes.

Finally, one point on general climate. I first stumbled across Gramsci in 1959, while working on Georges Sorel and transcribing the Sorel-Croce correspondence in *Critica* at the university of Turin. It now seems to me that it would be useful for people to adopt that approach consciously. I suggest as a starting-point, James H. Meisel, *The Genesis of Georges Sorel*, George Wahr, Ann Arbor, Michigan 1951 and Sorel's own *Matériaux d'une théorie du prolétariat*, Paris 1919. His essay on the decomposition of marxism is translated in I.L. Horowitz, *Radicalism and the Revolt Against Reason*, Routledge and Kegan Paul, 1961. Sorel needs to be re-assessed and re-possessed, particularly by anyone interested in Gramsci and 'Gramscianism'.

Of course, it depends *which* Gramsci you mean? But that's another story, and to quote Dylan Thomas, the fact that that goes without saying will in no way prevent me from saying it.

References

Chapter 1

1. *L'Ordine Nuovo*, 15 May 1919 (Feltrinelli reprint, Milan 1966: henceforth *ON*) published in *L'Ordine Nuovo*, p372, volume in A.Gramsci, *Opere*, Einaudi, Turin 1954.

2. Shepard B.Clough, *The Economic History of Modern Italy*, Columbia University Press, New York 1964, pp93-94, 182, 205; Christopher Seton-Watson, *Italy from Liberalism to Fascism*, Methuen, 1967, pp287, 488-89; Adrian Lyttelton, *The Seizure of Power*, Weidenfeld and Nicolson 1973, chapters 9 and 13. See, in particular, P.Spriano, *Socialismo e classe operaia a Torino dal 1892 al 1913*, Einaudi, Turin 1958 and *L'occupazione delle fabbriche*, Einaudi, Turin 1964.

3. For this section, as for all the economic material in this chapter, see Shepard B.Clough, *op cit* chapters 3-6 and appendix; Christopher Seton-Watson, *op cit* chapters 8, 10, 11, 12; Adrian Lyttelton, *op cit*, chapters 9 and 13. R.Romeo, *Breve storia della grande industria in Italia*, Milan 1961; R.Morandi, *Storia della grande industria in Italia*, Einaudi, Turin 1966; P.Spriano, the works listed above, particularly *L'occupazione delle fabbriche*.

4. C.Seton-Watson, *op cit*, pp282, 307.

5. All the major studies treat the southern problem: D.Mack Smith, *Italy*, University of Michigan, Ann Arbor 1959 sets the problem and that of Croce and the intellectuals in context. There is a useful introduction to Croce in H.Stuart Hughes, *Consciousness and Society*, London 1959; see the introduction to G.Nowell Smith and Q.Hoare, *Antonio Gramsci: Selections from the Prison Notebooks*, Lawrence and Wishart 1971.

6. For these figures, see S.B.Clough, *op cit*, appendix and ch. 4, 5, 6; C.Seton-Watson, *op cit* pp284-85 and notes.

7. *ON* 29 November 1919 (*L'Ordine Nuovo*, pp56-60).

8. See survey in P.Spriano, *L'occupazione delle fabbriche*, chapter 2.

9. On the Perrone brothers and Carrara, see Adrian Lyttelton, *The Seizure of Power*, pp206, 214-15.

10. See Adrian Lyttelton, *op cit*, pp210-11, commenting on R.de Felice, 'Primi elementi sul finanziamento del fascismo dalle origini al 1924', *Rivista storica del socialismo*, vii (May-August 1964).

11. Adrian Lyttelton, *op cit*, chapters 12 and 13; Roland Sarti, 'The Battle of the Lira 1925-27', *Past and Present*, 47 (May, 1970).

12. See Luigi Cortesi, *Le origini del PCI*, Laterza, Bari, 1972, p81. Cortesi's is an invaluable study of the period 1911-21. Its perspective is novel but correct. It is informed by a rigorously coherent analysis, which rehabilitates Bordiga but unduly diminishes Gramsci.

13. On the earlier history of Italian socialism, see R.Hostetter, *The Italian Socialist Movement, Origins (1860-1882)*, Princeton 1958; W.Hilton-Young, *The Italian Left*, London 1949. A good general introduction may be derived from C.Seton-Watson, *op cit* and material on the PSI before the War from A.W.Salomone, *Italy in the Giolittian Era*, Philadelphia, 2nd ed 1960. See also J.Cammett, *Antonio Gramsci and the Origins of Italian Communism*, Stanford 1967 and G.Nowell Smith and Q.Hoare, introduction to *Antonio Gramsci: Selections from the Prison Notebooks*, Lawrence and Wishart, London 1971. From the enormous output in Italian, central (and symptomatic) are the writings of Paolo Spriano, notably *Storia del partito comunista, i, Da Bordiga a Gramsci*, Einaudi, Turin 1967; *Socialismo e classe operaia a Torino dal 1892 al 1913*, Einaudi, Turin 1958 and *Torino operaia nelle grande guerra*, Einaudi, Turin 1960; L.Cortesi, *op cit*, Andreina de Clementi, *Amadeo Bordiga*, Einaudi, Turin 1971 and the numbers of the journal *Rivista storica del socialismo* (available at LSE).

14. In English, the emergence of the socialist and labour movements may be quickly assimilated from a correlation of the works of Hostetter, C.Seton-Watson and S.B.Clough cited above.

15. Labriola has been sadly neglected by English-language scholarship. There are English translations of some of his writing in *Essays on the materialist conception of history*, Charles H.Kerr, Chicago 1908 and *Socialism and Philosophy* (letters to Sorel), Chicago 1906.

16. The programmes are summarized in C.Seton-Watson, *op cit*, p198. Roberto Michels, *Storia critica del movimento socialista italiana*, Florence 1926, has detail, particularly on the bourgeois-worker split, which he elaborated on in his *Political Parties*, New York 1962.

17. On Sorel, see below.

18. Arturo, of course, is on no account to be confused with Antonio Labriola!

19. The position is summarized conveniently in C.Seton-Watson, *op cit*, pp297-306.

20. See P.Spriano, *Socialismo e classe operaia a Torino dal 1892 al 1913* and *L'occupazione delle fabbriche*.

21. Revealing quotation from speeches etc in A.W.Salomone, *op cit*, chapters 5, 6, 7 and see L.Cortesi, *op cit*.

22. Quoted in P.Spriano, *L'occupazione delle fabbriche*, p111.

23. Sorel seems to be known in Britain only for *Reflections on Violence*, The Free Press, USA 1950 (the American edition of T.E.Hulme's translation carries an essay by Edward Shils). From his many works *Matériaux d'une théorie du prolétariat*, Paris 1919 is perhaps most relevant. I have found most useful and precise James H. Meisel, *The Genesis of Georges Sorel*, George Wahr, Ann Arbor, Michigan, USA 1951; chapter 9 has in-

formation on Italy (Sorel's articles in a Bologna journal 1910-21 were published as *L'Europa sotto la tormenta*, Milan 1932). See also I.L.Horowitz, *Radicalism and the Revolt against Reason* (which has a translation of Sorel's 'Decomposition of Marxism'), Routledge and Kegan Paul 1961 and the relevant section in James Joll, *The anarchists*, Methuen 1964, and H.Stuart Hughes, *op cit*.

24. See H.Stuart Hughes, *op cit*, James H.Meisel, *op cit*, ch 9; C.Seton-Watson, *op cit* will open up this world. James Joll has an essay on Marinetti in *Intellectuals in Politics*.

25. On Mussolini and the Perrone brothers, see Adrian Lyttelton, *op cit*, p206: this is a marvellous study of fascism in its early days and essential. The major source is, of course, Renzo de Felice's massive study: see *Mussolini il rivoluzionario*, Turin 1965. In English there are G.Megaro, *Mussolini in the Making*, London 1938 and Laura Fermi, *Mussolini*, Chicago 1961. P.Monelli, *Mussolini: an Intimate Life*, London 1953 is funny and depressing. D.Mack Smith, *op cit*, while delightful, does not take him seriously enough, while E.Nolte, *Three Faces of Fascism*, London 1965 perhaps takes his ideology too seriously. The last days of fascism throw light on its origins, see the remarkable picture in F.W.Deakin, *The Brutal Friendship*, London 1962.

26. For this stupefying story, see F.W.Deakin, *op cit*, pp626-28, 811.

27. Alfred Rosmer, *Lenin's Moscow*, trans. Ian Birchall, Pluto Press 1971, p84.

Chapter 2

1. L.Cortesi, *Le origini del PCI*, pp5-6; A.W.Salomone, *Italy in the Giolittian Era*, p53, n49.

2. L.Cortesi, *op cit*, pp10-11.

2. L.Cortesi, *op cit*, pp3ff.

4. D.Mack Smith, *op cit*, pp275-76; on the crisis generally, see C.Seton-Watson, *op cit*, chapter 10.

5. On the congress, see L.Cortesi, *op cit*, pp16-28; A.W.Salomone, *op cit*, ch7.

6. L.Cortesi, *op cit*, pp31-55; A.W.Salomone, *ibid*.

7. Most of the works cited deal fully with this crisis and Mussolini's role. L.Cortesi, *op cit*, chapter 3, seems most effective.

8. The basic source is P.Spriano, *Torino operaia nelle grande guerra;* quotations are cited in J.Cammett, *Antonio Gramsci and the Origins of Italian Communism*, pp38-41.

9. Angelo Tasca, *I primi dieci anni del PCI*, p86; cited in G.Fiori, *Antonio Gramsci*, trans Tom Nairn, New Left Books 1970, p76.

10. See A.Tasca, *op cit*, ch1; in English, J.Cammett, *op cit*, ch2 and 3; G.Fiori, *op cit* ch9 and 10.

11. A.Tasca, *op cit*, pp91-92; J.Cammett, *op cit*, p34 mentions the Mussolini project, G.Fiori, *op cit*, pp94-95 does not.

12. Andreina de Clementi, *Amadeo Bordiga*, pp10-14; L.Cortesi, *op cit*, p57.

13. G.Berti, *Appunti e ricordi 1919-26*, Feltrinelli, Milan 1966, p19, quoted in A.de Clementi, *op cit*, p12.

14. Quoted in *Storia della sinistra comunista*, Milan 1964, pp186-87. This study, published by a 'Bordighist' group, the International Communist Party, assumes something of the character of a Bordiga anthology and is an element in the left-wing controversy over the historiography of the PCI. See Rosa Alcara, *La formazione e i primi anni del PCI nella storiografia marxista*, Jaca Book, Milan 1970: essential.

15. The best study of Bordiga, though it is highly controversial in its general argument, is A.de Clementi, *op cit*. She argues for a 'western' communism in opposition to the 'Russian', at least after 1921, and locates Bordiga in this context. She goes further than many contributors to the *Rivista storica del socialismo* eg Luigi Cortesi, whose book is also very useful on Bordiga, in her 'rehabilitation' of the Neapolitan and her diminution of Gramsci. In fact, she denies that Gramsci is a marxist. Her second chapter is the basis for this section, plus L.Cortesi, *op cit*, ch3.

16. *Storia della sinistra comunista*, pp213-15.

17. Fully treated in L.Cortesi, *op cit* pp 73-75 and A.de Clementi, *op cit*, pp29-33; *Storia della sinistra comunista*, pp229-35.

18. A.de Clementi, *op cit*, pp32-35.

19. For this section on Turin, see in English, J.Cammett, *op cit*, ch2. The basic source is P.Spriano, *Socialismo e classe operaia a Torino dal 1892 al 1913*.

20. The basic source is A.Tasca, *op cit*: J.Cammett, *op cit* and G.Fiori, *op cit*, give a full picture.

21. Tasca's study of fascism is available in English: A.Rossi (A.Tasca) *The Rise of Italian Fascism*, London 1938. The Italian edition of 1951, under his own name, *Nascita e avvento del fascismo*, Florence 1951, has more material.

22. This is not the place to attempt an analysis of Gramsci's early writing. From the vast bibliography in Italian, one may perhaps single out Leonardo Paggi, *Antonio Gramsci e il moderno principe*, i, Riuniti, Rome 1970. The introduction by G.Nowell Smith and Q.Hoare to *Antonio Gramsci: Selections from the Prison Notebooks* is very useful. On the years in Turin, S.F.Romano, *Antonio Gramsci*, Einaudi, Turin 1967 seems to have everything except his laundry bills; the best approach in English is through G.Fiori and J.Cammett, *op cit*. Gramsci's own writings, of course, are anthologized in the Einaudi, Turin, *Opere* volumes *Scritti giovanili*, 1958 and *Sotto la Mole*, 1960 and in Sergio Caprioglio(ed), *Scritti 1915-21*, Il Corpo, Milan 1968.

23. See G.Fiori, *op cit*, pp92-92.

24. See *Scritti giovanili*, pp21-22.

25. A.de Clementi, *op cit*, p28, n1.

26. The basic source is A.Tasca, *op cit*, pp92-94; for Togliatti's *pax britannica* see p96. Tasca's motives, at least with reference to Togliatti

were, of course polemical (and see Rosa Alcara, *op cit*) and he may have exaggerated Gramsci's interventionism, but there seems little reason to doubt his basic veracity on this issue.

27. See *Scritti giovanili*, pp3-7.

28. For obvious reasons, this period has been a trifle blurred in Gramsci biographies. I am grateful for information provided by my friend Stephen Overy, who is preparing a study of Gramsci's thought. The element of 'withdrawal' in 1914-15 has not always been clearly presented, but it can be detected in G.Fiori, *op cit*, pp97-99.

29. A.de Clementi, *op cit*, pp38-43.

30. C.Seton-Watson, *op cit*, pp393-95 and notes.

31. L.Cortesi, *op cit*, pp78-83.

32. The PSI's reaction to the outbreak of war is treated in most studies, but L.Cortesi, *op cit*, pp85-101 offers a rigorous and searching analysis.

33. For this incident, see F.W.Deakin, *The Brutal Friendship*, pp796-97.

34. This section is based on the relevant sections of S.B.Clough, *The Economic History of Modern Italy*, ch6; P.Spriano, *L'occupazione delle fabbriche* and *Torino operaia nelle grande guerra*, C.Seton-Watson, *op cit*, ch11 and footnotes, and the detailed information newly made available in Martin N.Clark, *The Failure of Revolution in Italy*, Dept of Italian Studies, University of Reading 1973.

35. *ON* 4 October 1919 (not included in Einaudi anthology: see translation in *New Edinburgh Review*, Gramsci-II, 1974).

36. C.Seton-Watson, *op cit*, p522 n1 and S.B.Clough, *op cit*, pp189-90.

37. See M.N.Clark, *op cit*, p2.

38. C.Seton-Watson, *op cit*, p489, n4, citing R.Romeo, *Breve storia delle grande industria in Italia*, p85; the figures are, of course, subject to dispute, but Romeo follows up in intricate detail, p88, for example.

39. M.N.Clark, *op cit*, p2 and n13 and see P.Spriano, *L'occupazione delle fabbriche*, pp40-41.

40. For an account of this system, see M.N.Clark, *op cit*, p9 and fuller details in the same author's thesis, 'Factory councils and the Italian labour movement', PhD London 1966.

41. M.N.Clark, *op cit*, pp11-12 and 'Factory councils . . .'; J.Cammett, *op cit*, ch4; P.Spriano, *Torino operaia nelle grande guerra*, pp298-301.

42. *ON* 9 October 1920 (*L'Ordine Nuovo*, pp158-63: translation *New Edinburgh Review*, Gramsci-II, 1974).

43. A.de Clementi, *op cit*, pp108-26, while arguing a controversial case in her treatment of Anton Pannekoek and the 'ultra-left', certainly opens up an area of discourse which, however, needs to embrace the war years as well and to take into account the western consequences of Brest-Litovsk. James Hinton, *The First Shop Stewards' Movement*, Allen and Unwin, 1973 also, by implication, poses the problem, and sharply.

44. See G.Haupt, *Socialism and the Great War*, Oxford 1972; Alfred Rosmer, *Le mouvement ouvrier pendant la guerre*, Paris, 1936.

45. See L.Cortesi, *op cit*, pp101-109, and on Bordiga's letter to Lenin in January 1920, pp208-11.

46. This section is based on P.Spriano, *Storia del partito comunista italiano* i, ch1 and L.Cortesi, *op cit*, ch4; A. de Clementi, *op cit*, pp49-58; see J.Cammett, *op cit*, ch3 and G.Fiori, *op cit*, ch12.

47. L.Cortesi, *op cit*, pp115-16 and M.N.Clark, *op cit*, p10, where the programme is set in a different context.

48. Quoted in P.Spriano, *Storia del PCI*, i, 8 and reproduced in *Storia della sinistra comunista*, p304.

49. P.Spriano, *op cit*, i, 9.

50. There is a good account of the Turin rising in J.Cammett, *op cit*, pp51-55; basic sources are P.Spriano, *Torino operaia nelle grande guerra* and D.Zucaro, 'La rivolta di Torino del 1917 nella sentenza del Tribunale militare territoriale', *Rivista storica del socialismo*, iii, (May-August 1960).

51. See Gramsci's account in his report to Comintern on the council movement, July 1920, published in the journal of the Comintern and reprinted in the daily *ON* 14 March 1921, now in *L'Ordine Nuovo*, pp181-82.

52. P.Spriano, *Storia del PCI*, i, 1-2; L.Cortesi, *op cit*, pp124-25.

53. See E. Soave, 'Appunti sulle origini teoriche e pratiche dei consigli di fabbrica a Torino', *Rivista storica del socialismo*, vii (January-April 1964); J.Cammett, *op cit*, pp72-74. For a description of the process, see Martin N.Clark, *The failure of revolution in Italy 1919-20*, pp11-12 and further details in his thesis, 'Factory councils and the Italian labour movement'.

54. On the Commission and the Pact of Alliance, see M.N.Clark, *op cit*, pp10-11; L.Cortesi, *op cit*, pp128, 138.

55. L.Cortesi, *op cit*, pp127-25.

56. L.Cortesi, *op cit*, pp142-43, 152-53.

Chapter 3

1. Quoted in C.Seton-Watson, *op cit*, p552.

2. P.Spriano, *L'occupazione delle fabbriche*, p39.

3. All major studies capture the climate of 1919-20; for a vivid and well-documented narrative, see C.Seton-Watson, *op cit*, ch12.

4. There is a terse, packed account in P.Spriano, *L'occupazione delle fabbriche*, ch2.

5. Martin N.Clark, *The Failure of Revolution in Italy 1919-20*, p2.

6. L.Cortesi, *Le origini del PCI*, pp164-66; C.Seton-Watson, *op cit*, p520, Martin N.Clark, *op cit*, pp13-14; and see A.Gramsci, *ON* 12 July 1919 (*L'Ordine Nuovo*, pp260-62).

7. See the discussion of Serrati's attitude in M.N.Clark, *op cit*, pp13-14 and L.Cortesi, *op cit*, pp166-67; for a comment by Gramsci, see *For the Communist International*, *ON* 26 July 1919 (*L'Ordine Nuovo*, pp19-22).

8. C.Seton-Watson, *op cit*, pp520-24, 552, 566-67; M.N.Clark, *op cit*, pp3-6; S.B.Clough, *op cit*, pp206-207; L.Cortesi, *op cit*, pp163-64, and see Adrian Lyttelton, *The Seizure of Power*, pp54-71.

9. See M.N.Clark, *op cit*, p4 for such a report.

10. C.Seton-Watson, *op cit*, pp512-15, and see Gramsci's comments in *ON*

1 November 1919 and 9 October 1920 (*L'Ordine Nuovo*, pp159-60, 284-86).

11. M.N.Clark, *op cit*, p4, 6; Adrian Lyttelton, *op cit*, pp37-38, 60-62.

12. See Serrati's interventions at the second congress of the Comintern and his celebrated letter to Lenin of December 1920 in *Lenin sul movimento operaio italiano*, Riuniti, Rome 1970, pp278-86, 290-301.

13. A.Gramsci, *Fascists and Legionaries*, ON 19 February 1921 (*Socialismo e Fascismo*, pp75-79); P.Spriano, *Storia del PCI*, i, ch9.

14. A.Gramsci, *The Leninism and Marxism of Rodolfo Mondolfo*, ON 15 May 1919 (*L'Ordine Nuovo*, pp373-75).

15. This section is based on L.Cortesi, *op cit*, ch5; A.de Clementi, *op cit*, ch3 and 4; P.Spriano, *Storia del PCI*, i, 1-4. Martin N.Clark, *The Failure of Revolution in Italy 1919-20*, discusses basic issues in a broad context. G.Nowell Smith and Q.Hoare explore the themes in their introduction to *Antonio Gramsci: Selections from the Prison Notebooks*.

16. L.Cortesi, *op cit*, pp143-46.

17. J.Degras(ed) *The Communist International: documents*, 2 vols, RIIA, 1956-60 gives much of the raw material; B.Lazitch and M.M.Drachkovitch, *Lenin and the Comintern*, Stanford, 1972 offer new material on the machinery of the Comintern; and see J.W.Hulse, *The Forming of the Communist International*, Stanford 1964.

18. L.Cortesi, *op cit*, pp148-49.

19. A.de Clementi, *op cit*, pp76-84; L.Cortesi, *op cit*, pp152-59; *Storia della sinistra comunista*, pp362-64, 371-74.

20. Martin N.Clark, *op cit*, p13 publishes this important document from the ministry of the interior archives.

21. L.Cortesi, *op cit*, pp164-66.

22. A.de Clementi, *op cit*, pp86-93; L.Cortesi, *op cit*, pp167-74; *Storia della sinistra comunista*, pp384-91, 394-96, 399-402.

23. L.Cortesi, *op cit*, pp171-72.

24. There is a very full account of the congress in L.Cortesi, *op cit*, pp174-96.

25. *Lenin sul movimento operaio italiano*, pp164-65; A.Gramsci, *The Professional Revolutionary*, ON 20 December 1919 (*L'Ordine Nuovo*, pp387-89). L.Cortesi, *op cit*, p201 prints the translation used by *Comunismo*.

26. For these two critical letters, see P.Spriano, *Storia del PCI*, i, pp38-40; L.Cortesi, *op cit*, pp208-13.

27. For a full treatment of the so-called ultra-left, Pannekoek and Gorter in particular, see A.de Clementi, *op cit*, pp108-32.

28. P.Spriano, *L'Ordine Nuovo e i consigli di fabbrica*, Einaudi, Turin 1971, pp88-98 and n; L.Cortesi, *op cit*, pp222-23; ON 17 January 1920; *Il Soviet*, 4 January 1920.

29. The report is now in *L'Ordine Nuovo*, pp176-86.

30. See J.Cammett, *op cit*, ch3, 4, 5; Paolo Spriano's studies of the city cited above, notably *Torino operaia nelle grande guerra* and his anthology *L'Ordine Nuovo e i consigli di fabbrica*.

31. Quoted in M.N.Clark, *op cit*, p11. M.N.Clark's work has added a

dimension to our understanding of the factory council movement in its working-class reality. Some of his findings are published in this booklet, *The Failure of Revolution in Italy 1919-20*, especially pp11-15; there is much detail in his unpublished thesis, 'Factory councils and the Italian labour movement', PhD London 1966.

32. L.Cortesi, *op cit*, p160 uses this to stress the marxist inadequacy of the Turin movement.

33. M.N.Clark, *op cit*, p12.

34. See Leonetti's own comments in his preface to *Bordiga-Gramsci: dibattito sui consigli di fabbrica*, Savelli, la nuova sinistra, Rome 1973.

35. E.Soave, *op cit*; J.Cammett, *op cit*, pp72-73.

Chapter 4

1. *ON* 6 September 1919 (*L'Ordine Nuovo*, p455).

2. *ON* 14 August 1920 (*ibid*, pp148-49).

3. See Angelo Tasca, *I primi dieci anni del PCI*, ch2.

4. *ON* 4 October 1919 (see the chronicle by Gramsci in *L'Ordine Nuovo*, pp458-59).

5. See below, chapters 6 and 7.

6. This section is based on my reading of *L'Ordine Nuovo* from May to December 1919.

7. *ON* 1 May 1919 (the programme not included in the anthology).

8. *ON* 1 May, 21 June 1919, 10 January 1920 and *passim*.

9. *ON* 22 November 1919.

10. All quotations in the first seven paragraphs of this section are from the article *The Ransom of History*, *ON* 7 June 1919 (*L'Ordine Nuovo*, pp6-10).

11. *ON* 1 May 1919 (*ibid*, p217).

12. *ON* 27 March 1920 and *ON* (daily) 1921 *passim (Socialismo e fascismo, passim)*.

13. *ON* 1 May 1919.

14. Article *Majority and Minority in Socialist Action*, *ON* 15 May 1919 (*L'Ordine Nuovo*, pp371-73).

15. *ibid*.

16. *ON* 21 June 1919 (*L'Ordine Nuovo*, pp10-13).

17. *Il Soviet*, 14, 21 September 1919; see below, ch7.

18. On the shop-steward system, see the excellent study, J.Hinton, *The First Shop Stewards' Movement*, Allen and Unwin, 1973, and review, *Proletarian*, 1, Edinburgh 1974.

19. On the Buozzi-Gramsci confrontation, see P.Spriano, *L'Ordine Nuovo e i consigli di fabbrica* (anthology with introduction) pp49-51.

20. *ON* 12 July 1919 (*L'Ordine Nuovo*, pp446-47).

21. *ON* 2 August, 20-27 September 1919 (*ibid*, pp447, 457-58).

22. *ON* 12 July 1919 (*ibid*, pp13-19).

23. *ON* 26 July 1919 (*ibid*, pp19-22).

24. *Guerra di Classe*, 7 January 1920; Ugo Fedeli, 'Breve storia dell'Unione Sindacale Italiana', *Volontà*, 1957.

25. On this controversy, see *ON* 16, 23 August 1919; not in the Einaudi anthology, but reprinted in Paolo Spriano's, *L'Ordine Nuovo e i consigli di fabbrica*, pp161-72.

26. *Towards new institutions*, *ON* 30 August 1919, reprinted in P.Spriano, *op cit*, pp173-79.

27. See below, ch7.

28. *ON* 13 September 1919 (*L'Ordine Nuovo*, pp456-57).

29. *ON* 13 September 1919; and see his greetings to the new commissars, *ibid* (*L'Ordine Nuovo*, pp27-34).

30. *ON* 11 October 1919 (*ibid*, pp34-39). There is a full English translation in *New Edinburgh Review*, Gramsci-II, 1974; *New Left Review* 51, 1968; *Soviets in Italy*, Institute of Workers' Control, nd.

31. For a quick assimilation in English, see B.Bolloten, *The Grand Camouflage*, 2nd ed Pall Mall 1968, part 1.

32. *ON* 25 October 1919 (*L'Ordine Nuovo*, pp39-44).

33. *ON* 8 November 1919 (*ibid*, pp44-48).

Chapter 5

1. *ON* 13 September 1919 (*L'Ordine Nuovo*, p31).

2. A.de Clementi, *Amadeo Bordiga*, p101; L.Cortesi, *Le origini del PCI*, p216.

3. *ON* 30 August 1919; P.Spriano, *L'Ordine Nuovo e i consigli di fabbrica*, pp43, 53.

4. Terracini wrote an article on the councils for *L'Almanacco socialista 1920*; see P.Spriano, *op cit*, pp48, 54.

5. See P.Spriano, *op cit*, pp53-54, *ON, passim*. The gains were recorded in *Avanti* (Turin). There is a full account of the growth of the movement in M.N.Clark, 'Factory councils and the Italian labour movement', PhD thesis, London, 1966, pp100ff and a summary in John Cammett, *op cit*, pp76ff.

6. *ON* 8 November 1919.

7. *Chronicles* of *ON* 25 October, 1 November 1919 (*L'Ordine Nuovo*, pp462-65); M.N.Clark, *op cit*, pp105-107.

8. It was published in *ON* 8 November 1919 (*L'Ordine Nuovo*, appendice, pp192-99).

9. This singles out the anarcho-syndicalist federation USI, as opposed to the catholic (CIL) and nationalist-interventionist (UIL) federations.

10. See above, chapter 4.

11. The report was published in *Internationale Communiste* (journal of the Comintern) in 1920 and reprinted in *L'Ordine Nuovo* (daily) 14 March 1921 (*L'Ordine Nuovo*, pp176-86).

12. See Togliatti's review of an article of 18 October by Castagno in *ON* 1 November 1919; M.N.Clark, *op cit*, pp171-72.

13. For the Fiat-Centro programme and the dissidents in Fiat-Centro, see *ON* 27 December and 22 November 1919; at the *camera* meeting in December, most of the Fiat-Centro delegates rallied to an *ordinovista* motion; see below. On the FIOM section meeting, see the article by Togliatti cited below and M.N.Clark, *op cit*, pp109-11.

14. Togliatti on the FIOM section meeting, *ON* 8 November 1919 (P.Spriano, *op cit*, pp197-202).

15. *ON* 15 November 1919 (P.Spriano, *op cit*, pp203-11).

16. See, for example, *ON* 6-13, 20, 27 December 1919, 3, 17, 24-31 January, 14 February, 28 February–6 March, 13 March 1920.

17. *ON* 6-13 December 1919; M.N.Clark, *op cit*, pp113-14.

18. *Chronicles, ON* 1 November, 1919, 28 February–6 March 1920 (*L'Ordine Nuovo*, pp463, 472-73).

19. *ON* 15, 29 November, 20, 27 December 1919.

20. See P.Spriano, *op cit passim* and M.N.Clark, *op cit*, p114.

21. *ON* 20, 27 December 1919; M.N.Clark, *op cit*, p122.

22. *ON* 20, 27 December 1919; P.Spriano, *op cit*, p86, n3; M.N.Clark, *op cit*, pp115-16; and see the echoes in the controversy between Tasca and Gramsci in the summer of 1920 in articles from *ON* reprinted in P.Spriano, *op cit*, pp261-300.

23. *ON* 3 January, 3-10 April 1920; P.Spriano, *op cit*, pp220-25; J.Cammett, *op cit*, p82.

24. *ON* 17 January, 13 March. 3-10 April 1920 (the essay on the historical function of the city is in *L'Ordine Nuovo*, pp319-22).

25. While most studies outline this process, the most detailed account is in M.N.Clark, *op cit*, pp170-78.

26. See below, chapters 6 and 7.

27. P.Spriano, *op cit*, p81.

Chapter 6

1. Gramsci-Leonetti, 28 January 1924 in P.Togliatti(ed) *La formazione del gruppo dirigente del partito comunista italiano*, p183.

2. L.Cortesi, *Le origini del PCI*, pp156, 172-73; P. Spriano, *L'Ordine Nuovo e i consigli di fabbrica*, p51.

3. See below, chapter 9 n11.

4. P.Spriano, *op cit*, p51, n1; M.N.Clark, 'Factory councils and the Italian labour movement', pp196-97.

5. Sergio Caprioglio(ed) *Antonio Gramsci: Scritti 1915-21*, appendix, p182.

6. P.Spriano, *op cit*, p51, n2, quoting the Turin *Avanti*.

7. *ON* 15 November 1919; *Il Soviet*, 18 May 1919.

8. *ON* 28 June–5 July, 12 July 1919 (*L'Ordine Nuovo*, pp257-62); L.Cortesi, *op cit*, p160.

9. Gramsci in *Avanti* (Turin) 21 August 1919, quoted in L.Cortesi, *op cit*, p172 and *ON* 13 September 1919.

10. L.Cortesi, *op cit*, p172; M.N.Clark, *op cit*, p121.

11. *ON* 4 October 1919.

12. *ON* 13 September 1919 (*L'Ordine Nuovo*, pp27-31); see above, chapter 4.

13. The most perceptive account is in L.Cortesi, *op cit*, pp171-72, 179ff.

14. *ON* 15 November 1919 (*L'Ordine Nuovo*, pp307-9).

15. *ON* 29 November 1919 (*L'Ordine Nuovo*, pp56-60): full translation in *New Edinburgh Review*, Gramsci-II, 1974.

16. Obituary in *L'Unità*, 14 May 1926, reprinted in *La costruzione del partito comunista 1923-26*, pp109-13.

17. See *Lenin sul movimento operaio italiano*, pp278-86, 290-301.

18. See P.Spriano, *op cit*, citations, pp84-85.

19. *ON* 3-10 April 1920; L.Cortesi, *op cit*, pp215, 217, 221 and *passim*.

20. Lenin, *op cit*, pp164-65 and reprint of translation used in *Comunismo* in L.Cortesi, *op cit*, p201.

21. Quoted in P.Spriano, *op cit*, p89 and see A.Tasca, *I primi dieci anni del PCI*.

22. *ON* 20 December 1919.

23. *ON* 6-13 December 1919 (*L'Ordine Nuovo*, pp61-67).

24. *ON* 20 December 1919 (*L'Ordine Nuovo*, pp387-89).

25. *ON* 27 December 1919 (*L'Ordine Nuovo*, pp67-71): full translation in *New Edinburgh Review*, Gramsci-II, 1974; *New Left Review*, 51, 1968; *Soviets in Italy*.

26. See, for example, the 'orthodox' response to the definition, become a 're-definition', of 'bourgeois revolution' in Miguel Vinas, 'Franquismo y revolutión burguesa', with the editorial *Prologo* in *Horizonte Español* 1972, Ruedo Iberico, Paris, 1972, vol iii.

27. See *ON* 17 January–13 March 1920 for polemic arising out of the Florence meeting; political background well handled in L.Cortesi, *op cit,* pp201-33; summary account in J.Cammett, *op cit*, pp90ff and full description in M.N.Clark, *op cit*, pp201-206.

Chapter 7

1. *ON* 24-21 January 1920 (*L'Ordine Nuovo*, pp389-96): full translation in *New Edinburgh Review*, Gramsci-II 1974.

2. *ON* 14 February 1920.

3. Gramsci-Scoccimarro 5 January 1924 in P.Togliatti(ed) *La formazione del gruppo dirigente del partito comunista*, p152.

4. *ON* 5 June, 14, 28 August 1920 (*L'Ordine Nuovo*, pp127-31, 146-54).

5. L.Cortesi, *Le origini del PCI*, pp222-23; P.Spriano, *L'Ordine Nuovo e i consigli di fabbrica,* pp88-98 and n; M.N.Clark, 'Factory councils and the Italian labour movement', pp123-25; *ON* 17 January 1920 (P.Spriano, *op cit*, pp231-36); *Il Soviet*, 4 January–29 February reproduced in A.Leonetti(ed) *Gramsci-Bordiga: dibattito sui consigli di fabbrica*, pp47ff.

6. *Il Soviet* 1, 15 February 1920; L.Cortesi, *op cit*, pp218-19; P.Spriano, *op cit*, p93 and n1.

7. *Il Soviet* 14 September 1919 (*Dibattito*, pp28-31).

8. From a long essay on councils, spread over *Il Soviet* 4, 11 January, 1, 8, 22 February 1920 (*Dibattito*, p56).

9. L.Cortesi, *op cit*, p222; *Il Soviet* 29 February 1920.

10. This is a vast and controversial subject. A. de Clementi examined one period of Gramsci-Bordiga relations in depth in, 'La politica del partito comunista d'Italia nel 1921-22 e il rapporto Bordiga-Gramsci', *Rivista storica del socialismo*, 1966 (May–August, September–December); she sets the council argument in a broader, European context in her *Amadeo Bordiga*, ch4; see also L.Cortesi, *op cit*, ch6 and P.Spriano, *Storia del partito comunista*, vol i. Here I merely wish to put an argument for some aspects of the Bordiga-Gramsci relationship; I intend to develop an analysis in a later study covering the period up to 1930.

11. *Il Soviet* 21 September 1919 (*Dibattito*, pp38-42).

12. *Il Soviet* January–February 1920 (*Dibattito*, pp47-70).

13. *ON* 3-10 April 1920.

14. *ON* 14 February 1920 (*L'Ordine Nuovo*, pp79-84).

15. *ON* 28 February–6 March 1920 for both articles cited here (*L'Ordine Nuovo*, pp91-101): full translation in *New Edinburgh Review*, Gramsci-II, 1974.

Chapter 8

1. The report is reprinted in *L'Ordine Nuovo*, pp176-86.

2. Anarchism and syndicalism during 1919-20 are neglected and ill-served by history. The general histories, L.Cortesi, P. Spriano, *op cit* have some material and more is scattered through the *Rivista storica del socialismo*. There is Armando Borghi, *Mezzo secolo di anarchia*, Naples 1954; Ugo Fedeli, *Un trentennio di attivita anarchica*, Cesena 1953; Enzo Santarelli, *Il socialismo anarchico in Italia*, Milan 1973; M.N.Clark, 'Factory councils and the Italian labour movement', carries detail from syndicate journals, p178ff. I am grateful to Joaquin Romero Maura and the Spanish libertarian movement for some suggestions.

3. E.Santarelli, *op cit*, pp14, 185-92.

4. Quoted in M.N.Clark, *The Failure of Revolution in Italy 1919-20*, p21.

5. Ugo Fedeli, 'Breve storia dell'unione sindacale italiana', *Volontà*, 1957, p647; I am grateful to Stephen Overy for drawing my attention to this source. For more detail, see M.N.Clark, 'Factory councils and the Italian labour movement', *op cit*, p178ff.

6. See P.Spriano, *L'occupazione delle fabbriche*, ch2; summary in M.N.Clark, *The Failure of Revolution in Italy 1919-20*, pp7-8.

7. M.N.Clark, 'Factory councils and the Italian labour movement', pp180-82.

9. *ON* 3-10 April 1920 (*L'Ordine Nuovo*, pp396-401): full translation in *Turin 1920: Antonio Gramsci, Factory Councils and General Strike*, Moulinavent press, 1970.

10. *Avanti* (Turin) 29 August 1920 (*L'Ordine Nuovo*, pp410-12).
11. P.Spriano, *L'Ordine Nuovo e i consigli di fabbrica*, pp93-94; *L'occupazione delle fabbriche*, ch1; M.N.Clark, *op cit*, pp128-31; and see the *ON* articles cited below.
12. *ON* 13 March 1920.
13. P.Spriano, *L'Ordine Nuovo e i consigli di fabbrica*, pp92-93; M.N.Clark, *op cit*, pp131, 183-84.
14. The speech was published in *ON* 15 May 1920 (*Dibattito, op cit,* pp93-99).
15. *ON* 27 March 1920.
16. P.Spriano, *op cit*, pp93-94. *Storia del partito comunista italiano*, i, 52; *L'Ordine Nuovo*, pp94-95; M.N.Clark, *op cit*, pp133-35 and ch4.
17. *ON* 27 March 1920 (P.Spriano, *L'Ordine Nuovo e i consigli di fabbrica*, pp236-41).
18. Published in *ON* 8 May 1920 (*L'Ordine Nuovo*, pp116-23): full translation in *New Edinburgh Review*, Gramsci-II, 1974; *New Left Review*, 51, 1968; *Soviets in Italy* and *Turin 1920*.
19. The best and fullest account of the struggle is in M.N.Clark, *op cit*, ch4; J.Cammett, *op cit*, pp98-104 has a more summary one in English. P.Spriano, *Storia del partito comunista italiano*, i, pp52-57 has important particulars. Several of Gramsci's articles during this period appear in English translation in *Turin 1920*.
20. *Avanti* (Turin) 3 April 1920 (*L'Ordine Nuovo*, pp105-107): translation *Turin 1920*.
21. See below, chapter 9.
22. *ON* 17 July 1920 (*L'Ordine Nuovo*, pp140-43).
23. J.Cammett, *op cit*, p98.
24. See Gramsci's article, *Superstition and Reality*, *ON* 8 May 1920 (*L'Ordine Nuovo*, pp108-14): translation in *Turin 1920*.
25. J.Cammett, *op cit*, p245, n4.
26. *ON* 8 May 1920, *Superstition and Reality*, see n24 above.
27. Details in M.N.Clark, *op cit*, ch4.
28. Quoted in J.Cammett, *op cit*, p246, n22.
29. He recurred to this theme constantly, even during 1921; *ON* (daily) 1921.
30. Bachi, Togliatti and Montagnana quoted in J.Cammett, *op cit*, pp100-101. I recollect Palmiro Togliatti making the point in a speech.
31. J.Cammett, *op cit*, p102 quotes Serrati; M.N.Clark, *op cit*, ch4 has plenty of others.
32. In his report to Comintern, now in *L'Ordine Nuovo*, pp176-86.
33. P.Spriano, *L'Ordine Nuovo e i consigli di fabbrica*, p99 and n1.
34. P.Spriano, *Storia del partito comunista italiano*, i, 55.
35. Interesting on this meeting are P.Spriano, *op cit*, pp53-57; J.Cammett, *op cit*, pp101-104; M.N.Clark, *op cit*, ch4.
36. *ON* 8 May 1920 (*L'Ordine Nuovo*, pp114-16): translation in *Turin 1920*.

Chapter 9

1. See L.Cortesi, *Le origini del PCI*, ch6; P.Spriano, *Storia del PCI*, i, ch5; P.Spriano, *L'occupazione delle fabbriche*, ch2; J.Cammett, *op cit*, ch5.
2. L.Cortesi, *op cit*, pp214-15; P.Spriano, *L'Ordine Nuovo e i consigli di fabbrica*, pp104-105.
3. P.Spriano, *L'occupazione delle fabbriche*, ch1 and n13; M.N.Clark, 'Factory councils and the Italian labour movement', p175.
4. The Tasca address and Gramsci's reaction to it fill much of *L'Ordine Nuovo* during the summer; see the articles on Tasca and the polemic over the programme of *L'Ordine Nuovo* in *ON* 29 May, 5 June, 14, 28 August and supplementary pieces 1920 (*L'Ordine Nuovo*, pp127-31, 146-54; P.Spriano, *L'Ordine Nuovo e i consigli di fabbrica*, pp106-109, 261-300); M.N.Clark, *op cit*, pp217-20.
5. *ON* 5 June 1920 (*L'Ordine Nuovo*, pp123-27; P.Spriano, *op cit*, pp254-60).
6. *ON* 12 June 1920 (*L'Ordine Nuovo*, pp131-35): full translation, *New Edinburgh Review* Gramsci-II, 1974; *New Left Review*, 51, 1968; *Soviets in Italy*.
7. See the detail in M.N.Clark, *op cit*, pp224-27 and his *The Failure of Revolution in Italy 1919-20*, pp2, 21.
8. Paolo Spriano, *L'occupazione delle fabbriche*, ch2 and see n27; for the details on Turin, see M.N.Clark, *ibid*.
9. *ON* 10 July 1920 (*L'Ordine Nuovo*, pp401-404).
10. *ON* 17 July 1920 (*L'Ordine Nuovo*, pp140-43).
11. P.Spriano, *L'Ordine Nuovo e i consigli di fabbrica*, pp115-18, quoting the education group's manifesto from the Turin *Avanti*, major source on the city; Gramsci-Scoccimarro, 5 January 1924, in P.Togliatti(ed) *La formazione del gruppo dirigente del partito comunista nel 1923-24*, pp151-52.
12. *ON* 3 July, 4 September 1920 (*L'Ordine Nuovo*, pp135-40, 154-58; P.Spriano, *op cit*, pp301-306); full translation of *The communist party*, *New Edinburgh Review*, Gramsci-II; of *Two Revolutions, ibid*, and *New Left Review*, 51, 1968 and *Soviets in Italy*.
13. This position I hope to elaborate in a further study *Gideon's Army*, on Bordiga, Gramsci and the PCI 1921-30.
14. *Il Soviet* 5 September, 3 October 1920; L.Cortesi, *op cit*, pp238ff.
15. On the Italians at the second congress there are many sources; basic – P.Spriano, *Storia del PCI*, vol i and L.Cortesi, *op cit*; there is an account in J.Cammett, *op cit*, pp104-107.
16. Central is P.Spriano, *L'occupazione delle fabbriche*; M.N.Clark, *op cit*, ch6 is good on the opening stages.
17. For the whole of this section, see P.Spriano, *L'occupazione delle fabbriche*, ch2 and 3 and M.N.Clark, *op cit*, pp235-50.
18. Bruno Buozzi's recollections, published in 1935, quoted in P.Spriano, *op cit*, see ch2, n14.
19. *Avanti* (Turin) 5 September 1920 (*L'Ordine Nuovo*, pp163-67).

Chapter 10

1. This chapter is based almost entirely on P.Spriano, *L'occupazione delle fabbriche*; my own translation was published 1975 by Pluto Press. There is a vivid account in J.Cammett, *op cit*, pp111-22 and further detail on Turin in M.N.Clark, 'Factory councils and the Italian labour movement', ch7.

2. See especially P.Spriano, *op cit*, ch4.

3. P.Spriano, *op cit*, p100, n1.

4. For opinion cited, see P.Spriano, *op cit*, pp100-101.

5. P.Spriano, *op cit*, p98, n3.

6. P.Spriano, *op cit*, p80, n5.

7. See the telephone conversations recorded in P.Spriano, *op cit*, appendix, pp192-94, and text, pp89-90, 93.

8. P.Spriano, *op cit*, pp73-74, 151-52.

9. *L'Ordine Nuovo*, pp163-66; P.Spriano *op cit*, pp81-82; M.N.Clark, *op cit*, p259.

10. On Turin, M.N.Clark, *op cit*, ch7 supplements the material in P.Spriano, *op cit.*

11. A point noted (from the Turin *Avanti*) in M.N.Clark, *op cit*, p255, n9.

12. P.Spriano, *op cit*, p70; M.N.Clark, *op cit*, pp255-57.

13. P.Spriano, *op cit*, p68, n1.

14. P.Spriano, *op cit*, p149, n1.

15. That gas-workers should obey the orders of FIOM seems a fact worthy of note and an indication of the general temper of workers. For the detail in this paragraph see M.N.Clark, *op cit*, pp256-57 and P.Spriano, *op cit*, p96. There was a full analysis of the situation a year later in *L'Ordine Nuovo* (daily) 2 September 1921, by Pietro Borghi.

16. P.Spriano, *op cit*, pp71-72.

17. P.Spriano, *op cit*, pp57-58.

18. P. Spriano, *op cit*, pp47 and n4, 78-80; M.N.Clark, *op cit*, p261.

19. P.Spriano, *op cit*, pp82-83.

20. P.Spriano, *op cit*, pp83-84.

21. P.Spriano, *op cit*, p86.

22. P.Spriano, *op cit*, pp100-102 and 100, n2.

23. Reproduced in P.Spriano, *op cit*, appendix, pp195-96.

24. P.Spriano, *op cit*, pp97-98, 102 and n2.

25. See P.Spriano, *op cit*, pp88ff.

26. From a letter of 6 March 1924 to his wife, published in *Rinascita*, 5 May 1962, quoted P.Spriano, *op cit*, pp87-88.

27. P.Spriano, *op cit*, p106 and n1.

28. A.Tasca, *Nascita e avvento del fascismo*, p121, quoted in P.Spriano, *op cit*, p89.

29. P.Spriano, *op cit*, pp90-92.

30. *Lenin sul movimento operaio italiano*, p222.

31. See telephone conversation Albertini-Amendola in P.Spriano, *op cit*, appendix, pp201-206 and text, pp139-42.

32. Quoted in P.Spriano, *op cit*, p111.

33. On these critical days, a valuable supplement in English to Spriano, are the reports of the International Labour Office (Geneva): ILO, *The Dispute in the Metal Industry in Italy*, Studies and Reports, series A, no2, 11; B, no7, 9 (September 1920 – April 1921); I owe this reference to Nina Stead. The meetings are covered in P.Spriano, *op cit*, pp103-15.

34. P.Spriano, *op cit*, pp103-106; *L'Ordine Nuovo* (daily) 7 September 1921.

36. P.Spriano, *op cit*, pp108-10; Terracini's speech to the third congress of Comintern is reproduced in *Lenin sul movimento operaio italiano*, appendix, pp308-12.

37. On the debate, see P.Spriano, *op cit*, pp111-13 and *ILO Report A2* (24 September 1920) pp16-17.

38. P.Spriano, *op cit*, p112 talks of the attitude of *Federterra*; there is a full treatment in R.Zangheri, *Lotte agrarie in Italia*, Feltrinelli, Milan 1960. For some analyses in English, see A.Lyttelton, *The seizure of power*, ch3 and C.Seton-Watson, *Italy from liberalism to fascism*, pp566-67.

39. Figures cited in P.Spriano, *op cit*, p17, n1.

40. Quotations in P.Spriano, *op cit*, pp112-13.

41. P.Spriano, *op cit*, pp118-19.

42. P.Spriano, *op cit*, pp119-21, 127 and see unpublished interview with Toeplitz in appendix, pp222-24.

43. P.Spriano, *op cit*, pp121-24.

44. P.Spriano, *op cit*, pp113-14 and n2.

45. M.N.Clark, *op cit*, pp275-76.

46. P.Spriano, *op cit*, pp124-25.

47. P.Spriano, *op cit*, pp125 and 128, n3; M.N.Clark, *op cit*, p270.

48. P.Spriano, *op cit*, p128 n1.

49. See P.Spriano, *op cit*, pp127-32 and appendix, pp198-211.

50. See the full range of comment in P.Spriano, *op cit*, ch8.

51. P.Spriano, *op cit*, p151, n1.

52. Quoted in P.Spriano, *op cit*, p138.

53. P.Spriano, *op cit*, p135.

54. M.N.Clark, *op cit*, pp273-74.

55. P.Spriano, *op cit*, p150 and n.

56. P.Spriano, *op cit*, pp132-33; *ILO Report A11* (5 November 1920) pp2-5.

57. Quoted from an article in *Stato Operaio* of 1930 in P.Spriano, *op cit*, pp147-48.

58. P.Spriano, *op cit*, p149.

59. See P.Spriano, *op cit*, p150 and n, M.N.Clark, *op cit*, pp278-79.

60. *Avanti* (Turin) 24 September 1920 (*L'Ordine Nuovo*, pp169-72); full translation in *New Edinburgh Review*, Gramsci-II, 1974; *New Left Review*, 51, 1968; *Soviets in Italy*.

61. P.Spriano, *op cit*, pp154-55; M.N.Clark, *op cit*, pp281-82.

62. See P.Spriano, *op cit*, pp151-53 and n.

63. M.N.Clark, *op cit*, pp281-82.

64. For details on the referendum, see *ILO report A 11* (5 November 1920) p8; P.Spriano, *op cit*, pp155-56; M.N.Clark, *op cit*, p283 and n97, 98.
65. P.Spriano, *op cit*, pp156, 158.
66. See especially, M.N.Clark, *op cit*, pp284-87 for detail on the Turin situation; P.Spriano, *op cit*, p157 on Agnelli.
67. This vivid description from Parodi's account is quoted in P.Spriano, *op cit*, pp156-57.

Chapter 11

1. *Avanti* (Turin) 24 September 1920 (*L'Ordine Nuovo*, pp172-76): full translation in *New Edinburgh Review*, Gramsci-II, 1974, *New Left Review*, 51, 1968, *Soviets in Italy*.
2. *ON* 26 April 1921 (daily: *Socialismo e fascismo*, pp150-51).
3. *ON* 18 February 1921 (daily: *Socialismo e fascismo*, pp80-81).
4. *Avanti* (Turin) 8 October 1920 (*L'Ordine Nuovo*, pp416-19).
5. *ON* 2 October 1920 (*L'Ordine Nuovo*, pp414-16).
6. *ON* 9 October 1920 (*L'Ordine Nuovo*, pp158-63): full translation, *New Edinburgh Review*, Gramsci-II, 1974.
7. The fullest account is in L.Cortesi, *Le origini del PCI*, pp250-63; see P.Spriano, *Storia del PCI*, i, ch6.
8. L.Cortesi, *op cit*, pp260-61.
9. A point made in M.N.Clark, 'Factory councils and the Italian labour movement', p294; see L.Cortesi, *op cit* and A.de Clementi, *Amadeo Bordiga*, ch5.
10. M.N.Clark, *op cit*, pp293-96.
11. L.Cortesi and M.N.Clark, *op cit*.
12. L.Cortesi, *op cit*, pp253ff; P.Spriano, *op cit* pp94ff: see *Lenin sul movimento operaio italiano*, *cit*.
13. L.Cortesi, *op cit*, pp252-57.
14. L.Cortesi, *op cit*, pp257-60; P.Spriano, *op cit*, pp94-98.
15. M.N.Clark, *op cit*, pp300-301.
16. On the Imola convention, see L.Cortesi, *op cit*, pp264-67 and P.Spriano, *op cit*, pp99-107.
17. On Livorno, see P.Spriano, *op cit*, ch7 and L.Cortesi, *op cit*, ch7.
18. *ON* 11 March 1921 (daily: article on Italy and Spain: *Socialismo e fascismo*, p103).
19. The most useful account is in International Labour Office (Geneva), *The Dispute in the Metal Industry in Italy*, Studies and Reports, series A, 2, 11; B, 7, 9 (September 1920–April 1921).
20. There are abundant accounts of the rise of fascism; for a quick, vivid survey, see Christopher Seton-Watson, *op cit*, pp570ff; for the figures, derived from Tasca's study, see p572, n2; see also Adrian Lyttelton, *op cit*, ch3 and P.Spriano, *op cit*, ch8.
21. See Christopher Seton-Watson, *op cit*, pp567ff.
22. M.N.Clark, *op cit*, pp305-306.

23. Christopher Seton-Watson, *op cit*, pp567-68.
24. There is a good account of the end of the factory councils in M.N.Clark, *op cit*, pp304-27, on which this section is based.
25. *ON* 10, 15, 25 February, 4, 6 March 1921 (daily: *Socialismo e fascismo*, pp67-71, 82-84, 89-92).
26. M.N.Clark, *op cit*, pp316-26.
27. G.Fiori, *Antonio Gramsci*, pp141-42, 150; M.N.Clark, *op cit*, p326; and see *ON* 17 May 1921 (daily: *Socialismo e fascismo*, pp166-67).
28. This whole section is based on P.Spriano, *op cit*, ch11 and 12; L.Cortesi, *op cit* and introduction to A.Tasca, *I primi dieci anni del partito comunista* and my reading of the sources usefully summarized in Rosa Alcara, *La formazione e i primi anni del PCI nella storiografia marxista*, Milan 1970. I hope to produce a further study on Bordiga, Gramsci and the PCI from 1921 to 1930. See the introduction by G.Nowell Smith and Q.Hoare to *A.Gramsci: Selections from the Prison Notebooks*, Lawrence and Wishart 1971.
29. P.Spriano, *op cit*, p261.

Epilogue

1. Quoted in P.Spriano, *op cit*, p265.
2. See P.Spriano, *Storia del PCI*, iii, 255-56.
3. This account, which I have tried to keep as 'neutral' as possible, is based on my reading (provisional) of the period 1921-30; see the valuable introduction to *Antonio Gramsci: Selections from the Prison Notebooks*; P.Togliatti(ed) *La formazione del gruppo dirigente del PCI nel 1923-24*; A.de Clementi, *op cit*; L.Cortesi, introduction to A.Tasca, *op cit*; Rosa Alcara, *op cit*. An essay on the historiography, *The Making and Unmaking of Antonio Gramsci*, appears in *New Edinburgh Review*, Gramsci-III.
4. *Men of Flesh and Blood*, *ON* 8 May 1921 (daily: *Socialismo e fascismo*, pp154-56).

Index

Acciaierie Fiat, 122,275

*Action Programme of the Turin
Socialist Section* (January 1920,
Ordine Nuovo), 171-3,174,192,196,
199

Address to the Anarchists (Gramsci
Ordine Nuovo, April 1920), 197,
203

Adler, Friedrich, 60,84

Agnelli, Giovanni, 12-13,200,204,
249,267,276,293,297; *see* Fiat

Albertini, Luigi, 250,254,266; *see
Il Corriere della Sera*

Althusser, Louis, 306

Amsterdam, bureau of Third International in, 79; closure, 210; trade
union international, 296; *see* International

Anarchism, 15,25,26-9,194,197,203;
in Turin, 63,141; *see* Anarcho-
syndicalism; Borghi, A; Ferrero,
P; Garino, M; Malatesta, E;
Umanita Nova; UAI; USI

Anarcho-syndicalism, 26-8,182
190-1,301; strength of, 194-6; and
post-war crisis, 68-9,71,74-5,81-2;
and council movement, 134,193-9;
and factory seizures, 199-200; and
Occupation of Factories, 236-40,
241-5,249,253,261,264,268-70,
273-5;and socialist crisis of summer 1920, 211-40; in Turin, 47-8;
in Naples, 44; and Mussolini, 53-4;
see Borghi, A.; Ferrero, P.; USI;
Garino, M.; *Guerra di Classe*

Ancona, Red Week and, 51; rising
in, June 1920, 217,238; and anarchists, 194; socialist congress in,
1914, 39,44-6,51

Ansaldo, 20,56,70,237-8,241,244,
266,276,292; *see* Perrone Ansaldo
Pomilio, 122; Ansaldo San
Giorgio, 122,264

Arditi, 11,74; *Arditi del Popolo*, 74

Avanguardia, 42,62,324; Bordiga
made editor of, 64; Leonetti article
in, 89-90

Avanti, 11,35,44,54,61,62,65,76,78,

80,83,90,146,283,285; move of, to
Milan, 38; Mussolini's editorship
of, 32,38,39,51-2; burning of, 11,
81, 146; and April struggle, 1920,
207; and Occupation of Factories,
249,268; Turin edition of, 49,97,
132,196,205,240,245,267,268,269,
272,285,325; foundation of, 89;
independence of, from PSI, 287;
important articles in: 'What do we
mean by demagogy' (Gramsci,
August 1920), 197-8; 'Political
capacity' (Gramsci, September
1920), 272,277-8,285

Bachi, Riccardo, 206

Bakunin, Michael, Bakuninist, 15,
22,23; *see* Anarchism

Balabanoff, Angelica, 38,52,60-2

Baldesi, Gino, 212,249,258,265,284

Banca Commerciale Italiana, 19-20;
and Occupation of Factories, 243,
263,265-6

Banca di Sconto, 19-20,70,292; and
Occupation of Factories, 263

Baratono, Adelchi, and Occupation
of Factories, 242; Gramsci on, 279

Barberis, Francesco, 40,61-3

Barbusse, Henri, 97

Battaglie Sindacali, 137,143-4,323;
see CGL

Bavaria, soviet republic in, 75,76

Benso, Nino, 255-6

Bergson, Bergsonian, 32,48,65,102,
163,285

Bertero, Oreste, 265

Berti, Giuseppe, 42,289

Bianchi, Mario, 44

biennio rosso, 68-76

Bissolati, Leonida, 23,34,35,43;
crisis of 1911-12 and, 36-7; expulsion of, from PSI,36-7

Blanc, Louis, 94,97

Blanqui, Auguste, 75

Boero, Giovanni, 40,62,134; as
abstentionist secretary of Turin
Socialist Section, 80,145-6,174,220;
and council movement, 123,138;

59; between Second and Third International, 77-9
The events of 2-3 December (Gramsci, *Ordine Nuovo*, December 1919), 159-60

The factory council (Gramsci, *Ordine Nuovo*, June 1920), 213-14
Fascist, fascism, 11,13,21,24,27,28, 30,50,69,73,74,261-2; 'left-fascism', 32-3; rise to power of, 268,292-4,296-7,300-1,303; *see* Mussolini, B.
Federterra (land-workers' federation), 25,74,323; and vote on revolution at Milan, September 1920, 260-2
Ferrero, Pietro, 9,195,197-8,330; and Occupation of Factories, 264, 269, 272-3; struggle of April 1921, 296-7; death of, 301
Ferri, Enrico, 26,33
Ferrieri (Piedmont), 247
Fiat, 12-13,30,46-7,101,217,247, 258,263,308; and the War, 56-7; and Turin, 86; and April struggle 1920,204; and struggle of April 1921,296-7; offer to turn firm into a co-operative, 70,267,276; *see* Acciaierie
Fiat, Garrone-Fiat, Fiat-Barriera di Nizza, Fiat-Centro, Fiat-Datto, Fiat-Lingotto; *see also* Agnelli, G.
Fiat-Barriera di Nizza, 122
Fiat-Centro, 13,98,112; workshop commissars in, 138,141,200,239-40; and Occupation of Factories, 246-7,248,252,253,264,271,274-6; unemployment in, 293; *see* Parodi, G.
Fiat-Datto, 122,275
Fiat-Lingotto, 122,244; arms in, 253
FIOM (federation of metal-workers), 9,29,39,59,98,109,110, 116,140,212,217,323; growth of, 46-8; and eight-hour day, 78,89; Rome congress of, 88; internal commissions and council movement in, 77,122-3,138-9,142, 212; and syndicalists, 29,39-40, 195,217; and April struggle 1920, 205; and summer crisis 1920, 236-40; and Occupation of Factories, 241-3,246-7,249,251,254,256-62, 264,269-70,272,276; and unemployment crisis, 293-4,296-7; and Turin, 57-8,65-6,87-8; *see* Buozzi, B.; Colombino, E.

First: renew the party (Gramsci, *Ordine Nuovo*, January 1920), 169-71,201-2
Florence, 62,63,65,146,193,273, 283,291; congress of abstentionist communist fraction in, 211; Socialist Party national council in, 166-7,169-72,180-1; Occupation of Factories in, 241,242,273, 275; syndicalists in, 207; revolutionary meeting in, November 1917, 65
For a Renewal of the Socialist Party (*Ordine Nuovo*, May 1920), 201-3,205,208,211; Lenin on, 235
Ford, Henry, 60
Fortichiari, Bruno, 62,286,288
Fournière, Eugene, 94,97
France, French, 39,42,53,74,110, 234; tariff war against, 18,24; union organization in, 24; socialist party and Third International, 287-8; general strike May-June 1968 in, 241,254-5; PSU of, 254; PCF and CGT in, 254; *Humanité*, 97; Jacobins, 225,229
Freemasons, 30,38,43-5,51
Freikorps, 74
Futurists, 32,91

Galetto, Leo, 89
Galleani, Luigi, 196
Garino, Maurizio, 138,141,195, 197-8; and Occupation of Factories, 251,264,269
Garrone-Fiat, 240
Gemelli, Agostino, 73
Gennari, Egidio, 62,79,82,211,283; and soviets, 167; and vote on revolution in Milan, September 1920, 258-60,262
Genoa, 13,17,237,298; Socialist Party congress in, 25-6,47,52,87, 193; syndicalists in, 195,207; *camere* in, 207,244; and Occupation of Factories, 241,244-5,251, 274
Gentile, Giovanni, 42,49
Germany, German, 39,53,57,62,74, 78,175; social democracy of, 162, 166; USPD in, 34,84,287; KAPD in, 84; and *Banca Commerciale*, 19,263; workers' movement in, 84,92,211,218,222
Giardina, Giovanni, 98,111
Giolitti, Giovanni, 11,15,18,19,26, 27,30,33,41,52,73,150,159-60,188, 199,283,330; pre-war system of, 18-19,21; and crisis of 1911-12,

143,175,177,190,193,201-2,216,
220; adherence of Italian Socialist
Party to, 79, 156, 210; representatives of, 78,83,157,180,181,214,
286,289; *L'Ordine Nuovo* as organ
of, 90,96-8,99-103; Amsterdam
bureau of, 79,210; French and
German parties in, 287; abstentionist communists and, 175;
second congress of, 84,150,199,
202-3,210-11,234-5; Twenty-One
Points of, 234-5,283,285,287-8,
290; and the Socialist Party 280-91;
and the Communist Party, 281,
287-8,298-304
ILO (International Labour Office)
260-1
Itala, 47,122
Italia, 250
Italy, 7,8,17,18, and *passim*;
Gramsci on Italianity, 278-80;
population of, 16-17; industrial
capitalism in, 12-22; agriculture
in, 15-17, 55; the South of, 15-19,
30; working classes of, 16-17,23-5,
55-8; unionization in, 23-5, 27-8;
imperialism of, 18,35-7; socialism
in, early history, 22-8; socialism in,
nature of, 28-34,178,183; anarchist
tradition of, 15,22-3,25-8; communism in, 220-36, 281-307;
crises of 1911-12 in, 35-40; and the
War, 51-67; crisis of 1917 in,
59-66; post-war crisis in, 68-85
(*biennio rosso*); food troubles of
June-July 1919 in, 68,71,146;
elections of November 1919 in,
68,71-2,73,83-4,152; Occupation
of the Factories in, 236-76; unemployment crisis in, 292-4, 296-7;
fascist victory in, 292, 294; Salò
republic in, 32-3; heroism of
working class of, 308

Jacobins, 225,229

KAPD, 84
Kamenev, Lev, 287
Kautsky, Karl, 60,84,97
Kienthal, 60
Kipling, Rudyard, 278-79
Kornilov, General, 282
Kuliscioff, Anna, 23,194,217

Labriola, Antonio, 25,31,48
Labriola, Arturo, 26-7,39,44,
248-9
The Land of Pulcinella (Gramsci,
Ordine Nuovo, October 1920),
280

Lanzillo, Agostino, 27,29
Lazzari, Costantino, 24,26,38,40,
51,63-5,67,79
Legionaries (D'Annunzio), 74
Lecco, 253
Lenin, Leninism, 12,14,33,43,52,
59,60,62-4,82,97,100,106,111,149
150,156,162,173-4,181,184,194,
255,279,304; *State and Revolution*, 188,191,198,202,229; *Left-
wing Communism: an infantile
disorder*, 84,193,210,235; letter to
Italy, 1919, 83; and Serrati, 74-5,
78-9,156,157,234-5,287-8; and
Bordiga, 84-5,159,167,177; and
ultra-left, 210-11; and Gramsci,
177-8; praise of *For a Renewal
of the Socialist Party*, 202-3; on
Occupation of the Factories, 254
Leone, Enrico, 27,39,166
Leonetti, Alfonso, 89-90,98-9,109,
145,146
Levi, Paul, 269
The Liberator, 92
Liebknecht, Karl, 227
Liguria, 20,28,71,89,98,237,298;
councils in, 142; syndicalists in,
195,207; factory seizures in, 199;
Occupation of the Factories in,
241, 244-5, 250-1
Livorno, 193,274; Socialist Party
congress in, 149,289-91,298;
syndicalists in, 207
Ljubarsky, Nicolai (Carlo Nicco-
lini), 157,180,181
Lombardy, 16,17,47,72,98,194,237,
298
La Lotta Operaia, 195,244
Lusignoli, Alfredo (prefect of
Milan), 248-9,263,265,273
Luxemburg, Rosa, 14,114,155,227
Luzzatti, Luigi, 36

Machiavelli, 225,229
*Majority and minority in socialist
action* (Gramsci, *Ordine Nuovo*,
May 1919), 101-3
Malatesta, Errico, 51,81,89,90,194,
196,208,268
Mao Tse Tung, 255
Marabini, Anselmo, 289
Marinetti, Filippo, 32
Marx, Karl, Marxism, 22,25,31,41,
48,90,94,109,133,174,183,219,277,
305; of the Second International,
31; of the Socialist Party, 29,33-4,
37,40-2; absorption of Marxism,
31; Marxist-Leninism, 178, 307;
Karl Marx circle, Naples, 44

238,265; and Mussolini, 32; *see*
 Ansaldo
Petri, Carlo (Pietro Mosso), 98,123,
 139-40,195
Petrograd, Petersburg, 33,61,234
Piedmont, 17,18,43,47,83,85,121-2,
 224,288,298; and council move-
 ment,140,142; factory seizures in,
 199; April struggle in, 1920,206,
 208
Pirandello, Luigi, 31,91
Pirelli, 13,122,250
La Plebe, 23
Po, 16; Lower Po, rural workers in,
 22,23,68
Pogliani, Achille, 263
Polano, Luigi, 283,286
Political capacity (Gramsci, *Avanti*,
 September 1920), 272,277-78,285
Pope, Papacy, 16,72; *Rerum
 Novarum*, 97
Il Popolo d'Italia, 32,68; founda-
 tion, 53-4
Popular Party (*popolari*), 68,71,
 72-4,154,156,184,188,267,292,328
Popular front, 231,254,303,305
Prampolini, Camillo, 23
*The problem of the internal com-
 missions* (Pastore, Giardina,
 Gramsci, *Ordine Nuovo*, August,
 1919), 110-12
The problem of power (Gramsci,
 Ordine Nuovo, November 1919),
 152-5,164
The professional revolutionary
 (Gramsci, *Ordine Nuovo*, Decem-
 ber 1919), 160-1
A Programme of work (*Ordine
 Nuovo*, October 1919), 147-9
*The Programme of the Workshop
 Commissars* (*Ordine Nuovo*, Octo-
 ber 1919), 99,120,123-136,138,
 150,182,196
Proletarian unity (Gramsci,
 Ordine Nuovo, March 1920),
 185-91,202,220
Propaganda, 44

Quaglino, Corrado (For Ever),
 98

Rabezzana, Pietro, 40,49,61-3,297
The ransom of history (Gramsci,
 Ordine Nuovo, June 1919), 99-
 101
Ransome, Arthur, 98
Red Army, 170
Red Week, 22,46,51-2
Reed, John, 98,123

Repossi, Luigi, 62,286
Revolutionaries and the elections
 (Gramsci, *Ordine Nuovo*, Nov-
 ember 1919), 150-2
Rigola, Rinaldo, 27-8,35,39,66,331
Risorgimento, 18,25,142,305
Rolland, Romain, 92,97,174,203
Rome, 15,16,25,39,44,52,82,85-6,
 194,204,270,287; Occupation of
 the Factories in, 241,274
Romeo, 13,217,239
Romita, Giuseppe, 47,48,247
Rosmer, Alfred, 33
Rotigliano, Edoardo, 238,249
Rousseau, Jean-Jacques, 162
Russell, Bertrand, 98
Russia, Soviet, 31,32,71,75,76,77,
 78,79,82,109,110,118-19,213,217,
 224,247,257,287; revolution, Feb-
 ruary, 59,61-3; delegation to
 Italy 1917, 63; revolution, Octo-
 ber, 64,66; in *L'Ordine Nuovo*,
 99-103; communist party of, 302-3;
 electoral law of, 176

Salandra, Antonio, 52,60
Salvemini, Gaetano, 19,48,49,98,
 267; and Socialist Party, 30,38,42;
 offered a seat in Turin, 30,42; and
 culture debate within Socialist
 Party, 42,43; and the War, 53
Santhia, Battista, 219,307; and
 Occupation of Factories, 270-1
Schiavello, Ernesto, 259-60,274
Scoccimarro, Mauro, 295
Seassaro, Cesare, 97
Serrati, Giacinto Menotti, 33,34,
 37,38,51,141-2,150,181,257,331;
 editor of *Avanti*, 54; and the War,
 54,56,59-65; and post-war crisis,
 78,79,81-2,83,84; and Socialist
 Party, 155-8; and CGL, 157; and
 Gramsci, 279-81; and Lenin, 74,
 75,218,234-5; and council movement, 157; in April struggle, 1920,
 206-8; in summer of 1920, 210;
 and Third International, 283-91,
 303
Sestri Ponente, 195,207; factory
 seizures in, 199-200; and Occupation of the Factories, 241,244
Social democracy, 12,59,162,166,
 300-1,304
Socialist Party (PSI), 104,138,153,
 155,324-8; early history of, 25-8;
 nature of, 28-34; intellect of, 29-32,
 40-43; Marxism of, 29,33-4,40-2;
 Freemasons in, 30,38,43-4,51; and
 the South, 30,42,45-6; Congresses,

366 / Index

Viglongo, *Ordine Nuovo*, August 1919), 112-14
trasformismo, 18
Treves, Claudio, 35,37,38,52,60,62, 88,249,284
Trotsky, Leon, 60,255,303
Tunis, 18
Turati, Filippo, 25,26,29,33,36,37, 52,156,159,194,210,235,332-3; early formation, 23; and the War, 53,54,60-1,64,66,67; and post-war crisis, 29,76,78,81,83; and Occupation of the Factories, 249,254, 263-4; and the PCd'I, 283,285-7
Turin, 7,8,9,11,12,13,29,30,37,38, 52,81,89,90,93,137,145,176,210,265, 280; growth of, 46-7,56,58,86-7; socialism in, 40-2,47-50; co-operative alliance ACT in, 46-7,64,87, 248; youth section under Tasca in, 47-8; Francisco Ferrer school, 47; insurrection of August 1917 in, 61-4; Socialist Section in, 108-9, 122,145-6,217,219-20; Action Programme of January 1920, 167-73, 192; Bordiga in, for Section elections, 174-5; *camera* in, 87,122,123, 212,297; council movement in, 69,77,83-90,121-3,136-44,181-4; capture of *camera* and FIOM section by council movement, 123, 138,141; *Programme of the Workshop Commissars* of, 123-32; *L'Ordine Nuovo* and city, 85-8, 90-9; Libertarian Group in, 195, 201; the April struggle 1920 in, 193-209; Occupation of the Factories in, 237,238-40,241,244-8, 249-50,252-3,256-7,258,262-3, 264-6,268-76; unemployment crisis in, 292-93,296-7; last struggle of councils in April 1921, 296-7; elections in, 293,297; heroism of working-class city of, 308
Twenty-One points (Comintern), 234-5;283,285,287-8,290
Two revolutions (Gramsci, *Ordine Nuovo*, July 1920), 222-31

Ultra-Left, 78-9,83,199,210-11; Lenin's *Left-wing communism*: 84,193,210,235
Umanità Nova, 194,196,217,328; and Occupation of the Factories, 243,264; *see* Malatesta, E.
Unions and Councils (Gramsci, *Ordine Nuovo*, October 1919), 116-19; (Gramsci, *Ordine Nuovo*, June 1920), 214-16

UAI (Italian Anarchist Union), 194, 195,328-9; *see* Anarchism, Malatesta, E.
UIL (Italian Labour Union; interventionist), 53,134,324
USI (Italian Syndicalist Union, Anarcho-syndicalist), 12,28,35,37, 38,134,152,299,323-4; formation, 1912, 28; growth of, 159,194-6; and the War, 39,52,53,66; and post-war crisis, 69,71,75,77-8,81,82, 84; and proposed united revolutionary front, 81,195,217; and FIOM, 194-6; council movement and Parma congress of, December 1919, 195-6; and summer crisis, 236-40; and Occupation of Factories, 241-5,249,253,261,264,268-70, 273-5; branch of, in Turin, July 1920, 217; *see* Anarcho-syndicalism, Borghi, A.; Ferrero, P.; Garino, M.
L'Unita, 30; Salvemini's journal, 38,41
United front, 231,300-1,303-4
USA, 77,92,109,257,293
USPD (German Independent Socialist Party), 84,287
Utopia, 39, 326

Venice, Venetia, 17,241,298
Viareggio, prize, 305
Viglongo, Andrea, 98,112-13,114, 116,122,139,167,176,196,199-200, 307; rally to Gramsci, summer of 1920, 219-20
La Voce, 38,41,48,122

War, World, 12,19-20; and Italian industry, 19-20; impact on Italy of, 52-67; Socialist crisis of, 59
What do we mean by demagogy? (Gramsci, *Avanti*, August 1920), 197-8
Whitley councils (British), 88
Whitman, Walt, 97
Wilson, Woodrow, President, USA, 59,60,61,73,77,81
Workers' Democracy (Gramsci, *Ordine Nuovo*, June 1920), 103-8

Yudenich, General, 33

Zanetta, Abigaille, 62
Zibordi, Giovanni, 22
Zimmerwald, 60,61,280
Zini, Zino, 97,140
Zinoviev, Gregory, 283,285,287-8
Zocca, Elvira, 41,62